CW00664408

'SORRO

INTO PRIDE...'

The story of a Staffordshire 1914-1919 war memorial

(Elmore Green High School, Bloxwich)

by Ken Wayman & Barry Crutchley

Reveille
PRESS

'SORROW INTO PRIDE...'

2012

*"In unveiling the tablet, 'to those who gave their lives for justice and freedom,' we must remember those dear to them. We can do no less than pray God to transform their **sorrow into pride** – pride in the wonderful work they performed. We owe it to these splendid men not to sorrow too much. If we could hear them speak they would say, 'Sorrow not at all. We have our reward; you carry on. We only did our duty; you do yours."*

Major H. Lord of the 1/5th South Staffordshire Regiment, at the inauguration of the Elmore Green High School Old Boys' war memorial on 25th March 1922.

Best wishes

Ken Wayman

Dedication

This book is dedicated to the Elmore Green Old Boys whose sacrifice is commemorated on the school war memorial, and to their descendants.
It is also dedicated to the pupils and staff of the present Elmore Green Primary School who warmly welcomed the memorial back into their community.

Special Dedication

The sad passing of Elaine Box

'…*Elaine started her 37-year career at Walsall Council in Catering Services and then moved to Property Services.*

It was while she was working in Property Services that she became Asset Management Support Officer for the Council, and she took particular pride in her responsibilities for the War Memorials in the Borough. She felt it was an honour to ensure that they are preserved, and she loved that part of her job.

Elaine, together with now-retired colleague Mike Gaffney, was instrumental in returning the Elmore Green School War Memorial to its rightful place in that fine old Bloxwich school in March last year.

…Elaine, who had been unwell over the last few months, was diagnosed with cancer only at the beginning of April this year. She passed away aged just 58.

Like so many Council officers, she worked away quietly, tirelessly, out of the limelight, doing the best she could for local people and the borough.
She deserves to be remembered for that, and much more.'

Stuart Williams, 25 April 2012

Originally posted on
'thebloxwichtelegraph.wordpress.com'

Barry Crutchley and Ken Wayman wish
to be fully associated with Stuart's words.

Reveille Press is an imprint of
Tommies Guides Military Booksellers & Publishers

Gemini House
136-140 Old Shoreham Road
Brighton
BN3 7BD

www.tommiesguides.co.uk

First published in Great Britain by
Reveille Press 2012

For more information please visit
www.reveillepress.com

© 2012 Ken Wayman and Barry Crutchley

A catalogue record for this book is available from the
British Library.

All rights reserved. Apart from any use under UK
copyright law no part of this publication may be
reproduced, stored in a retrieval system, or transmitted,
in any form or by any means, without prior written
permission of the publisher, nor be otherwise circulated
in any form of binding or cover other than that in which
it is published and without a similar condition being
imposed on the subsequent publisher.

ISBN 978-1-908336-44-6
Cover design by Reveille Press

Typeset by Graham Hales

Printed and bound by
CPI Group (UK) Ltd, Croydon, CR0 4YY

Contents

PRELUDE

Lists of Maps, Tables & Illustrations .12

Foreword 17

Preface 21

About the authors 25

Thanks & Acknowledgements 27

INTRODUCTION 31

PROLOGUE A sad gathering... 35

Unveiling ceremony for the Elmore Green Memorial in 1922

PART I

Bloxwich before the storm... 39

Chapter One   The town before 1914 41

Chapter Two   Elmore Green School – from Board School to High
                 School and beyond .51

Chapter Three   The 'Parker Street Boys' 57

Chapter Four   A Tradition of Military Service – other wars 61

Chapter Five   Pre-1914 Soldiering in Bloxwich 69

PART II

The storm breaks, summer 1914... 73

Chapter Six   The Road to War 75

Chapter Seven British Forces in 1914 93
 How the army was organised, 1914-1918 93
 Branches of the Army in 1914. .97
 From Tommy's point of view .97
 Sea Power: the navy's role in 1914 99
 Air power: RNAS, RFC and RAF 99

Chapter Eight General Mobilisation and Recruitment 103
 Royal Navy mobilisation 104
 Regular Army mobilisation 105
 Pre-war role of the Regular Army 106
 Mobilising reservists and Territorials 110
 Recruitment, 1914-1918. 113
 Pre-war and 1914 Elmore Green Recruitment 125
 Army Basic Training – what faced the volunteers? 127
 Note: The main theatres of war, 1914-1918. 128

PART III
The 'Boys' who really did the job. 129

Note: How to Read a Short Obituary Entry. 130

Chapter Nine 1914: *Regulars, Reservists, Old Contemptibles and 'Wipers'.* 133

Chapter Ten 1915: *Gas, Gallipoli, 'Weekend Soldiers' Blooded and the New Army Bloodied.* 157

Chapter Eleven 1916: *Into the Cauldron of the Somme..* 197

Chapter Twelve 1917: *Arras, Passchendaele and the World Bled Dry.* . . 245

Chapter Thirteen 1918: *Through Hell to an Expensive Victory.* 313

Chapter Fourteen 1919-20: *Home to a Battle Unfinished..* 363

PART IV
Tribute to a lost generation…. 395

Chapter Fifteen   The School community and the rededication 397

Chapter Sixteen   The re-dedication ceremony – 11 November 2011 . . .401

Full Roll of Honour – extended list of servicemen traced in the
    memorial story 404

PART V
'Never again..?' 407

Chapter Seventeen   Peace and post-war Bloxwich 409

Chapter Eighteen   Reflection and a thought for the future 415

Appendices
1. Burials and Commemorations. 419
2. Campaign & Bravery Awards 425
3. Tracing Servicemen and their Descendants 429
4. Battlefront chronology of war deaths 432
5. Elmore Green Servicemen – units & service dates 436

Glossary of terms used in the book 440

Bibliography 450

List of Maps

Map 1 Western Front, main locations 1914-1918 134

Map 2 August-September 1914 Battlefields 136

Map 3 First Ypres: 21 October-11 November 1914 145

Map 4 Hohenzollern Redoubt: 13-18 October, 1915 177

Map 5 The Somme: 1 July 1916 (to November) 216

Map 6 Arras Offensive: 9 March 1917 and Beyond 255

Map 7 Operation 'Michael': 21 March 1918 318

List of Illustrations

NB: Every obituary summary bears the serviceman's photograph, if available.

Silk card, *'South Staffordshire'*, French origin
46th Division memorial, Hohenzollern Redoubt 16
Memorial unveiling in March 1922, *'Walsall Observer'* 35
Old Boys' Memorial in T.P. Riley School, 1980s 36
Bloxwich Public Hall, pre-1914 42
Bloxwich High Street, pre-1914 43
'Snap time', Great Wyrley Colliery, 1 January 1914 47
South Staffs Territorials, Walsall, 11 August 1914 48
'Your King & Country Need You', 15 August 1914 49
'Our Soldiers at the War – How Women can help' 50
Elmore Green Primary School today 51
TF Pre-war: 2 Platoon, 'D' Coy, 1/5 S. Staffs 71
Declaration of War, *'Daily Mirror'*, 5 August 1914 77
'They shall not pass', cartoon, *'Punch'*, March 1914 78
H.M.S. *'Warrior'*, revolutionary ironclad warship 82
'Chain of Friendship', cartoon, *'Brooklyn Eagle'*, July 1914 91
'A Call to Arms', recruiting poster, August 1914 114
'VC Winners', recruiting poster, December 1914 117
Imperial Service Obligation, conditions of service 124
'Out since August 1914' – L/Cpl James Dawson
      Dress uniform: James Dawson, 2/South Staffs 133
1914 'Mons' Star 139
'Coxy' Lavender, bare-knuckle fighter 141
Menin Gate: Pte. William Groves commemoration 148
Imperial Service Obligation – Territorial assent 150
Cloth Hall, Ypres, on fire, 22 November 1914 153
'Tower Bridge', pit-head, Loos Battlefield, 1915 157
Emblem: Motor Machine Gun unit 170
Hohenzollern Redoubt, simplified diagram 178
'London Gazette', Sgt. F. Lloyd M.M. 182
Thiepval Memorial, Cross and Cemetery 198
Military Medal – Thomas Eccleston .212
'London Gazette', Gnr. T.F. Eccleston, M.M. 213
7th Division, Christmas card 1916 .232
Ypres skyline from Hill 62 at sunset 246
Shrine Cemetery, Bucquoy 251
Commemoration, J.J. Davies, Thiepval Memorial 253

Rossignol Wood, Cemetery, near Hébuterne 253
Commemoration, W.A. Bullock, Arras Memorial. 263
'Walsall Pioneer', L/Cpl. Albert Stych M.M.. 265
'With his army pals on leave', Gnr. Alfred Sleigh 269
Emblem: Royal Naval Volunteer Reserve 270
German concrete blockhouse, Hill 60, Ypres 277
Ricqueval Bridge: 46th Division, St. Quentin Canal 314
Ploegsteert Memorial to the Missing 323
Lt. Wilkes memorial, All Saints Church, Bloxwich 328
Vis-en-Artois Memorial to the Missing 338
Bloxwich burials: Frank Lloyd, Leon Beech, Alf Main 363
Sopwith *'Camel'* 367
Leonard Beech, Remembrance Card, 1920 369
Emblem: Silver War Badge 369
'Home at last!' Old Boys' memorial in Elmore Green 399
Holly Bank Colliery, near Bloxwich 411
Bloxwich ex-servicemen's Peace Celebrations, 1919 416
A 'Dead Man's Penny' or Bronze Death Plaque 427
Medal Roll Index Card and explanation 457

List of Charts & Tables

Chart: 'Standards of Education, 1872' 53

1911 Census – data for Parker Street, Bloxwich 59

Tudor Militia/Old Boys' memorial – comparison 62

Elmore Green Roll of Honour 1939-1945 64

Search for European Security, 1873-1907 88

The Two Alliances in 1914 and after 92

A Soldier's Units, September 1916 98

Principal Army Ranks 98

1914 Royal Navy, sea-going strength 99

Great Powers – relative naval strengths, 1914 104

Great Powers – relative army strengths, 1914 105

Table: Volunteers and Conscripts, totals 1914-1918 123

Table: Pre-War and 1914 volunteers 125

1914 Recruits, Elmore Green Old Boys 151

1914: Chronological Roll of Honour .154

1914: Alphabetical Roll of Honour 154

Old Boys at the Front, 1915 155

Hohenzollern Redoubt, 137th Bde. Casualties. 182-183

1915: Chronological Roll of Honour .187

1915: Alphabetical Roll of Honour 187

1916: Chronological Roll of Honour .232

1916: Alphabetical Roll of Honour 233

Bullecourt: casualties by division, spring 1917 268

U-Boat War: Merchant ship losses, 1917 289

Old Boys – arrivals at the Front, 1917. 292

1917: Chronological Roll of Honour .293

1917: Alphabetical Roll of Honour 294

Old Boys – arrivals at the Front, 1917-18 346

1918: Chronological Roll of Honour .347

1918: Alphabetical Roll of Honour 347

1919-20: Chronological Roll of Honour 370

1919-20: Alphabetical Roll of Honour 371

Full Roll of Honour – all seventy-eight names 404-405

Units and Service dates of the Old Boys 436-439

46th '1st North Midland' Division memorial recently raised near the site of the Hohenzollern Redoubt. 13th October 1915 saw four Elmore Green Old Boys perish in the attempt to storm the German stronghold.

Foreword

WHEN THE authors of this work invited me to write the Foreword for a book commemorating the men on the Elmore Green School War Memorial, it was with mixed emotions that I accepted the honour. As a Bloxwich lad born and bred, my roots here are deep. I have tried my best to promote our local history, and I have always been strongly affected by the story of those who, serving King and country, made so many sacrifices in the Great War.

My late grandfather, Harry Williams of Walsall Wood and Brownhills, was a soldier in the Lincolns during 1914-18; remarkably he survived both that war and service in our local regiment, the Staffords, during the Second World War. I was very young when I knew him, and he always kept his memories of those terrible conflicts to himself, as did so many old soldiers, sailors and airmen. My maternal grandfather, Charles Taylor of Bloxwich, who was too young to fight in the Great War, later did his duty serving the war effort in the mines of the Cannock Chase coalfield, on long shifts at the coal face during World War II.

This ancient Anglo-Saxon village, including both Little Bloxwich and Great Bloxwich, has long been closely associated with Leamore, Blakenall Heath, Harden and nearby places. Medieval Bloxwich, in the county of Staffordshire, was an agricultural village of around 600 people, expanding in the 1700s with coal mining, when cottage industries thrived. By the early 1800s Bloxwich was surrounded by canals, encouraging expansion, and on what is now Beechdale Estate, some of England's earliest blast furnaces were built as the industrial revolution gained unstoppable momentum. Much small-scale coal mining and brick making took place and the village became justly famed for its light metalwork, especially *'awl blades of Bloxwich repute'*.

Bloxwich in 1914 was small but very independent-minded and pugnacious, with its own unique character partly formed by a long-standing rivalry with

Walsall dating as far back as the English Civil War, when Walsall had been for Parliament, and Bloxwich was Royalist. It will come as no surprise that the favourite dog of Bloxwich folk was traditionally the Staffordshire Bull Terrier, and you will often see them proudly patrolling the High Street today. By the beginning of the Great War, the village was a place of contrasts. Much of the land surrounding the busy High Street and the maze of smaller thoroughfares and close-packed houses intertwined with surprising green spaces, was still agricultural, notably to the north and east. But the west was a hive of industry astride the railway running between Walsall and Cannock Chase, and was distinctly Black Country, strewn with the remains of small pits, tips, foundries, workshops and factories encroaching on the village centre.

The centre of Bloxwich village was always of a green and leafy character, though, despite the incessant rattle of the trams and motor buses along the High Street and beyond, with many historic buildings, as it mostly remains today, despite the scars of 20th century redevelopment. Here, the heart of a close-knit community could be found around its parks and within its churches, its pubs – and its schools.

Bloxwich Park was the old village green, with several pubs nearby, many workers' cottages and terraces especially on The Sandbank and the Coneygrey Estate, and the village's first real school, 'The National' (now Bloxwich CE Primary), expanded in 1862 from an 1828 building. The 1857 Music Hall next door also served as a drill hall for volunteers in time of war. At the other end of High Street was Elmore Green, originally Chapel Green, with the parish church, All Saints, nearby and its own quota of pubs, the old library and police station, houses great and small, and schools, notably Elmore Green School, which had its origins as a mixed and infants board (council) school opened in 1882. In 1908 that establishment became a higher elementary school, as it was throughout the Great War and until 1922-3 when it became a selective central school. After 1944 it became Elmore Green High School.

So as you can see, Elmore Green School, in its 'high' days and long before, was one of the main historic centres of the always close Bloxwich community, and that tradition was to be carried on by its successor when in 1958 Elmore Green High School's pupils, staff – and its war memorial – moved to Lichfield Road, Bloxwich, to help form the nucleus of the newly-built T. P. Riley Comprehensive School. Like Elmore Green High School before it, whose coat of arms and school song it inherited, T.P. Riley had a strong community focus – and an army cadet force. In the 1970s the Elmore Green buildings were used as the annexe to T.P. Riley, which is how I remember it, studying as I did in that very Annexe in 1972-3 and latterly at Lichfield Road, which is where I first saw the historic memorial from Elmore Green. But the rest of the remarkable tale of that monument to the Old Boys of Elmore Green School who died in the Great War, and how it returned to its rightful home in 2011, you will read later.

Now, all those who fought in the Great War are gone, and it is up to us to keep their memory alive, whether through the preservation of memorials such as that at Elmore Green School, in ceremonies, or through the writing of books such as this. It is a sacred trust. Remembrance and history is at the heart of what makes Bloxwich, Bloxwich. Bloxwich, Leamore and Blakenall Heath folk do not forget. They see their history every day, and keep it close in their hearts.

I would like to end with some verse from Bloxwich's own Great War poet, 2nd Lt. Harold Parry of '*Croxdene*', not far from Elmore Green, who was killed in action at Ypres on 6th May, 1917. He was just twenty years old.

Time

I looked into the eyes of Time,
And musingly I said,
"There'll come a day when you and I
Will both of us be dead.
"But I shall rise again, to count
No hours that come and go,
And quiet you will ever bide
With Death as bedfellow."

Stuart Williams
Bloxwich, October 2012

Preface

IT IS not often that one war memorial, essentially unaltered, is unveiled and dedicated on two occasions eighty-nine years apart and both in the self-same location. What is more, this particular memorial is now quite well-travelled, was twice rescued, was once shunned by an expensive, modern institution and was finally brought home by the community, A community that had produced it in order to grieve for and to honour its fathers, sons, brothers and husbands, so arbitrarily taken by war.

As will be later explained, the Bloxwich area has across the years contributed more than its share of servicemen to the defence of the realm. This book is not intended to relate the story of *all* the Bloxwich lads who went to the Great War and never returned. It is the story of a few of those lads, young men whose shared experience included being educated at Elmore Green School and who, as a consequence, now share pride of place on the Old Boys' war memorial. The lads' stories necessarily include their wider family connections, as many of their fathers, brothers, uncles and cousins also enlisted in the ranks of the Great War military – unsurprisingly, some of these relatives suffered death, wounding or other trauma. As far as the present researches have uncovered, only one former pupil of Elmore Green School who lost his life while serving his country in the Great War is not actually commemorated on the Old Boys' memorial – Arthur Parkes of Providence Lane attended Elmore Green School and was killed in action during September 1918. Sadly, his name was not put forward for inclusion on the memorial. Arthur's older brother, William Parkes, was also killed in action, near Ypres in June 1917, though William did not attend Elmore Green.

In tracking down the memorial, our aim was to return the lads to the community that produced them. In this respect the process itself was fruitful, with many descendants of the Old Boys coming forward in response to newspaper appeals and kindly offering invaluable background information, photographs and remarkable family memorabilia that could be found nowhere else. In some cases, family members had already pursued their own research; there were other cases in which descendants knew almost nothing of their ancestor's service life. In some instances, our research processes turned up family connections that had been lost to the mists of time, as in the case of the six Goodall lads who lost their lives in the Great War.

Some of the lads were more easily traced than others, their photographs and military stories being broadly related in the local press and thus offering many vital clues for further investigation. A very small minority of the lads' service records survived Hitler's bombers during the Second World War and some of these offer surprising detail. The existence of Royal Naval Volunteer Reserve service records (that escaped the fires of London in wartime) furnished information about their subjects (Harold Goodall and Tom Rowbotham) that had, until then, been thin on the ground.

One or two lads proved to be frustratingly elusive. Prime among these was 'Malpass, L.', whose name revealed more than one Medal Index Card but would not cross-reference with Commonwealth War Graves information nor with information from 'Soldiers Died in the Great War' database. Local newspapers related no demise of a Malpass, L. The riddle was solved by Graeme Clarke whose hitherto unpublished research on Walsall Servicemen provided him with a clue. Graeme painstakingly examined Census returns, newspaper reports and photographs, 'Soldiers Died…' and numerous other sources. He finally discovered that Leonard Malpass in fact served under his sister's married name! He was, in fact, Leonard Morris and his death *was* reported in the 'Walsall Observer'. His *actual* Medal Index Card is in the name of Morris not Malpass.

As the men's stories came together, there remained three who offered more than one possible identity. The three in this category who had defied positive identification were 'Hill, H., Smith, J., and Yates, J.'. This problem was publicised locally and was almost immediately resolved by the skill of Paul Ford, archivist at Walsall Local History Centre in Essex Street. He kindly consulted Elmore Green School registration books for the twenty years preceding 1918 and, again cross-referencing against rates/housing records and National Census returns, established beyond doubt the identities of the three 'mystery men'. They are: Horace Hill who attended Elmore Green while residing with his maternal grandmother in Stafford Road; James Smith of Alfred Street; John Yates of Providence Lane.

We do not claim that the stories and information that we have related in this book is the definitive version – it is the best we can do with the resources presently available and represents the *story so far*. A number of the lads' graves or memorials are still to be visited although in some cases headstone photographs have been obtained from other sources. Ken Wayman, Barry Crutchley and Graeme Clarke will happily receive further information on any of the lads mentioned in this book.

Thanks to the wonderful efforts of Elmore Green head-teacher, Jane Humphreys, who stepped forward when a home was being sought for the memorial and who kindly arranged the impressive ceremony of rededication in November 2011, the pupils of Elmore Green are now reconnected to their doughty predecessors. The Old Boys' war memorial is now in the school's keeping and will most certainly be acknowledged as each November brings another Armistice Day to stir proud memories of pupils past.

About the authors

Barry Crutchley

Barry was born and raised in Bloxwich and attended Harden Primary school followed by Bloxwich 'National' secondary school. He emigrated to Canada with his parents and sister in January 1957 where he attended Patterson Collegiate Institute in Windsor, Ontario, returning to Bloxwich in September 1961 with a High School Diploma. Barry spent a year as a student teacher at Busill Jones Primary School, Bloxwich, then entered teacher training college in Birmingham, qualifying as a Secondary School teacher in July 1965. His first post was as a teacher of P.E. (he was an outstanding footballer) and history at Tynings Lane Secondary School in Aldridge. Eighteen months later, accompanied by his wife Mary and son Gary, Barry took up a three-year teaching engagement in Zambia. On his return to England in January 1970, he took up a teaching post in Birmingham and spent the remainder of his career in the city teaching English to students and adults newly arrived from overseas and reaching the level of head-teacher. Barry retired in 2008 and lives locally.

Ken Wayman

Ken Wayman was born in Hertfordshire and was, according to his early school reports, a 'poor student of history'. He studied History and French at Bournemouth University and in 1971 moved to the Midlands and took up a post, contrary to earlier expectations, teaching history at T.P. Riley School in Bloxwich in 1972. He taught there for the next 26 years. Over that time, Ken accompanied several groups of GCSE students on study-trips to visit the battlefields and cemeteries of the Great War in Flanders and Northern France – still among the most satisfying times of his career. Following early retirement in 1999, he was drawn into local research on the Great War and still regularly visits the old Western Front. His first book, *'The True and Faithful Men'*, traces the stories of the lads on the Pelsall war memorial; he managed to uncover sixty more Pelsall lads who have now been added to supplementary panels at the foot of the memorial. His second book *'Thank God I Am Trying to Do My Little Bit'*, traces the brief military career of a Walsall soldier, Private Jim Elwell who served first in 1/5 South Staffordshire and then with 7/Suffolks. The story relies heavily upon Jim's original letters and cards from France.

For many seasons Ken played cricket for Bloxwich C.C. He is married to a teacher, Sue, and has two grown-up children, Vicki and David. He lives locally.

Graeme Clarke

Graeme served for many years in the police force. Since retiring, Graeme has spent many years researching in detail the war dead of the wider Walsall area and he is now a leading authority on the subject. Without Graeme's invaluable contribution, the compilation of the Elmore Green Old Boys' stories would have proved infinitely more difficult. His research on the Walsall lads deserves publication in its own right – for its quality and as a fitting tribute to those who lost their lives.

Graeme lives locally.

Thanks &
Acknowledgements

WE WOULD like to thank the following individuals and organisations, and thus to acknowledge the part they have played in bringing this book to completion:-

Graeme Clarke, without whose extensive research of Walsall servicemen who died on the Great War the book would not have been possible. His detailed discoveries deserve to be published in their own right!

Head-teacher Jane Humphreys and the Elmore Green Primary School staff and pupils for adopting the war memorial and for the part they played in the rededication ceremony.

New Horizons Community Enterprise at Blakenall Village Centre: we are especially indebted to individuals Mike Brice, Terri Wall and Tom Perrett for providing the enthusiasm for and funding of the book project.

Former Walsall Councillor Ian Robertson.

Council employees, particularly Elaine Box and Mike Gaffney, who both kindly contributed to the recovery of the war memorial.

Stuart Williams and Paul Ford of Walsall Local History Centre: Stuart for his generosity in writing an excellent Foreword, for kind permission to incorporate his report from the *'Bloxwich Telegraph'* and for providing a rare 1919 photograph of Bloxwich ex-servicemen; Paul for his skill in tracking down three lads [H. Hill, J. Smith and J. Yates] who had proved most difficult to identify.

Andrew Weller of Pelsall Local History Centre who gave us access to microfilm copies of the *'Walsall Observer'* (and always put a smile on our faces!).

Edna Marshall and her sister Jean [descendants of Corporal Tom Eccleston M.M.] who happily shared their earlier efforts to track down the 'missing' Elmore Green war memorial.

Journalist Deborah Stewart who kindly highlighted the search for the memorial. Her thoughtful articles stimulated much local interest.

Roger Butt, former head-teacher of Bloxwich Church of England School (known locally as 'The National').

Alan Hawkins of Hednesford for allowing us access to a rare copy of the '1919 *Walsall Peace Celebrations.*'

Anyone who has provided photographs: all are acknowledged in the book but, if anyone has been missed, we apologise.

David Scripps of Trinity Mirror plc (London): thanks for valuable support in respect of raising the profile of the lads on the memorial.

Cannock Chase Mining Museum, Hednesford.

The Coal Authority (Mansfield).

Peter Barker, Mick Drury and Trevor Matthews of Cannock Chase Mining Historical Society.

'*Bloxwich Telegraph*' website, created and maintained by Stuart Williams. A 'must' for Bloxwich history-lovers.

Commonwealth War Graves Commission '*Debt of Honour*' website.

'*Great War Forum*' website created by Chris Baker.

'*Cannock Chase Mining Historical Society.co.uk*' – website.

'*Coalmine.proboards.com*' – website discussion forum.

'*Archives.Staffordshire.gov.uk*', county historical website.

Any current copyright-holders not mentioned by name – our apologies and we request your forbearance.

Last but by no means least, we extend our grateful thanks to the descendants and friends of the following men who have contributed so many invaluable sources of information, photographs, stories, memorabilia and above all their time and interest – they kept us going when the trail was difficult to follow. We hope they think their support was worthwhile:

John	BATE
Harold	BAUGH
Leonard	BEECH
Alfred	BULLOCK
William	BULLOCK
Alfred	BUSHNELL
George	BUSHNELL
James	DAWSON
George	Dawson**
Charles	Dawson**
Howard	Dawson**
Thomas	ECCLESTON, M.M.
Edgar	GOODALL
Harold	GOODALL
John	Goodall**
Samuel	Goodall**
J. William	GOODALL
David	Goodall**
Bill	GRIMSLEY
Frank	GROOM
George	GROVES
William	GROVES
Bill	HAYCOCK
Edward	JONES
James	Jones**
Arthur	KITSON
Ernest	Lavender**
William	Lavender**
Arthur	LINNELL M.M.
Frank	LLOYD M.M. & bar
Alfred	MAIN
George	Main**
Wm Edw	PICKIN
Tom	ROWBOTHAM
Ambrose	SQUIRE

[A surname in lower case followed by ** indicates a serviceman not named on the Old Boys' memorial but related to one of those commemorated.]

Introduction

by Ken Wayman & Barry Crutchley

OUTSIDE THE main library, at the back of the Sixth Form study area in T.P. Riley Community School in Bloxwich, and to the left of the staffroom door, there stood for many years a beautifully-carved alabaster war memorial. It did not commemorate lads who had attended T.P. Riley – the school was too young for that, built in 1958 – though many of the family names on the memorial had passed through the school for at least two generations. The dedication read:

> *"1914-1919 – TO THE GLORY OF GOD & IN MEMORY OF THE OLD BOYS OF THIS SCHOOL WHO FELL IN THE GREAT WAR. THEIR NAME LIVETH FOR EVERMORE."*

Unsurprisingly, the memorial originated elsewhere in Bloxwich. When T.P. Riley opened in 1958, it duly replaced Elmore Green High School that had been located in the centre of Bloxwich since 1908 and had, since 1918, been a selective school.

When war came in 1914, many Old Boys of Elmore Green School immediately volunteered for military service or were already regular soldiers, Special Reservists or members of the local Territorial Force in Bloxwich. The Great War was a brutal conflict that, by 1920, had left at least sixty-seven of the Old Boys dead and many more scarred physically or psychologically. After the Armistice, the Old Boys' Committee set about organising a local appeal to pay for an appropriate memorial to those who had lost their lives. Money was raised mainly by the strenuous efforts of the Old Boys' Committee and by the children then attending the Elmore Green School, many of whom were related to the dead servicemen or, at the very least, knew their families.

During the final week of March 1922 the memorial was proudly unveiled in the hall of the Elmore Green Central High School and both the memorial and the dedication service reflected both the deep sorrow and the burgeoning pride felt by the local community. And there the memorial stood for years, watching over successive generations, one of which again went to war in 1939.

The memorial remained in the High School, a resplendent testimony to the sacrifices made by an earlier generation of the school's pupils, until its closure in 1958. Changing circumstances in the organisation of local education led, in the 1970s, to the erstwhile Elmore Green High School buildings, complete with war memorial, being handed over to the overflowing T.P. Riley School for use as a lower school annex from 1971 to c.1990. Came the day when T.P. Riley required even more extensive accommodation and a move to the Richard C. Thomas site in Field Road was necessitated. Rather than leave the war memorial in an empty building, the decision was taken to re-locate the memorial to the rear of the library in T.P. Riley main school in Lichfield Road.

Early in the 21st Century (2003), with the roll falling, T.P. Riley closed and the buildings were replaced by the expensive new Walsall Academy that found it could provide no home for the Elmore Green School war memorial. And so the memorial temporarily passed from sight…but not from mind.

The 'rebuild' apparently entailed the removal of the memorial with the intention of relocating and rededicating it at an appropriate place in Bloxwich, though this was not widely known. Ken Wayman asked a colleague who had transferred to the new Academy of the whereabouts of the memorial and soon became concerned that no one seemed to know what had happened to it. It increasingly appeared that the memorial had been 'forgotten'.

In November 2009 Barry Crutchley asked a local councillor where we should begin to search in our efforts to find the memorial. He suggested we begin at the Council Depot in Norfolk Place, North Walsall. At the reception we were fortunate to come across an employee who heard us explaining our problem and he pointed us to the Regeneration Department at the Council House. Barry rang the department and arranged to meet Ms. Alison Butcher who showed great interest and said she would present the search as a project to one of the junior members of the department. Within a week Alison reported that the memorial had been found, in storage at a stonemason's yard in Cannock. Over the Christmas and New Year break Alison said she would try to arrange for Ken and Barry to be able to visit the yard and see the memorial in person. As January came and went there was no news from Alison and it later transpired that Alison had left the Council's employment – thus the proposed visit failed to materialise.

In March Barry visited the Local History Centre to ask the advice of Stuart Williams, at whose suggestion Barry wrote to Miss Evans, Head Teacher of The Walsall Academy, asking her to enquire of the 'old T. P. Riley' teaching staff if anyone had information that could be of help in the search for the memorial. Within a week her reply produced the name of Brian Jackson who had exercised a 'Clerk of Works' role during the building of The Academy.

Shortly afterwards Barry again contacted the Regeneration Department and was directed to speak to Ms. Elaine Box in the Properties Department. Elaine quickly discovered the original letter to Alison Butcher but more importantly located the now-retired Brian Jackson and learned from him the whereabouts of the safely stored memorial. It was indeed in a stonemason's yard in Cannock and remained in good condition. Unknown to Barry and Ken, a relative of Corporal Thomas Eccleston. M.M. (whose name is commemorated on the war memorial), had also been searching for the memorial. Following protracted enquiries Edna Marshall had also tracked it, by a different route, to the stonemason's yard in Cannock.

To Ken and Barry, the recovery of the memorial offered an opportunity to help Bloxwich families remember the sixty-seven Old Boys of Elmore Green School whose names were inscribed on the alabaster memorial. From Ken's years at T.P. Riley and Barry's own memories of Bloxwich National School, surnames of friends and pupils were recognised, demonstrating that descendants of many of the families from 1918 still live in Bloxwich today. Here was a rare opportunity to help repay the great debt of gratitude owed to those men by returning their memorial to a place where their families and other citizens of Bloxwich could pay tribute to the sacrifice they had made. The present Head Teacher at Elmore Green Junior School, Jane Humphreys, happily agreed that the memorial could return 'home' to the school in which it was originally dedicated in 1922.

At the initial dedication ceremony in 1922, Councillor Edward Shelley, chairman of Walsall Education Committee, had promised:-

> *"In the name of the Walsall Education Committee I gratefully accept this memorial and will solemnly charge that body to see that it is ever preserved."*

In 2011, the Elmore Green School war memorial was finally relocated to a permanent home back in the school where the young men whose names adorn the memorial had learned, laughed and grown towards manhood.

The memorial was proudly re-installed in the main hall of Elmore Green Junior School and was re-dedicated on Friday, 11th November 2011 – Armistice Day. The full circle had at long last been closed.

This book is the story of the memorial and of the men whose names are thereon inscribed. We trust it will do them justice.

Prologue

A Sad Gathering…

'SCHOOL WAR MEMORIAL

Elmore Green's Tribute to Sixty-Seven Old Boys who
gave their lives
[*'Walsall Observer', 1st April 1922]*

A BEAUTIFUL tablet which has been placed in the
hall of the Elmore Green Central High School
at Bloxwich as a memorial to the 67 old boys who
gave their lives in the war was on Saturday unveiled
by Major H. Lord of the 5th South Staffords, and
dedicated by the Vicar of Bloxwich (the Rev. J.C.
Hamilton). The ceremony was largely attended, many
of those present being relatives of the fallen or old boys
of the school. Councillor E. Shelley (chairman of the
Walsall Education Committee) presided.

An interesting fact about the tablet is that the
alabaster was quarried in Staffordshire at a place
named Fauld, near Tutbury; while the sculptor, Mr.
Frederick T. Perry, although now living in Lichfield, is
a native of Bloxwich, and received his education at the
National Schools there. On the left side of the tablet is
a figure of a sailor and on the right side that of a soldier
– all very beautifully carved. Both figures are in repose,

35

suggesting that their work is finished and they are having a well-earned rest. At the top are the figures, '1914-1919', with a black cross in between. Immediately beneath are the words,

> 'To the glory of God and in memory of the old boys of this school who fell in the Great War.'

The names of the dead occupy a large space below the inscription. Each letter of these has been incised and then filled with a special black mastic which, it is said, is absolutely imperishable. At the bottom are inscribed the words,

'Their name liveth for evermore.'

The cost of the tablet was £130, and the money was raised mainly by the strenuous efforts of the Old Boys' Committee, who arranged whist drives, and the children, who gave entertainments.

The short memorial service before the unveiling was conducted by the Vicar, It opened with the hymn, *'For all the saints who from their labours rest'*, followed by prayers for the fallen and for the bereaved families. The Rev. A.G. Kick, M.C. (Wesleyan minister), read the lesson from Wisdom iii, 1-6, and v, 15-16, and the school choir, under Mr. Middleton, sang the anthem, *'Lift thine eyes.'*

The names on the roll of honour were then read by the headmaster (Mr. J. Sixsmith).

In unveiling the tablet, *'to those who gave their lives for justice and freedom,'* Major Lord said:

> *"We must remember those dear to them. We can do no less than pray God to transform their **sorrow into pride** – pride in the wonderful work they performed. We owe it to these splendid men not to sorrow too much. If we could hear them speak they would say, 'Sorrow not at all. We have our reward; you carry on. We only did our duty; you do yours.'"*
>
> *The memorial had proved that the boys of the school in the last generation were heroes, and he looked to the boys now attending it to prove themselves worthy of them.*
>
> *"They were splendid men," he added; "...let us try to follow in their steps that we may not be ashamed when we meet them again."*

After the dedication of the tablet by the Vicar, Mr. Sixsmith formally presented it to Councillor Shelley, who replied:

> *"In the name of the Walsall Education Committee I gratefully accept this memorial and will solemnly charge that body to see that it is ever preserved." Continuing, he congratulated the sculptor on the very excellent result of his work.*
>
> *"We must," he said, "feel ourselves highly honoured that we have been able to secure the services of a native of Bloxwich to carry out the work."*

Supporting Major Lord's remarks, he said that he hoped the coming generation would be no less enthusiastic than the past one and be as anxious to do what they could when the occasion arose.

Two buglers from the Queen Mary's School Cadet Corps sounded, *'The Last Post'* and *'Reveille'*, and the proceedings closed with the *National Anthem.'*

The sixty-seven Elmore Green Old Boys whose names are recorded on the school Great War memorial are as follows:

ANDREWS, I

BEECH, L

BULLOCK, AC

BUSHNELL, GB

COPE, JH

DOWNES, H

EVANS, T

GOODALL, E

GRIMSLEY, WE

GROVES, JW

HARPER, F

HAYCOCK, WA

HEELEY, J

JONES, E

LAWLEY, WH

LLOYD, F, MM & Bar

ORGILL, J

PERKS, HV

ROWBOTHAM, J.T.

SIMMONS, AJ

SMITH, J

STYCH, A., MM

WILLETT, J

BATE, J

BRICKNALL, TV

BULLOCK, WA

COCKAYNE, WC

DAVIES, JJ

ECCLESTON, TF, MM

FRANCE, H

GOODALL, H

GROOM, FJ

HALL, AG

HARRISON, SG

HAYWARD, A

HILL, H

JORDAN, H

LESTER, F

MAIN, AL

PARTON, JE

PICKIN, WE

SARGENT, G

SLEIGH, A

SMITH, S

SYLVESTER, R

YATES, J

BAUGH, H

BRYAN, J

BUSHNELL, AJ

COOPER, AE

DAWSON, J

ELKS, BL

GILL, B

GOODALL, JW

GROVES, GA

HANDY, JH

HARVEY, F

HAYWOOD, E

HOOPER, BC

KITSON, A

LINNELL, A., MM

MALPASS.L

(served as MORRIS.L)

REVITT, H

SHARRATT,W

SMITH, G

SQUIRE, A

WILKES, AV

PART I

Before the storm…

Chapter One

The town before 1914

ALTHOUGH BLOXWICH was in the Black Country, and proud of it, it was a borderline case. It was full of countrymen who could spend all day down the pit or in the factory and the evenings in the fields or along the canals. It should not be forgotten that the term Bloxwich includes its satellite communities of Leamore, Harden, Goscote, Blakenall and Little Bloxwich. Bloxwich men and women always had a reputation for sturdy individualism and local patriotism. Although a district or parish of the nearby borough of Walsall, there was always a sense of rivalry with its much larger neighbour. The Bloxwich 'nobility' who lived in Stafford Road or Lichfield Road had got there by hard work not like the 'softies' down Walsall!

The colliers often started their shifts at 6 a.m. and finished about 4 p.m. They would usually walk to work across fields carrying their 'snap' of dry bread and cheese or bacon and a bottle of cold tea. They would walk home, indistinguishable from one another with their faces blackened by coal dust, to their outdoor lives of pigeon fanciers, fishermen or gardeners. Their loyalty to each other was fierce and they reserved their bitterness for their bosses and the mine owners. By the turn of the century the mines near to Bloxwich had been worked out so miners had to travel to neighbouring villages and towns like Essington, Great Wyrley, Cannock, Walsall Wood and Aldridge. At least half the men on the Elmore Green School memorial had employment at one time or another in collieries, the most popular being Holly Bank near Essington. As well as Bertie Gill, Robert Sylvester and George Sargent, of Parker Street, four others worked at Holly Bank, Alfred Bullock, Joseph Davies, Frank Lloyd and Wm Edw Pickin.

Accompanying Frank Harvey to Allen's Rough were John Bate, George Bushnell and Harry Perks. Leonard Morris (served in the war as L. Malpass), Bertie Elks, Horace Downes and Joseph Handy all worked at the Great Wyrley Colliery. James Goodall and J. T. Smith worked at the Lea Croft Colliery (Cannock). James Dawson worked at the Aldridge Colliery. Edgar Goodall, 'Ted' Jones and Arthur Kitson worked at the Wood Farm Colliery (between Busill Jones Primary School and the M6 motorway). John Cope and William Lawley worked at the Huntington Colliery. Samuel Harrison worked at the Hawkins Colliery in Cheslyn Hay. Albert Stych was employed at the 'Fair Lady' pit in Heath Hayes and George Smith, who had moved to Yorkshire worked at the Castleford Colliery. Harold Baugh, John Yates, Aaron Hayward, Frank Groom and Thomas Eccleston (before joining the Police Force) were described as 'miners' (though no colliery was specified).

Day-wage men earned an average of £1 a week with deductions of 2d for insurance, 3d for a savings club and 1d for an 'old age fund' (the total of 6d. equals 2½ pence).

Of the men who didn't work at the pit, 21 worked in local factories like Wiggins, Talbot Stead and BOAK.

The *'Kelly's Directory'* for Bloxwich in 1912 tells us that there was a Public Hall, known locally as the Music Hall, on the corner of Wolverhampton Road. As well as concerts it was the drill hall for the Territorials of 'D' Company 5th Staffordshire Regiment. Charles Bullock, Horace Downes, George Groves,

Bloxwich Public Hall

and George Sargent of the Elmore Green boys would have been regulars here. The 'Terrors' were led by Captain W. Burnett and their Sergeant Major was Eli Walker who lived at 197, High Street with his wife and seven children.

The Registrar for Births, Deaths and Vaccinations was at 7, Harrison Street and the Registrar for marriages was next door at 5, Harrison Street. There was a Central Picture Palace in Park Road and the Electric Palace further down the High Street. Prices for seats ranged from 3d. to 1 shilling. The free reading room was open daily from 9 a.m. to 10 p.m. and on Sunday from 2 p.m. to 9 p.m. An isolation hospital was situated in Sneyd Lane. The convent of St. Paul of Chartres stood on the Stafford Road at Wallington Heath. In 1911 all the nuns were French and the only Bloxwich woman in the convent was the cook.

The focus of the town was naturally the High Street. It began at the Bell Inn in the north and ended at Field Street, later Field Road, at the Pinfold. It reflected the times. Trams linked the town to Walsall otherwise there were horse-drawn vehicles and only the occasional motor vehicle.

Bloxwich High Street

The most important businesses in those pre-supermarket days were the grocers, of which there were eleven and the same number of butchers. There were more than three dozen varieties of other businesses. Boot makers and boot repairers were popular (nine) and there were six clothiers or tailors. Some trades have survived the last one hundred years: bakers, chemists, fishmongers, hairdressers, newsagents, stationers and even offices for solicitors and estate agents would not look out of place in 2012. Others were more a product of their times: iron-monger, salt dealer, brush maker, surgeon, lamp oil dealer, tea dealer and a more recent loss would be a tobacconist.

Lloyds and Metropolitan provided the banks while the Spread Eagle, Kings Arms, George Inn, The Swan and the Prince of Wales provided liquid refreshment.

Bloxwich 1914 January to July

The Bloxwich Strollers football team was comfortably sitting in the top half of the Midland Combination at the start of 1914 and was playing teams like Stafford Rangers, Hednesford Town, Tamworth Castle and Birmingham Trams.

Fund raising events and 'benefit' meetings were regularly held in local pubs. The Sir Robert Peel held a benefit concert in mid-January for the widow of Mr. F. Bough who had been drowned in the canal locks in Walsall. It was organized by the Society for Canal Men and a special vote of thanks was given at the end of the evening to the landlord Mr. Perry for his 'support and service'.

At the end of January the Tobacconists' Association held a 'smoking evening', which attracted about sixty people to the Spread Eagle. The occasion enabled the association to award prizes to its members.

At the same time the Red Lion hosted a meeting of the Imperial Prize Band. Unfortunately, the prize band was *"…badly in need of some new instruments"*, so a variety of fundraising events were suggested including a charity football match at Easter and a number of Sunday engagements for the Birmingham Parks Committee. The monetary target for the replacement instruments was £120.

A natural consequence of the pub-centred social life was the occasional case of overindulgence. On February 11th Robert Hughes of Victoria Terrace, Bloxwich boarded the tram at the Bridge in Walsall heading for Bloxwich. The tram conductor was upstairs collecting fares when Mr. Hughes got on the bus. On descending the stairs the conductor observed Mr. Hughes *"…dancing backwards and forwards",* on the lower deck. Upon being told to behave himself Mr. Hughes declared that he had no money for the fare and that the conductor must pay it for him. A scuffle ensued. In court Mr. Hughes said he was sorry for what he had done and he was ordered to pay the costs.

On April 18th Bloxwich All Saints Church held a Bazaar in order to raise £1,000 for a new organ, to provide electric lighting for the church and to pay debts arising from repairs to the church roof. Lady Cooper, the wife of the Walsall MP Sir Richard Cooper, declared the bazaar open.

Whitsun, in early June, provided families with the first opportunity of the year for their summer excursions. Whit Monday was traditionally a day to get out. Favourable weather was predicted and there were record bookings for the many excursion trains. The London and North Western Company reported that their most popular trips were to Wolverhampton (872 passengers), Lichfield (576 passengers), North Wales (480 passengers) and Blackpool (233 passengers). The Midland Train Company had by far the most popular destination with 3,200 passengers booked to go to Sutton Park. This was followed by 750 to Malvern and 500 to Matlock.

Huge queues also gathered near the County Court for the arrival of the increasingly popular motor-buses with the ensuing eager scramble for the seats on top.

Throughout the months until the declaration of war on 4th August the local theatres and cinemas offered constant relief from the hardships of life. Her Majesty's Theatre was the pre-eminent entertainment venue with many national and international artists performing there. Built in 1900 it was an imposing building at the top of Park Street known as Town End Bank. Its only serious rival was The Grand Theatre near the station. A seat in the stalls cost 1/- and a private box could be had for 7/6.

Citizens of Bloxwich had the Electric Theatre on the High Street. Its feature film for the first week in August was *"The Doctor's Honour"*, a heart-stirring Drama of Army Life in the Tropics. But more importantly, they could ready themselves for the Pat Collins' Grand Fete and Gala at the Wakes ground, now the site of the Asda Supermarket and the Pinfold Health Centre. People were promised *"…A grand amalgamation of new and novel amusements"*.

Local news inevitably reflected the adversities and tribulations of Bloxwich people. A street disturbance caused by an argument over football led to Robert Harvey of Blakenall Lane and Walter Jenkinson of Bridgtown, Cannock coming to blows. Jenkinson fell and hit his head on the tramlines. He died later in hospital. Harvey pleaded self defence and was convicted of manslaughter.

On February 3rd 1914 an explosion rocked the home of William Summerton at 69, Station Road, Bloxwich. He was charged with causing an explosion likely to endanger life and property. As a miner he could have had access to explosive materials and when under the influence of drink, *"…he was like a madman"*. In William's defence it was stated that the explosion, *"…was a very small matter and did not even blow the grate out"*. The prisoner was remanded in custody. John Holden of Reeves Street was arrested abusing his wife outside the Lamp Tavern on February 7th. Police Inspector Haycock found Holden trying to hide behind a telegraph pole – he was, *"..under the influence of drink at the time"*. Holden's wife, Dora, said she didn't hear her husband use bad language!

Mid-March saw a dispute at Holly Bank Colliery which was arguably the single highest employer of men from Bloxwich at this time. The disagreement centred on the employment of non-union labour. The recent history of the mining industry told of constant conflicts between miners and mine owners and managers over many issues, not just pay but also hours of work, safety and conditions of employment. In this instance the company was given a fortnight's notice of a stoppage of work by 1,200 miners unless steps were taken to greatly reduce the numbers of non-union workers. At the last minute a strike was averted by the disclosure that since the issuing of the ultimatum most of the non-union workers had, in fact, joined the union and those that hadn't would be interviewed by the miner's agent, Mr. Dean as they left work.

April saw William Evans of Parker Street charged with an offence against the Coal Mines Act by having cigarettes hidden inside his cap as he entered Leacroft Colliery. He was fined 10/- with costs. James Goodall of the Elmore Green Memorial also worked at Leacroft Colliery.

By June Walsall Wood Colliery was in dispute. Miners' agent Mr. Dean was again at the forefront. The cause of the conflict was 'difficult and involved' but it had arisen with regard to the lease and Lord Bradford. Obviously not wanting to antagonize Lord Bradford a public meeting appealed to him to be aware of the "...*calamitous results that will fall upon it (the local community) in the event of a stoppage*".

Mr. Dean was also present at a meeting of about 1,000 people on Pelsall Common in July. Many Bloxwich miners had joined the Pelsall and District Miners Union who had organized the meeting because it was the strongest of the local federations at that time. Unusually, the miners of the district were given a day's holiday to attend the meeting. Two years earlier they had 'won the principle' of a minimum wage at great sacrifice and wanted to build upon that success. The meeting was addressed by three local Members of Parliament and representatives of mining federations from North Staffordshire and Cannock Chase.

Before the end of the month there were two reported deaths of Bloxwich miners. George Davis of Little Bloxwich died twenty months after being thrown down between the tubs full of coal and the wall of the mine. The cause of the accident was a startled horse pulling the tubs. He had had treatment at Walsall hospital and at the Birmingham orthopaedic hospital where he had several operations. It was following an operation that he haemorrhaged and died from loss of blood.

On July 16th Joseph Athersmith (59) of New Street, Bloxwich died after a roof fall at Harrison's Colliery, Great Wyrley. The Inspector of Mines, the representative of the Miner's Association and colleagues working with him agreed that they did not think that, "...*Joseph Athersmith or any other man could have avoided the accident.*" A verdict of 'Accidental Death' was returned and

Snap time at Great Wyrley Colliery (The Plant) New Year's Day 1914. From the left: Deputy Tom Smith, George Hawley, Fred Sivorn, Cyril Deakin, Frank Hunt, Mr Hemingsley and at the front Tom Smith Junior. (Source:Mr Mick Drury, CCMHS)

sympathy was expressed. Len Malpass named on the Elmore Green Memorial was a fellow worker at Harrison's.

The *Walsall Observer's* apparent policy to be non-political meant that little national news was published which may explain why events leading up to the outbreak of war were hard to find; indeed, as late as May 21st 1914 an article was published extolling the virtues of the German education system. Mr. R. R. Carter, Principal of Walsall School of Art, delivered a lecture at a meeting of the Educational Society at the Masonic Hall. He had recently been to Germany to visit some of their Trade Schools. Entrance to the English equivalent of Trade Schools from the age of fourteen to sixteen was voluntary whereas in Germany it was compulsory. He was also impressed by the 'lavish expenditure' on equipment everywhere.

Earlier in the year Elmore Green School was the venue for a meeting organized by the Women's Social and Political Union. The *Observer's* headline "Suffragette Heckled: Lively Meeting at Bloxwich" seemed a little understated. Miss Barbara Wylie of London had trouble delivering her speech, being subjected to frequent interruptions from a large audience mostly comprised of miners.

Miss Wylie's assertions that, *"Men thought that they had got the right to vote by some divine right"*, and that, *"...all men today were born with a golden spoon in their mouth."* produced raucous laughter. Miss Wylie was made of stern stuff, she ended with, *"I am not surprised that the status of British workmen is as low as it is. The remarks I have heard made tonight have been an explanation of the fact that the British workman requires more education before he is fit to use the vote."*[1] (followed by laughter, applause and disorder).

Finally, on 1st August, under the heading Local Notes it was reported that, *"…The war cloud which is hanging over the Continent promises to envelope Britain also, with what terrible consequences none can say."*

August 1914

Following the example of central government the local council was urged by Sir R. A. Cooper MP to, *"…lay aside all domestic political controversy until danger has passed."*

Monday August 3rd 1914 was a bank holiday but the centre of Walsall was crowded with people eager to have news and those who stayed until evening were surprised to see the local Territorial units arrive home prematurely from their camp in North Wales. The excited crowds continued to gather on Tuesday particularly after the King's Proclamation calling up the reserves of the Army. Large crowds gathered near the station expecting to see the Territorials depart by train but they were disappointed.

The Bridge, Walsall town centre on 11th August 1914, as 1/5th South Staffordshire parades prior to departure for war training.

---

1   *'Walsall Observer'* 21st March 1914

On Tuesday, 11th August the Territorials of the 5th South Staffords assembled on the Bridge for a civic farewell. Led by Lieutenant-Colonel C. Fiddian Green the twenty three officers and eight hundred and ninety two men proceeded to Lichfield and then Burton. Ninety eight men and sixteen non-commissioned officers comprised 'D' Company from Bloxwich.

The first advertisement appealing for volunteers appeared the following week, on August 15th 1914.

Local war items, also on the 15th included a notice that men employed by John Shannon, wholesale clothiers, *"…who have volunteered to 'go to the front'"* will be paid half wages while the war lasts. Walsall Corporation and the Walsall and District Co-operative granted the same concession while Lambert Bros agreed to pay 8/- a week to the family of each man plus 1/- per child.

Walsall Football Club announced that the proceeds of their first practice match would go to the Prince of Wales Fund. Meanwhile, the assistance of the police was requested by the parents of several girls who were said to have 'followed' the 5th South Staffords.

A warning was issued under the title, 'RUMOURS GIVEN THE LIE'. It asked the public not to place any reliance on rumours regarding alleged victories or defeats since they are baseless.

"The public may be confident that any news of successes or reverses to British arms will be communicated officially without delay."[2]

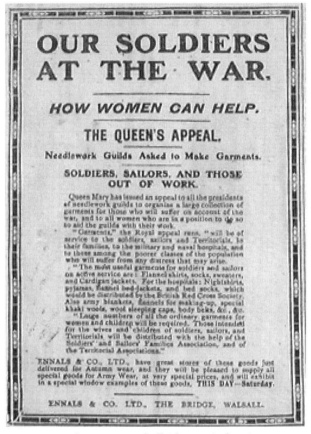

August 15th 1914. A 'Walsall Observer' advertisement
asking for the help of women.

---

2   From the *'Walsall Observer'*, August 15th 1914

Chapter Two

Elmore Green School – from Board School to High School and beyond

ELMORE JUNIOR and Infants' School, Elmore Row, Bloxwich, was opened at Elmore Green in 1882. It was an Elementary Board School providing a basic standard of education for working class children aged from five to fourteen but it was compulsory for a child to attend only until they were ten years old. A School Board, funded by the local rates, had been created in Walsall

Elmore Green Primary School today

to overcome the problem of having many more school age pupils than the existing schools (mainly church schools) could accommodate. These Boards were given the task of providing elementary education for these 'shortfall' pupils. The curriculum was restricted to the three R's, reading, writing and arithmetic, but schools were encouraged to instil social behaviour such as acceptance of the teacher's authority, and the need for punctuality, obedience and conformity. As the right to vote extended to more people it was thought necessary to educate people so they could use their vote wisely. Some objected to the idea of 'universal education' on the grounds that it would make the working class 'think' and become dissatisfied with their lives and encourage them to revolt. Many landowners and industrialists were against compulsory universal education because they would lose a great reservoir of cheap labour. Others feared that these new pupils would be open to indoctrination by the state; however, employers soon saw the benefits of having workers who could now read, write and do simple mathematical computations.

Elementary education became compulsory in 1880; even then, education was compulsory only to the age of ten and only became 'free' in 1891. For the first nine years Elmore Green pupils had to pay weekly 'pence' to attend school. This was usually two pence for the first child and one penny each for siblings. After Elmore Green opened in 1882 the Headmaster of the National School (Bloxwich C. of E.) had to reduce his charges which had increased to three pence and two pence to avoid being undercut by the new school and thereby losing pupils. (Source: R. C. Butt, *The 'National Schools, Bloxwich'*)

The 1891 Elementary Education Act decreed that elementary education was to be provided free. The Act provided for ten shillings (50p) a year to be paid as a 'fee grant' by Parliament for each child over three and under fifteen attending a public elementary school. The schools were forbidden to charge additional fees except in certain circumstances. Parents were finally relieved of the task of providing the 'pence' each week.

In 1893 the minimum leaving age was raised to eleven and in 1899 it rose to the age of twelve. However, if they wanted to get a job before the age of fourteen they would have been required to show a certificate that they had reached Standard IV (see table on page 53).

Funding for Elmore Green School depended to a large extent on average attendance and examination results, though attendance was affected, initially, by the parent's ability to pay the 'pence'. Times of sickness, industrial strikes, recessions and inclement weather were reflected in the school's registers. In many respects, despite its mines and factories, Bloxwich was still a rural community and attendance was often affected by 'picking' and 'harvesting'.

Examination results were measured by pupils reaching defined standards. The following are the six '*Standards of Education*' contained in the *Revised code of Regulations, 1872*:

STANDARD I	
Reading	One of the narratives next in order after monosyllables in an elementary reading book used in the school.
Writing	Copy in manuscript character a line of print, and write from dictation a few common words.
Arithmetic	Simple addition and subtraction of numbers of not more than four figures, and the multiplication table to multiplication by six.
STANDARD II	
Reading	A short paragraph from an elementary reading book.
Writing	A sentence from the same book, slowly read once, and then dictated in single words.
Arithmetic	The multiplication table, and any simple rule as far as short division (inclusive).
STANDARD III	
Reading	A short paragraph from a more advanced reading book.
Writing	A sentence slowly dictated once by a few words at a time, from the same book.
Arithmetic	Long division and compound rules (money).
STANDARD IV	
Reading	A few lines of poetry or prose, at the choice of the inspector.
Writing	A sentence slowly dictated once, by a few words at a time, from a reading book, such as is used in the first class of the school.
Arithmetic	Compound rules (common weights and measures).
STANDARD V	
Reading	A short ordinary paragraph in a newspaper, or other modern narrative.
Writing	Another short ordinary paragraph in a newspaper, or other modern narrative, slowly dictated once by a few words at a time.
Arithmetic	Practice and bills of parcels.
STANDARD VI	
Reading	To read with fluency and expression.
Writing	A short theme or letter, or an easy paraphrase.
Arithmetic	Proportion and fractions (vulgar and decimal).

The result of these Standards of Education regulations was the organisation of elementary schools on the basis of annual promotion. Only if a pupil reached the standard could they move to the next level. Classes in the senior department were named standards I to VI, roughly corresponding to ages seven to twelve.

From the beginning there was much opposition to these arrangements. Teachers objected mainly to the principle of 'payment by results' because it linked money for schools with the pupils reaching a minimum standard. There was no incentive for schools to widen the curriculum beyond the three R's, thus the higher primary work which was beginning to appear before 1861 in the best elementary schools was seriously discouraged. The only form of practical instruction that survived was needlework.

Furthermore, the standards themselves were defective because they were based not on any educational research into what children of a given age might understand, but on an 'idea' of what they ought to know.

Over the years the initial strict conditions were gradually relaxed: more freedom was allowed. The tests were made more flexible and the exams were taken by sample only. From about 1892 the standards system began to fall into disuse and it was finally abandoned by the Board of Education around the turn of the century, much to the joy, no doubt, of the teaching staff of Elmore Green.

Families who wanted their children to be educated beyond elementary level had the choice of grammar schools in Walsall or Lichfield. Queen Mary's School in Walsall was the obvious choice and, significantly, an important part of its funding came from the coal bearing lands of Little Bloxwich and Fishley. Deeds left by Richard Francis in 1657 awarded Queen Mary's the considerable mining royalties of this area. It was no surprise therefore that Bloxwich people were up in arms when in 1871 Queen Mary's proposed that a minimum fee of £6 a year must be paid by every scholar. A Bloxwich miner working a twelve-hour shift at that time earned about 2 shillings (10p) a day. There was great resentment that Grammar School education would only be available for the children of the rich (i.e. Walsall) and at a public meeting in September 1871 it was observed:

> *"The high fees proposed will necessarily exclude the majority of rate payers from any participation in the benefits of this wealthy foundation."*
> (Source: E. J. Homeshaw, 'The Story of Bloxwich')

A resolution was passed demanding the erection of a branch of the Grammar School in Bloxwich.

Elmore Green Elementary school proved to be too small and in 1902 the lack of space at the school compelled the transfer of the younger boys to temporary accommodation in High Street, Bloxwich. A building for a junior mixed school was subsequently added to Elmore Green in 1904. Two years later, the schools were re-organised into what we now know as Primary and Secondary schools.

The Elmore Green secondary school became a Higher Elementary school in 1908.

Higher Elementary schools received a higher rate of grant than the ordinary public elementary schools on the condition that they provided a four-year course for promising children aged ten to fifteen. The report of the Government Consultative Committee affecting higher elementary schools was published in May 1906. It argued that a higher elementary school should continue the general education which a child had already received in the ordinary elementary school. The first need was,

> *'...to secure for each child as much humanity, as much accurate knowledge of general elementary fact and as much mental power and manual aptitude, as could be expected during a short course of instruction extending over three years at a comparatively early age.'*

The course should consist of three strands: humanistic, scientific and manual, and, in the case of girls, domestic. The curriculum included drawing, theoretical and practical science, a foreign language and elementary mathematics.

Those pupils attending school after 1906 were to get the benefit of school meals for the first time. A new act of Parliament empowered Local Education Authorities to provide meals for undernourished elementary school children. One LEA which quickly took advantage of this new power was the City of Bradford. In an Education Committee Report, Medical Superintendent Ralph H. Crowley reported on a *'Course of Meals given to Necessitous Children'* between April and July 1907:

> *The meals, consisting of breakfast and dinner were given in a School in one of the poorest quarters of the city, about thirty of the children coming from this school, and ten from an adjacent one. The children were selected out of Standards I. to IV. by the Head Teacher and myself. ... Every effort was made to make the meals, as far as possible, educational. There were tablecloths and flowers on the tables; monitresses, whose duty it was to lay the tables and to wait on the other children, were appointed, one to each group of ten children; they were provided with aprons and sleeves and had their meals together after the other children. ... The tablecloths, it is true were very dirty at the end of the week, but this was chiefly due to the dirty clothing of the children, and owing to the very inadequate provision at the school for the children to wash themselves, it was difficult to ensure that even their hands were clean.* (The National Archives: 'School Dinners')

Eventually, the 1918 Education Act changed Elmore Green to a selective Central School. This provided an improved general education of a practical character, sometimes with a slight industrial or commercial bias, for pupils between the ages of eleven and fourteen or fifteen.

Although Bloxwich pupils were still able to take entrance examinations for Queen Mary's they now had their own selective school.

Chapter Three

The 'Parker Street Boys'

PARKER STREET has the distinction of being home to the largest number of 'memorial boys'. At some point before leaving Bloxwich for the last time Bertie Gill, Frank Groom, Frank Harvey, Alfred Main, George Sargent, Albert Stych and Robert Sylvester all lived there. Indeed, Frank Groom and Frank Harvey both lived at number 92 but at different times. Frank Groom lived there in 1911 and Frank Harvey was there at the time of the 1901 Census.

The houses in Parker Street had been built about 25 years before the outbreak of the Great War and only the west side of the street had residences. The 62 houses give an excellent reflection of Bloxwich as a whole. The 1911 Census tells us that of the 168 people employed, 101 (60%) of them worked in the coal mines. The remaining 67 worked in such diverse jobs as chain making (5), carpentry (4), tailoring (4), leather stitching (4), domestic service (4), and 3 each in awl blade making, spring hook makers, errand boys, bricklayers' labourers, bakers and assistant bakers and locksmiths.

Although all the houses were 'three up, two down' they were occupied by as many as fourteen persons (as with Thomas Lawrence's family at number 44) and as few as one (at number 126 where Elizabeth Dudson lived as a woman of 'private means').

The average occupancy of the 62 houses was seven persons. 46 of the heads of households were born in the Bloxwich/Walsall/Wolverhampton area while others came from places such as Wales, Cumbria, Devon, Yorkshire and Ireland.

Five of the seven Parker Street boys named on the memorial worked in the 'pits'. The exceptions were Alfred Main, whose father was a 'miner, hewer,' enlisted in the army before the war and Frank Groom who enlisted in April 1918. There is no record of his employment before that although his father, Thomas, worked in a local colliery as a 'stallman'.

Frank Harvey was employed at the Allen's Rough Colliery as a blacksmith's striker. This was an appropriate job for a young sportsman with a particular talent for boxing. The colliery was easily reached from Parker Street being near the site of the present Allen's Rough Primary School, New Invention.

Albert Stych was employed as a miner at the Fair Lady pit, Coppice Colliery which was sited on the south west corner of Five Ways island at Heath Hayes. The 'Fair Lady' in question was Lady Bowering-Hanbury who took great interest in the welfare of the workers at the pit providing food in times of strikes and organising trips to Blackpool for her mining families.

Three of the five men worked at the Holly Bank Colliery which was situated on the Bloxwich side of Essington village. This pit employed many men from Bloxwich, particularly from Parker Street and Sand Bank. The period between 1895 and the outbreak of war saw the manpower numbers rising at Holly Bank from 532 to more than 1,220. The Holly Bank Colliery established in 1895 had begun life as the Essington Wood Colliery (1855) and would end its life as the Hilton Main (1924) as the sinking of shafts moved gradually northwest following the deepening seams of coal.

Bertie Gill's father Jonah had actually been born in Essington and worked as a coal miner. Bertie also became a miner at Holly Bank until he voluntarily enlisted in January 1915. In the 1911 Census, while living at 100, Parker Street, he was described as being a 'coal miner driver below'. Drivers were usually young boys who drove the pit-ponies on the 'main roads' underground.

George Sargent, who lived at number 60 was a colliery labourer 'on top' at Holly Bank, as was his younger brother, Harry.

Finally, Robert Sylvester who had lived in Parker Street as a young boy, worked with his father William at Holly Bank until he enlisted in 1914. They probably worked together in a team of four. Two hewers would get the coal and put in timber to support the roof. A loader would put the coal into trucks and a driver and pony would take away the full trucks and return with empty ones. Each truck would be marked so that when it was weighed it would be 'booked' to the stall that had mined it. Usually a single wage packet was given to each stall reflecting the amount of coal it had produced. After deductions for powder and fuses, the money was shared out among the team.

Of course, Parker Street was also home to many men who had not attended Elmore Green and seven of these were among those never to return.

Samuel Stych, brother of Albert, had moved from Parker Street to Pontefract, Yorkshire looking for work. Married with three children he was killed at Festubert on 9th March 1916 aged 26.

Harry Taylor lived at 50, Parker Street and had attended the Bloxwich National School. He had been a member of 'D' Company of the Territorials before the war and was killed on 13th October 1915 while attacking the Hohenzollern Redoubt. He left a widow and one child.

Charles George Millington had lived with his mother at 44, Parker Street while working at Allens Rough Colliery. He was an early volunteer in August 1914 joining the South Staffords. He never married and was killed in action on the same day and in the same attack as his neighbour three doors away, Harry Taylor.

Arthur Smith at number 86, Parker Street had been a Holly Bank miner before volunteering in December 1914. While fighting for the Royal Field Artillery, he was killed in action near Arras on 28th May 1917, aged 26. He left a widow and three children.

Alfred Evans of 2, Parker Street had been in the same battalion as Harry Taylor and Charles Millington but, unlike them, had survived the attacks on the Hohenzollern Redoubt in 1915. After being wounded twice he eventually died on 4th January 1918 near Béthune.

Henry (Harry) Ball was the son of the newsagent in Parker Street living at number 104. Leaving his job at Bloxwich Colliery he volunteered with the 1/5 South Staffordshire in 1914. In the same battalion as Alfred Evans, Charles Millington and Harry Taylor he died shortly after his battalion returned from Egypt. He was killed on Sunday, 2nd April 1916 when a mine exploded under trenches at Ecoivres and he is commemorated on the Arras Memorial to the Missing,

Parker Street – data from the 1911 Census

- 62 Residences
- Holding 441 people
- The largest household had 14 persons (number 44).
- The smallest household held one person, a 76 year old widow of 'private means' (number 126).
- 168 were employed
- 60% (101) of those were employed in the coal mines.

The other 67 were employed in 26 different occupations including:

Chain making	5
Carpenters	4
Tailoring	4
Leather stitching	4
Domestic servants	4
Polishing	3
Awl blade makers	3
Spring hook makers	3
Errand boys	3
Bricklayers' labourers	3
Bakers and assistants	3
Locksmiths	3

Chapter Four

A Tradition of Military Service

DURING THE twentieth century, many lads from Bloxwich, most willingly, some reluctantly, served in the British armed forces during the two world wars. In excess of three hundred Bloxwich men lost their lives in the Great War (1914-1918); rather fewer died in the second war against Germany (1939-1945). Men from the town continue to join the services and more, sadly, have paid the ultimate price. Many have survived the wars, damaged in body and health, though their names are rarely publicly celebrated in the same way as those on Bloxwich's war memorials.

Similarly to most parts of the country, lads from this area have sought military service for a wide range of reasons – not the least of which has been to avoid the dangerous, exhausting grind of the coal-mines. Sometimes, joining the military was a release from the poverty of typically large families; infrequently, it was offered by a local magistrate as a means to avoid prison; just occasionally it might well have been a career of choice, though a poorly-paid and harsh one.

Back in Tudor times (1487-1603), numerous Bloxwich lads were numbered among the members of the local home guard or militia. Most of these men would have been given little choice by their social 'betters', who, in their turn, were required to provide partly-equipped soldiers (or at least bodies) when the Crown demanded. During the reign of Henry VIII (1509-1547), every man over the age of sixteen was expected to possess and practise skills with the legendary longbow and the more bucolic, though deadly billhook or pike. The impetus for such a militarily-trained populace originated as a consequence of

Henry's determination to pass on the crown of his newly-established dynasty to a male heir. His wife, Queen Katherine of Aragon, had only one child, a daughter, Princess Mary. As Katherine was very unlikely by dint of her age to conceive again, Henry demanded an annulment to the marriage so that he might marry a woman who could provide him with a male heir. Only the Pope could grant the king's wish for a divorce but at that time the Papacy was in thrall to the powerful Habsburg Emperor, Charles V and the emperor was Katherine's uncle!

As is now common knowledge, Henry ignored the Pope's jurisdiction, declared himself head of the Church in England, and duly granted his own divorce. In 1538 Pope Paul IV excommunicated Henry from the Catholic Church and encouraged Charles V and Francis I of France to settle their differences and unite to invade England in the name of the Church. Recognising the real possibility of invasion, the king ordered a muster of his kingdom's armed forces. This really meant an audit of every locality – who had what weapons, who was skilled in their use, who owned a horse and harness (this makeshift 'cavalry' was an early forerunner of the yeomanry that fought in 1914-1918).

Ironically, this militia was never called upon to fight but the audit has survived to provide a record of the military predecessors of modern Bloxwich lads. Some of the names among the militia mirror those whose names are recorded on the Elmore Green Old Boys' memorial that commemorated the school's dead of the Great War.

ELMORE GREEN 1914-18 MEMORIAL:	BLOXWICH TUDOR MILITIA 1539:
Samuel George Harrison *(Territorial, infantry volunteer)*	**John Haryson** *(possessed protective leather doublet; owned a bow and was a skilled archer)*
	Thomas Harryson *(similar to John Haryson, above)*
	Wylliam Harryson *(owned a bow and was a skilled archer)*
	Wylliam Harryson *(a skilled archer)*
Joseph Orgill *(Territorial; CAMC volunteer)*	**Thomas Orgyll** *(owned a gorget – a metal or leather collar to protect the throat; arrows and a bill)*
	Richard Orgyll *(possessed metal armour to protect the man from vulnerability of sleeveless jacket)*

Aaron Hayward
(*Regular; infantry volunteer*)
John Bate
(*Guardsman, volunteer*)

George Smith
(*Infantry volunteer*)

J. Smith
(*Presently unidentified*)
Samuel Smith
(*Territorial; volunteer; driver,
then infantryman*)
George Alexander Groves
(*Territorial, infantry volunteer*)
(John) William Groves
(*Regular; infantry volunteer*)
William Amos Bullock
(*Infantry volunteer*)
Alfred Charles Bullock
(*Territorial, infantry volunteer*)

Thomas Heyward
(*a skilled billman*)
John Bett
(*leather jerkin, with metal arm-protectors, a
gorget, poleaxe and his own horse*)
Robert Smyth
(*leather jerkin, with metal arm-protectors; a
bow and half a sheaf of arrows*)
William Smyth
(*skilled billman*)
Robert Smythe
(*skilled billman*)

Thomas Grove
(*skilled billman*)

William Bulok
(*leather jerkin, with metal arm-
protectors*

This tradition undoubtedly would have continued into later centuries, notably with local men serving in the army and navy during the wars against Revolutionary and Napoleonic France (1792 to 1815), during the worldwide British Colonial and Imperial actions of the Victorian era and during the struggles against the Boer settlers in South Africa (1899-1902). The latter war was the first after which numerous local war memorials commemorated those who had fought and fallen – seemingly making soldiering a more 'respectable' profession.

The First World War (1914-1918) caused more traceable local casualties than any other conflict in history, though it was far from the last in which local lads lost their lives 'for King and Country'. Although there is no war memorial to the Elmore Green Old Boys killed during the Second World War (1939-1945), that conflict led to many former pupils serving in various branches of the armed forces and at least twenty-one did not return home.

Elmore Green Old Boys' Roll of Honour, 1939-1945

Dennis Frank ALVES
Sergeant 550539 (Air Gunner)
17 Operation Training Unit, Royal Air Force
Died (age 21) in England on Wednesday, 7th August 1940.
Buried in plot B.22 of Bury Cemetery, Huntingdonshire.

Ralph Charles BURTON
Sergeant 1584576
40 Squadron, Royal Air Force Volunteer Reserve
Died (age 21) on sortie over Yugoslavia on Sunday, 4th February 1945.
Buried in plot XII.D.8 of Bari War Cemetery, Puglia, Italy.

Norman Henry COLEBATCH
Sergeant 1578101
156 Squadron, Royal Air Force Volunteer Reserve
Died on sortie to Germany on Monday, 3rd January 1944.
Commemorated on panel 227 of Runnymede Memorial to the Missing,
Surrey, England.

Albert John DARBY
Sub-Lieutenant (A)
H.M.S. *'Argus'*, Royal Naval Volunteer Reserve
Died (age 22) on Wednesday, 1st March 1944.
Commemorated on Bay 5, Panel 5 of the Lee-on-Solent Memorial to the
Missing, Hampshire.

William HAMER
Guardsman 2611470
3rd Battalion, Grenadier Guards
Died (age 35) in Italy on Wednesday, 9th August 1944.
Buried in plot VI.E.14 of Arezzo War Cemetery, Tuscany, Italy.

Leslie William HARVEY
Gunner 974417
88th Field Regiment, Royal Artillery
Died (age 27) as a P.o.W. in Thailand [Burma-Siam railway] on
Sunday, 4th July 1943.
Buried in collective grave 10.F.2-10.L.4 of Kanchanaburi War Cemetery.
Thailand.

John Amos HENDEN
Lance Corporal 4916310
1st Battalion, South Lancashire Regiment
Died (age 22) in Holland on Monday, 6th November 1944.
Buried in plot VIII.C.13 of Mierlo War Cemetery, Noord-Brabant,
Netherlands.

Victor John HORNE
Signalman 4917513
6th Armoured Division Signals, Royal Corps of Signals
Died (age 23) in Italy on Sunday, 11th March 1945
Buried in plot I.E.6 of Florence War Cemetery, Tuscany.

Raymond Robert HUMPHREYS
Private 14654939
4th Battalion, King's Shropshire Light Infantry
Died (age 20) in Germany on Friday, 13th April 1945
Buried in plot II.H.3 of Becklingen War Cemetery, Niedersachsen, Germany.

Noah LAW
Petty Officer Stoker C/KX 75431
H.M. Submarine *'Olympus'*, Royal Navy
Died (age 36) at sea on Friday, 8th May 1942
Commemorated on Panel 61,1 of Chatham Naval Memorial, Kent.

Sidney Joseph MALABAND
Sergeant 1819794
106 Squadron, Royal Air Force Volunteer Reserve
Died (age 22) on sortie over Germany on Thursday, 22nd June 1944
Buried in plot V.A.1 of Uden War Cemetery, Noord-Brabant, Netherlands.

Jeffrey MARSH
Trooper 7905072
15/19th King's Royal Hussars, Royal Armoured Corps
Died (age 22) in Holland on Wednesday, 18th October 1944
Buried in plot II.E.2 of Venray War Cemetery, Limburg, Netherlands.

Cecil Charles NEVILLE
Sergeant 1343367
Army Educational Corps
Died (age 24) in Singapore on Friday, 13th February 1942.
Commemorated on column 111 of Singapore Memorial to the Missing,
Kranji War Cemetery, Singapore.

Thomas Josiah PRITCHARD
Sergeant 655945
40 Squadron, Royal Air Force Volunteer Reserve
Died (age 24) on sortie over Tunisia on Thursday, 31st December 1942.
Commemorated on Panel 4, Column 2 of Malta Memorial to the Missing,
Floriana, Malta.

Randolph Frank RINGROSE
(A) Sub-Lieutenant
H.M.S. *'Dipper'*, Royal Naval Volunteer Reserve
Died (age 20) in England on Monday, 8th November 1943
Buried in Section Q, Grave 152 of Rushall (St. Michael) Churchyard,
Walsall, Staffordshire.

Geoffrey Joseph SMITH
Aircraftman 2nd Class 1582768
Royal Air Force Volunteer Reserve
Died (age 22) in South Africa on Sunday, 6th February 1944
Buried in Section K, Grave 18 of Queenstown Cemetery,
Eastern Cape, South Africa.

Richard WALTERS
Private 4916686
5th Battalion, South Staffordshire Regiment
Died (age 30) in France on Friday, 18th August 1944
Buried in plot VIII.E.20 of Bayeux War Cemetery,
Normandy, France.

John William WHITTAKER
Private 14780321
6th Battalion, King's Own Scottish Borderers
Died (age 19) in Germany on Sunday, 18th February 1945.
Buried in plot 12.F.4 of Rheinberg War Cemetery,
Nordrhein-Westfalen, Germany.

John WITHNALL
Lance Corporal 4928645
Hallamshire Battalion, York and Lancaster Regiment
Died (age 29) in France on Wednesday, 23rd August 1944.
Buried in plot V.D.12 of St. Desir War Cemetery,
near Lisieux, Normandy, France.

Frank WOODFIELD
Sergeant 954449
144 Squadron, Royal Air Force Volunteer Reserve
Died (age 25) in England on Saturday, 11th April 1942.
Buried in Section 37, Grave 9 of Walsall (Ryecroft) Cemetery, Staffordshire.

Norman Alfred YARDLEY
Telegraphist D/JX 330244
H.M.S. *'Copra'*, Royal Navy
Died (age 21) in Belgium on Thursday, 2nd November 1944.
Buried in plot 9, Row 6, Grave 38 of Oostende New Communal Cemetery,
West-Vlaanderen, Belgium.

Since 1945 local lads have continued to serve in the forces and some have paid the ultimate price in Korea (1950-1953), various Imperial actions, during the 'Troubles' in Northern Ireland and latterly in the South Atlantic, Iraq and Afghanistan. No doubt the tradition of honourable service will continue into the future.

Chapter Five

Pre-1914 Soldiering in Bloxwich

IN 1870, Edward Cardwell was appointed Secretary of State for War in Mr. Gladstone's first Liberal government and commenced a series of reforms aimed to modernise the British Army, partly as a response to the shock successes of Prussia over Austria (1866) and France (1870-71) and partly as a logical development of Gladstone's liberal principles. The reforms would continue, somewhat piecemeal, under subsequent administrations.

Among the aspects addressed by the reforms that continued under various governments at least until 1908 was the abolition of the purchase of commissions, a process that had ensured that the officer class was populated by many of the younger sons of the aristocracy and gentry, sometimes regardless of ability. Terms of enlistment for the ordinary soldier were changed to twelve years (part active service, part reserve, often 'six and six') in place of 'life' enlistment; this would be adjusted again before the onset of the First World War. New equipment was introduced, though prior to 1914 the British Army was slow to appreciate the possibilities of the machine-gun. Even in 1914 in the higher echelons, the army was still dominated by generals of cavalry background as opposed to infantry or artillery.

As part of the reform process, the naming of infantry regiments replaced the traditional numbering system in 1881, though regimental seniority was maintained so the First Regiment of Foot, the Royal Scots, remained the senior regiment in the British Army. Most regiments were named on a 'County' basis, with a 'local' regimental depot to aid recruitment and create 'local' ties.

Staffordshire was deemed a large enough county to warrant the creation of two named regiments – locally the 38th and 80th Regiments of Foot became the First and Second Battalions of the South Staffordshire Regiment, with the regimental depot in Lichfield.

In the north of the county, the 64th and 98th Regiments of Foot became the Prince of Wales (North Staffordshire) Regiment. So from 1881 most regiments had two regular battalions, one or two militia battalions and one or two battalions of Rifle Volunteers.

In 1908 the naming and function of battalions within each regiment was regularised. In the South Staffordshire Regiment, the two regular, professional battalions were 1st and 2nd, one of which was nearly always on overseas service. By then, regular army enlistment was known as 'seven and five' for the infantry[3], that is seven years with the Colours and five in the army reserve (remaining liable to be recalled in time of emergency). A volunteer had to be between 18 and 38 years old, taller than 5 feet 3 inches and pass a medical examination; as a volunteer, he was allowed a say in his choice of regiment or corps. In 1914, some of the Elmore Green lads were professional soldiers on overseas service while others had served their seven years with the Colours and were on the National Army Reserve when war was declared; these men were James Dawson, Ernest Lavender, Joseph Bullock, Aaron Hayward, George Stych and possibly John Bullock.

In 1908 there were two forms of 'part-time' soldiering available, the Special Reserve and the Territorial Force. The Special Reserve had its origins in the militia and written records in Bloxwich may be traced to the reign of King Henry VIII's Tudor Militia; it has been suggested that the idea of the militia may date back to the Anglo-Saxon 'Fyrd' that was raised from the local population in time of national emergency. By 1908 the Special Reserve existed to supplement the regular army reserve with partly-trained men who could easily be fed into the front-line battalions in wartime. The Special Reservist enlisted for a six-year term, initially trained full-time for six months (on full regular army pay) and thereafter was free to resume his civilian occupation but had to train for up to four weeks per year and was paid a small annual 'retainer' by the army. One or two Elmore Green lads gained military experience in the South Staffordshire Regiment's Special Reserve (3rd and 4th Battalions) but it was a system unpopular with employers and locally could not compete with the attraction of the newly-formed Territorial Force. Even so, at least five Elmore Green lads enlisted in the Special Reserve, namely John William Groves, Frank Harvey, Timothy Taylor, Joseph Orgill and Alfred Main.

---

3   For artillerymen, known as 'gunners', it was still 'six and six.'

Pre-war, likely 1914. 1/5 Battalion, South Staffordshire Regiment: No.2 Platoon, 'D' Company.

The above photograph includes George Sargent (middle row, five from right), Charles Bullock (middle row, three from left), Bill Haycock (middle, three from right), Arthur Linnell (front, four from left). Albert Stych and Len Morris (served as Malpass) may also be present.

Most local lads with any military inclination were attracted to enlist for a four-year term with the South Staffordshire Territorials – 1/5th Battalion covered the Walsall area while 1/6th Battalion covered the Wolverhampton area. During the six years prior to 1914, each 'Terrier' battalion comprised eight companies – the Bloxwich 'Terriers' were officially 1/5th Battalion's 'D' Company, based at the local Drill Hall (otherwise known as Bloxwich Public Hall on the corner of Wolverhampton Road). While still retaining his civilian job, a lad could enlist at 17 for the Terriers (younger than for the Regular Army) and would train in the evenings or at the weekend, thus obtaining a taste of army life without the long-term dislocation from home and workmates. Enlistment conditions demanded the same of 'Terriers' as of regulars but the Territorial Force could not be forced to serve overseas without an individual's assent – its function was to serve where needed within the United Kingdom. The lads from the Elmore Green story who are known or thought to have served with the local Territorials were William 'Coxy' Lavender, Horace Downes, Leonard Malpass, George Sargent, Jack Parton, , Joseph Handy, George Groves, Arthur Linnell, Albert Stych, Joseph Stych, Frank Lloyd, John Orgill, Robert Sylvester, Bill Haycock, Ben Haycock and Edward Smith.

Sadly, for the entire generation an opportunity and even necessity for full-time soldiering was looming on the horizon. When asked to sign the Imperial Service Obligation allowing a 'Terrier' to serve overseas, most lads jumped at the chance to prove they were not merely 'weekend warriors'. When the time came, they did not let down their king and country.

PART II

The storm breaks, summer 1914...

Chapter Six

The Road to War, June to August 1914

"One day the great European War will come out of some damned foolish thing in the Balkans." (Count Otto von Bismarck)

Sunday, 28th June

Archduke Franz Ferdinand, heir to the thrones of Imperial Austria and of Hungary, and his wife Sophie, were assassinated in the Bosnian town of Sarajevo. Several of the assassins, including Gavrilo Princip who fired the fatal shots, were arrested; Austria claimed that the plot had been hatched by Serbia, an avowed enemy of Austria.

Saturday, 5th July

the German emperor, Kaiser Wilhelm II, promised his Austrian counterpart, Emperor Franz Josef, *"…full support"* if action were to be taken against Serbia. Wilhelm then went on a holiday cruise in the Baltic Sea.

Thursday, 23rd July

an Austrian ultimatum, provocatively worded, was delivered to the Serb government in Belgrade at 6 p.m. Agreement to all points of the ultimatum was demanded by Austria by 6 p.m. on Saturday, 25th July, just 48 hours later.

Friday, 24th July

Germany repeated its support for Austria's harsh ultimatum to Serbia.

Britain proposed an international conference in order to avoid war.

Belgium announced that in the event of war, it would remain neutral, *"…whatever the consequences."*

Saturday, 25th July Serbia sent a conciliatory reply to Austria, agreeing to all but one of the demands. Even so, Serbia also mobilised its army, just in case!

Sunday, 26th July Austria mobilised its army towards Serbia.

Monday, 27th July France and Italy supported Britain's proposal of a peace-saving conference.

Tuesday, 28th July Austria declared war on Serbia (exactly one month after the assassination of Franz Ferdinand in Sarajevo.)

Vienna, 28th July 1914, Count Berchtold:
"…The Royal Serbian Government not having answered in a satisfactory manner the note of July 23rd, 1914, presented by the Austro-Hungarian Minister at Belgrade, the Imperial and Royal Government are themselves compelled to see to the safeguarding of their rights and interests, and, with this object, to have recourse to force of arms. Austria-Hungary consequently considers herself henceforward in a state of war with Serbia."

Also, Germany rejected the idea of a conference.

Wednesday, 29th July As a threat to Austria, Russia mobilised its army in support of Serbia.

Thursday, 30th July Britain rejected a German request for British neutrality in the case of a European war.

Friday, 31st July Belgium and Russia ordered a general mobilisation of their armed forces; Austria also ordered general mobilisation.

Germany sent an ultimatum to Russia – *"…stand down your army or prepare to fight a war."*

Saturday, 1st August Britain mobilised the Royal Navy.

Germany ordered general mobilisation, declared war on Russia and invaded.

France ordered general mobilisation.

Sunday, 2nd August Germany demanded safe passage through Belgium, in order to attack France.

Monday, 3rd August Britain promised support for Belgium if
[UK Bank Holiday] Germany invaded that neutral country.

Germany declared war on France.

	The British Cabinet met late in the morning and the House of Commons met in special session in the afternoon; just after 5:00 p.m., Britain ordered general mobilisation.
	Italy announced its neutrality, although it was technically an ally of Germany and Austria.
Tuesday, 4th August	Following an ignored ultimatum objecting to the German invasion of neutral Belgium, Britain declared war on Germany at 11p.m.
	Germany declared war on Belgium and invaded the small, hitherto neutral country.
Wednesday, 5th August	Austria declared war on Russia.
	Serbia declared war on Germany.
Friday, 7th August	First units of the British Expeditionary Force (BEF) landed in France.
Wednesday, 12th August	Britain and France declared war on Austria.

'Great Britain Declares War on Germany'

"…Great Britain is in a state of war with Germany. It was officially stated at the Foreign Office last night that Great Britain declared war against Germany at 11.00 p.m. The British Ambassador in Berlin has been handed his passport. War was Germany's reply to our request that she should respect the neutrality of Belgium, whose territories we were bound in honour and by treaty obligations to maintain inviolate."

The following statement was issued from the Foreign Office last night:

"Owing to the summary rejection by the German Government of the request made by his Majesty's Government for assurances that the neutrality of Belgium would be respected, his Majesty's Ambassador in Berlin has received his passport, and his Majesty's Government has declared to the German Government that a state of war exists between Great Britain and Germany as from 11.00 p.m. on August 4th."

['*Daily Mirror*', front page on Wednesday, 5th August 1914]

In the official announcement from the Foreign Office in Whitehall, the '*casus belli*' (cause of war) was thus clearly given as Germany's invasion of Belgium, a small, independent nation, whose neutrality Britain had committed itself to uphold according to the international Treaty of London (1839). Ironically Germany, also a signatory to this treaty, referred to it as a, "*…scrap of paper*". Britain's defence of 'Little Belgium' was immediately construed in the British press as taking the part of the underdog against an 'international bully'. The most famous example of this view appeared in *'Punch'* magazine in August 1914; drawn by F.H. Townsend, the magazine's art editor, it was captioned, *'They shall not pass'*, and showed *'Brave little Belgium'* standing up to the *'Prussian bully'*. The cartoon was always likely to appeal to the British love of fair play. [By coincidence, in 1916 France's blood-soaked, nine-month defence of Verdun was also noted for its rallying cry of, *'Ils ne passeront pas'* - They shall not pass]. Even so, was this violation of Belgian neutrality the real reason for war? Was it sufficient reason to change forever so many Bloxwich

"They shall not pass." Brave Little Belgium defies the Prussian Bully.
[F.H. Townsend, 'Punch', March 1914]

families' lives? How might conversation have gone in the greengrocer's on the High Street or over a pint in the bar of the 'Sandbank Tavern' or in the smoke room of the 'Spring Cottage'?

On the evening of 4th August, crowds gathered in London. As Big Ben struck 11 p.m. (midnight in Berlin) they sang *'God Save the King'*, and then ran home crying: *'War! War! War!'* [Similar such scenes were also played out by patriotic crowds in Berlin]. As British Foreign Secretary Sir Edward Grey watched the crowds leave London's Parliament Square, he observed:

"The lights are going out all over Europe: we shall not see them lit again in our lifetime."

Yet it had been a lovely late summer in Bloxwich. The August Bank Holiday (Monday, 3rd August) had released hundreds of hard-working family-men from the endless grind of their labours to spend a few precious leisure hours with wives and children. There were rumours of grave problems, even a crisis, on the continent; something about one of the Austrian royals being murdered. Yet over the previous ten years crisis had followed crisis in North Africa and in the Balkan Mountains; there had been a couple of wars out there but nothing to really involve good old England! Everything had always been resolved without the Great Powers *really* falling foul of each other – after all, this was the twentieth century and the European nations had spread their culture and civilisation throughout their extensive empires. Why would any nation put all that peace and prosperity at risk? Nevertheless, by way of precaution the government kept the banks closed beyond the normal Bank Holiday. Even so, as the last days of July gave way to early August, these rumours about Germany persisted; there might just possibly be a war. But surely that was unthinkable in such civilised times? Anyway, Britannia ruled the waves – the all-powerful Royal Navy would keep us safe, just as it had for centuries past… As an island nation, separate from and immune to the foibles of continental Europe, the British regarded the English Channel as the world's most effective 'Moat and Drawbridge', and it was the task of the navy to ensure that the drawbridge was in perfect working order!

Britain was accustomed to being 'top' nation. Over the course of centuries, the British had built an extensive overseas empire (about a quarter of the world) on which it was said, *"…the sun never set…"*. Such was the global extent of the British Empire. During the nineteenth century, the European nations' quest for overseas empire had been fired by the demand for raw materials required by new technology that was taking to new heights the Industrial Revolution whose origins were in Britain. Such imperial expansion also provided exclusive markets for finished products. Of course, obtaining colonies demanded the protective military power of modern armies, and as soldiers could at that time reach far-off colonies only by sea transport, modern sea-power was crucially important. As steam-powered ships gradually replaced sail, so strategically-located coaling-stations (and later, oiling-stations) round the globe became a necessity. With such opportunities for wealth creation and the sophistication of modern culture, it was often said that war was *'unthinkable'*. What is more, the principal royal families of Europe were closely inter-related by blood and marriage.

Britain's was not the only old-established empire but was the only one not distracted by direct control of territories on the European continent, as were the Ottoman (Turkish), Russian, Habsburg (Austro-Hungarian) and French Empires. The nineteenth century witnessed the rise of the 'new' nationalist states of Germany (rising from the military power of Prussia), and Italy (emerging from the power of Piedmont). These vibrant, young nations were ambitious to emulate the example of their longer-established 'elders and betters' in seeking their place in the sun, particularly in Africa and the Far East. Along with political independence came the need for economic and military independence. In the Balkan region, this new factor was replicated in smaller states such as Serbia where, by definition, nationalism threateningly challenged the old order and the old empires *within* the boundaries of Europe. The long-anticipated decline and possible break-up of the Ottoman Empire (essentially European Turkey), consequently known as the 'Sick Man of Europe', was mirrored to the west of the Balkans by the potential decline of Austria-Hungary, an ancient empire comprising a dozen separate, subject nationalities and languages. Thus the Balkan region, fired by Serb ambitions for a 'Greater Serbia' (Serbian nationalists hoped to unite all Serbs by absorbing Bosnia-Herzegovina, Macedonia, Montenegro, Croatia and Dalmatia), was located between two old, crumbling empires and posed many dangerous, unanswered questions.

To a great extent, nineteenth century nationalism had its origins in the French and American Revolutions of the late eighteenth century. In northern Europe, Prussia's military quest for German unification achieved its goal in January 1871; on the southern fringe of Europe, Italian unification was completed in 1870 with the annexation of Rome and the adoption of that city as capital the following year; in Balkan south-eastern Europe, Slav nationalism witnessed the example of Serbia gaining independence from the Ottoman Turks in 1878 thanks to Russian victory in the Russo-Turkish War of 1877-1878; and, on the Channel coast of western Europe, a precedent had been set by Belgian nationalists who attained independence from the Dutch in 1839. Each politico-military change was to have a major bearing on the course of events that unfolded in the eighty years prior to 1914.

The favourable resolution of international disputes that affected spheres of political and military influence was an indicator of a state's standing among its rivals. Beyond the bounds of Europe, colonial disputes, more often than not involving British overseas interests, could usually be settled by diplomatic wheeling and dealing but *within* Europe's boundaries territorial clashes would actually threaten the peace of the 'old order'[4].

Updating military hardware to reflect the benefits of new technologies has always been standard procedure among leading nations. When two nations, or two blocs of nations, introduce new hardware at much the same time, it generally gives rise to the term 'arms race', though new weaponry is usually researched or developed with the aim of solving problems that have arisen during a nation's most recent conflict, or in order to maintain a vital, existing advantage. The latter was true of Britain's regard for the importance of the Royal Navy, where colonial expansion had stimulated military expansion both on land and at sea. New industrial technologies were effectively adapted to transport networks and to military purposes; and so the whirlpool of perceived

---

4   The 'old order' refers to the days when Europe was dominated by the old-established, huge empires – the Habsburg Austrian Empire, the Russian Empire, the Ottoman Turkish Empire and the British Empire.

rivalry intensified. In terms of naval shipping, British-designed ironclad warships, armed with ever-improving guns and gunnery, came to dominate the latter years of the nineteenth century. During the same century on land, accurate repeater rifles employing cartridges replaced single-shot, slow-reloading, smooth-bore muskets; the first machine-guns[5], though not widely appreciated, came into use; barbed-wire, born of the range wars of the U.S. cattle-lands, soon revealed a defensive military application. Artillery pieces moved on from cannon firing largely iron-shot to effective, cartridge-style high explosive shells fired rapidly from breech-loading guns whose power and range increased apace. Chemical technology was later to produce myriad poison gases and flamethrowers for the battlefield. The methods of killing soldiers on an industrial scale quickly outstripped methods of defence and in consequence, casualty figures for all armies were to far exceed that which civilians could reasonably comprehend. And civilians themselves would, for the first time, come under aerial bombardment from the new-fangled flying machines in the form of Zeppelins and bomber aircraft. In short, 1914 raised the curtain on the century of 'total' warfare.

During the century prior to 1914 methods of warfare had evolved considerably in respect of tactics as well as equipment. Back in June 1815, on the muddy battlefield of Waterloo, red-coated squares of musket-equipped infantry held off and defeated circling cavalry, the entire battle being overlooked and directed by the Duke of Wellington on one side and Napoleon on the other. Thereafter, the British army carried out essentially colonial 'policing' actions, albeit world-wide, until the wake-up call afforded by the guerrilla tactics of the Boers during the South African conflict of 1899-1902. In both strategy and tactics, the Great War of 1914-1918 was to bear very few similarities to the British army's experiences of the previous century of battle. In some respects, the sole conflict that bore much resemblance to the nature of the Great War (and one that did not directly involve Britain), was fought in the USA between 1861 and 1865. In terms of strategy and tactics, the American Civil War proved to be a transition between the old and the new – cavalry, infantry and artillery all featured, though so did trenches and Dr. Richard Gatling's innovative but primitive, hand-cranked, multi-barrel machine-gun. Crucially, as the years passed, new military technologies gradually loaded the battlefield advantage heavily in favour of the defence, employing trenches, barbed wire, machine-guns, advanced artillery pieces, air-spotting as well as

---

5   The first emerged during the American Civil War of 1861-65. The Gatling Gun, invented by Dr. Richard Gatling, was hand-cranked and could fire up to 200 rounds per minute. The first true, automatic machine-gun was the Maxim Gun, invented by Hiram Maxim in the 1880's. Its water-cooled recoil-operated firing mechanism could deliver up to 600 rounds per minute.

extensive railway networks for rapid reinforcement and re-supply. However, on land little occurred that encouraged extensive change in the technologies and tactics of the British army – the cavalry remained the elite branch of the army, while the possibilities of the machine-gun remained largely unexplored and unrecognised by many of the military's policy-makers. Ironic, then, that the Great War of 1914-1918 should come to be dominated by technological advance in the form of heavy artillery, machine-guns, air-power and chemical warfare.

In 1914, the most recent conflict between major powers had been between Russia and the industrially-emergent Japan. The Russo-Japanese War of 1904-05 was decided largely at sea in three principal actions, fought in what were, effectively, 'home' waters for the Japanese. The Imperial Russian Navy, comprising its Baltic Fleet, Black Sea Fleet and Pacific Fleet, totalled a greater number of warships but they were widely dispersed. During July 1904, the first clash saw the Russians defeated in the Yellow Sea; then in January 1905, the Russian Pacific fleet was attacked in Port Arthur and badly damaged. In consequence, seven of Russia's European fleet of twenty battleships, considered to be a war-winning weapon, sailed round the globe only to suffer a surprisingly decisive defeat at the hands of Admiral Togo's Japanese fleet in the Battle of Tsushima (14th-15th May 1905). This war more than confirmed Britain's long-held belief in its sea power principle – that the Royal Navy was expected to be stronger than the next two most powerful hostile navies in the world, thus guaranteeing island Britain's freedom from invasion.

The British fleet had progressed from wood and sail to iron hulls, armour-plate, breech-loading heavy guns and steam power, such as the revolutionary H.M.S. 'Warrior' (1860).

HMS 'Warrior', known to and feared by the French (Britain's traditional enemy) as the 'Black Snake of the Channel.'

However, the growth of industrialised Germany, and the accession of Kaiser Wilhelm II in 1888, gave rise to a new naval challenge to Britain's supremacy. The long-time German Chancellor, Otto von Bismarck, whose policies had not only secured the establishment of the unified German nation in 1871 but had also subsequently maintained an advantageous peace in Europe for twenty years, was relieved of office by the new emperor in 1890. In 1897, the Kaiser appointed Admiral Alfred von Tirpitz as Secretary of State of the German Imperial Naval Office; his task was to implement Wilhelm II's ambition to make Germany a world power – 'Weltpolitik' – and for that a strong navy was essential. In 1898 and 1900, Von Tirpitz pushed through the Reichstag (the German Parliament) two Navy Laws which set out the emperor's maritime intentions; the laws specified the types and numbers of warships required and also earmarked finance for the plan. Tirpitz justified such vast expense by naming a specific and powerful naval enemy:

> 'For Germany, the most dangerous naval enemy at the present time is England.... Our fleet must be constructed so that it can unfold its greatest military potential between Heligoland (Bight) and the Thames...' [in effect, the area of the North Sea and the entrance to the Channel – the implicit threat to Britain was clear].

British attention had already been attracted to Germany's naval ambitions by the eight-year construction of the Kiel Canal (cutting through the base of the Jutland Peninsula) that was opened in 1895. The canal furnished a more rapid and safe passage of German warships between the Baltic Sea and the North Sea. In 1907 the Kiel Canal was widened and by 1914 could accommodate Germany's most modern battleships, thus enhancing the threat to Britain's domination of the seas.

When it was launched on 10th February 1906, HMS 'Dreadnought' was the most powerful battleship in the world – the first all-big-gun battleship to enter service, and the first battleship to be powered by Parsons turbines. As a result she was two and a half knots faster than her rivals, and carried twice the firepower of earlier battleships.

After 1906 the world's battle fleets were divided into Dreadnoughts and pre-Dreadnoughts. Unsurprisingly, a new 'race' to construct Dreadnoughts broke out between Britain and Germany, which served to raise the level of tension in Europe. The money spent on modernising the fleet might protect Britain from invasion but could not defeat major potential land enemies. Germany had long been at the cutting edge of military development and Wilhelm II, with the co-operation of his navy minister, Admiral Tirpitz, attempted to replicate this superiority at sea – they could hardly have been unaware of how this ambition would likely be interpreted in Britain.

Since the 1640's, military preparedness, optimum modernity and tactical acuity had been the life-blood of the rise of Brandenburg-Prussia, the forerunner of the German nation. In fact, it was once observed that, *"… most states had an army but the Prussian army had a state."* One of the rulers of Brandenburg-Prussia had commented on the power of the military, *"…you can do anything with bayonets, except sit on them!"* With the brief but notable exception of the supremacy of Revolutionary and Napoleonic France (1789-1815), the army had continued to dominate first Prussia and had then been instrumental in Bismarck's unification of Germany during the 1860's and 1870's[6]. As beneficial to Bismarck's aims as had been the Prussian army, even the Chancellor of the new German Empire recognised that peace was essential for the new German economy to flourish and that a war on two fronts might, at worst, cripple the infant state. To the detriment of the balance of power in Europe, in 1890 Kaiser Wilhelm II saw fit to dismiss the experienced Bismarck. To Germany's detriment, the new Kaiser had great ambitions for his nation but sadly lacked the diplomatic or strategic understanding necessary to bring anything but disaster to his people.

In 1913, Krönprinz Wilhelm, the son of Kaiser Wilhelm II, summed up both Germany's vulnerability and her belief that, if all else failed, force of German arms would prevail, as it had in the recent past. The timing was unfortunate:

> *"Our country is obliged more than any other country to place all its confidence in its good weapons. Set in the centre of Europe, it is badly protected by its unfavourable geographic frontiers, and is regarded by many nations without affection.*
>
> *"Upon the German Empire, therefore, is imposed more emphatically than upon any other peoples of the earth the sacred duty of watching carefully that its army and its navy be always prepared to meet any attack from the outside. It is only by reliance upon our brave sword that we shall be able to maintain that place in the sun which belongs to us, and which the world does not seem very willing to accord us."*

However, no nation's army can remain indefinitely at peak readiness and modernity; such peaks come and go in 'cycles', depending on factors such

---

6   The Prussian army defeated Austria-Hungary in just six weeks in 1866 and proceeded to defeat the French in the Franco-Prussian War of 1870-71. By the subsequent peace treaty, France was forced to cede the border territories of Alsace and Lorraine to Germany – a source of perennial bitterness, resentment and potential for future conflict.

as recruitment methods, training, financial constraints, new weaponry and transport, mobilisation plans, political will and ambition. The German army was due to reach a cyclical peak in 1914; thereafter, Britain and France would catch up in 1915-16; and Russia not until 1917. So from the German generals' perspective, '...*if war must come, better it comes in 1914*'. Also for Germany, a vital influence in political and military decision-making was the Bismarckian fear of a war on two fronts, against the traditional enemy France in the west and her likely Russian ally to the east. Every country's military prepares its plans against the likelihood of war and thus Germany's was intended to deal with the spectre of a two-front war. Every country's war plans had to make provision for the mobilisation[7] of soldiers and sailors, plus a wide range of reservists, equipment and supplies.

In this respect, ever-improving railway networks facilitated the initial rapid deployment of troops towards vulnerable frontiers and the later transport of reinforcements. The principal war plans in the summer of 1914 were broadly as follows:–

Germany:

The plan drawn up by von Schlieffen in 1896, (later revised and implemented by von Moltke in 1914) required a relatively small force to hold back the slow-mobilising Russians in the east, while a smaller force held the frontier with France. The main German force would demand passage through neutral Belgium in order to attack the French capital, Paris, from the vulnerable north.

Russia:

For the lumbering, Russian military, and in a country where distances to enemy borders (particularly Germany to the west and Austria to the south) were so great, mobilisation meant war as such a process was very slow to put into reverse. This was a vital factor in the slide into war.

France:

France had often modified its war plans and in 1914 the current one was Plan Seventeen (XVII). The plan required a minor French force in the east to hold an 'unlikely' German assault through the Ardennes Mountains while the major French units would attack in full force (*'attaquer à l'outrance'* was the French term for this) into the 'lost' provinces of Alsace and Lorraine. For the French army, the Napoleonic by-words were attack, glory and élan.

---

7   Mobilisation (highly over-simplified) is the process of putting the military on a war footing, calling up reservists and moving them to the likely points of enemy contact.

Austria-Hungary:

The Austrians were in a situation similar to their German allies. The Austro-Hungarian army was divided into three elements covering the Russian front, the Serbian front and providing a reserve element to reinforce wherever necessary. 'Part-mobilisation' was thus difficult for Austria-Hungary.

Great Britain:

For the island nation, the war plan logically assumed that sea transport (protected by the ubiquitous Royal Navy) was essential, whether against Germany or France[8]. Once across the Channel, road, rail and Shanks's Pony[9] would move troops to the point of enemy contact.

Considering the reliance of most countries' relatively inflexible mobilisation plans on railway transport networks, it is understandable that one eminent historian, A.J.P. Taylor, made a case for the outbreak of war being, *"…war by railway timetables."* Given that in major nations war plans of some nature were always in existence, that modernisation of armies and fleets was an accepted safeguard, that politicians (sometimes backed by weaponry) not infrequently pushed diplomacy to the limit, why then did the Sarajevo crisis lead to Elmore Green lives being put at risk in the summer of 1914?

In respect of the long-term causes of war, the answer, widely debated, owes much to the secret negotiations of diplomats and politicians that gave rise to complex treaty obligations during the thirty-five years prior to 1914; in the shorter term the '*…staggering and stumbling games of bluff*' of those officials during the six weeks directly following the assassinations at Sarajevo may be seen as culpable.

The pattern of secretly-negotiated European alliances and understandings that had evolved since 1879 is sometimes cited as a major cause of war. Even in peacetime nations usually conclude alliances if they feel exposed to or under implicit strategic threat from rivals and the period 1879-1914 witnessed a time of major insecurity among the European 'Great Powers'. As previously suggested, the rise of nationalism in nineteenth century Europe dramatically affected the balance of power on the continent. The long-established empires (Great Britain, Russia, Habsburg Austria-Hungary and Ottoman Turkey) had for centuries vied for advantage amongst themselves; during the latter half of the seventeenth century France had also been thrust into the front line of the power struggle by Louis XIV's aggressive foreign policy, a role emphasised by

---

8   It was not unknown for soldiers of the British Expeditionary Force to be close to the front line before they were certain which enemy they were due to fight!

9   This is a traditional English term for travelling on foot.

the French Revolutionary Wars and by Napoleon Bonaparte's bid for military domination of the continent.

According to the text of the 1919 Treaty of Versailles[10], Germany was forced to accept responsibility for causing the Great War and paying for its attendant destruction. However, this is too simplistic an explanation. Essentially, Germany was guilty of supporting its ally, Austria-Hungary. Ultimately, more blame attaches to Austria, Serbia and Russia whose intransigent attitudes to negotiation left no room for peaceful manoeuvre.

"Dropping the pilot…"The new Kaiser, Wilhelm II, dismisses the experienced politician, Otto von Bismarck. [By Sir John Tenniel, 'Punch' magazine, 1890].

However, Germany *was* at the root of the quest for diplomatic security that obsessed the Great Powers between 1879 and 1907. Born of internal military conflict (under the auspices of Count Otto von Bismarck's resurgent Prussia) and international war against Austria (1866) and France (1870-71), the German state sought the means to secure diplomatic solidarity with like-minded neighbours. The fact that Germany's first major alliance in 1879 (the Dual Alliance) linked it with a former mortal enemy, the Habsburg[11] Austro-Hungarian Empire, was symptomatic of the 'Realpolitik'[12] of the time. This secret treaty was expanded three years later to the Triple Alliance, encompassing another international newcomer, Italy. During the late 1880's, Bismarck even secured an unlikely secret 'Reinsurance Treaty' with Russia to ensure neutrality in war against a third party (with the respective exceptions of Austria-Hungary and France). In many respects Bismarck's Europe, in which France was isolated and Britain uninvolved, was diplomatically quite stable. The threat to that stability came with the accession of the new

---

10 One of five treaties that, together, constituted the Paris Peace Settlement at the end of the Great War. The Treaty of Versailles was the treaty between the Allies and Germany.

11 The Habsburgs were the royal family of Austria-Hungary.

12 'Realpolitik' was the name given to Bismarck's practice of pursuing policy and diplomacy in which the end achieved justified the means employed.

Kaiser, Wilhelm II, in 1888[13]. Dismissing the elderly but massively experienced Chancellor Bismarck and renouncing the treaty with Russia, Wilhelm put his hands firmly on the reins of government. And promptly pushed Russia towards the welcoming arms of France, a new friendship that was confirmed by the defensive military alliance of 1893. Yet outside the circle of alliances, revelling in its *'Splendid Isolation'*[14], lurked Britain whose international influence lay in its economic strength and sea-based, worldwide Empire. Undoubtedly, Britain had more in common with Germany, with whom it shared a royal family, than with France or Russia but solutions to colonial differences with each of these states and increasing naval rivalry with Wilhelm II pushed Britain away from Germany. 1904 saw the *'Entente Cordiale'* lubricate Anglo-French relations, to be followed in 1907 by an Anglo-Russian Entente[15]. While these were not military alliances, they would have provided a strong diplomatic indicator for a head of state more perceptive than Wilhelm II. The 'system' of alliances did not cause the war but did create the crucial mutual support between states that embarked upon a fateful game of bluff in the summer of 1914. Politicians caused the confrontations, and generals were usually left to fight the resultant wars.

The Search for European Security, 1873 - 1907

1873 – *'DreiKaiserBund'* or *'Three Emperors League'* (Germany, Austria-Hungary and Russia).

1879 – Russia withdrew from the *'DreiKaiserBund'*; so, in the same year…

1879 – German-Austrian Dual Alliance (Vienna, October 7th). The treaty was signed by Germany and Austria-Hungary, promised aid to each other in the event of an attack by Russia, or if Russia aided another power at war with either Germany or Austria-Hungary.

1882 – Triple Alliance, Germany/Austria/Italy (May 1881). Germany and Austria-Hungary promised to assist Italy if she were attacked by France, and vice versa: Italy was bound to lend aid to Germany or Austria-Hungary if France declared war against either.

1887 – Germany's secret *'Reinsurance Treaty'* with Russia. Aimed to protect against its possible break-up by a combined two-front attack from French and Russia.

---

13 The ambitious, headstrong, twenty-nine year old William II did not directly succeed William I. Frederick III ruled for ninety days but died of cancer. Such are the quirks of history.

14 *'Splendid Isolation'* was a phrase coined by Lord Salisbury to describe Britain's desire to remain free from continental commitments, using the Royal Navy as Britain's shield.

15 An 'Entente' was, derived from French, an 'understanding' between nations. It was *not* a binding, military alliance.

1890 – *'Reinsurance Treaty'* allowed to lapse by Wilhelm II.
1914-1918 – known as the **TRIPLE ALLIANCE** or the **CENTRAL POWERS**.

V.

1839 – (19th April) Treaty of London – between Great Britain, Austria, France, Prussia, and Russia, on the one part, and The Netherlands, on the other.
"Belgium, within the limits specified in Articles 1, 2, and 4, shall form an Independent and perpetually Neutral State. It shall be bound to observe such Neutrality towards all other States" (Article 7).
1893 – Franco-Russian defensive military alliance.
1902 – Just five months after the latest renewal of the Triple Alliance, Italy reached an understanding with France that each would remain neutral in the event of an attack upon the other.
1902 – Anglo-Japanese Alliance was primarily directed against the potential shared menace posed, it was believed, by France and (most probably) Russia in the Far East. The alliance obligated either power to remain neutral if one or other found itself at war. However, should either power be obliged to fight a war against two or more powers, the other signatory was obliged to provide military aid.
1904 – Anglo-French *'Entente Cordiale'*. Settled colonial rivalries in North Africa. This was not a military commitment.
1907 – Anglo-Russian Entente. Safeguarded British colonial interests in India and Afghanistan. This was not a military commitment.
1914-1918 – known as the **ALLIES** or the **ENTENTE**.

Yet, for all the complex, secretly-negotiated alliances and ententes, the outbreak of war owed more to the strength of Serbian nationalist ambitions to create a 'Greater Serbia' (comprising Serbia, Bosnia-Herzegovina, Macedonia, Montenegro, Croatia and Dalmatia) than to the rival militaries of the Great Powers. What the latter did contribute was a litany of misguided support and convoluted, error-strewn diplomacy based on the idea that a Europe-wide war had not occurred since Waterloo in 1815 and was thus unlikely to occur in the more modern, civilised Europe of 1914. Austria-Hungary fully expected to be allowed to punish Serbia for the assassinations of June 1914; the outbreak of a general European war was a consequence of diplomatic bluff and miscalculation. Some states regarded mobilisation merely as a threat or diplomatic 'tool' but others interpreted it as a virtual declaration of war. In many ways, Europe '… *staggered and stumbled into war'* – it was not pre-planned or expected, and when it happened it was certainly expected to be short and decisive. The coming of the Great War was a poor recommendation for political vision and diplomatic skill. For Elmore Green and Bloxwich it would destroy families; for Europe, it would herald a century characterised by 'total' war. 1914-18 was the first war to affect the entire community and in no way compared to the Boer War of 1899-1902, a decade previously. Just as the Industrial Revolution gave rise to an urbanised society, so industrialisation meant that war itself would never be the same – the battlefield was to become a mechanised killing ground on an undreamt scale.

When the German government failed to respond to Britain's ultimatum relating to Belgium's neutrality, expecting that Britain would not go to war, *"… for a scrap of paper"*,[16] Britain declared that a state of war with Germany existed from 11:00 pm on 4th August 1914. Sadly, the outbreak of war was celebrated in every European capital – they did not understand what was coming. The following report sets out the German government's attitude on 4th August, 1914:

Official Report of the Breaking of Diplomatic Relations and of the *"Scrap of Paper"* by Sir Edward Goschen, British Ambassador to Berlin:

> *"…In accordance with the instructions contained in your telegram of the 4th instant, I called upon the Secretary of State that afternoon and inquired, in the name of His Majesty's Government, whether the Imperial Government would refrain from violating Belgian neutrality."*
> *"Herr von Jägow at once replied that he was sorry to say that his answer must be '…No,' as, in consequence of the German troops having crossed the frontier that morning, Belgian neutrality had been already violated."*
> *"I informed the Secretary of State that unless the Imperial Government could give the assurance by 12 o'clock that night that they would proceed no further with their violation of the Belgian frontier and stop their advance, I had been instructed to demand my passports and inform the Imperial Government that His Majesty's Government would have to take all steps in their power to uphold the neutrality of Belgium."*

The *'Walsall Observer'* of Saturday, 8th August 1914, reported the mood and reactions of people in Walsall:

---

16 The 'scrap of paper' referred to was the 1839 Treaty of London by which Belgium's neutrality was guaranteed. Both Britain and Germany had signed it.

'A Chain of Friendship'. The caption read: "If Austria attacks Serbia, Russia will fall upon Austria, Germany upon Russia, and France and England upon Germany." [This cartoon appeared in the American newspaper the 'Brooklyn Eagle' in July 1914.]

"In Walsall, in common with every other town in the kingdom, the news that England[17] would almost immediately be involved in war caused intense and widespread excitement. Rumours that this would be the case were circulated on Monday morning (3rd August), and as that was a Bank Holiday, it appeared as though everyone had decided to stay at home and learn whatever news there was to be learnt. The streets were crowded from an early hour, The Bridge seeming to be the centre on which most of the people concentrated. The streets in that neighbourhood were crowded to such an extent that at times it was difficult for passers-by to get along. Throughout the day the same interest was evident and many people were about until quite late at night and saw with intense surprise the Territorials [1/5th Battalion TF South Staffordshire Regiment] arrive thus prematurely from their training camp at St. Asaph. The more positive news that came through then caused still further excitement and for hours the streets in the centre of the town were more or less thronged with people. On Tuesday morning (4th August) the excitement was rendered still deeper by the King's Proclamation and by the fact that

---

17 A typical error, overlooking Wales, Scotland and Ireland!

the various banks were closed for three more days; hundreds of people assembled in the hope of seeing the Territorials marching to the Station. In this, however, they were disappointed, as the men did not leave the town and, indeed, have not done so up to the present time. The Town Hall and other buildings, where the men have been accommodated, each proved a centre of attraction for the crowds who assembled in front of them from time to time. The Railway Station was, however, the supreme point and near it hundreds gathered, crowding both sides of Park Street. Largely this interest was due to a desire to see the Territorials if they should start but partly it was caused by anxious friends desiring to see those who had been out of town, it having become known that the Government had temporarily taken over the railways and that the ordinary traffic was suspended, except so far as it could be worked without interfering with the War Office needs. Few, if any, of the manufactories in the town were open, but by Thursday morning (6th August) those which had to do leather work for the government were re-opened and have been working more than full time, various orders having been received for material required by the Army[18]. Since that time – and especially since the banks reopened yesterday morning – the streets have resumed very much their usual appearance."

The die was cast and Europe's fate passed into the hands of generals and admirals. The opening gambits were played out by the following combination of alliances:-

The protagonists took the following sides:

The Triple Alliance or Central Powers

GERMANY   **AUSTRIA-HUNGARY**

ITALY (nominally a member but refused to fight Britain; first declared
   neutrality then completely changed sides in 1915).

OTTOMAN TURKEY joined the Central Powers in October-November
   1914.

BULGARIA later joined the Central Powers.

The Triple Entente or Allies

FRANCE   **RUSSIA**   **GREAT BRITAIN & HER EMPIRE**
BELGIUM   **SERBIA**   **JAPAN**

MONTENEGRO later joined the Entente Powers.

RUMANIA later joined the Entente Powers.

---

18   Such orders in Walsall largely comprised horse leathers and metals.

Chapter Seven

British Forces in 1914

How the Army was organised

In the summer of 1914, the army consisted (just as it had done for decades) of three main offensive elements – cavalry, infantry and artillery – though none of the lads on the Elmore Green memorial served in the cavalry. Consequently, the chart below attempts to show how the infantry units of the British Army were organised and where the artillery fitted into the pattern in August 1914, from the smallest unit (known as a 'section') at the top of the chart, to the largest unit (an army) at the bottom[19].

Section
- Four sections of 12 to 15 men, each commanded by a sergeant or a corporal, made up a **platoon**.

Platoon
- Four platoons of 50 to 60 men, each commanded by a subaltern (a lieutenant or 2nd lieutenant) made up a 'rifle' **company**.

Company
- Four rifle companies (usually 'A', 'B', 'C', 'D') each of 250 men and a Headquarters company of 100 men, each usually commanded by a major or temporarily a captain, made up a **battalion**.
- The most experienced (and often most important) soldier in a company was the Company Sergeant Major – he set the standards.
- In 1914 each battalion went to war with but two machine-guns, initially equipped with two Maxim (later Vickers) heavy machine guns.

---

19   For each of these army units, the figures quoted represent peacetime maximum (known as 'establishment') numbers – in wartime few, if any, of these units would be anywhere near to full strength.

Battalion

- A battalion was commanded by a lieutenant-colonel or, temporarily, a major. The optimum peacetime establishment of a battalion was between 1,000 and 1,100 men.
- Every battalion, whether of Regular Army, Territorial Force or New Army origin, belonged to a 'parent' regiment that had a long-established headquarters and depot in the United Kingdom that were responsible for the raising and training of recruits and their subsequent deployment.
- The regiment had previously been the standard fighting unit of the British Army until the Army Reforms of 1881 by which regiments' numbers were replaced by (mainly) county-style titles. For example, the old 38th and 80th Regiments of Foot were allied to create the 1st and 2nd battalions respectively of the new South Staffordshire Regiment.
- From that time, regiments were 'county' based and recruited largely from their own region, although a few regiments, such as the King's Royal Rifle Corps and the several Guards regiments recruited on a national scale.
- The majority of regiments had two 'regular' battalions (career soldiers) and these were designated the 1st and 2nd battalions, although some larger regiments like the Middlesex and the Worcestershire could support four regular battalions. On the other hand, smaller counties found difficulty in raising and maintaining a single front-line battalion and sometimes had to combine with a neighbouring county, as in the case of the Oxfordshire and Buckinghamshire Light Infantry. After 1908, each regiment maintained one or two Special Reserve battalions numbered in sequence after the regular battalions and a variable number of Territorial Force battalions, numbered in continuing sequence after the reserve battalions but prefixed by a Territorial Force identifier, such as (first-line TF) 1/5th and later (the second and third-line TF) 2/5th, 3/5th.
- So, in August 1914, the numbering and naming sequence of the South Staffordshire Regiment was:-

1st	(Regular) Battalion	} Full-time professional
2nd	(Regular) Battalion	} soldiers in August 1914
3rd	(Reserve) Battalion	} Special Reserve
4th	(Extra Reserve) Battalion	} " "
1/5th	(Territorial Force) Battalion	} Territorial Force
1/6th	(Territorial Force) Battalion	} " "

Lord Kitchener gradually raised a volunteer 'New Army' for war service only. When the South Staffordshire 'Service' battalions were numbered, they were as follows:-

7th (Service) Battalion } 'New Army' or 'Service'
8th (Service) Battalion } Battalions.
9th (Service) Battalion }
10th (S) and 11th (S) were Training Battalions
12th (Labour) Battalion, transferred to the Labour Corps.

- Until February 1918, four battalions made up a **brigade**. However, as from February 1918, just three battalions constituted a **brigade**. This measure was implemented to cope with the shortage of trained soldiers being released from Britain into the front line. As a result, some battalions were disbanded and their men redistributed; however, the number of divisions remained as before.

Brigade
- In 1914 a brigade was normally commanded by a brigadier-general and comprised four battalions and a brigade headquarters, thus until February 1918 a brigade ideally contained over 4,000 men.
- Some battalions remained with the same brigade for the duration of the war, whilst others were transferred between brigades several times. The latter often occurred when it was considered necessary to 'stiffen' a particular under-performing brigade with a proven and battle-hardened battalion.
- In 1914 and throughout the war, three brigades[20] usually constituted a **division**.

Division
- A division (with its own headquarters) was commanded by a major-general and normally contained twelve battalions until February 1918 and nine battalions thereafter.
- A division usually comprised three brigades and thus contained about 12,000 infantry. These were further expanded by three Royal Engineers companies, field ambulances (not the transport but the RAMC staff themselves), units of the ASC (Army Service Corps), a sanitary section and transport units that totalled another 6,000 men.
- In addition, in 1914 each division was assigned three 18-pounder field-gun[21] artillery brigades[22] (which in terms of manpower were significantly smaller than infantry brigades), one 4.5-inch howitzer brigade and one heavy battery of four 60-pounder breech-loading guns of the Royal Garrison Artillery.
- Adjustments to the division were made during the war, such as the addition of a pioneer battalion, a machine-gun company (1917) and a

---

20 This varied under some circumstances.

21 A shell fired from a field-gun described a low arc; one from a howitzer, a high arc.

22 An artillery brigade comprised three batteries, each of six guns.

trench mortar unit. This was partly counter-balanced by the loss (to Corps control) of the heavy artillery.

- During the course of the Great War, the British Army was expanded from just six divisions to seventy-six.
- At least two divisions, with about 18,000 men in each (made up of 12,000 'fighting' men or 'rifles' and about 6,000 men of other units, such as RE, ASC, RFA, Field Ambulances), constituted a **corps**.

Corps

- A corps was commanded by a lieutenant-general. A corps comprised in 1914, a headquarters and normally two divisions, thus containing slightly fewer than 25,000 infantry and over 10,000 support troops.
- As the war progressed and the numbers of troops in the field increased, so the corps could and did contain more than two divisions.
- The divisions themselves were often moved from corps to corps as battles wore on. At least two corps, sometimes more, constituted an **army**.

Army

- **An** army (the largest single unit and comprising at least two corps) was commanded by a full general; **the** army (as opposed to the navy) was often commanded by a Field Marshal, the highest rank in the British army.
- In August 1914 the British Expeditionary Force that was sent to France was of sufficiently small size to constitute just *one* **army** (commanded by Field Marshal Sir John French), comprising the **I Corps** (commanded by Lt.-Gen. Sir Douglas Haig) containing 1st Division and 2nd Division; the **II Corps** (commanded by Lt.-Gen. Sir Horace Smith-Dorrien) contained 3rd Division and 5th Division.
- As regular troops were brought back from overseas stations and reservists called up, so more divisions reached France and Flanders. The **III Corps** was formed in France on 31st August 1914 – it was commanded by Maj.-Gen. William Pulteney and contained 4th Division and 6th Division; the **IV Corps** was formed on 9th October 1914 – it was commanded by Lt.-Gen. Sir Henry Rawlinson and contained 7th Division and 3rd Cavalry Division.
- As Territorials were asked to forego their right to serve on home stations only, and Kitchener's volunteers (known as the 'New Army') were slowly turned into soldiers, so the original one army of 1914 grew to five armies by the time of the Armistice in November 1918. Such was the scale of the war

Branches of the Army in 1914

- Contained within the above unit structure was a wide range of military functions.
- The front line fighting troops comprised the infantry (including machine gunners), the artillery and the cavalry, though all the other branches frequently found themselves in the zone of shot and shell and so were trained to fight when necessary.
- The vital 'support' services, if they may thus be described, were the Royal Engineers, the pioneer battalions, the medical services, the veterinary services, the Ordnance Corps, the Labour Corps and the Army Service Corps (logistics) – without these, the fighting units simply could not have functioned.

From Tommy's point of view

- The battalion was the most significant unit in his daily life; he would have known the name of, and occasionally would have seen, the lieutenant-colonel (usually just referred to as 'the colonel') who commanded his battalion. The second-in-command, generally known as 'the adjutant', and usually holding the rank of major, would have been a familiar face.
- More familiar would have been the major or captain in charge of the soldier's company (usually 'A', 'B', 'C' or 'D') of about 200 men. The Company Sergeant Major (CSM) was often the backbone of the company (and the terror of the Tommy!).
- In his platoon of 50 or 60 men, the leader, usually a Lieutenant or 2nd Lieutenant, would have known most Tommies by name and would have been aware of their strengths and weaknesses as soldiers.
- The section of about 15 men, which was the largest unit run by a non-commissioned officer (usually a sergeant), would have contained the soldier's closest friends and was the everyday working unit to which he belonged. While there was always loyalty towards and pride in the traditions and achievements of the 'regiment', every Tommy really fought for his mates and dreaded the idea of letting them down
- Every soldier (though there were slight differences for the likes of the artillery, engineers and later the machine-gunners) technically belonged to eight units at varying levels of importance.
- If asked, the ordinary 'Tommy' would have struggled to tell you his corps and army numbers, less still the names of those who commanded them. He would, of course, have known whether he served as a regular, a Territorial, a reservist or a 'duration man' (New Army).

Overleaf is an Elmore Green example of a 'New Army' volunteer soldier's units during the Battle of Thiepval, on the Somme, 26th-28th September 1916:–

40171, Private
Edward 'Ted' Jones

Section unknown (rarely found on service records)

Platoon unknown (rarely found on service records)

'D' Company (Company C.O. unknown)

7th (Service) Battalion, the South Staffordshire Regiment (C.O. Lt.-Col. D.T. Seckham)

33rd Brigade (under Br.-Gen. J.F. Erskine)

11th 'Northern' Division (under acting-G.O.C. Br.-Gen. O. de l' E. Winter)

The II (Two) Corps (under Lieutenant-General Claude W. Jacob)

Reserve Army (under General Sir Hubert Gough) renamed Fifth Army

(30/10/16)

Principal Army Ranks: A brief guide

Commissioned Officers: (appointed by Royal Commission)

    Field Marshal

    General

    Lieutenant-General

    Major-General

    Brigadier-General

    Colonel

    Lieutenant-Colonel

    Major

    Captain

    Lieutenant

    2nd Lieutenant

Warrant Officers: (appointed by Royal Warrant)

    Sergeant-Major [RSM; CSM; BSM]

    Quarter Master Sergeant [CQMS]

Non-commissioned officers: (appointed by senior officers)

    Sergeant

    Lance-Sergeant

    Corporal

    Lance-Corporal, 2nd Corporal, Bombardier

    Private, Rifleman, Guardsman, Sapper, Pioneer, Gunner, Driver

Sea Power – the vital role of the Royal Navy in 1914

The Royal Navy had a truly powerful, modern fleet, built on the premise that should be capable of outfighting the combined fleets of its two largest potential enemies.

When questioned in 1798 in the House of Lords as to the likelihood of invasion of these islands by Napoleon's all-conquering *'Grande Armée'*, Earl St. Vincent (Admiral John Jervis) produced the memorable answer:

> *"I do not say the French cannot come, my Lords - I only say they cannot come by sea."*

1914 RN sea-going strength

22 Dreadnoughts

40 Pre-Dreadnoughts

9 battle-cruisers

108 lighter cruisers

215 torpedo-boat destroyers

28 gunboats

106 torpedo boats

7 minelayers

75 submarines

one seaplane-carrier

Such words explained why Britain placed its faith, not to say its money and research, in the development of the Royal Navy. Equally, it explains why the British army of 1914 was, in comparison to its continental counterparts, so much smaller and less of a threat in international diplomacy. The principle of the seas providing a natural moat against invasion still held good in 1914. The advent of air power was soon to see the age-old maritime principle come under severe challenge.

Air Power – the Royal Naval Air Service, the Royal Flying Corps and the Royal Air Force

When the call went out to mobilise, the least regarded (except among a perceptive tiny minority) were the brave pilots of the strange machines of the Royal Flying Corps and the Royal Naval Air Service. Even those original few, enthusiastic fliers as they were, could not have believed that within the span of twenty-five years air power would supplant the Royal Navy as Britain's prime defence against invasion. War, or sometimes even fear of it, is often a stimulus to advance in weapons technology – pre-war, the Royal Navy had seen the advent of the 'revolutionary' high-speed, fully-armoured heavy weapons platform in the shape of the *'Dreadnought'* class of battleship. The army was to experience rapid battlefield developments in the form of better machine-guns and more accurate heavy artillery, the terror of increasingly noxious, toxic gases, the horrors of liquid fire or flame-throwers and the supposed invulnerability of 'land battleships' or tanks. Of course, every effective battlefield development saw the 'boffins'[23] working feverishly to find a military counter-measure. Yet the most rapid advances came in the new field of air power; not only did the technology change at a dizzying pace but also did air power's battlefield tactical role and it even contributed to a change in war strategy by virtue of the introduction of long-distance heavy bombing. After the unreliable 'kites' and 'string-bags' of 1914, more powerful and efficient engines, stronger airframes, extensive bomb-racks, high-quality cameras and interrupter-gear machine-guns turned aircraft into killing machines that could 'spy' over enemy territory and could 'observe' for the artillery.

Royal Flying Corps (RFC)

Not until 1st April 1911 did the government show strong interest in the military application of powered flight[24], when the Corps of Royal Engineers was ordered to set up the Air Battalion, (ABRE), based at Farnborough, commencing a long association. The new unit comprised 154 officers and men, divided into No.1 Company (airship) and No.2 Company (aeroplane). The first pilots had to have already obtained their flying licence through private means. On 13th May 1912, just a year after its inauguration, the ABRE was converted by royal warrant into the Royal Flying Corps (comprising an army element, the RFC, and a naval element, the RNAS). As a branch of the Army, the RFC retained army ranks. At the outset, the role of the RFC was to act as the 'eyes of the ground troops', directing artillery fire by rudimentary methods and carrying out photographic reconnaissance. When it deployed to France in 1914 the RFC sent four Squadrons (Nos. 2, 3, 4 and 5) each with 12 aircraft, which together with extra aircraft in depots, gave a total strength of 63 aircraft supported by 900 men. In 1914, the RFC mainly used the de Havilland BE-2, Farman MF-7, Avro 504, Vickers FB5, Bristol Scout, and the (Royal Aircraft Factory) F.E.2. A year later, in September 1915 at the start of the Battle of Loos, the Royal Flying Corps had 12 squadrons and 160 aircraft in France and Flanders. Therefore, as the French '*Aéronautique Militaire*' had 1,150 aircraft available, the vast majority of the early operations on the Western Front had to be carried out by Britain's allies.

---

23 A slang term broadly covering scientists, engineers and inventors.

24 With the exception of balloons and their derivatives. The Air Battalion developed from the School of Ballooning in 1911.

Royal Naval Air Service (RNAS)

The RNAS was the naval element of the Flying Corps; ironically, the navy had use of a permanent airfield, the Royal Aero Club's Eastchurch field on the Isle of Sheppey, before the RFC was officially constituted. On 1st July 1914, the Admiralty made the Royal Naval Air Service part of the Military Branch of the Royal Navy so, unlike the RFC, the RNAS opted for navy-related ranks – in the long term, these formed the basis of Royal Air Force ranks in 1918. By the outbreak of the First World War in August 1914, the RNAS had ninety-three aircraft, six airships, two balloons and seven hundred and twenty-seven personnel. The Navy maintained twelve airship stations around the coast of Britain and not until August 1915 did it come under the direct control of the Royal Navy. Although there was rivalry between the air services, the two co-operated to the benefit of the war effort.

Royal Air Force (RAF)

The Royal Air Force did not exist in 1914, though the RNAS and RFC were both in existence at the outbreak of hostilities. Not until 1st April 1918 did the separate flying services of the army and navy merge to form the new air branch – the Royal Air Force. As far as is known, no Elmore Green lad joined either the RFC or RNAS early in the war. However, Frank Lloyd, who earned the Military Medal and bar[25] with 'D' (Bloxwich) Company of the 1/5th Battalion, the South Staffordshire Regiment, was commissioned from the ranks in 1918 and joined the newly-formed RAF as a Second Lieutenant with 61st Squadron. He remained in the service after the war ended, was killed in a flying accident and was laid to rest in Bloxwich Cemetery.

---

25   This shows he won the award on two separate occasions.

Chapter Eight

General Mobilisation and Recruitment, August 1914

MOBILISATION MEANT differing levels of threat to each of the Great Powers – for **Germany**, mobilisation could be used as a measured threat and, thanks to an excellent railway network, could be reversed within 48 hours. For **Russia**, mobilisation was akin to a declaration of war and could not be easily reversed in a matter of hours as the railway lines towards the east (the German frontier) and towards the south-west (the Austro-Hungarian frontier) were of very limited capacity, So, Germany's demand on 31st July that Russia de-mobilise within twenty-four hours was near-impossible to achieve. In the eyes of the **British** government, an order for the mobilisation of the Royal Navy would normally precede general mobilisation as the sea had always provided an effective 'moat' against invasion. General mobilisation in Britain would follow the:

> '…declaration of war with a first-rank European Power…..and would entail the complete mobilisation of the whole of the naval and military forces of the Crown.'

Self-evidently, Germany was a, '…*first-class European Power*', so Britain's declaration of war on **4th August** triggered general mobilisation. The process was organised so as to put the regular army on a war footing, to recall regular army units from overseas garrison duty (and to arrange for their replacement), to alert regular army reservists and special reservists to report to regimental depots, and to embody the Territorial Force. Beyond raising the troops, mobilisation required governmental takeover of the all-important railway network, the requisitioning of vehicles, of animals (particularly horses), of all manner of seaworthy vessels and of the few aircraft that were available. The protection of ports and sea approaches was almost 'second nature' to the British.

Relative naval strengths in July 1914

GB	22 Dreadnoughts; 40 Pre-Dreadnoughts; 9 Battle-Cruisers 108 light cruisers; 215 torpedo-boat destroyers; 28 gunboats 106 torpedo boats; 7 minelayers; 75 submarines; one seaplane-carrier.
France	4 Dreadnoughts; 21 Pre-Dreadnoughts; 28 various cruisers 67 submarines; 81 destroyers.
against	
Germany	16 Dreadnoughts; 30 Pre-Dreadnoughts; 54 various cruisers 30 submarines (U-Boats); 152 destroyers.
Austria-Hungary	16 Battleships (mostly pre-Dreadnoughts); 13 cruisers; 5 torpedo-gunboats; eighteen destroyers; eleven submarines 91 torpedo-boats

Royal Navy mobilisation

Royal Navy Regulars (RN)   Royal Fleet Reserve (RFR)
Royal Navy Reserve (RNR)   Royal Naval Volunteer Reserve (RNVR)
Royal Naval Division (RND)

In 1914, when the Royal Navy was mobilised, the Admiralty soon became aware that on drafting the required men into ships of the fleet, rather than suffering a shortage of manpower like the army, the Senior Service would more than likely enjoy a substantial surplus of reservists. The **Royal Fleet Reserve** (RFR) had been established under the Naval Forces Act of 1903, to provide a regular reserve of trained men for service in time of emergency; the **Royal Naval Reserve** (RNR) produced a nucleus of professional seamen from the merchant and fishing fleets; and the **Royal Naval Volunteer Reserve** (RNVR) was established by the Naval Forces Act of 1903 to allow the naval training of civilians. Any civilian who volunteered for the RNVR had to agree to serve either ashore or afloat – unlike the army's Territorial Force of 1908 that required volunteers to serve only within the Home Command. The resultant flood of all types of reservists produced between 20,000 and 30,000 men more than it required for the ships available – some volunteer reservists were to receive an unwelcome surprise. The Admiralty's solution, given the desperate need for infantrymen at that time, was to create three land-based brigades, two of them RN and one Royal Marine within a **Royal Naval Division**[26]. Initially unpopular with naval reservists who had expected to go to sea in wartime, members of the division retained their naval ranks and the battalions that composed the various brigades had obvious naval or marine connotations[27]. The erstwhile reluctant 'soldiers' of the RND served with great distinction at Antwerp in 1914, on Gallipoli in 1915 and on the Western front thereafter, sustaining nearly 45,000 casualties.

As the war progressed and merchant vessels became easy prey for German U-Boats, many merchantmen were armed and a number of RNVR sailors joined merchant ships as gunners. At least two lads recorded on the Elmore Green war memorial, Tom Rowbotham of the S.S. 'Kilmaho' and Harold Goodall aboard S.S. 'Ottokar', served with the RNVR on merchant vessels and died doing their duty.

Regular Army mobilisation

More than half of the nation's **regular soldiers** and thus most of the hardened, front-line battalions of many regiments were deployed on normal overseas garrison duties, anywhere from Gibraltar to South Africa to India to China or Bermuda, protecting the far-flung corners of the Empire – it would take many weeks to transport them to Britain, re-equip and re-supply them and move them to the European battle-front.

Existing armies against Britain in August 1914

Germany	2 million	modern equipment; conscription
Austria-Hungary	1 million	outdated equipment

Existing armies in Britain & the Entente in August 1914

GB	100,000	available as BEF; very professional
France	1,000,000	quite modern equipment; conscription
Russia	1,300,000	slow to mobilise; ill-trained, ill-equipped
Belgium	117,000	of varying quality, many in forts in 1914
Serbia	150,000	unpredictable, poorly equipped

---

26 In May 1916, the RND arrived on the Western Front and in July 1916, at the time of the Battles of the Somme, was incorporated into the British army and renamed 63rd (Royal Naval) Division.

27 The RN battalions were named Anson, Benbow, Collingwood, Drake, Hawke, Hood, Howe and Nelson.

The pre-war role of Britain's Regular Army

By way of an extended local example, in mid-1914 the soldiers of 1st Battalion[28] the South Staffordshire Regiment were garrisoning Fort Napier, overlooking the city of Pietermaritzburg in Natal province, South Africa. The preceding fifteen years had provided 1st South Staffordshire with a wealth of experiences, some of which are recounted below.

1st Battalion, the South Staffordshire [formerly 38th Regiment of Foot]
Until the War Office army reforms of 1881, 1st South Staffordshire was known as 38th Regiment of Foot[29] and was to play a considerable part in Britain's first major colonial war of the twentieth century, although on the outbreak (1899) of the Boer War the battalion was on duty in Kinsale, Ireland. From there, 1/South Staffordshire was ordered to Gibraltar for garrison duty until January 1900, when the battalion was ordered to England where it would mobilise for active service in South Africa. Hectic preparations ensued, landing at Southampton in early February and proceeding to Aldershot for posting to 17th Brigade of 8th Division. It was a replenished 1st Battalion that sailed for South Africa on March 17th with 25 officers and 1,049 men aboard the S.S. *'Aurania'*. The ship docked at Cape Town on April 8th, moving on to Port Elizabeth the following day, where the battalion disembarked. A week later 1/South Staffordshire entrained for the front and was involved in numerous actions until peace returned after 31st May 1902. Casualties in South Africa were:

Killed	4 officers and 23 other ranks
Missing	23 other ranks
Wounded	one officer and 53 other ranks
prisoners of war	9 other ranks
died of disease	90 other ranks.

[Note: 4/South Staffordshire, although an Extra Reserve (former militia) Battalion, served in South Africa. It saw action and carried out garrison duties, guarded prisoners of war, provided reinforcements for 1/South Staffordshire and protected lines of communication – a vital task in such a huge landscape.]

Following its battle exploits, 1/South Staffordshire remained on duty in South Africa until autumn 1904 when it was posted back to the Curragh, Ireland, until November 1906. During its Irish posting, in January 1905

---

28 2nd Battalion had served in India until 1907, then sailed to South Africa to serve for four years at Pretoria.

29 Also in that year, 80th Regiment of Foot was 'linked' to 38th and became 2nd Battalion, the South Staffordshire.

Lichfield Cathedral unveiled a stained glass window in commemoration of the Regiment's officers and other ranks who lost their lives in the South African War – a large number of 1st Battalion were allowed to travel to the ceremony to honour their fallen comrades. By November 1906, the battalion had been posted to Aldershot, prior to moving to Devonport in October 1908. It was in Aldershot in 1907 that two newly-trained lads from our story were posted to the battalion – nineteen year-old Private Aaron Hayward, a native of Stoke-on-Trent but later an Elmore Green schoolboy, had joined 'D' Company of 1st Battalion and twenty-four year-old Harry Lavender, a native of Bloxwich, arrived to serve eventually in the capacity of Military Policeman. With the exception of one day, the battalion remained at Devonport until February 1911. On one occasion during that posting, 20th May 1910, the entire battalion decamped to London for duty in Hyde Park for the funeral of His Majesty King Edward VII. Whilst the battalion was based in Devonport, another Bloxwich lad and former Elmore Green schoolboy, (John) William Groves, went through basic training and, as a nineteen year-old Private, joined his new mates in 1st Battalion. He had become part of the South Staffordshire Regiment as Europe's Great Powers were approaching a dangerous crossroads.

1st South Staffordshire departed Devonport on 9th February 1911 aboard H.M. Troopship *'Plassey',* bound for Gibraltar. Privates Hayward and Groves were together on the first leg of their new posting but, after duty in Gibraltar, would not meet again until Lyndhurst Camp in September 1914. En route to Gibraltar, in the Bay of Biscay the troopship passed H.M.T. *'Soudan'*, the latter carrying the regiment's 2nd Battalion on their return journey from duty in Pretoria, South Africa. Landing on 13th February 1911, 1st South Staffordshire relieved 2nd Norfolk in Gibraltar and while on 'The Rock' received new 'Colours' from H.M. King George V (January 1911) and welcomed a new C.O., Lt.-Colonel R. M. Ovens, who replaced the retiring Lt.-Colonel J. W. Sears (December 1912). Within a fortnight of taking command, the Colonel oversaw his new battalion embark on H.M.T. *'Rohilla'*, bound for South Africa. Prior to departing Gibraltar, a draft of 223 other ranks reinforced the South Staffordshire, bringing battalion strength up to 21 Officers and 884 other ranks. Already, young Private Groves had had a close view of the King and was on his way to South Africa where his battalion had made a name for itself during the Boer War. Private Hayward, however, was on his way home to England. He was not hurt nor was he in trouble; he had signed his army engagement papers in Bloxwich in 1907 on what was termed a 'seven and five' – seven years with the Colours and five years in the Army Reserve (and thus liable to be mobilised in time of emergency). Hayward's time in the army would expire long before the battalion's posting to South Africa ended, so from Gibraltar he was sent back to serve with 2nd Battalion or at the Regimental Depot. Little did he expect that soon after his demobilisation to the Army Reserve[30] he would be recalled to the Colours.

The troopship *'Rohilla'* docked in Durban, South Africa, on 2nd February 1913 and the battalion disembarked next day, finally arriving at Pietermaritzburg where they garrisoned Fort Napier. The role of the Staffordshire men in Natal was more policing than soldiering – in July 1913 during the great mining strike on the Rand, half the battalion's strength assisted the civil authorities of Johannesburg and Bramfontein by occupying the Post Office, Telephone Exchange, railway stations, and some of the principal mines. This duty lasted until 5th August 1913, when the Staffordshire men returned to Fort Napier. Private Groves might well have wondered whether this was *real* soldiering. It was, nevertheless, typical of the British army's role in the garrisons of Empire.

However, just as the next twelve months unrolled as a more peaceful posting, so dark war clouds loomed in far-off Europe. In consequence, on 7th August 1914, 1st South Staffordshire received orders to embark for England on warning for active service. The long, slow journey to England, to an unknown future on the battlefields of Europe, began on 21st August aboard slow train transports from Pietermaritzburg to the docks at Capetown – the recall to England must have filled with foreboding some of the families who had accompanied their menfolk to South Africa. The battalion boarded H.M.T. *'Briton'* and awaited the embarkation of the other units of what today might be termed a 'battle-group', namely 10th Hussars, 1st Royal Dragoons, and three Batteries of 22nd Brigade, Royal Field Artillery. The flotilla of six troop transports, escorted by two cruisers, H.M.S. *'Hyacinth'* and H.M.S. *'Astra'*, left Capetown on 27th August. The convoy paused for one night at St. Helena though no-one was allowed to land on the island where Napoleon Bonaparte lived out his lonely exile. The voyage continued without incident, arriving at Southampton on 19th September. Soon the incidents would come thick and fast.

At Southampton docks came the parting of the ways – on landing, the wives and children were sent directly to their homes while their men were ordered to march to Lyndhurst Camp in the New Forest, to become the final battalion to join 22nd Brigade of the 7th Division. On arrival at the camp, most men were issued with new clothing and new, 'unbroken' boots[31], replacement of worn and damaged kit and webbing; once re-equipped, the battalion underwent a short but intense period of training, especially marching stamina and fitness.

---

30 In 1914, there were more than 145,000 men on the Army Reserve; the most skilled and experienced 6,000 received pay of one shilling per week; all others were paid sixpence per week.

31 For soldiers, new boots meant the pain of blisters.

Finally, as the men were most certainly going to war, a short leave was granted, allowing William Groves to bid farewell to family and friends. Sadly, he would not return. One soldier who had had much more preparation time than most of the battalion was Private Aaron Hayward. He had been recalled to the Colours from the Army Reserve in August and had had the opportunity to regain his fitness and break in new boots; he actually rejoined 1st Battalion whilst it was re-fitting and re-equipping at Lyndhurst Camp in the New Forest. Undoubtedly he would have renewed his acquaintance with William Groves, perhaps even swapping tales of their school escapades.

On Sunday, 4th October the Division was inspected by Major-General Capper (Divisional Commanding Officer) and orders came for 7th Division to embark that day at Southampton. In cold, wet weather that was to become familiar in Flanders, 1/South Staffordshire marched to Southampton and to war. A soaked and weary battalion, including the two Elmore Green lads John Groves and Aaron Hayward, embarked in the pre-dawn hours on H.M.T. *Lake Michigan*. The battalion was up to establishment[32], though not every man was aboard that troopship. An advance billeting party, comprising the Quartermaster and four Company Quartermaster-Sergeants, went ahead on the first divisional transport to arrange billets for the battalion on its arrival in Belgium – many a tired or seasick Tommy was soon to be grateful for the efforts of the billeting officers. In addition, a further captain and two subalterns along with 100 other ranks remained at Lyndhurst Camp as the first reinforcement and to provide a leavening of experienced soldiers for future new drafts – when some of them eventually reached the front line, a few old friends would no longer be among the ranks.

On the night of October 5th, the heavily-laden transports reached Dover where they collected Sealed Orders, few lads knowing whether they would land in France or Belgium. However, at dawn on Wednesday, 7th October, their landfall was Belgium, in the shape of the port of Zeebrugge. The men disembarked at noon, closely followed by horses, transport and essential kit, disappointed to find they were the last battalion to arrive. Remarkably, loading the troop trains took less than two hours and even less to reach the beautiful, medieval city of Bruges where they detrained and marched to Oost Camp. It was there that a few kind words would, for once, have been heard about the billeting officers who had made every provision for the men's arrival but the battalion was very soon sent forward to Lophem on outpost duties. Worse still, next morning the battalion was ordered to march the twenty-six miles to the seaward end of the Ostend-Bruges Canal; again, the weather was foul.

---

32   Establishment meant full peacetime strength of 29 Officers and 1,013 other ranks.

On 9th October, the Staffordshires marched into the town centre of Ostend and entrained for the city of Ghent where Captain Dunlop's 'B' Company was put on outpost duty – still in drenching rain. 7th Division had been allotted the vital task of covering the withdrawal from the port of Antwerp where the remnants of the Belgian army and Churchill's[33] Naval Brigade had attempted to stall the German invasion. Although Antwerp was surrendered on 10th October, the delay cost the Germans easy access to the vital Channel ports of Calais and Dunkirk and certainly changed the fate of the British Expeditionary Force. The soldiers of 1st Battalion, the South Staffordshire Regiment could never complain that life was dull!

2nd Battalion, the South Staffordshire [formerly 80th Regiment of Foot] The army reorganisation of 1881 created mainly two-battalion[34] regiments with 'County'-style titles and permanent regimental depots in their recruiting areas. Normally, one battalion would serve overseas while the other would serve at home – the two 'linked' battalions of a regiment would alternate as the overseas battalion. 2nd Battalion of the South Staffordshire Regiment had itself served many times overseas:

1881 Ireland	Tralee (detachment actions against Irish nationalists)
1883 England	Lichfield Depot (sent drafts to 1st Bn in Egypt)
1886 England	Pymouth then Devonport (from March)
1889 Ireland	The Curragh, Dublin (from September)
1891 England	Aldershot (from December)
1893 England	miners strike in Yorkshire, civil unrest (detachments – August, September)
1893 Egypt	Alexandria (to October 1895)
1895 India	Madras (south-eastern coast of India, to October 1897)
1897 Burma	Thaytemyo (on the Irrawaddy River in central Burma – now known as Thayet in Myanmar. To December 1899, though some detachments had remained in India.)
1900 India	Agra (on the Yamuna River, central northern India, west of Cawnpore)
1904 India	Allahabad (confluence of Rivers Ganges and Yamuna in central northern India, east of Cawnpore)
1907 South Africa	Pretoria (from November; inland on the High Veldt, near Johannesburg)

---

33 Winston Churchill had been First Lord of the Admiralty since 1911 and had advocated a staunch defence of Antwerp. He visited the beleaguered port on 5th October – five days before the city fell.

34 Some counties, such as Worcestershire and Middlesex could sustain **four** regular battalions.

1911 England	Lichfield (Regimental Depot, Whittington Barracks from February)
1911 England	strike duty in Manchester and Liverpool.
1912 England	Windsor Castle (Guard duty from 24th August-20th September)
1913 England	Aldershot in 6th Infantry Brigade, 2nd Division (from September to outbreak of war.) As a result of the Aldershot posting, 2/South Staffordshire was the first of the regiment's battalions to serve with the BEF in the Great War.

Regular Army Reserve

When on home duties, most regiments' second-line regular battalions were somewhat under-strength, comprising newly-trained recruits awaiting their first overseas posting, soldiers recently recuperated from illness, injury or wounds, 'old sweats' whose role was to mentor new arrivals and soldiers whose army term had all but expired (known as 'time-expired' men) such as Elmore Green's Private Aaron Hayward. In time of war emergencies, these home-based battalions were to be bulked out by men of the regular army reserve and regimental special reserves. Posters proclaiming the mobilisation of regular reservists were displayed in the windows of Post Offices throughout the towns and villages of Britain and also each reservist was individually notified by telegram that he was to follow the written instructions already issued to him on qualifying for the regular reserve. He would know where to report for duty and would have a money order by way of pay advance and a travel warrant for the railway. Regulars (other ranks) on leave from home battalions were to immediately report to their units, while men on leave from overseas battalions usually reported to the regimental depot for posting.[35] The depot held responsibility for processing all men of the regiment who were not already on duty with a battalion.

Each reservist had to be medically examined and would be classified 'fit for duty', 'unfit for duty' and immediately discharged, 'temporarily unfit' and placed on the reserve or 'unfit for overseas duty' and retained for home duties or placed on the reserve. At that busy time, only those fit for immediate service remained in the depot, whereas all others were for the moment sent home. All fit men were then issued with their kit and blankets, for which they signed, prior to being fed, watered and temporarily quartered for the night.

---

35 Officers on leave from overseas battalions had to report to the War Office.

Special Reserve

The processing of the Regular Reserve was intended to be largely accomplished within three days; then commenced the processing of the Special Reservists[36] of each regiment. The Special Reservists, it was hoped, would enable a regiment's regular battalions to be brought up to 'establishment numbers'[37] at the time of mobilisation. In order to attract volunteers, Special Reservists received six months basic infantry training and then returned to civilian life while enjoying part-pay from the army, thus the 3rd and 4th battalions were effectively training battalions. Like their regular reserve counterparts, the Specials were sent individual 'call-up' telegrams. In addition, on mobilisation, any regular reservist who was temporarily unfit for overseas service along with any soldier not yet nineteen years of age, would be posted to a Special Reserve battalion. Within a few days, most Reserve battalions had been deployed to wartime stations, initially ports and vital transport hubs. It was expected that the men of the Special Reserve would gradually be fed into the regular battalions as much-needed reinforcements and thus the Territorial Force would assume the role of home defence, especially counter-invasion duties on the East Coast. According to their terms of service, a Territorial soldier was not obliged to serve overseas but on the outbreak of war Lord Kitchener hoped the Territorials would sign the Imperial Service Obligation and thus make many more battalions available to replace the regular battalions returning from imperial garrison duties.

Territorial Force

Territorials were frequently termed 'Saturday night soldiers' on account of their weekly Drill Hall parades and training allied to an annual summer training camp. Even the renowned Secretary of State for War, Lord Kitchener, in reply to an offer that,

> "…the Territorial Forces Associations are ready to help you to the utmost of their powers", commented tersely, "…I don't want Territorials – I want soldiers."

The Territorial Force rightly felt insulted and when later given its chance, contributed impressively to the war effort overseas. A good number of Bloxwich lads were already pre-war members of the local 'D' [Bloxwich] Company of the

---

36 For most regiments, the Special Reserve battalions were numbered 3rd (Reserve) Battalion and 4th (Extra Reserve) Battalion. For a few, large regiments such as the Worcestershire that had four front-line battalions, the Special Reserves were numbered 5th and 6th Battalions.

37 'Establishment numbers' was the ideal size of the battalion in peacetime – rarely achieved in wartime. By November 1914, casualty rates reduced some battalions to as few as 100 men.

1/5th Battalion of the South Staffordshire Regiment and felt that with more training they could 'do their bit' on the front line.

Recruitment, 1914-1918

The various branches of the army were recruited on differing bases. The regular infantry was raised on a county basis, such as the South Staffordshire Regiment and the Northumberland Fusiliers; notable exceptions were the regiments of Foot Guards and two rifle regiments (the King's Royal Rifle Corps and the Rifle Brigade) that recruited on a nationwide basis. The regular cavalry and various corps such as artillery, engineers and medics, were also recruited nationwide. Territorial infantry and territorial cavalry (the latter known as yeomanry), recruited on a passionately local and county basis, usually at the local drill hall.

From 5th August 1914 until the end of 1915, all recruits were volunteers and as such, were allowed a fair degree of latitude in respect of which branch of the forces they joined, and, if opting for the army, in which regiment they served. Unless unfit, all volunteers were expected to serve overseas – this was automatic for those who joined the regulars, the 'New Army' or from the reserve. Men already serving in the Territorials in 1914 had signed up for Home service and could not be compelled to serve overseas. They were almost immediately asked to sign the Imperial Service Obligation, thus consenting to serve abroad. Any man who refused to sign, for whatever reason, usually was posted to their regiment's new second-line Territorial battalion (such as 2/5th South Staffordshire) that was raised to supply trained recruits for the first-line 'Terriers' (in this case 1/5th South Staffordshire).

Kitchener's Army or New Army

For his part and out on something of a limb, Lord Kitchener envisaged a war of at least three years duration[38] and would not entrust the safety of the Realm into the hands of what he termed 'amateur soldiers.' So, on 6th August, Kitchener decided to raise a new volunteer army of 100,000 men who were to be trained along regular army lines and were not to be confused with existing reservists and Territorials. The new recruits, initially between nineteen and thirty-one years of age[39], signed up for '…three years service or the duration of the war,' and their new battalions were accordingly designated 'service battalions'. Within two days newspaper appeals and the poster campaigns began their famous call for the 'first hundred thousand volunteers', creating in December

---

38 Many observers were of the opinion that the war would be, '…over by Christmas.' This popular view explains the flood of recruits for Kitchener's New Army.

39 The upper age limit was raised to 39 in September 1914. Many recruits also lied about their ages.

1914 in one of the best-known and most imitated posters of all time – the face-on image of Kitchener announcing, "Your Country Needs You." One of the forerunners first appeared in August, 1914.

Lord Kitchener's hope to raise 100,000 volunteers for the New Army over a period of six months proved to be a serious underestimation – the public's response was stunning, as 500,000 men came forward in the first month alone and by Christmas 1,180,000 volunteers had swamped the army's capacity to cope with the new recruits' training. There were grave shortages of accommodation, mess-rooms, parade-grounds, uniforms, webbing, rifles and ammunition. As temporary measures, recruits wore their own, civilian clothing and footwear (and in an unpopular move, spare, blue Post Office uniforms) while some recruits lived at home and learned their drill in local parks and other open spaces using walking sticks and broom handles in place of rifles. Slowly, khaki uniforms and rifles reached the recruits, while tents and huts provided basic if minimal shelter as autumn gave way to winter.

During the first month of war, fifteen of the lads whose names appear on the Elmore Green war memorial stepped forward to offer their services in defence of their country, adding to the four serving regulars and reservist already mentioned. By Christmas 1914 yet another twelve lads had volunteered, thus accounting for almost half the names engraved on the memorial. These volunteers joined a variety of units and signed on under varying terms – Regular Army volunteers went to regimental depots such as the South Staffordshire's Whittington Barracks near Lichfield; Regular Army Reservists and Special Reservists reported to their regiments; Territorials settled their affairs and then renounced the right to serve solely in home defence by signing the Imperial Service Obligation; raw but willing civilians, fired by feelings of patriotism and a thirst for the adventure of a lifetime, turned the work of the 'New Army' recruiting sergeants into a busy but 'cushy' number.

The Pals' (Service) Battalions

Today, one seemingly familiar aspect of Lord Kitchener's 'New Army' is that of the Pals' battalion that allowed for men who lived, played or worked together to volunteer together, train and serve together. The scheme came about thanks to the 17th Earl of Derby who was strongly opposed to the concept of conscription. Derby's idea was first aired in Liverpool where, through the local press, through local businessmen and through a speech on the Pals theme on

28th August 1914, he appealed for volunteers to attend St. George's Hall, Lime Street in Liverpool on Monday, August 31st. The result was again remarkable as more than three thousand men, enough to complete three new battalions, volunteered. Subsequently, the scheme was promoted throughout the country, though with its greatest take-up in the industrial north and midlands[40]. Such was the attraction of the 'Pals' idea that, until the casualty disaster of The Somme in 1916, they would contribute 145 battalions[41] to the 'New Army'. September produced close on another half million further volunteers and, though numbers fluctuated in following months, by the end of 1914 almost 1,200,000 Britons had answered the nation's call to arms.

Standards, Requirements and Conditions for Recruits

Any man who enlisted for military service in 1914 or 1915 was a volunteer and, as such, was allowed to join his preferred service. In the case of the army, a man could, within certain constraints, opt for a branch of the army (infantry, cavalry, artillery, engineers) and choose his regiment; moreover, he could sign on with the Regulars, the Territorials or the New Army. Given this latitude, he still had to satisfy specific terms and conditions of service and these were clearly outlined on recruiting posters and in newspaper appeals. As the war progressed and the need became more urgent, so requirements were gradually relaxed.

Age, Height and Fitness – Males over 5 feet 3 inches, medically fit and aged from 19 to 39 were urged to join the Colours. Old soldiers could be up to 45 years. In the initial appeal the age limit was 19-30 but was then extended to 39 in September 1914, though many under-age and over-age men managed to slip through a colluding recruiting officer's net! No-one under the age of 19 was supposed to be sent to the front[42], though this regulation was relaxed when the losses became critical later in the conflict. From November 1914, men below the minimum height (though otherwise fit) were allowed to join so-called 'Bantam' battalions.. Older soldiers were also used on Home Service for coastal defence, training, recruiting and regimental depot service.

---

40 Logically, most of the Pals-type battalions were raised in urban areas.

41 There were no Pals-type battalions in the South Staffordshire Regiment but the nearby Royal Warwickshire Regiment produced three – 14th, 15th & 16th Battalions, known as the 1st, 2nd & 3rd 'Birmingham Pals'.

42 The youngest soldier known to have died in the British army was, ironically, an Irish lad, Private James Condon of the Royal Irish Regiment, who was aged just fourteen. He is buried in Poelcapelle British Cemetery, near Ypres, Belgium.

Pay – this was ordinary Army pay of 7 shillings[43] a week (less 1½ d. Insurance) plus free food, clothing, lodging and medical attendance. Nationally, the average manual worker's pay in 1914 for a 72-hour week was less than £2.

Terms – if he preferred, a man signed on for the duration of the war only (known as 'War Service') and was assured, *"Then, as soon as the war is over, you will be able to return to your ordinary employment."*

Separation Allowances – these allowances were intended to help the soldier's family to cope with his absence. The Army provided, for a wife only, 12s. 6d, of which the soldier must contribute 3s. 6d.; for a first child, an additional 5s. 0d was granted; for a second child 4s. 0d. and for each subsequent child, 2s. 0d.

Pensions – a man disabled by service was entitled to normal Insurance Benefits as well as a War Office pension for varying degrees of disablement.

Provision for Widows and Children – the death of a soldier on active service entitled a widow to a continuation of Separation Allowance for up to 26 weeks. Afterwards, subject to certain conditions, a variable-rate pension would be allowed.

How to Enlist – at his nearest Post Office or Labour Exchange a man could obtain the address of the local recruiting office.

Maintaining the Flow of Recruits in 1915

It is easily imagined, given the rush of volunteers to the Colours during the five months of 1914, that British military manpower would rapidly expand. As ever, the truth is far more complicated. During those first months of the war, the British Expeditionary Force (BEF) sustained in excess of 95,000 casualties, chillingly close to the *total* number of men that comprised the entire BEF in August 1914. The government stepped up its efforts to increase the flow of volunteers. The original call to arms was replaced by a poster bearing Kitchener's image and the legend, *"Your Country Needs You!"* – it became one of the most successful and most imitated posters of all time. The recruiting machine went to work on the importance of family ties with the likes of, *"What did you do in the war, Daddy?"* – starkly emotional blackmail certainly, but the means was felt to justify the ends. Women, particularly those of marriageable age, were made to feel guilty if their, *"Best boy was not in khaki…"*. The young men themselves were subjected to appeals to their 'manliness' and to 'winning glory' as in an appeal that occupied the centre of the front page of the *'Walsall Observer'* on 12th December, 1914:-

---

43   One pound contained 20 shillings; one shilling contained 12 pennies.

These Soldiers Have Won the Victoria Cross

August 1914	Charles Jarvis	Royal Engineers
August 1914	Maurice Dease	Royal Fusiliers
August 1914	Sidney Godley	Royal Fusiliers
August 1914	Ernest Alexander	Royal Field Artillery
October 1914	John Hogan	Manchester Regiment
October 1914	James Leach	Manchester Regiment
October 1914	Arthur Martin-Leake	Royal Army Medical Corps
Nov'ber 1914	Spencer Bent	Leicestershire Regiment
Nov'ber 1914	John Vallentin	South Staffordshire Regiment
Nov'ber 1914	Walter Brodie	Highland Light Infantry

There's room for your name here on this Roll of Honour.
These heroes would never have won the V.C. by staying away
from the Recruiting Office. They enlisted for their Country's
sake and fought as only brave men do.

Enlist Today!

The More Men We have, The Sooner The War Ends

National Registration (spring 1915)

As a first move between voluntary and compulsory (conscription) enlistment, in July 1915 the Government introduced the National Registration Act with the aim of discovering how many men between the ages of 15 and 65 were engaged in each trade or profession. By mid-September 1915 the scheme revealed that there were still nearly 5 million civilian men of military age in Britain. One and a half million men worked in vital, reserved occupations and were exempted from enlistment, unless they chose to volunteer. Just over half the available men were induced to come forward under the following scheme introduced by Lord Derby.

The Derby Scheme (autumn 1915)

Although the pressure on men to volunteer in 1915 was intensifying, many married men were concerned as to how their families would cope if the 'breadwinner' joined the forces. So, Prime Minister Asquith who had been greatly impressed by Lord Derby's 'Pals' recruiting idea in Liverpool, appointed him Director-General of Recruitment on 11th October 1915. In both government and among the population there was still strong resistance to military conscription, so on 16th October Derby announced a policy by which men could give voluntary 'assent' to being called up if necessary; in its turn, the government endeavoured to call up men in age groups, with single men before married. Men aged 18 to 40 were informed that they could still enlist voluntarily, or attest their willingness to serve when their group was called up. A 'Derby' man would remain at home and in his job until called – to avoid a being given a white feather, an 'attested' man would wear an official grey armband bearing a red crown emblem. As an obvious financial incentive for a man to leave hearth and home, a military pension was introduced for the dependants of a man killed on service.

In the event, the Derby Scheme led to the actual enlistment of fewer than 350,000 men, though upwards of two million men attested for later service. Consequently, the government dropped the Derby Scheme in December 1915 and decided to turn to conscription.

Conscription (The two Military Service Acts, January and May 1916)
In January 1916 the volunteer system of enlistment was replaced by conscription under the terms of the First Military Service Act. By this, single men between 18 and 41 years must join the armed services when called up, youngest group first; the first of these conscripts (nineteen year-olds) were sent for in March 1916[44]. Two months later, in May 1916, the Second Military Service Act accepted that conscripting single men would not slake the thirst for recruits and so married men were also to be required for military service.

Catching the 'Draft Dodgers'
In the wake of the Second Military Service Act, checks on male civilians of military age increased in stringency. For example, on 10th June 1916, the *'Walsall Observer'* carried the following announcement:-

> *"Every man who has been or ought to have been registered under the National Registration Act (NRA) is liable, under the Defence of the Realm Acts, to a penalty of a fine of £100 or six months in prison if he fails to produce his certificate of registration when duly required to do so at his place of residence. Any such person who has lost his certificate or for any reason has not been registered, should apply forthwith to the Clerk to the borough, urban or rural district in which he is residing."*

By way of practical implementation of the new acts, a Walsall Tribunal put

---

44   At the same time as the first 'attested' men, as a matter of fairness.

into effect in February 1916 – its task was to carry out the provisions of the 1st Military Service Act (Conscription) by investigating all applications for exemption from military service. The volume of applications for exemption necessitated the expansion of the Tribunal to two courts in order to cope. Contrary to modern belief, in its 262 sittings, of the 8,769 applications that were heard, exemption was refused to just 1,579 men. Twenty-five others were granted conditional exemption on conscientious or religious grounds, becoming in the dismissive parlance of the day, 'Conchies'.

Reserved or 'Starred' Occupations

A number of skilled, specialist occupations were vitally important to the national economy. A list was drawn up of all jobs and those considered essential were denoted by a star or asterisk (hence the nickname, 'starred occupations') – among these were mining, food-production and transport. A man employed in such an occupation was entitled to remain at his work in this country, with the consequence that over 1,600,000 men would thus remain outside the armed services for the duration of the conflict. Yet a man working in a 'starred' occupation was still entitled to volunteer for military service if he so wished. Many did, creating a labour 'gap' and such shortfalls were made good by the large-scale employment of women.

Among the lads whose names appear on the Elmore Green war memorial, and also related men whose stories are told, almost half were miners. The men included twenty-nine miners and another seven who worked in metal-casting industries.

That these lads volunteered for service when they might have remained in Bloxwich may be ascribed to a number of factors, among which were:-

- The heavy, repetitive nature of their work in pit or foundry.
- The strong pull of patriotism, still powerful in 1914.
- An opportunity for travel beyond their own parish.
- Wanting not to 'miss out' on the adventure of a lifetime.
- Escape from the pressure of the 'daily round' and the possibility of improved pay (for some) in comparison to civilian employment.
- In a few cases, the chance of a 'fresh start'.

Today, it is too easy to underestimate the importance at that time of coal and coke in the vast majority of industrial processes, in domestic heating and not the least in keeping the fleet at sea. It is also necessary to recognise that many aspects of mining were not only skilled but required strong nerve and not a little courage. So, it is unsurprising that on 4th November 1916, the 'Walsall Observer' carried a short statement, tucked away at the bottom of an inside page:-

> *"No More Miners as Soldiers – The Home Secretary announced on Tuesday night that about 11,000 men have been returned to the mines. As output of coal is still too low, there can be no question of releasing other miners for enlistment in the Army."*

Nevertheless, several Elmore Green-educated miners enlisted in the army in the wake of the government announcement, so it seems that a man's stated occupation was not too carefully checked. In any case, the decision was rescinded early in 1918 in response to the acute need for soldiers.

The Call to Arms in the Walsall area

On 8th August 1914, the *'Walsall Observer'* carried a call to arms that included the phrase, *"For the location of local Recruiting Offices, enquire at local the Post Office or Labour Exchange."* This appeal was for new recruits to the army and the effects were anticipated elsewhere in the same edition of the newspaper announcing, *"…The rash of recruits in Walsall has been as great as in any other town; in fact it has been impossible to deal with all the applicants."* Evidence from, *'Soldiers Died in the Great War'*, indicates that there were recruiting offices located not only in Walsall Town Hall but all over the local area. Nineteen year-old Ted Jones, a miner from Marlborough Street, walked no further than the Bloxwich recruiting office to sign up for Lord Kitchener's 'New Army', joining 7th Battalion, South Staffordshire; another Kitchener volunteer was Elmore Green's twenty-four year-old George Smith who enlisted in Castleford, Yorkshire for the 12th (Service) Battalion of the West Yorkshire Regiment.

Apart from volunteers seeking recruiting sergeants, many local reservists were hastening to join their units. The *'Walsall Observer'* editions of 8th and 15th August both carried reporting instructions for Regular Army Reservists – these men, as trained soldiers, would be among the first of the existing civilians to go into the firing-line. From the Elmore Green memorial lads, Alf Main went from the a reserve battalion to join the Regulars of 2nd Battalion, South Staffordshire; with four years' experience in the Special Reserve, James William Goodall was posted to 1st Battalion, South Staffordshire, while Aaron Hayward, as a member of the Regular Army Reserve automatically rejoined his former battalion, 1st South Staffordshire.

The outbreak of war coincided with the annual summer training camp for the two Territorial battalions of the South Staffordshire Regiment. 1/5th Battalion was the Walsall-based battalion and 1/6th Battalion was the Wolverhampton-based battalion but the two came together on Sunday, 2nd August to *'…proceed to St. Asaph,'* in North Wales. Hardly were the men settled into the camp and their kit (for which they were individually responsible) checked, than the battalions were recalled and mobilised in Walsall (1/5th) and Wolverhampton (1/6th). For six days 1/5th Battalion then was stationed at the Town Hall, affording locals the bizarre sight of sentries, with bayonets fixed to their rifles, marching up and down Tower Street. For the duration, the troops were billeted in local schools as the pupils were enjoying their sunny, summer vacation.

This is how the *'Walsall Observer'* reported the events of that momentous week.

The clearest indication that Walsall was about to play its part in a major war came with the departure on Tuesday, 11th August from the town centre of the Walsall, West Bromwich, Lichfield and Sutton contingents of the Staffordshire Yeomanry[45] – this amounted to about one hundred cavalrymen. On leaving Walsall, the mounted troops made their way to Stafford, to link with other county contingents, and then on to Grantham in Lincolnshire to sharpen their training. For most townspeople, the majority of whom appeared to be gathered in Walsall centre on that day, the big event was to be the departure of the Territorials of the 1/5th Battalion of the South Staffordshire – whereas few locals knew anyone enlisted in the cavalry, most people had a loved one or a friend or neighbour in the infantry. In fact, 'D' Company[46] of the 1/5th Battalion had been raised in Bloxwich.

The *'Walsall Observer'* edition of 15th August carried a photo of the battalion on parade on The Bridge and described the scene thus:

> *"From Lloyd's Bank to within a few feet of Sister Dora's statue and from Bridge Street to Bradford Street, was a mass of khaki, and many compliments were paid as to the smart appearance of the men as they stood in full marching order, with bayonets glittering in the brilliant sunshine. A platform decorated with Union Jacks and a banner inscribed, 'God Save The King', had been erected in front of the statue, and upon which were the Mayor and Mayoress as well as Lieutenant-Colonel Green (the C.O. of the battalion). Many other prominent citizens were present."*

Unidentified in the khaki ranks but undoubtedly present in the centre of Walsall on 11th August were several lads from the Elmore Green school memorial – among Captain F.C. Hughes's 'A' (Walsall) Company was

---

45 The County Yeomanry was, effectively, the Territorial Force of cavalrymen.

46 In August 1914 Territorial battalions still maintained the eight-company system; this was later brought in line with the four-company system of the regular army.

seventeen year-old Jack Parton of Cope Street, Leamore; in Captain C. Lister's 'B' (Walsall) Company was nineteen year-old Joseph Handy of Marlborough Street, Bloxwich, a lad with over two years experience in the Territorials; and among the one hundred and fourteen men of Captain H. Lord and Lieutenant L. Cozens's 'D' (Bloxwich) Company were miner Len Morris (recorded as 'Malpass' on official documents), seventeen year-olds Horace Downes and George Groves, married man Corporal Bill Haycock, mining engineer Frank Lloyd, Albert Stych (who would be wounded on the first day of the Somme in 1916), boat-builder's son Arthur Linnell and a Territorial with eight years experience in 'D' Company, George Sargent. Between them, they would earn four Military Medals and be recommended for one Distinguished Conduct Medal. None of them would return after the war.

The battalion and a huge crowd of well-wishers heard the mayor, Alderman Peter Bull, deliver a complimentary and encouraging farewell speech. The '*Walsall Observer*' edition of 15th August, portayed the scene in the town centre as follows:

> "*For a week Walsall has borne the appearance of a garrison town. Since the mobilisation of the forces on Tuesday week, khaki-clad men have been here, there and everywhere, and we have had the unique experience of seeing men posted with fixed bayonets at the entrances to the George Hotel, the Town Hall and other points. But all that is now at an end. On Tuesday, the officers and men of the 5th Battalion of the South Staffordshire Regiment, under the command of Lieut.-Colonel C. Fiddian Green, left, after a civic farewell, for Lichfield, whence they proceeded to Burton on Wednesday and were still there yesterday. Where they are to go next is not known, but in view of the request made by the War Office[47] in a letter received by the Commanding Officer on Tuesday, it is likely that some of them, at any rate, may eventually have experience of the more serious side of warfare.*"

All stood and the men uncovered their heads as the band had played the National Anthem; the troops fell into line, four deep and, to the strains of '*Tommy Atkins*', set off along Bridge Street and Lichfield Street *en route* for the regimental depot at Whittington[48]. The 'Terriers' were off to war and 46th 'North Midland' Division would be sent to France early in March 1915 – the

---

47 This letter, sent to all Territorial battalions, asked the volunteers to forego their right to serve only in Britain and to sign the Imperial Service Obligation.

48 Whittington Barracks, Lichfield was (and still is for its modern successor, the Mercian Regiment) the home of the South Staffordshire Regiment.

first *complete* TF division to join the BEF[49]. Individual TF battalions had been sent to the continent early in the war to relieve regular battalions of the task of 'lines of communication' duties but it was not long before the TF lads of the London Scottish (14/London) were in action at Messines, south of Ypres.

Where Elmore Green men enlisted

Locally, most Elmore Green men volunteered at recruiting offices in Bloxwich, Darlaston, Hednesford, Walsall, Willenhall and Wolverhampton. Three even volunteered in Birmingham (of these three lads, two joined the Royal Field Artillery and the other joined the Royal Army Medical Corps). A number of men 'enlisted' at Whittington Barracks, Lichfield, reporting for their previously attested 'call-up' to the South Staffordshire Regiment. It seems that some Bloxwich men had, for a variety of reasons, drifted to other parts of the country, probably following the availability of some kind of mining work. Into the latter category came George Smith who, though born in Bloxwich, volunteered in Castleford, Yorkshire, having moved there in search of pit-work. Another youngster, David Goodall, was born in Bloxwich and lived most of his adult life in Chesterton (near Newcastle-under-Lyme) where his father was a stone-hewer, but David had returned to Bloxwich to volunteer. One lad, educated at Elmore Green, enlisted as far away as Valcartier in Canada, having emigrated to Quebec Province in 1913.

Results of National Recruitment

Any man joining the army in 1914 or 1915 was technically a volunteer, and any man enlisting from January 1916 was more than likely a conscript, with the exceptions of the Derby Scheme men who had attested their willingness to serve when called up in their age group. During the five calendar years of the war, recruiting figures were as follows:-

Volunteers		Conscripts	
To 31st Dec. 1914	1,186,357	To 31st Dec. 1916	1,190,000
		To 31st Dec. 1917	820,646
To 31st Dec. 1915	1,280,000	To 11th Nov. 1918	493,562
	2,466,357		**2,504,208**

Nationally, by November 1918, nearly 6 million men had passed through the Army. When war was declared, the battalions of the South Staffordshire Regiment were scattered to the four winds. 1st (Regular) Battalion was at

---

49 TF divisions had already been sent abroad to replace 'Regular Army' garrisons – 42nd 'East Lancashire' to Egypt (September 1914); 43rd 'Wessex', 44th 'Home Counties' and 45th '2nd Wessex' to India (between October and December 1914).

Pietermaritzburg, in South Africa; 2nd (Regular) Battalion was at Aldershot. 3rd (Reserve) and 4th (Extra Reserve) Battalions, constituting the Special Reserve, were in training at Whittington Barracks, Lichfield. 1/5th and 1/6th Battalions (Territorial Force) had left their Drill Halls in Walsall and Wolverhampton respectively, on the 2nd August, for their Annual Camp at St. Asaph in North Wales, only to be brought back again next day to Walsall and Wolverhampton, when they were mobilised. Each type of battalion had slightly differing priorities – 1st Battalion was faced with the logistics and frustrations of a long journey back to England from South Africa, then fitting out for transfer to the British Expeditionary Force in France and Flanders; 2nd Battalion, already part of 2nd Division's 6th Brigade, had to put to the test existing mobilisation

CONDITIONS OF SERVICE.

1. On undertaking the liability to serve abroad in time of national emergency, an officer or man of the Territorial Force will be required to sign an agreement, on Army Form E. 624, in the presence of the Officer Commanding the Territorial unit to which he belongs, and, unless notification to the contrary is given to the Commanding Officer, the liability will continue as long as the officer's or man's engagement in the Territorial Force lasts.

2. The engagement on Army Form E 624, of an officer or man of the Territorial Force to accept liability for service outside the United Kingdom in time of national emergency, will be to serve with his own unit, or with part of his own unit, only. He cannot, under this agreement, be drafted as an individual to any other unit.

3. Except as regards liability for foreign service, the conditions of the officer's or man's service in the Territorial Force will not be affected by this agreement.

4. A badge will be awarded to each individual accepting such liability for service outside the United Kingdom. This badge will be worn, when in uniform, on the right breast of the officer or man so long as the liability continues.

Army form E.624, commonly known as the Imperial Service Obligation (terms and conditions), by which a TF man gave his consent to serve overseas during the national emergency.

plans, move to the south coast, cross the Channel and bolster the left wing of the French Fifth Army and the right wing of the remaining Belgian Army; the men of the Special Reserve had to accustom themselves to the fact that they were about to leave home and be tested as reinforcements for the hard-pressed regulars; and the immediate priority of the Territorials was to decide whether or not to sign the Imperial Service Obligation [Army Form E.624 on page 124'] that would take them from Britain into harm's way. At Whittington Barracks, the training corporals would soon have to cope with the influx of 'Kitchener volunteers' who would become the basis of three new 'Service' battalions, the 7th, 8th and 9th.

Pre-war and 1914 Elmore Green Recruitment

The local 'Old Contemptibles', under fire before 22nd November 1914

John Bullock	1st (Reg) Battalion, South Staffordshire Regiment
Joseph Bullock	2nd (Reg) Battalion, South Staffordshire Regiment
James DAWSON	2nd (Reg) Battalion, South Staffordshire Regiment
William GROVES	1st (Reg) Battalion, South Staffordshire Regiment
Aaron HAYWARD	1st (Reg) Battalion, South Staffordshire Regiment
Ernest Lavender	2nd (Reg) Battalion, South Staffordshire Regiment
William Lavender	1st (Reg) Battalion, Lincolnshire Regiment

Men who were under fire between 23rd November and 31st December 1914

Edgar GOODALL	1st or 2nd (Reg) Battalion, South Staffordshire Regiment
James Jones	1st (Reg) Battalion, South Staffordshire Regiment
Timothy Taylor	1st (Reg) Battalion, South Staffordshire Regiment

Men who enlisted between 4th August and 31st December 1914

Charles BULLOCK	1/5th TF Battalion, South Staffordshire Regiment
Alfred BUSHNELL	1st (Reg) Battalion, King's Own Scottish Borderers
George BUSHNELL	1/5th TF Battalion, South Staffordshire Regiment
Joseph DAVIES	1/5th TF Battalion, South Staffordshire Regiment
Horace DOWNES	1/5th TF Battalion, South Staffordshire Regiment
Thomas Dunn	89th Field Company, Corps of Royal Engineers
William GOODALL	2nd (Reg) Battalion, South Staffordshire Regiment
Samuel Goodall	13th (S) Battalion, Northumberland Fusiliers
George GROVES	1/5th TF Battalion, South Staffordshire Regiment
Joseph HANDY	1/5th TF Battalion, South Staffordshire Regiment
Frank HARVEY	4th (Sp. Res) Battalion, South Staffordshire Regiment

Bill HAYCOCK	1/5th TF Battalion, South Staffordshire Regiment
Ted JONES	7th (S) Battalion, South Staffordshire Regiment
Arthur KITSON	1st (Reg) Battalion, Royal Welch Fusiliers
William LAWLEY	3rd (Reg) Battalion, Grenadier Guards
Arthur LINNELL	1/5th TF Battalion, South Staffordshire Regiment
Frank LLOYD	1/5th TF Battalion, South Staffordshire Regiment
Alfred MAIN	2nd (Reg) Battalion, South Staffordshire Regiment
Leonard MALPASS	1/5th TF Battalion, South Staffordshire Regiment
John Orgill	1/5th TF Battalion, South Staffordshire Regiment
Joseph ORGILL	2nd Fld. Amb., Canadian Army Medical Corps
Jack PARTON	1/5th TF Battalion, South Staffordshire Regiment
Harry PERKS	1st (Reg) Battalion, Worcestershire Regiment
Simon Perks	1/5th TF Battalion, South Staffordshire Regiment
Wm Edw PICKIN	2/5th TF Battalion, South Staffordshire Regiment
George SARGENT	1/5th TF Battalion, South Staffordshire Regiment
Edward Smith	10th (S) Battalion, West Yorkshire Regiment
George SMITH	12th (S) Battalion, West Yorkshire Regiment
Albert STYCH	7th (S) Battalion, Suffolk Regiment
George Stych	2nd (Reg) Battalion, South Staffordshire Regiment
Samuel Stych	17th (S) Battalion, West Yorkshire Regiment
Robert SYLVESTER	2/5th TF Battalion, South Staffordshire Regiment
Harry WILLETT	3rd (Reg) Battalion, Grenadier Guards
John YATES	2nd (Reg) Battalion, South Staffordshire Regiment

UPPER CASE surnames indicate men whose names are commemorated on the Elmore Green school memorial.

Lower case surnames indicate men *related* to those who are commemorated on the Elmore Green school memorial.

(Reg)	indicates a Regular Army battalion.
TF	indicates a Territorial Force battalion.
(S)	indicates a Service or 'New Army' battalion.
(Sp. Res.)	indicates a Special Reserve or Extra Reserve battalion.

Why did men serve in regiments other than their 'local' battalions?

By far the greatest proportion of Elmore Green men served with one or more battalions of the South Staffordshire Regiment, though it is not difficult to uncover one or two surprises. Before the advent of conscription in January 1916, most volunteers were allowed their preference as to the arm and branch of the services in which they would serve. Consequently, some lads on the school memorial opted for famous regiments such as the Grenadier Guards that was the choice of Bill Lawley, John Bate and John Willett; Isaac Andrews served with the Royal Scots but, as he enlisted in 1916, he had no choice and many Englishmen were being sent north to reinforce the decimated Scots' battalions. Once in the army, soldiers might be transferred to other regiments according to need; Albert Stych and Robert Sylvester both enlisted in the South Staffordshires but Albert was killed in action with the Suffolk Regiment and Robert died of wounds serving with the Gloucestershire Regiment. More than one Elmore Green lad joined the army as a private and later earned a commission as an officer; for many reasons, such men were transferred to different units. Albert Wilkes enlisted in the South Staffordshire Territorials in 1916, was commissioned 2nd Lieutenant in October 1917 and thereafter served with three battalions of the Sherwood Foresters; Frank Lloyd was a pre-war Territorial with the South Staffordshires and earned gallantry medals with that Regiment and was commissioned 2nd Lieutenant and was posted to 6th Battalion the Worcestershire Regiment. Further still, near the end of hostilities Frank transferred to the Royal Air Force and served with 61 Squadron.

Army Basic Training – what faced the volunteers?

Army training facilities in autumn 1914 in the United Kingdom took many months to cope with the overwhelming flood of recruits. Initially, there were drastic shortages of kit, equipment and accommodation.

On arrival at his first camp, a recruit would be issued with his army kit for which he became responsible; often ill-fitting, the boots, uniform and webbing had to be kept in pristine condition, requiring monotonously long hours of attention. Day on day, physical fitness was built up as were the near-automatic responses on the drill square; above all, discipline was hammered home – individual discipline, group discipline, march discipline, weapons discipline. Discipline began to forge the soldier from the raw civilian, above all purging the man of individuality and instilling standard responses.

Whatever his unit, every soldier would have to learn basic field-craft skills and musketry, then more specialised skills specific to his role; many men received initial training to equip them as signallers, bombers, machine-gunners and the like. Finally, as the day approached for a man's draft to prepare for overseas service, the troops were given their first taste of front line survival skills in trench digging, wiring and revetting, anti-gas defence and very basic first aid.

Basic training was, for most 'civilians', a dispiriting, uncomfortable six-month course under the auspices of sergeants and corporals who often resembled foul-mouthed bullies who demanded the impossible. Only when a man reached the front line did he appreciate some of the things he had been forced to do as a raw recruit. As every soldier new to the trenches would find out, they would all still have much to learn the hard way in the mud of France and Flanders.

The Main Theatres of War, 1914-1918

On enlisting in the armed forces, a man might, according to his branch of the services, be sent to fight in any of the following theatres of war:

Western Front	France and Flanders
Eastern Front	Russia, Poland, Galicia, Austria
Southern Front	North Italy, Austria, Alpine region
Salonika	Serbia, Macedonia, Greece
Gallipoli/The Dardanelles	An attempt to force Turkey out of the war
Egypt/Suez Canal Zone	British effort to maintain the security of vital trade route to the east
Palestine	Late but successful effort to force Turkey to sue for peace
Mesopotamia	Attempts to secure modern-day Iraq and its oilfields
Sub-Saharan Africa	East Africa West Africa
Imperial outpost garrisons	India was the most likely

Royal Navy Fleet war

Royal Navy coastal defences

Armed Merchant Ships

The U-Boat War: Submarine Service, Minelayers and Minesweepers

PART III

The 'Boys' who really did the job...

Note:
How to read an obituary/record entry

Note: not every serviceman will have *all* the following information available. What appears is the best from the research sources at the time of publication. Items shown below in bold print appear as such in the obituary/record

Serviceman's full name [**MM** indicates award of Military Medal; **CdeG** indicates award of French Medal, Croix de Guerre].

- A photo (sometimes poor quality!) from a relative or from a newspaper report.
- Date (sometimes just approximate year) and place of birth.
- Residence in August 1914 and/or former local residence.
- Parents' names and residence; brothers/sisters.
- Where educated (most cases this will be Elmore Green).
- Marital status, if known, and children.
- Nature and place of employment at time of enlistment.
- **Date** and place of **volunteering or enlisting** – 'volunteered' usually refers to pre-war enlistment in the regular army and up to the end of 1915; 'enlisted' usually refers to the 1916-1918 period of conscription according to age and marital status.
- Pre-war military service, if any.
- **Regimental number; rank; company** if known (usually preceded by a letter or number e.g. 'D' or '3' Company).
  Battalion number and type (Regular Army, Territorial Force or Service/New Army; the last indicates 'war service duration' only) plus any **battalion informal names or nicknames** (e.g. 'Church Lads Brigade' Battalion):-

  '**7257, Corporal,**
  '**3' Company**
  16th (Service/New Army) 'Church Lads Brigade' Battalion'

- **Regiment or Corps** (e.g. Worcestershire Regiment, Grenadier Guards or Corps of Royal Engineers).
- **Battalion's brigade and division** at time of soldier's death or end of service, if survived (divisions were often assigned a number *and* a regional name, such as 46th *'1st North Midland'* Division or 16th *'Irish'* Division) though a man's brigade and division may have varied during his service:-

  '**King's Royal Rifle Corps** (often shown as 'KRRC'),
  (100th Brigade, 33rd Division)'

- In a very few cases the service details will refer to **rank and service branch**, such as 'Royal Navy Volunteer Reserve' or 'Royal Air Force' in addition to any reference to **squadron or ship**:-

  'Bristol Z/9639, Able Seaman
  S.S. *'Kilmaho'*
  Royal Naval Volunteer Reserve'
  OR...

  '2nd Lieutenant
  61st Squadron
  Royal Air Force'

- Service details at time of death are sometimes preceded (*not* in bold type) by details of former unit(s) and any transfer(s):-

  '11456, Private
  South Staffordshire Regiment. Transferred to... [date given when known]

  86336, Sapper
  173rd Tunnelling Company
  Royal Engineers'

- In the Unit History, comes the detailed war service of a man's unit (sometimes including actions before a man joined it):-
- ➢ Date when a man first landed in a theatre of war (e.g. France, Mesopotamia).
- ➢ Main battle actions experienced – theatre of war or major offensive (e.g. Gallipoli, Somme) is underlined, followed by main battles and their duration dates in that theatre or offensive (e.g. 26-28/9/16 Battle of Thiepval). Battles within an offensive are separated by semi-colons; the end of an offensive is marked by a full stop.
- ➢ Details of actions are followed by record of wounds, illness, gassing or injury (aside from that which led to death). Note: wounds usually indicate that a man was not present in all his unit's battle engagements.
- **How died** ('killed in action', 'died of wounds', 'died from illness or accident'), **day and date of death, age**, incident/action that led to death and where died:-

  'Died of wounds (age 22) on Thursday, 27th April 1916, having been severely wounded near Poperinghe by counter-battery artillery fire on 10th April 1916.'

- **Place of burial** or **commemoration** (with burial plot number or commemoration reference), region and country of burial or commemoration:-

    'Buried in plot V. B. 15A of **Etaples Military Cemetery**, France.'

OR...

    'Commemorated on panels 73-76 of the **Loos Memorial to the Missing**, Dud Corner, near Lens, France.'

- Medal entitlement – awards and recommendations for bravery such as Military Medal, Mention in Despatches *plus* campaign medals such as 1914 'Mons' Star, 1914-15 Star, British War Medal and Victory Medal. [Most servicemen were entitled to the last two in the list.]:-

    'Entitled to the Military Medal, awarded in June 1916 for brave action when a shell hit a gun-pit (award posted in the *'London Gazette'* supplement edition of 10th August 1916, page 7887), British War Medal and Victory Medal (Medal Roll – TF/RFA/147B, p.9561).'

- Location and type of local commemoration (e.g. Bloxwich War Memorial, Rushall section of the Staffordshire Roll of Honour); location and nature of personal memorials; location and nature of memorials beyond the local area. Widow's name and number of children. Relatives who served, their units and their fates:-

    'Commemorated on the Elmore Green School Roll of Honour (formerly located in the T.P. Riley School library), on the Walsall and Bloxwich Rolls of Honour and the Roll of Honour at All Saints Church, Bloxwich.'

- Family connections, whether wife and children; indication of relations who served:-

    'Family – an older brother, 200822, Private Charles Bullock of 1/5 South Staffordshire was killed in action on 23rd April 1917 at Arras; a second brother, 7745, Private John Bullock of 1/South Staffordshire was held prisoner in Germany from November 1914; a third brother, 6285, Private Joseph Henry Bullock of 2/South Staffordshire served on the Western Front and survived the war.'

'Medal Roll' references in the records

In the section 'Medal entitlement', the example includes "British War Medal and Victory Medal (Medal Roll – TF/RFA/147B, p.9561)." The reference to the Medal Roll is an official record, kept on microfilm in the National Archives at Kew in London. This record may be consulted in person at Kew. The medal roll offers variable information, from home address to regiment/battalion details, occasionally information that no longer exists in official form about the serviceman.

Chapter Nine

1914:

'The Regulars and Reservists go to War – the Old Contemptibles, Mons, 'Wipers' and the first Casualties…'

August
Mons and the Retreat

September
The Marne and The Aisne

October
La Bassée, Messines and Armentières

October/November
First 'Wipers' – Ypres

August to December
Volunteering back home

'Out since August 1914…'
Professional soldier,
James Dawson, 2/South
Staffordshire,
eventually killed in action on
the Somme, November 1916.

Map 1: Western Front – Main Locations, 1914-1918

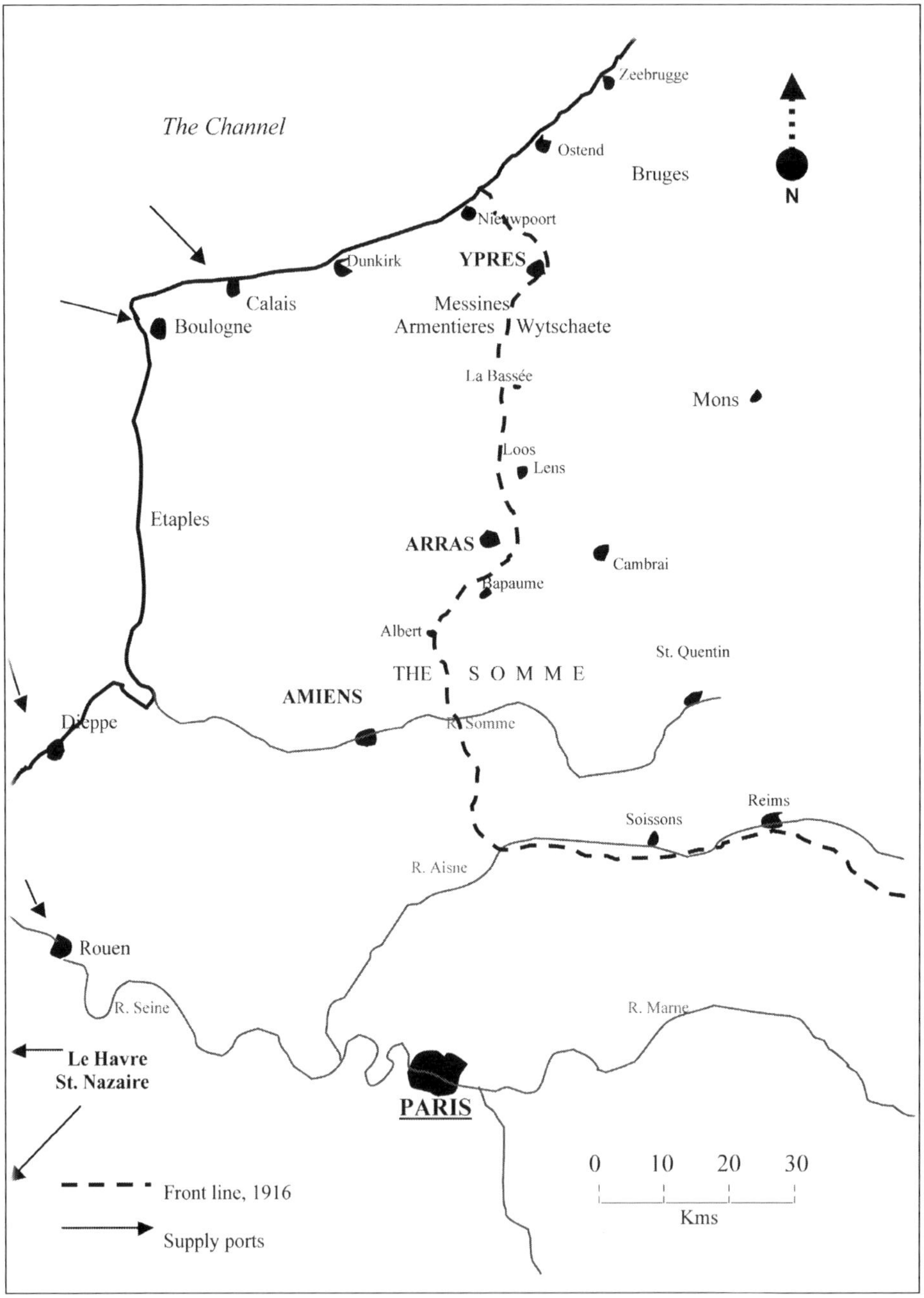

The Channel

Zeebrugge

Ostend

Bruges

N

Nieuwpoort

Dunkirk

YPRES

Calais

Messines

Boulogne

Armentieres | Wytschaete

La Bassée

Mons

Loos

Lens

Etaples

ARRAS

Cambrai

Bapaume

Albert

St. Quentin

THE SOMME

AMIENS

Dieppe

R. Somme

Reims

Soissons

R. Aisne

Rouen

R. Seine

R. Marne

Le Havre
St. Nazaire

PARIS

0   10   20   30

Kms

- - - - Front line, 1916

———► Supply ports

August

Following the declaration of war with Germany on 4th August 1914, the vanguard of the British Expeditionary Force (BEF) that prepared to board troopships and cross the English Channel consisted of just four divisions of highly-professional, regular soldiers reinforced by a notable proportion of Regular and Special Reservists – in all, the whole force totalled about 50,000 infantrymen accompanied by 25,000 men in support units. By way of example, 2nd Battalion, the South Staffordshire Regiment was one of twelve infantry battalions[50] in the three brigades of Major-General C.C. Monro's 2nd Division[51]. The infantry battalions of the three brigades in 2nd Division, were drawn from all over the country and were all Regular Army:

4th (Guards) Brigade – 2 & 3/Coldstream, 2/Grenadier and 1/Irish Guards.
5th Brigade – 2/Worcesters, 2/Ox & Bucks, 2/HLI and 2/Connaught Rangers.
6th Brigade – 1/King's (Liverpool), 2/S. Staffs, 1/KRRC and 2/Royal Berkshire.

The units other than infantry that composed the division were:-
    'B' Squadron, 15th (The King's) Hussars [about 220 men]
    2nd Cyclist Company [composed of 2nd Division infantrymen]
    34th Brigade, Royal Field Artillery [795 all ranks, eighteen 18-pounders]
    36th Brigade, Royal Field Artillery [795 all ranks, eighteen 18-pounders]
    41st Brigade, Royal Field Artillery [795 all ranks, eighteen 18-pounders]
    44th (Howitzer) Brigade, Royal Field Artillery [755 all ranks, eighteen
    4.5-inch howitzers]
Each field artillery brigade had its own Brigade Ammunition Column; each BAC contained 158 all ranks.
    35th Heavy Battery, Royal Garrison Artillery [four 60-pounder guns; 166 all ranks] with its own Heavy Battery Ammunition Column [fewer men than a field artillery BAC].

    2nd Division Ammunition Column (for Small Arms and Artillery re-supply)
    5th Field Company, Royal Engineers [about 220 men]
    11th Field Company, Royal Engineers [about 220 men]
    2nd Divisional Signal Company [about 160 men]
    4th Field Ambulance, RAMC [about 230 men]
    5th Field Ambulance, RAMC [about 230 men]
    6th Field Ambulance, RAMC [about 230 men]
    3rd Mobile Veterinary Section AVC [28 all ranks]
    11th Company, Army Service Corps }

---

50 For more explanation of battalions, brigades and divisions, please see Chapter 7, British Forces in 1914.

51 2nd Division and 1st Division constituted the I Corps that was commanded by Lieutenant-General Sir Douglas Haig, who was destined to replace Sir John French as Commander-in-Chief of the BEF after the catastrophic Battle of Loos in the autumn of 1915.

Map 2: August/September 1914
Battlefields

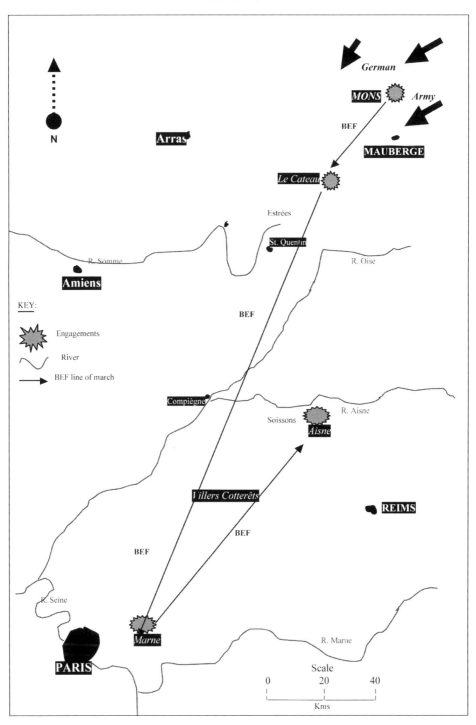

28th Company, Army Service Corps } 2nd Divisional 'Train' (or Supply
    Column)
31st Company, Army Service Corps }
35th Company, Army Service Corps }

Each A.S.C. (Horse Transport) Company contained 430 all ranks, responsible
for 378 horses, 17 carts, 125 G.S. (General Service) wagons and 30 bicycles.

Four Elmore Green 'memorial' lads crossed the Channel in 1914 – two were
serving regular soldiers, one was an old soldier called up from the regular
reserve and a fourth was a regular army volunteer with 1st or 2nd South
Staffordshire. However, five 'related' soldiers[52] also crossed the narrow strip
of sea before Christmas. The first Elmore Green soldier to reach France
was Private **James Dawson**, a regular with 2nd South Staffordshire; aboard
the same troopship, the 5,000-ton S.S. *'Irrawaddy'*, were the **Groves boys'**
uncle, Private **Ernest Lavender** and one of the four Bullock brothers, Private
Joseph Bullock. Also aboard the packed troopship was a second battalion
of 6th Brigade, 1st (King's) Liverpool Regiment. The other two battalions in
6th Brigade, 1st Royal Berkshires and 1st King's Royal Rifle Corps, crossed in
another transport, the two ships keeping close station. They landed at Le Havre
on 13th August to a memorable welcome from the local populace, described
thus in a first-hand account:

> *"We landed, and…..proceeded to march to the* [No.1] *Rest Camp…..*
> *about six miles away on the summit of a hill commanding the harbour.*
> *We had to march through the town most of the way, and our reception*
> *was truly terrific, banners welcoming 'les braves Anglais' were displayed*
> *on all sides, and our march became a triumphal procession between*
> *cheering crowds. We had been to some pains in teaching the men 'La*
> *Marseillaise' and there were a good many mouth organs amongst the*
> *Company, so that, when we struck up, there was a tremendous burst of*
> *enthusiasm, and the crowds nearly went mad, flinging flowers down for*
> *us to walk over."* [Even so, the march did not end very gloriously and
> alcohol, the curse of many a soldier, played its unexpected part.] *"The*
> *men had had two bad nights and little food on the boats; the heat was*
> *absolutely terrific, and the march between dense crowds through narrow*
> *streets was almost suffocating. In addition, the weight of the equipment*
> *carried was found very trying by the Reservists, and it was a steady pull*
> *up steep hills over cobble stones the whole way. The men soon became*

---

52 'Related' soldiers do not appear on the school memorial but their stories are included as a means of
    illustrating the harrowing effects of war on wider family groups.

exhausted, and it was impossible to prevent the well meaning populace from pouring wines and liqueurs down their throats whenever there was a halt. Tommy is not used to either wines or liqueurs. The natural result was that a great many men collapsed, and a large number fell out. These were increased when the men in the ranks passed those who had fallen out and saw them being fanned, bathed with eau de Cologne and revived with brandy by pretty French girls. When we finally arrived, we rested the whole afternoon and allowed our soaking shirts to dry in the sun."
[James P. Jones]

Into the third week of August, the French and Belgian *'pavé'*[53] rang loud to the hobnails of thumping British army-issue boots as clouds of summer dust bore witness to the arrival of 1st, 2nd, 3rd and 5th Divisions of the small British Expeditionary Force (BEF). The khaki-clad battalions, hailing from South Wales to Northumberland and from Staffordshire to the Scottish Highlands, were on the move (first by troop train then in marching order) to take position on the left flank of the French Army, inside the Belgian border and near to the unattractive, industrial town of Mons.

Accompanying the infantry units could be heard the clatter of horse-drawn General Service wagons, the rattle of smart cavalrymen and the rumble of a variety of artillery; now and then the infantry ranks would falter as men avoided the inevitable by-product of so much horse transport. Regular halts were called as the hot sun caused men's throats to dry and feet to swell in stiff new boots; after a few minutes rest, the route march resumed. Unknown to the British, they were heading directly into the path of the strongest element of the vital and powerful right wing of the so-called Schlieffen Plan. 4th Division would follow much the same route, though only as far as Le Cateau, by 24th August; 6th Division reached the Aisne by 16th September and 7th Division (containing 1st South Staffordshire and more Elmore Green lads) landed at Zeebrugge in Belgium on 6th October.

A mere ten days after their initial culture shock in Le Havre, 2nd South Staffordshire was in the front line at Harmignies (south-east of Mons) with 2nd Grenadier Guards on its left and 1st Royal Berkshire on its right. To their front was the daunting prospect of the German 17th Reserve Division and part of the cavalry of General von Boehn's IX Reserve Corps. On 19th August, from his Headquarters at Aix-la-Chapelle, Kaiser Wilhelm II issued an Army Order to his troops in Belgium that were soon to confront the BEF:

---

53 'Le Pavé' was similar to the British cobblestone surface and with a similar painful effect upon 'unhardened' feet wearing the unforgiving leather of new army boots.

"It is my Royal and Imperial command that you concentrate your energies, for the immediate present, upon one single purpose, and that is that you address all your skill and all the valour of my soldiers to exterminate first the treacherous English and walk over General French's contemptible little army." [Kaiser Wilhelm II, August 1914]

The insult clearly illustrated the weakness in numbers of the BEF and fully justified Lord Kitchener's decision to raise a 'New Army'. Equally, though, the German emperor's words rankled with the Tommies of the BEF who typically turned the phrase to their advantage and adopted the name, *'The Contemptibles'*, later to become the famous, *'Old Contemptibles'*, that would be held as a badge of honour among its participants, as was the more tangible honour of receiving the 1914 'Mons' Star (shown below) after the war[54].

The 1914 'Mons' Star

Massively outnumbered at Mons, the BEF had no option but to fight the field-grey clad masses, delay as long as possible and then attempt to execute a fighting retreat. At that time, the lads of the BEF did not suspect that there would be much more retreating than fighting over the ensuing ten days of the Great Retreat from Mons. Fortunately for 2/South Staffordshire, the battalion had suffered no casualties at Mons, despite coming under sporadic artillery fire. By comparison, the retreat was sheer torture. Taking into account the final march towards Mons on 21st August, the battalion covered nearly 240 miles from the battlefront, through Bavai, Landrécies, Le Cateau and Guise to La Fère. The day's march between Guise and La Fère passed quite close to St. Quentin on the division's right flank – there were rumours of German troops massing near St. Quentin (there are always rumours in the ranks of an army) and in a minor clash on 27th August **Jimmy Dawson** became the first of the memorial lads to be wounded. The first of his eventual five wounds was suffered near St. Quentin when he was struck in the head and hands by shrapnel that also smashed his rifle to pieces. Invalided home, he returned to his battalion in December 1914 but later that same month he was again invalided home suffering from diphtheria. From La Fère, the wearied, marching troops passed through Soissons, Villers-Cotterêts, Château-Thierry

---

54 Sadly, very few of the 'originals' survived the war; a fact hardly surprising when considered against 95,000 British casualties (killed, missing or wounded) by the end of 1914.

and finally to Chaumes and the turning of the tide in battle at the River Marne. The heat and dust created a thirst that the sparse water supplies could not hope to slake; rations were unpredictable and it is fair to assume that 'Tommy' did not religiously obey the orders to not 'forage' for food; for Reservists with new boots, as yet not fully broken in, horrific blisters were commonplace, while the regulars' seasoned boots fell apart under the pressure of the forced marches – by the time the Grand Morin River was crossed near Coulommiers, 2/South Staffordshire was truly 'blood-shod'.

September

Weary and aching, the Bloxwich contingent of **Ernie Lavender** and **Joe Bullock**, like most of their compatriots in the BEF, were undoubtedly looking forward to 'having a crack' at the enemy that had pursued them since Mons. From Chaumes, the British and their allies, refreshed and reinforced, advanced towards the River Marne where soon their thirst for action was sated. As advanced guard, 2/South Staffordshire crossed the River Marne at Charly on 10th September and, just to the south of Hautesvesnes, fell upon an enemy rear-guard column. Supported by unanswered artillery, the 6th Brigade's infantry carried the day and took 300 prisoners at relatively light cost[55]. Again, the Bloxwich lads came through unscathed. Shaken by the Allies' success at the Battle of the Marne (6th to 9th September), the German army made a determined and successful effort to halt their enemy's advance at the River Aisne (13th to 26th September).

The stalemate which followed the Aisne led each side to attempt to outflank the other, in what has been mis-named the 'Race to the Sea', the failure of which brought into play two more factors – first, the digging of trenches to strengthen defensive lines and, second, the town of Ypres where more British and Empire blood would be spilt than anywhere else on the Western Front. Of the 250,000 British dead in and around the Ypres Salient, ten are men whose names are inscribed on the Elmore Green school memorial – **John William Groves, Aaron Hayward, Bill Grimsley, Fred Harper, Joe Orgill, Bernard Hooper, Wm Edw Pickin, Horace Downes, John Yates** and **Bertie Elks**. In addition, **William 'Coxy' Lavender** (John Groves' uncle) was killed in the Salient and **John Bullock** was captured there; a number of other local lads were wounded at Ypres. The First Battles of Ypres (19th October to 22nd November) were chaotic, blood-drenched affairs that did much to forge the dark reputation of the Ypres Salient; every Tommy dreaded his unit being

---

55   2/South Staffordshire lost just one man killed in action, 9325, Private Ben Purslow, a reservist from Wolverhampton; 6875, Private Tom Stringer of Walsall died of his wounds next day. Five men were wounded.

posted to 'Wipers'[56] and it may be safely assumed that the Elmore Green boys were typical Tommies.

October and November

Yet there was a major prologue to the chaos and carnage of the First Battles of Ypres. Just to the south of the Salient, units from 3rd, 4th, 5th and 6th Divisions, supported by Indian infantry and various cavalry brigades, first engaged the enemy as early as 10th October near La Bassée Canal, then two days later on the higher ground at Messines and finally on 13th October at Armentières. Each of these actions provided a view of future engagements, grinding on until 2nd November when increasingly serious clashes in the Ypres Salient demanded reinforcement by both sides. None of the memorial lads was killed in this prelude to First Ypres (as the forthcoming battles were to be known) but one of the families, the **Groves** of Park Road and Bell Lane in Bloxwich, suffered one of four terrible blows that the war would deal them. [John and Annie Groves would lose two sons to the war; Annie was about to endure a brother (**John Brown** of the Worcestershire Regiment) being twice wounded and to lose a son, **John William Groves**, and his father-in-law, **William Lavender**].

First we will turn to **William Lavender**. Like many a pre-war Bloxwich lad, William followed his father down the pit, and coal-mining was later to

William 'Coxy' Lavender (front, middle right) with opponent Billy Smith after a bare-knuckle contest in Bloxwich.

---

56 British Tommies found French and Flemish names hard to pronounce and soon produced their own versions, so Ypres was 'Wipers', Le Cateau was 'Lee Catoo', Wytschaete was 'Whitesheet' and Ploegsteert was 'Plugstreet'.

take him, his wife and three children to live in Mansfield in Nottinghamshire. In Bloxwich, though, William was well-known as **'Coxy' Lavender**, a bare-knuckle boxer as tough as the coal seams he hewed. 'Coxy' volunteered for the Lincolnshire Regiment as soon as war was declared in August 1914, training with 3rd Battalion and being sent to France with a draft of reinforcements for 1/Lincolnshire (9th Brigade, 3rd Division) on 22nd October 1914. Following the Battle of the Aisne, far to the south, the BEF had been moved north to slot into the front line to the left of the French, between Béthune and Ypres. By 11th October, 1/Lincolnshire reached billets on the south bank of La Bassée Canal; next day, 3rd Division was on the attack, attempting to turn the German right flank. When 'Coxy' reached his battalion, he found soldiers exhausted both by attacks and marches in appalling conditions but on 29th October the Lincolnshire was glad to be relieved by a newly-arrived Indian battalion. Private Lavender did not have to wait long for his first (and only) taste of battle. 1/Lincolnshire moved to Estaire on 30th and thence to Kemmel (inside Belgium), two miles behind the front line at Wytschaete ('Whitesheet' in Tommy's parlance), in preparation for its part in the short but vicious Battle of Messines. Possession of Mount Kemmel, Kemmel village, Wytschaete and Messines was vital as they provided higher ground that overlooked Ypres to the north and would furnish the German artillery with an ideal location for its gun-line to bombard the British-held town. On 31st October, 1/Lincolnshire and 1/Northumberland Fusiliers of 9th Brigade were ordered to Kemmel in support of the troops holding Wytschaete village – those troops were the hard-pressed 2nd Cavalry Division[57] fighting as dismounted infantry. Two miles to the south, 1st Cavalry Division held part of Messines village. Between the two villages, the London Scottish[58] battalion held the enemy advance at bay – these Territorials, much-maligned by the Secretary for War, quickly forged an enviable reputation on the Western Front. During the night, the thinly-held British trench lines and the two villages were pounded ceaselessly by the German artillery, causing massive damage and heavy casualties; at 1 a.m., nine German infantry battalions assaulted Wytschaete (adverse odds of twelve to one) and the British were pushed to the edge of the village; at 1:45 a.m. 1/Lincolnshire and two companies of Northumberland Fusiliers with the survivors of 3rd Hussars were tasked to recapture Wytschaete. The first attempt was beaten back at great cost by heavy machine-gun and rifle fire; as dawn broke, the British infantry was caught in the open and, again pounded by artillery and rifle fire, the British troops were forced to retreat.

---

57   At 1914 establishment, a British cavalry division comprised about 6,000 men; at Messines in October 1914, action had greatly reduced 1st and 2nd Cavalry Divisions' available men.

58   Their official title was 14th Battalion, the London Regiment, a Territorial Force unit.

When the roll-call was taken back in Lindenhoek village, the Lincolnshire had suffered 301 casualties (killed, wounded or missing); the 'Saturday-night soldiers' of the London Scottish, now back in La Clytte village, had sustained 394 casualties[59].

One of the 1/Lincolnshire men recorded as 'missing in action' on 1st November was Private **'Coxy' Lavender**; his death orphaned three young children and left Lucy widowed. His name is engraved in the Lincolnshire Regiment section (panel 21) of the splendid Menin Gate Memorial to the Missing on the north side of Ypres. The first of the legendary 'Old Contemptibles' was gone.

Ironically, 'Coxy' Lavender was still in England with 3/Lincolnshire when, on 4th October, as part of 22nd Brigade of 7th Division, 1st Battalion, the South Staffordshire Regiment (containing Coxy's nephew, William Groves) had left Southampton aboard the S.S. *'Lake Michigan'* to disembark two days later at Zeebrugge in Belgium. From the port, the battalion entrained for the city of Bruges[60] and next day was marched to the coast at Oostende. Unlike the arrival at Le Havre of the regiment's 2nd Battalion back in early August there was no public welcome; neither was there sunshine, rather there was pouring rain and late autumn temperatures. From Oostende the Staffords moved inland again to Ghent, covering the withdrawal of Allied forces (including the Royal Naval Brigade as well as the remnants of the Belgian army) from the major port of Antwerp. On 11th October the battalion had its first experience of constructing trenches; the next day they were again on the move, necessitated by the enemy concentrating about 30,000 men to threaten the British. 1/South Staffordshire was now forced to retreat, marching 32 miles in 24 hours with little rest, little food, in thick mist and low temperatures. It was their version, albeit much shorter, of the 2nd Battalion's retreat from Mons. Through Ghent to Thielt, then on another 24 miles to Bevering on muddy roads; at Roulers, a hub of the railway network, 1/Queen's and 2/Royal Welch Fusiliers entrained for Ypres. The Staffords and 1/Royal Warwickshire again trudged the seventeen miles of uneven road that took them to Ypres and a date with destiny. For the first time in living memory the two regular battalions of the South Staffordshire would fight on the same major battlefield. 1st Battalion arrived in Ypres on 14th October (the anniversary of the Battle of Hastings) and 22nd Brigade was ordered to press eastwards along the Menin Road towards the town of Menin itself, a task that was abandoned when the enemy, in corps strength (this meant adverse odds of about ten to one), poured forward. The Staffords were pushed

59   In comparison, 2nd Cavalry Division sustained 723 casualties in four days.

60   The Flemish name for the city is Brugge; connected by canal, Zeebrugge is its port.

back and dug themselves into defensive positions to the east of Gheluvelt village; by the morning of 20th October, defending the furthest point of the Allied salient, 1/South Staffordshire prepared to meet a German onslaught aimed at capturing Ypres and driving the British out of the Channel ports. On the same day, 20th October, 2/South Staffordshire were marching into Ypres, and,

> *"…by a curious coincidence, occupied the same billets held three days previously by the 1st Battalion…"* (James P. Jones)

– the latter battalion was now in the front line about two miles to the east of 2nd Battalion.

The gathering German storm-cloud burst onto British and French lines around Ypres on Wednesday, 21st October – 'Trafalgar Day' would again see the testing of British mettle as, often outnumbered by six or more to one, the defenders came close to being overrun. The First Battles of Ypres represent both the Germans' and Allies' final efforts to outflank each other in their attempts to reach and protect (respectively) the vital Channel ports of Zeebrugge, Dunkirk, Calais and Boulogne. The fighting around Ypres was both desperate and savage; trenches were no more than three feet deep and often little more than connected, muddy shell craters; the battlefield was a very complex and confused area that defied any commander's effective overview and planning. One of the few discernible facts is the numerical superiority of the German attackers, as high as six to one.

For one of the few occasions in the Regiment's history, the divisions to which the South Staffordshire regulars belonged were side by side on a battlefield – 1/South Staffordshire's 7th Division faced the German 53rd Reserve Division's advance from Dadizeele towards Polygon Wood, while on the 7th's immediate left 2/South Staffordshire's 2nd Division faced the German 52nd Reserve Division's advance from Passchendaele Ridge. This first clash became known as the Battle of Langemarck and is identified as lasting from 21st to 24th October, though battles in the Ypres area were rarely clearly defined but were marked by short lulls in the fighting while each side seemed to take a deep breath before resuming hostilities. At least five local lads, **Ernest Lavender** and **Joe Bullock** of 2nd Battalion along with **Aaron Hayward, John Bullock** and **William Groves** of 1st Battalion, were present on the battlefield, though 2/South Staffordshire was initially in (6th) brigade reserve. As far as is known, all the lads came through this first encounter relatively unscathed; this was not to be repeated at Ypres. In the official record, the follow-up attack on Gheluvelt village lasted from 29th to 31st October but 1/South Staffordshire

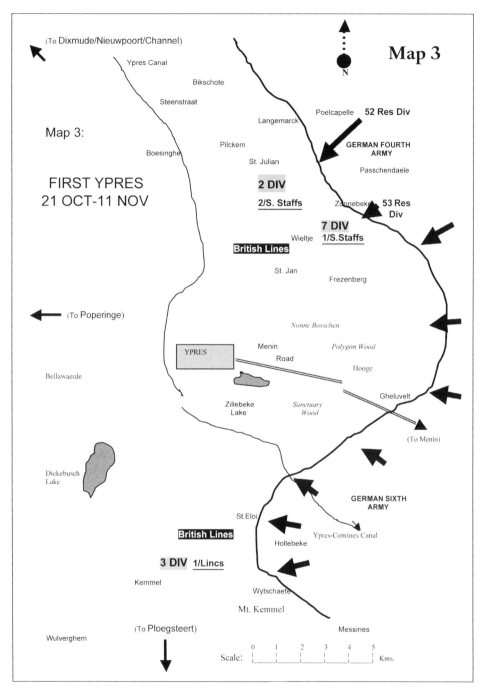

Map 3

Map 3:

FIRST YPRES
21 OCT-11 NOV

was rarely out of the line except to adjust its position. Heavily committed to repelling the initial German offensive north of Ypres at Langemarck, Private **Aaron Hayward**'s 1st Battalion advanced to support positions in Polygon Wood, east of Ypres, on Friday, 23rd October. Two days later a move was made to Kruiseecke, north east of Gheluvelt where the battalion held a ridge of ploughed land. During this period the battalion found itself under incessant artillery fire. Private Leonard Faulkner[61], who lived at Wisemore but was born in Willenhall, wrote home with details of his comrade Aaron's experiences on the battlefield. He stated that following some heavy fighting on Monday, 26th October, Aaron had been badly wounded in the arm and leg. Like many of 1/South Staffordshire that day, Aaron had been captured by the Germans who, it would appear, had taken him to Lille Hospital where he later succumbed to his severe injuries.

1/South Staffordshire battalion war diary records the following:

> *"25 October 1914 - At 4 a.m. the regiment moved off towards Kruiseecke where we were attached to the 20th Brigade. 'D' Company was left….. the rest of the battalion entrenched at the bottom of the hill behind the Grenadier Guards section and near the Brigade HQ."*

It is unfortunate that Aaron's company is not known, for it is well recorded how members of 'D' Company were captured. On the night of 25th-26th October, the company reinforced the Grenadier Guards and were approached by a body of men calling out:

> *"Don't shoot, we are Scots Guards and South Staffords."*

The fact that they were Germans was soon apparent as few of the Staffords escaped the subsequent rifle fire. Following this the enemy unleashed a terrible bombardment and when it ceased the company found that the Germans had used the cover of darkness, rain and shelling to reach and enter the British trenches. The only surviving officer and a handful of men were captured.

> *"26 October 1914 – 'B' Company was used on patrol in rear of the Grenadier Guards trenches, where they patrolled all night and retired from there at 7 a.m. on the 26th going into our original barracks. We remained there until 10 a.m. about which hour we received orders to reinforce 'C' Company. Two platoons were sent forward under Lieutenant Hume for this purpose and during the heavy firing several men were killed or wounded including Lieutenant Hume who did so well.*

---

61 Leonard Faulkner himself lost part of his arm and was captured with Aaron Hayward. Early in 1915 he was one of a number of prisoners whom the Germans and British exchanged. Subsequently he rose to the rank of Sergeant and was killed in action on 31st August 1916 in the attacking Delville Wood on the Somme.

'C' Company advanced at 7.30 p.m. to reinforce the Border Regiment under very heavy rifle fire.

About 2 p.m. a party under Colonel Ovens and Captains Bonner and White took up a position along a ridge of ploughed land, also along a road and wood running north east to Gheluvelt......enemy were then bursting their shrapnel beautifully on this ridge and 'Jack Johnsons' were falling beside our hasty entrenchments dug with the small entrenching tool and even hands alone."

Bearing in mind Hayward's injuries and capture, it is most likely that he was a member of 'D' Company (commanded by Captain John Franks Vallentin who was subsequently to be killed on 7th November and to be awarded a posthumous Victoria Cross). Hayward was possibly taken to the notorious prison fortress nicknamed by those who experienced it, *'the black hole of Lille'*, but more likely he was held in a ward in Lille Hospital. Private **Aaron Hayward**'s wounds to his arm and leg were so severe that the twenty-four year-old died of his injuries on 2nd November. He was subsequently buried in Lille Southern Cemetery, France, in a plot reserved by his captors for prisoners of war. Aaron had been born in Fenton, Stoke-on-Trent but soon after the turn of the century his family had moved to Bloxwich where they lived on High Street and Aaron attended Elmore Green School. Enlisting in Bloxwich in 1907, Aaron had become a very experienced, professional soldier, who had served eight years in the South Staffordshire before the war – a second of the illustrious 'Old Contemptibles' had, in the Tommies' description, 'gone west'.

When 1/South Staffordshire was eventually withdrawn from the line on 7th-8th November, of the 1,100 men who had faced the enemy on 21st October, only 78 other ranks and a handful of officers had survived. Private **William Groves**, who managed to survive the engagements at Langemarck and Gheluvelt would find his luck running out before the battalion was withdrawn from the front line. As for the local lads, including Privates **Ernest Lavender** and **Joe Bullock** of 2/South Staffordshire, repeated heavy German attacks were beaten back at high cost to the Staffords. Unlike their sister battalion, 2/South Staffordshire would remain in the line until 13th November when they would be relieved by 2/Highland Light Infantry.

7th Division's role in holding at bay the German offensives at Langemarck and Gheluvelt had been pivotal but by 31st October 1st Division on their left was being forced back, threatening 7th Division's left flank – only a desperate defence ensured that the line held. For five long days the battle developed into an artillery duel, ironically giving 1/South Staffordshire some breathing space. James P. Jones, in his *'History of the South Staffordshire Regiment'*, takes up the story:

"On November 5th the line was readjusted and some relief was given to the 7th Division....now reduced from 12,000 men and 400 officers to a little over 3,000. 1st South Staffordshire had lost quite eighty per cent of their effectives in this fighting. They had been relieved for a few days but were back in the line again on November 7th."

This time 1st Battalion attacked an enemy trench to the north-west of Klein Zillebeke – it was taken and held, capturing three German machine-guns. Once more **William Groves, Ernie Lavender** and **John Bullock** went forward under the command of Captain Vallentin who won the Victoria Cross, *"for conspicuous bravery on 7th November at Zillebeke."* No battalion war diary exists for this period, a direct consequence of the massive losses sustained on 7th November 1914 – neither **William Groves** nor **John Bullock** were among the 78 other ranks who survived to answer their names; 22 year-old **Private Groves** was posted 'missing believed killed in action' and his name is commemorated on an addendum panel on the Menin Gate in Ypres:

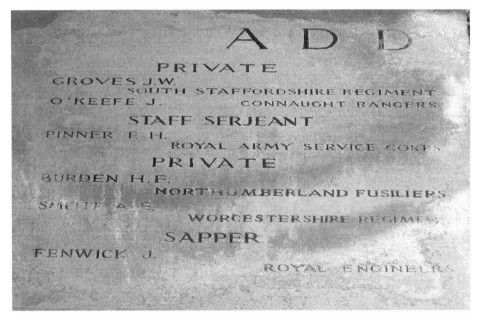

Private Bullock had been taken prisoner but would eventually return to Bloxwich after the war. By the evening of 7th November, the battered but proud remnants of 1/South Staffordshire had mercifully been relieved from the battle-line.

In 2/South Staffordshire and 6th Brigade **Ernest Lavender** and **Joseph Bullock** supported 7th Division and later 1st Division, in a flexible support role devised by Corps Commander, General Sir Douglas Haig, a fluid process known as 'putting up' – in effect, the battalions of the support brigade were directed wherever the need was most pressing. For day after day in early November, 2nd Battalion remained under shellfire and, on the 11th, took part in the Battle of Nonne Bosschen (Nun's Wood); however, on the extreme left of the British line, the Staffords did not face the daunting assaults of the Prussian Guard as much as the weight of German shelling. The local lads came through this ordeal, although it is possible that Private **Ernie Lavender** received one of his three wounds during this action that signified the last major German assault on Ypres before the end of the year. These lads had more than earned their place in the annals of the legendary 'Old Contemptibles'[62].

December

The story of the locals with the British Expeditionary Force in 1914 is not quite done; two more lads, one recorded on the school memorial and one related, joined the regulars of the South Staffordshire before the turn of the year. **Edgar Goodall**, a married miner who had been educated at Elmore Green, volunteered for the South Staffordshire as soon as war was declared in August 1914. It is not certain whether Edgar served with 1st or 2nd Battalion but he definitely landed in France on 18th December 1914; in action with his battalion, though not before the New Year, he had one remarkable escape when a bullet hit him but was deflected by a knife he was carrying in his tunic. During the spring of 1915, Edgar applied for a transfer to the newly-formed Tunnelling Companies of the Royal Engineers – it paid better than the infantry but was intensely dangerous. We shall return to the Goodall family in due course. Private **Timothy Taylor** (a miner from Alfred Street, Bloxwich and a cousin of the two Bushnell lads whose names appear on the memorial) most certainly joined 1st Battalion, landing on the business side of the Channel on 17th December. However, he did not arrive in time to take part in the battalion's final action around Ypres that year, an unsuccessful attack on 18th December on Well Farm in which the South Staffordshire gave fire support to 2/Royal Warwickshire. Taylor's story will re-emerge during the spring battles of 1915. On account of the date of their arrival on the Western Front, neither Edgar Goodall nor Timothy Taylor was a member of that exclusive club, the 'Old Contemptibles'.

Volunteering back home (August to December)

In the meantime, back in 'Blighty', Elmore Green and Bloxwich lads were volunteering in remarkable numbers to serve their country. By 31st December

---

62 To qualify for the 1914 'Mons' Star and thus be one of the 'Old Contemptibles', a man had to come under enemy fire before midnight on 22nd-23rd November 1914.

1914, thirty-two of the lads whose names are engraved on the Elmore Green memorial had volunteered for the British army, or were pre-war serving regulars – two had already died in their country's service. At least another eleven 'related' lads had volunteered. Many existing Bloxwich Territorials such as **Albert Stych, George Groves, Horace Downes, Joseph Handy** and **George Sargent**, immediately accepted the Imperial Service Obligation

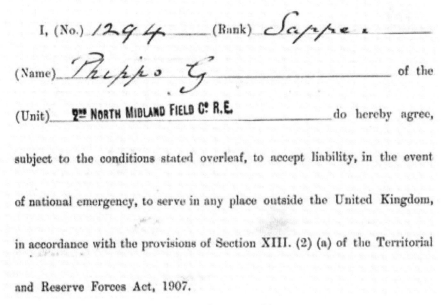

AGREEMENT to be made by an officer or man of the Territorial Force to subject himself to liability to serve in any place outside the United Kingdom in the event of National Emergency.

I, (No.) *1294* (Rank) *Sapper*

(Name) *Phipps G* of the

(Unit) 2ᴺᴰ NORTH MIDLAND FIELD Cᵒ R.E. do hereby agree,

subject to the conditions stated overleaf, to accept liability, in the event

of national emergency, to serve in any place outside the United Kingdom,

in accordance with the provisions of Section XIII. (2) (a) of the Territorial

and Reserve Forces Act, 1907.

Territorial Force: Imperial Service Obligation assent

(shown here), signing away their right to serve only within the United Kingdom and eagerly went into the full training that was designed to bring their Territorial units up to front-line standard. Two serving Bloxwich Territorials (of 1/5th TF South Staffordshire) decided, for a variety of possible reasons[63], to not sign

---

63 Such reasons included fear of poverty for a family left behind, unwillingness to give up a hard-earned or vital job, the arrival of a new baby, pregnancy or chronic illness in the close family; it is quite possible that some men were afraid, a very natural reaction.

the overseas service waiver and thus became a founding, integral part of their second-line unit (2/5th TF South Staffordshire in the case of Bloxwich) that would initially train reinforcements and would itself go into the front line in February 1917; some would later be posted to 1/5th Battalion.

By the end of 1914 many lads whose stories will be told were wearing khaki, as indicated in the following list (as far as may be ascertained from written records and family information). For many volunteers, it was to be a massive step into the unknown – patriotism, adventure, travel or simply a change of scenery were among the motivations for making the journey to the recruiting office:

The local 'Old Contemptibles', under fire before 22nd November 1914:

James DAWSON	2nd (Reg) Battalion, South Staffordshire Regiment
William GROVES	1st (Reg) Battalion, South Staffordshire Regiment
Aaron HAYWARD	1st (Reg) Battalion, South Staffordshire Regiment
Ernest Lavender	2nd (Reg) Battalion, South Staffordshire Regiment
William Lavender	1st (Reg) Battalion, Lincolnshire Regiment
John Bullock	1st (Reg) Battalion, South Staffordshire Regiment
Joseph Bullock	2nd (Reg) Battalion, South Staffordshire Regiment

Men under fire between 23rd November and 31st December 1914:

Timothy Taylor	1st (Reg) Battalion, South Staffordshire Regiment
Edgar GOODALL	1st or 2nd (Reg) Battalion, South Staffordshire Regiment
James Jones	1st (Reg) Battalion, South Staffordshire Regiment

Men who enlisted between 4th August and 31st December 1914:

Charles BULLOCK	1/5th TF Battalion, South Staffordshire Regiment
Alfred BUSHNELL	1st (Reg) Battalion, King's Own Scottish Borderers
George BUSHNELL	1/5th TF Battalion, South Staffordshire Regiment
Joseph DAVIES	1/5th TF Battalion, South Staffordshire Regiment
Horace DOWNES	1/5th TF Battalion, South Staffordshire Regiment
Thomas Dunn	89th Field Company, Corps of Royal Engineers
William GOODALL	2nd (Reg) Battalion, South Staffordshire Regiment
Samuel Goodall	13th (S) Battalion, Northumberland Fusiliers
George GROVES	1/5th TF Battalion, South Staffordshire Regiment
Joseph HANDY	1/5th TF Battalion, South Staffordshire Regiment
Frank HARVEY	4th (Sp. Res) Battalion, South Staffordshire Regiment
Bill HAYCOCK	1/5th TF Battalion, South Staffordshire Regiment
Ted JONES	7th (S) Battalion, South Staffordshire Regiment

Arthur KITSON	1st (Reg) Battalion, Royal Welch Fusiliers
William LAWLEY	3rd (Reg) Battalion, Grenadier Guards
Arthur LINNELL	1/5th TF Battalion, South Staffordshire Regiment
Frank LLOYD	1/5th TF Battalion, South Staffordshire Regiment
Alfred MAIN	2nd (Reg) Battalion, South Staffordshire Regiment
Leonard MALPASS	1/5th TF Battalion, South Staffordshire Regiment
John Orgill	1/5th TF Battalion, South Staffordshire Regiment
Joseph ORGILL	2nd Fld. Amb., Canadian Army Medical Corps
Harry PERKS	1st (Reg) Battalion, Worcestershire Regiment
Simon Perks	1/5th TF Battalion, South Staffordshire Regiment
Wm Edw PICKIN	2/5th TF Battalion, South Staffordshire Regiment
George SARGENT	1/5th TF Battalion, South Staffordshire Regiment
Edward Smith	10th (S) Battalion, West Yorkshire Regiment
George SMITH	12th (S) Battalion, West Yorkshire Regiment
Albert STYCH	7th (S) Battalion, Suffolk Regiment
George Stych	2nd (Reg) Battalion, South Staffordshire Regiment
Samuel Stych	17th (S) Battalion, West Yorkshire Regiment
Robert SYLVESTER	2/5th TF Battalion, South Staffordshire Regiment
Harry WILLETT	3rd (Reg) Battalion, Grenadier Guards
John YATES	2nd (Reg) Battalion, South Staffordshire Regiment

UPPER CASE surnames indicate men whose names are commemorated on the Elmore Green school memorial.

Lower case surnames indicate men *related* to those who are commemorated on the Elmore Green school memorial.

(Reg)	indicates a Regular Army battalion.
TF	indicates a Territorial Force battalion.
(S)	indicates a Service or 'New Army' battalion.
(Sp. Res.)	indicates a Special Reserve or Extra Reserve battalion.

Where local volunteers might serve on the front line – theatres of war and garrison commitments in 1914:

Western Front	in France and Belgium against the German army.
West Africa	Togoland and Cameroon against German colonials.
East Africa	in Rhodesia, Nyasaland, Zanzibar, Tanga against German troops and German colonial troops.
Mesopotamia	(Iraq) in Basra and Qurna against Turkish troops.

Imperial Garrisons and Royal Navy coaling stations throughout the Empire – Africa, Suez Canal Zone, India, West Indies, Gibraltar, Hong Kong and many others. Regular troops were gradually replaced by local 'native' and TF troops.

At sea   U-Boat war

Main Square, Ypres – the Cloth Hall on fire after the German bombardment of 22 November 1914.

Chronological Roll of Honour for 1914

November 1st	William	Lavender**	Ypres
November 2nd	Aaron	HAYWARD	Ypres
November 7th	William	GROVES	Ypres

** Indicates a name related to those that appear on the Elmore Green School Old Boys War Memorial.

Alphabetical Roll of Honour for 1914

(John) William GROVES *'One of the Old Contemptibles'*
Born between January and March of 1892 in Walsall and lived with his parents, first at 53, Park Road, Bloxwich and later at 72, Bell Lane, Bloxwich. Son of a brass caster, John William, and Annie (née Brown) Groves. One of six children, five of whom were living at home in 1911 – four younger brothers (George, Alfie, Ernest and Charles) and one sister (Effie). Educated at Elmore Green School. Single. Formerly a locksmith, employed by Mr. Appleby of Old Lane; then a regular soldier. **Volunteered in 1909** in Wolverhampton. As a regular, he saw service in Gibraltar and South Africa and returned to England at the outbreak of war with his regiment and disembarked in Belgium on Sunday, 4th October 1914. One of the *'Old Contemptibles'*. **8605, Private, 1st (Regular) Battalion, South Staffordshire Regiment, (22nd Brigade, 7th Division).** *Unit History* – 4th October 1914 landed at Zeebrugge, Belgium. Defence of Antwerp (Bruges). 1st Ypres, 21-24/10/14 Battle of Langemarck and 29-31/10/14 Battle of Gheluvelt. **Killed in action (age 22) on Saturday, 7th November 1914** near Klein Zillebeke in the Ypres Salient. Commemorated on addenda panel 60 of the **Menin Gate Memorial to the Missing**, Ypres, Belgium. **Entitled** to the 1914 'Mons' Star and Clasp 2/2692, (Medal Roll – F/2/4/, p.40), British War Medal and Victory Medal – the trio known as 'Pip, Squeak and Wilfred', (Medal Roll – F/101B3, p.236). Commemorated on the Elmore Green School Roll of Honour (formerly located in the T.P. Riley School library) and on the Walsall and Bloxwich Rolls of Honour and on the Roll of Honour in All Saints Church, Bloxwich. **Family** – a younger brother, George, took John's service number

when he enlisted. 8605, Private George Groves of 'D' Company, 1/5th South Staffordshire died from illness on 18th June 1916 near Doullens in France. An uncle, John Brown of the Worcestershire Regiment, was twice wounded. An uncle by marriage, 14114, Private William 'Coxy' Lavender (see below) of 1/Lincolnshire was killed in the Ypres Salient on 1st November 1914.

Aaron HAYWARD *'One of the 'Old Contemptibles'*

Born in 1888 or 1889 in Stoke-on-Trent to James (a coalminer) and Fanny Hayward of 5, William Street, Fenton, Stoke on Trent and later of 44, High Street, Bloxwich. Educated at Elmore Greeen School. Single. Regular soldier then army reservist. **Volunteered in 1907** in Bloxwich. Pre-war, served in Gibraltar and in Pietermaritzburg, Transvaal, South Africa. **7979, Private [possibly 'D' Company], 1st (Regular) Battalion, South Staffordshire Regiment, (22nd Brigade, 7th Division).** *Unit History –* 4th October 1914 landed at Zeebrugge, Belgium. Defence of Antwerp (Bruges). 1st Ypres, 21-24/10/14 Battle of Langemarck; 29-31/10/14 Battle of Gheluvelt. One of the *'Old Contemptibles'.* **Died (age 24) in a Lille hospital on Monday, 2nd November 1914 of wounds to his arm and leg sustained near Ypres. Buried** in plot III. A. 10 of **Lille Southern Cemetery,** France (plot III being used by the Germans for the burial of prisoners of war). **Entitled** to the 1914 'Mons' Star (Medal Roll – F/2/4/44), British War Medal and Victory Medal (Medal Roll – F/101B2, p.183). Commemorated on the Elmore Green School Roll of Honour (formerly located in the T.P. Riley School library) and on the Walsall and Bloxwich Rolls of Honour. **Family** – a brother, James, served in the Royal Army Medical Corps.

William 'Coxy' LAVENDER** [not Elmore Green Mem] *'One of the 'Old Contemptibles'*

Born in 1887 in Bloxwich to William (a miner) and Mary A. Lavender of 47, Portland Street (1891 Census). Two sisters – Alice (born 1897) and Dora R. (born 1900). Married to Lucy Lyons (three children) and lived at 22, Harden Lane, Blakenall. Miner employed at a pit in Langworth, Mansfield, Nottinghamshire.

Locally, a very capable bare-knuckle boxer of note, hence the nickname; he fought 'Catty' Rhodes, Reece and Billy Smith. Pre-war served several years in the local 'D' Company of the 1/5th Territorial Battalion, South Staffordshire Regiment. **Volunteered** for the Lincolnshire Regiment in **August 1914** in Mansfield. **14114, Private, 1st (Regular) Battalion, Lincolnshire Regiment (9th Brigade, 3rd Division).** *Unit History –* 'Coxy' crossed the Channel on 22nd October 1914. Battles in Flanders, 10/10-30/10/14 Battle of la Bassée. 31/10/14-2/11/14 Battle of Messines. One of the *'Old Contemptibles'.* **Killed in action (age 28) on Sunday, 1st November 1914** in a counter-attack at Wytschaete (south of Ypres) during the Battle of Messines. **Commemorated** on panel 21 of the **Menin Gate Memorial to the Missing, Ypres**, Belgium. Commemorated on the War Memorial in St. Peter's RC Church, Bloxwich. **Entitled** to the 1914 'Mons' Star (Medal Roll – F/1/3/87), British War Medal and Victory Medal (Medal Roll – F/105B8, p.1003). **Family** – left a widow, Lucy, and three children. One brother, Ernest (born 1893) served in the South Staffordshire and was wounded three times and eventually invalided from the army. Another brother, Henry 'Harry' (born 1889), served in the Royal Military Police – after the war, Harry (army Private, 1/SS in 1911) became a chief of police in Walsall. A third brother, Charles, possibly served in the South Staffords. William was an uncle by marriage to the Groves brothers.

Chapter Ten

1915:

'Gas, Gallipoli, 'Weekend Soldiers' Blooded and the New Army Bloodied…'

Winter 1914-15
Digging in – trench lines

March
Neuve Chapelle

May
Aubers Ridge and Festubert

April/July
The Gallipoli Campaign begins

April/May
2nd Ypres and Poison Gas

Spring /summer
Territorials and New Army arrivals

July
Death on Hill 60
September
Death by accident

September/October
Ordeal at Loos

September /October
The Hohenzollern Redoubt

Towards autumn and winter 1915

La Guerre 1914-15-16
Visé Paris

Panorama de Loos (P.-de-C.)
The Panorama of Loos

Edition Deschamps à Béthune

Loos Battlefield – pit-head winding gear known as 'Tower Bridge'.

Digging in (winter 1914-15)

Until the 1914 battles of Ypres reached their muddy stalemate in December, most fighting had been above ground in a difficult war of movement. Initially, the Germans would not 'dig in' as their war was intended to be one of invasion and conquest – time and pace was of the essence for the Armies clad in field grey. The French were loath to 'dig in' as they were fighting on the soil of 'La Belle France' and to entrench would leave much of their beloved *'patrie'* under German control, just as the Franco-Prussian War of 1870-71 had ultimately left the French borderlands of Alsace and Lorraine in German hands. Besides, the watchwords of the French military, inheritors of Napoleonic reputation, were *'en avant'*, *'la gloire'* and *'attaquer à outrance'*.[64] However, the battles around Ypres were fought by protagonists who were attempting to outflank each other, the one to defend possession of the Channel ports, the other to achieve their capture and thus cut short the war. The British Expeditionary Force had only recently taken responsibility for the Ypres sector, extending their line northward across the valley of the River Lys from La Bassée. Massively outnumbered and facing numerous artillery pieces, the BEF had performed heroically in frustrating General von Kluck's efforts to envelop the

---

64 Translated as, 'Forward', 'Glory' and 'Press the attack to the hilt'.

Allies' left wing and to drive the British into the Channel. As soon as the two sides accepted the reality of a hard-fought stalemate, both dug in – the Germans to consolidate their gains and the BEF to bolt the gate to the Channel. Before long, the trench lines scarring the landscape would stretch almost six hundred miles from the Swiss frontier to the English Channel. And trench warfare favoured the defenders by making artillery and machine-guns the kings of No Man's Land. Over by Christmas? The war seemed set for a much longer run.

It was during the harsh winter months of 1914-1915 that the opposing armies addressed themselves to the cold, wet and back-breaking task of transforming temporary trenches (at times they were little more than ditches and shell-holes) into a coherent front line that would better enable defenders to withstand vigorous enemy assaults. According to the Official History[65]:

> *"January [of 1915] was a month of rain, snow and flood…"*

Inevitably, the required heavy labour[66] was provided by resentful infantrymen who were nominally 'at rest'; technical expertise was offered by the field companies of Royal Engineers attached to each division. These early trenches were rudimentary compared to the complex features that would develop over the ensuing three years of static warfare.

During the Revolutionary and Napoleonic Wars (1792-1815), most armies had accepted that there was a distinct 'campaigning season' and that during the harsh continental winter armies would go into 'winter quarters'. By 1914-15 this convention was long gone and, although the winter weather removed from everyday trench-life the likelihood of major attacks, each side did what it could to disrupt its enemy's attempts to strengthen the front line. These regular, though short-lived, artillery duels were popularly referred to as the 'daily hate' and, while it might only comprise a few shrapnel or high explosive shells, they exacted a steady toll of the nerves and lives of the men living in the often squalid trench conditions. The greatest enemy during the winter months was the weather – frequent rain, snow and hard frost turned earth to mud or iron, causing bronchitis, pneumonia and trench foot among the most common illnesses. **James 'Jimmy' Jones**, older brother of **Ted Jones** (who will feature during the battles of the Somme in 1916), was one of the local lads in 1/South Staffordshire who fell victim to the pain of frostbite but James was to be one of the fortunate lads who would survive the war.

---

65 In this case, *'Military Operations, France & Belgium, Volume 1'*, by Brig-Gen. JE Edmonds & Capt GC Wynne.

66 Such labour would later be furnished by Pioneer Battalions (created early in 1915) and even later by the Labour Corps..

Trench warfare, favouring as it did defenders rather than attackers, developed a dedicated body of weaponry that was considered most appropriate to static fighting. Below surface level and protected by a trench parapet reinforced by rolls of barbed wire, an enemy was difficult enough to locate let alone to kill or capture. This would remain the case until aerial photography attained sophistication sufficient to provide effective intelligence to inform the planning of attacks.

Identifying the direction of an enemy gun-line[67] was easier but establishing its distance was a fine art for the experienced artilleryman. Trench mortars and howitzers whose shells described a high trajectory were more suited to trench bombardments than field guns whose trajectory was shallow; machine-guns were the deadly partner to trench artillery and two or three well-positioned machine-gun nests might hold at bay an entire battalion. Subsequent weaponry developments to break through strongly-defended trench systems would include poison gas, flame-throwers, mine-works and tanks. For the individual infantryman, 'appropriate' weapons included the bayonet, hand-grenades, knuckle-dusters, knives and the sharpened edges of entrenching tools. Trench fighting was in every sense a dirty business and a man's life expectancy was short when his unit was in a 'lively' sector.

March

Our story now returns to 2/South Staffordshire and March of 1915 when the battalion played a diversionary but costly part in the first British attack of the New Year. Following the struggles around Ypres, the bloodied but still-strong German armies had decided to establish a solid defensive line from which to conduct future offensives. They had also reinforced the Russian Front where their enemy's resistance had proved greater than anticipated. The French military commander, General Joseph Joffre, was planning a major offensive against the German line between Lens, Vimy Ridge and Arras; he believed that the BEF was too small to play any significant part but Sir John French wanted to carry out a British attack in their own sector for a number of reasons. He felt that 'Tommy' needed the boost gained from a successful offensive – Mons and the subsequent retreat had not been too good for morale. Naturally enough, Sir John was keen to prove Joffre wrong in his unflattering view of the BEF; the latter now had some experience and was being reinforced every week, most recently by the Empire troops of the Indian Corps. Military intelligence also suggested that the German defences were particularly thin in the sector that Sir John had chosen for the attack – the village of Neuve Chapelle in the Lys

---

67 A gun-line was the carefully-sited location of an artillery battery. It had to be close enough to the front line to facilitate finding its target but back far enough in case of an order to retreat.

valley. The Official History ('*Military Operations, France & Belgium, Volume 1*') suggests that the entire sector was less than ideal. The front line trenches in the Lys Valley and the low-lying Flanders Plain had a clay sub-soil, so the water table was only two feet below the surface. The River Lys was seven feet higher than usual, creating floods up to one hundred yards across. Some flooded trenches had had to be abandoned, while most trenches had to be supplemented by raised earth parapets. Too often,

> "…*men in many parts of the line stood knee-deep in mud and water, and had to be relieved twice a day.*"

As a direct result, illness, disease and trench foot caused almost as many casualties as did battle.

The main players in the four-day Battle of Neuve Chapelle (10th-13th March 1915) were 7th Division (containing 1/South Staffordshire), 8th Division, alongside the Meerut Division and the Lahore Division of the Indian Corps. The South Staffords' 1st Battalion was in divisional reserve for two days and on 12th March attacked the Pierre Redoubt in a muddy fiasco that cost a few lads their lives. For Elmore Green the main story lies with 2/South Staffordshire that was tasked to prevent German troops and artillery being moved the short distance from the Givenchy sector to reinforce Neuve Chapelle village. 2nd Battalion had been in this area since the turn of the year when,

> "…*the weather conditions were very bad, the snow and floods preventing any active operations, and with the exception of the usual shelling and sniping, no infantry attacks were made on the 2nd Division during the month of January,*" (J.P. Jones).

As for the condition of the trenches in which they existed rather than lived,

> "*The trenches were indescribable, almost waist deep in water in many places. Under these conditions daily relief was a necessity, and the Companies interchanged daily. Two days in trenches and two days in billets was the order. During the month of January, sickness in the Battalion was rather heavy, 2 Officers and 96 men going sick, nearly all suffering from severe cold, rheumatism and swollen feet……the filth and dirt of the trenches transformed the usually smart men into dirty scarecrows, but it was difficult for men burrowing in the ground to preserve anything like an aspect of cleanliness.*" (J.P. Jones).

The battalion would remain there for most of 1915. **Jimmy Dawson, Joe Bullock** and **Ernie Lavender** had come through several major tests with the Staffords during 1914 and in that dreadful January they were joined by two more Elmore Green lads – Special Reservist **William Goodall** (mid-month) and **John Yates** (end of the month). Throughout January 1915, the battalion alternated between the front line, reserve trenches and rest billets north and east of Béthune – the only German attack was launched on 25th-26th January to celebrate the Kaiser's birthday. The battalion finally moved into the Givenchy sector on 4th February where trench life settled into a regular pattern; however, on 20th February, the battalion carried out a trench raid, losing a young 2nd Lieutenant, which did little to encourage those new to the front line.

On 10th March the battalion received orders to attack the enemy lines known as the 'Duck's Bill' to the north east of Givenchy and the preparatory bombardment began at 7:30 a.m. The German front line trench was eighty yards distant and, as the first wave of men went 'over the top' at 8.45 a.m., they were hit by cross-fire from two well-sited German machine-guns. A number of the Staffords reached the German trench but were unable to remain there. Despite a second preparatory bombardment, the German wire remained uncut and the trenches were largely undamaged by shellfire, thus at 2.45 p.m. the attack was renewed by 'C' and 'A' Companies, with similar results and so, at 3:45 p.m. the attack was called off and the battalion retired to the original trench line after collecting all the wounded and their equipment. The assault at Givenchy cost the battalion 137 casualties, killed or wounded or missing.

One of those killed on **10th March** was a twenty-three year-old Elmore Green Old Boy, **Private William Goodall** of Clarendon Street, Bloxwich – the unmarried miner would never again 'clock on' at Leacroft Colliery. Like so many of his battalion comrades, William's body was never identified and therefore he was, a year on, presumed killed in action and his name is now commemorated on Le Touret Memorial to the Missing at Richebourg-L'Avoué near Festubert. He had been in France just six short weeks. William's father Edward Goodall and his stepmother Emma thus received the first of many pieces of family bad news from the war years.

Another Elmore Green Old Boy, twenty-two year-old **Private John Yates** was a native of Pelsall though his family moved to live in Bloxwich when John was a toddler. During the failed assault on the 'Duck's Bill' at Givenchy, John Yates was gravely wounded and, although he was treated by number 4, 5 or 6 Field Ambulance, it was to no avail as his injuries proved fatal two days later on **12th March**. Within a few more days the much-dreaded telegram would have been delivered to his parents' home in Providence Lane, Leamore; they would later hear that their son had been buried in France in Béthune Town Cemetery.

Once again **Jimmy Dawson, Ernie Lavender** and **Joe Bullock** came through a testing time and made their way to rest billets in the town of Béthune.

The Battle of Neuve Chapelle marked a first for many more of the Elmore Green lads. This time it was the turn of the local Territorials to enter the fray. The only unit available to act as reserve division for the battle was 46th 'North Midland' Division, the first complete Territorial Force division[68] to arrive on the Western Front, thus 1/5th and 1/6th Battalions, South Staffordshire made their bow on the big stage. In the ranks of the Territorials were eleven Elmore Green Old Boys and a few related names that descended the gangplanks from the S.S. *'Empress Queen'* when she docked in Le Havre on 3rd March 1915. Excitement must have been mounting as the much-derided but confident 'weekend soldiers' left far behind any thoughts of the local Drill Hall. Of the eleven who first set foot on French soil that March, seven (**Horace Downes, Charles Bullock, George Groves, Joe Handy, Len Malpass, George Sargent** and **Jack Parton**) would serve and die with 1/5th Battalion, while two (**Frank Lloyd** and **Albert Stych**) would transfer and die with other units; just two, **John Orgill**[69] (older brother of Canadian emigrant **Joseph Orgill**) and **Simon Perks** (younger brother of **Harry Perks**[70]) would return to Bloxwich after the peace.

Although the village of Neuve Chapelle was captured and held, it was at the cost of 11,000 British and Empire (Indian) casualties. The failure to advance onto and to capture Aubers Ridge brought criticism down on Sir John French who promptly offset the blame on to a 'shortage of shells'. The subsequent 'shell scandal' in Britain caused political conflict, the upshot of which brought in a coalition government under the existing Liberal Prime Minister Herbert Asquith; as for the shells, a new Ministry of Munitions was created under the control of David Lloyd-George. One of his first solutions in 1915 was to limit licensing hours in pubs in order to prevent workers in vital industries from turning up drunk; such 'temporary' measures lasted for more than seventy years, so the Battle of Neuve Chapelle cost Bloxwich at least two of its soldiers and the freedom to drink alcohol all day, not that many people could afford it!

The late spring of 1915 saw local lads involved in the fighting in two sectors of the Flanders front and in the Mediterranean theatre at Gallipoli; to some

---

68 Individual TF battalions had reached France and Belgium in late 1914, though no 'New Army' units were deemed ready for action.

69 John Orgill transferred to the 172nd Tunnelling Company, R.E. in October 1915; 1st January 1917 he was posted to 174th Tunnelling Company, R.E. He survived the war.

70 Harry Perks would himself soon arrive in France – on 29th March with 48th 'South Midland' TF Division.

extent the time-scale of these battles overlapped, so they will not necessarily be examined in their actual chronological order.

May

In many ways, the Battles of Neuve Chapelle (10th-13th March), Aubers Ridge (9th May) and Festubert (15th-25th May) may be viewed as three attempts to capture the Ridge on which stood the village of Aubers. A mere seventy feet high, the ridge afforded the troops in possession good observation across the muddy, often-flooded plain to the west and north-west. On 9th May, the only local unit involved was 1/South Staffordshire that was in reserve lines near Fromelles, supporting 8th Division. That the Battle of Festubert was launched just six days later is adequate comment on the outcome of the Aubers Ridge assaults which left more than 11,000 Allied casualties.

In the wake of a thirty-six hour preparatory bombardment, 22nd Brigade of 7th Division advanced either side of Rue des Cailloux (five hundred yards north of Festubert village). 1/South Staffordshire, south of the road, was in close support of 2/Queen's (Royal West Surrey) and would play an active and costly part in the battle. The dawn attack that went in at 3:15 a.m. on Tuesday, 16th May saw 2/Queen's held up by heavy defensive fire but a renewed artillery barrage enabled the supporting Staffords, thanks to the bravery of their bombing parties, to enter and hold the German front trenches. Over the following two days the Germans rained artillery fire on the Staffords, though no German infantry counter-attack materialised. When 1/South Staffordshire was relieved during the night of 18th May, their casualty list showed 270 men killed, wounded or missing. Twenty-four year-old **Private Timothy Taylor**, a cousin of Elmore Green Old Boys **Alf** and **George Bushnell**, was posted missing, believed killed in action on **16th May**. Pre-war, he was employed as a miner at Holly Bank Colliery but had volunteered for the Special Reserve of the South Staffordshire Regiment. When war came, Timothy was trained up to regular standards and went out to France a week before Christmas 1914. Back home at 53, Alfred Street, Bloxwich, his mother Mrs. Ann Titley received the devastating news in a personal letter from Company Sergeant-Major A. Baker[71] who explained that her son died instantly when a bullet pierced his brain. He wrote,

> *"Always remember that he died an honourable death, doing his duty for King and Country like the brave soldier he was."*

---

71 8281, CSM A. Baker of 1/ South Staffordshire had previously been Mentioned in Despatches for his brave conduct – it had been announced in the *'London Gazette'* edition of 17th February 1915, page 1664].

Private Taylor's body was never identified, a probable consequence of the artillery bombardment, so he is commemorated on Panel 21 or 22 of the Le Touret Memorial, Richebourg-L'Avoué, near Festubert.

April to July – Gallipoli Campaign in the Mediterranean

Ten days after his cousin Tim Taylor was fighting and dying in the Battle of Festubert, Private Alf Bushnell was landing at Cape Helles on the Turkish peninsula of Gallipoli in the Mediterranean. Alf had volunteered for the Highland Light Infantry as soon as war was declared in August 1914 but had soon transferred to the 1/King's Own Scottish Borderers[72]. In April 1915 an Anglo-French naval force attempted to force the Dardanelles Straits[73] with the aim of easing the pressure on their Russian ally but the fleet was crippled by mines and by hits from shore batteries. On the day of Alf's arrival in theatre, 25th May 1915, a German submarine torpedoed and sank the battleship HMS 'Triumph'; next day it was the turn of HMS 'Majestic' to suffer the same fate. The result was that naval presence was abandoned and the troops that had been landed on Gallipoli (including 1/KOSB in 87th Brigade of 29th Division) would no longer enjoy support from the heavy guns of the Royal Navy's ships. The name Gallipoli was to become synonymous with poor military planning, senseless slaughter and crippling levels of disease and illness. Toeholds at Helles and Anzac Bay were restricted to the coast while a subsequent landing at Suvla Bay in August met a similar fate; the struggle turned into an infantry assault on an area of narrow beaches backed by steep cliffs. Attempts to break out were continually frustrated by the German-directed Turkish troops [The Commander-in-Chief was the astute German General, Otto Liman von Sanders. Among his divisional commanders was a Lieutenant-Colonel by the name of Mustafa Kemal (later known as Kemal Ataturk), who was to become an impressive leader of Turkey in 1923] and heat-fuelled disease began to ravage the tightly packed Allied divisions. By mid-December, the decision had been taken to evacuate the peninsula, a plan that was executed with virtually no casualties – one of the few successes of the entire campaign.

1/KOSB had suffered heavy casualties at Helles in April[74] and again in early June at Twelve Tree Copse and so was taken out of the firing line on 12th June for a week's 'rest' that amounted to little more than fatigues. From the 18th to 23rd, the battalion was back in the firing line then, on 27th they assembled for an attack the next day on enemy trenches near Gully Ravine (Saghir Dere). Minor successes cost the battalion eight officers and 223 other ranks but, after

---

72   1/KOSB had been in Lucknow, India on outbreak of war.

73   The only entrance to the Black Sea.

74   In excess of 330 all ranks were recorded as casualties.

just two days' rest, 1/KOSB went into the line again on Wednesday, 30th June. On 5th July, General Liman von Sanders ordered his Turkish troops to attack the full length of the British line. **Private Alf Bushnell** was killed the following day, **6th July**, while the Turkish trenches were on high alert and snipers were very active. A letter from Lieutenant A.A. Whittel informed Alfred's family that the lad had been shot by a sniper while getting tea from a 'dixie'.

1/KOSB battalion war diary records the following:

> *"5 July 1915 - Companies in fire trench, continued to improve the Sap. 5 p.m. – 'C' and 'D' Companies relieved 'A' and 'B'. 1 officer wounded. 8 p.m. - One platoon and machine guns of 5/Argyll and Sutherland Highlanders were attached to our companies in the fire trench for the night.*
>
> *"6 July 1915 – 2 a.m., 2/South Wales Borderers rushed an enemy sap covered by our machine guns. 5 p.m. – 'C' and 'D' Companies relieved 'A' and 'B'."*

Twenty-one year-old **Alf Bushnell** was buried in Twelve Tree Copse, near the village of Krithia; however, his grave was later disturbed by shellfire and it is now commemorated by a 'Special Memorial' that indicates that he is, 'known to be buried' in the cemetery. Sadly, Alf and Tim Taylor were not to be the last of the Bushnell family's losses during their grim year of 1915.

April and May on the Western Front

Our tale of 1915 now returns to the Western Front in Flanders and to the German army's second major attempt to 'pinch out' the salient at Ypres and to break through British lines to reach the Channel ports. The 2nd Battles of Ypres (22nd April to 25th May) now favoured the defenders even though the original professionals of the BEF had all but disappeared as casualty figures soared. Of the seven Bloxwich lads in our story who fought with the BEF, **Aaron Hayward, William Groves** and **'Coxy' Lavender** had already been killed, while **John Bullock** had been taken prisoner. Surprisingly, three lads (**Jimmy Dawson, Joe Bullock** and **Ernie Lavender**) who had been 'out' since 12th August 1914 with 2/South Staffordshire had survived longest, through Mons, the Retreat, the Marne, the Aisne, 1st Ypres and Cuinchy.

Second Ypres was launched by the Germans on Gravenstafel Ridge in the north-eastern sector of the salient, while 2nd Division and 2/South Staffordshire were still on the La Bassée front contributing to the attack at Festubert. By April of 1915, Ypres had been reinforced by Empire troops of the Indian Corps and the Canadian Division, along with the British Regulars of 27th and 28th Divisions and the Territorials of 50th 'Northumbrian' Division; nevertheless, the German attackers still retained the advantage of numbers. Breakthrough in trench warfare had already proved difficult but each side had prepared a few surprises for the other. German pioneers had exploded a mine under British trenches back in February of 1915 and, inspired, organised and cajoled by an engineer, Major John Norton-Griffiths, the Royal Engineers raised a number of specialist Tunnelling Companies, initially trying out their art in the vicinity of Hill 60, a mile south of Zillebeke in the Ypres Salient. On 17th April, five mines dug by 171 Tunnelling Coy, RE, were detonated and a form of medieval warfare was thus revived. An Elmore Green lad and a former miner at Wood Farm Colliery, **Edgar Goodall**, who had come out to the Western Front in December of 1914 with a regular battalion of the South Staffordshire, had transferred the following February to 173rd Tunnelling Company, RE. He had chosen a dangerous but well-paid job, though he probably thought that it couldn't be much more perilous than life in the infantry, where he had had one narrow escape from death by a fraction when a bullet hit him but was deflected by a knife he was carrying in his tunic. Would his luck hold? The odds were against him.

Another Elmore Green lad was involved in defending the first German attack on Gravenstafel Ridge. **Joseph Orgill** was born in Pelsall, educated at Elmore Green School and served three years in the Bloxwich ('D' Company) Territorials with his older brother John before, in 1913, emigrating to Canada. With such recent experience in the British military, Joseph volunteered on 23rd September 1914 in Valcartier, Canada for the first Canadian contingent to train for overseas service, joining 2nd Field Ambulance of the Canadian Army Medical Corps. The Division left Canada on 3rd October 1914 and arrived at Plymouth, England on 14th of the month. After a cold, wet winter in tents and huts on Salisbury Plain the 1st Canadian Division embarked in February at Avonmouth and landed at St. Nazaire in France. Their baptism of fire was to be Second Ypres in April 1915, unaware then exactly what they would face. What they *would* face was unprecedented even in a war as harsh as this one. In the late afternoon of 22nd April 1915, an opaque, greenish mist crept over and into the Allied lines near Bikschote on the northern edge of the Ypres Salient. Along a four-mile sector of the front stunned, terrified and choking soldiers of the French 87th Territorial Division and of the 45th Algerian Division fell back or were overrun in their trenches. These French soldiers were victims of the first major use of poison gas[75] and understandably many had broken and fled but the situation was salvaged by a desperate and heroic effort by the Canadian Division from the right flank who, at great cost, plugged the gap. Joseph Orgill,

---

75 This first-used gas was chlorine gas.

a medic with the Canadians, received a most extreme initiation to the Western Front. On the German side, it was a missed opportunity to break through. In respect of the new chemical warfare, the genie was out of the bottle and would be used by both sides as the months passed. By late May, the battles of Ypres staggered to a stalemated close, with British losses amounting to 59,000. Amazingly, there were no Elmore Green lads among these fatal casualties.

Spring into summer – Territorials and New Army arrivals

In the southern sectors of the Ypres Salient and beyond, towards La Bassée, several divisions new to the front line had arrived from 'Blighty' during the spring and early summer. Among the Territorial newcomers were 46th 'North Midland', 47th 'London', 48th 'South Midland', 49th 'West Riding' and 51st 'Highland' divisions. The first of Lord Kitchener's 'New Army' divisions had also arrived in Flanders, among them 9th 'Scottish', 12th 'Eastern', 14th 'Light' and 15th 'Scottish' divisions (10th 'Irish', 11th 'Northern' and 13th 'Western' divisions all served at Gallipoli in 1915). The next two Elmore Green Old Boys to die would be local Territorials. 46th 'North Midland' Division contained 1/5th and 1/6th Battalions of the South Staffordshire, while 1/5th Battalion contained the lads of 'D' Company who had started their soldiering with the Bloxwich Territorials. 46th 'North Midland' landed at Le Havre on 5th March 1915, the first complete TF division deemed ready to be sent to the Western Front. 1/5th Battalion went into the front line in early April near Wulverghem and then in late June moved to billets at Ouderdom in the Ypres Salient and manned the trenches at Hill 60 – this was one of the most nerve-wracking tasks in the Salient on account of the artillery bombardments, trench raids and mines that were occasionally exploded under the British trenches. To make the situation worse, when out of the front line, the battalion sheltered in dugouts still within range of German artillery – technically, this was 'brigade reserve'. The Staffords held this tough sector for almost three months then, when relieved, they moved south to train for their part in the Battle of Loos in October – most surely a case of 'out of the frying pan into the fire'. However, two lads, **Horace Downes** and **Leonard Malpass**[76], were doomed never to leave the sector between Mount Sorrel (towards Sanctuary Wood) and the dreaded Hill 60; both formerly worked at local Collieries, nineteen year-old Downes was employed as a horse driver at the Wyrley Plant Colliery while twenty-five year-old Malpass worked underground as a coal-hewer at Harrison's Colliery, Wyrley Grove, Pelsall. Both had been educated at Elmore Green School, though the age difference meant they would probably not have met until both

---

76   His actual name was Leonard Morris – he had enlisted under his sister's married name.

joined the Bloxwich Territorials; both would be severely wounded in the same incident and both would die from their injuries several days later.

July

Hill 60[77] was a low ridge made from the spoil removed during the construction of the nearby Ypres-Comines railway line cutting. As it was a small area of elevated land in a flat landscape, Hill 60 obviously had strategic importance in the conflict in the Salient and both sides struggled to gain control of it and the daily fighting there was savage. On Monday, 5th July, 1/5th Battalion moved from bivouac in Ouderdom to relieve 1/5th Leicestershire in trenches in Armagh Wood, one mile east of Zillebeke. Six days later, on Sunday, 11th July, **Horace Downes** and **Len Malpass** were severely wounded by a shell that burst over their company's trenches. The same shell also killed two other Bloxwich lads, 7849, Private James Perry and 9014, Private Godfrey Fletcher. 1/5th South Staffordshire battalion war diary for 11th July records:

> *"Two enemy aeroplanes over our lines yesterday evening and one from 3.45 to 4.20 a.m. this morning. Enemy fired four trench mortars at about 8.30 p.m., damage slight. Retaliated with 16 rifle grenades but 7 failed to explode. Our guns (artillery) also opened fire. Suspect enemy sapping towards us from new redoubt. Enemy have lowered parapet opposite [trench locations] A1 and A2. [Our]...snipers report accounting for a German officer.*
>
> *"Enemy shell burst over A5 Support (Trench) about 10 a.m. inflicting six casualties. Our artillery shelled wood opposite A5. Enemy replied by shelling Sanctuary Wood."*

Horace's wounds were almost certainly treated in No.5 Casualty Clearing Station in Poperinghe but no avail; he died on **17th July** and was subsequently buried in the nearby huge military cemetery at Lijssenthoek just to the south of Poperinghe. It appears that the serious shrapnel wounds to his abdomen required **Len Malpass** to be moved down the line to 13th General Hospital at Boulogne; there, he clung tenaciously to life until **30th August** when he finally succumbed to his injuries. He is buried nearby in Boulogne Eastern Cemetery. Interestingly, although Len served under the surname Malpass, his actual surname was Morris – for reasons unknown, Len enlisted under the surname of his married sister, Emily Malpass, with whom he resided in Pelsall Lane, Little Bloxwich. Many men served under assumed names, for many differing reasons.

---

77 The '60' indicated it was sixty metres (about 175 feet) above sea level; the hill was a low ridge about eighty metres in length.

September

One Elmore Green lad who served in a specialist army unit that gives us an insight into his character was **Horace France** of Bloxwich Road, Leamore. It appears that his skill as a motor-cyclist led him to enlist in Birmingham during

May 1915 in the Motor Machine Gun Service (a section of the Royal Field Artillery). Horace France was part of 14th Battery that was attached to 20th 'Light' Division; Horace's skill as a rider meant that he spent rather less than the usual time in basic military training and arrived in France on 20th July 1915. A Motor Machine Gun battery comprised six Vickers Machine Guns, with eighteen motorcycle combinations to transport the guns, ammunition and gun

spares; there were eight solo motor cycles (usually 'Triumph') and a few wagons or motor trucks. The MMG rider's uniform was distinctive – weatherproof clothing, gauntlets, goggles and leather gaiters.

Unlike so many of his contemporaries, **Horace France** was killed in an accident. The infantry of 20th 'Light' Division received its trench warfare tuition in the Fleurbaix sector, just south of Armentières; the MMG battery was then at Estaires and it was from there that Horace set out on his last journey on 20th September. His Captain wrote to Horace's parents to explain what had occurred:

> *"He was riding a motor cycle on duty this afternoon testing the machine after having made some slight adjustments; and very shortly afterwards news was brought that he had met with a very serious accident, having collided with a tree. In an unconscious condition he was at once taken to the hospital, and died about five minutes after arrival. The cause of the accident is, and will remain, a mystery. His loss is deeply felt by officers and men who all liked him."*

The hospital mentioned was either No.7 or No.54 Casualty Clearing Stations that were then at Merville. However, his injuries were too severe and **Horace France** died the same day, Monday, **20th September** 1915. He is buried in Estaires Communal Cemetery near Merville, to the north of Béthune.

September and October

Elmore Green lads were about to endure the greatest test of their resolve and character in the offensive that came to be known as the Battle of Loos (25th

September to 8th October). A year later, on 1st July 1916, many towns' Pals battalions would suffer appalling losses on the first day of the Somme but for Bloxwich and the wider Walsall area it was to be their local Territorials that experienced the 'worst ever day' in the follow-up to Loos at the Hohenzollern Redoubt (13th to 18th October). It is no coincidence that the Territorials' brave yet unsuccessful attempt to storm the powerful Redoubt is the subject of one of the two huge murals at the rear of the platform in Walsall Town Hall; the subject of the other mural is the Territorials' successful breaking of the Hindenburg Line at the St. Quentin Canal in September 1918. The names of those who died in those two actions are, appropriately, commemorated on the Roll of Honour plaques that adorn the walls of the Town Hall's lofty interior.

The French commander, General Joseph Joffre, judged that July 1915 was a propitious time to make a breakthrough on the Western Front. The French would attack in the Lens-Arras sector while the British were required to assault the German lines in the La Bassée-Loos sector. The French would also make a parallel attack in the Champagne region and a number of minor diversions would also inhibit German reinforcements from being moved to the main target areas. The timing did not appeal to Sir John French (it was ultimately deferred to 25th September) and certain British generals expressed strong reservations about the choice of battleground – one Corps commander for the assault, General Sir Henry Rawlinson, commented prophetically,

> "…my new front at Loos is as flat as the palm of my hand. Hardly any cover anywhere. Easy enough to hold defensively but very difficult to attack. It will cost us dearly and we shall not get very far."

Even after the shell scandal and the subsequent political changes that followed Neuve Chapelle, the British were still noticeably short of artillery and ammunition; this goes a long way to explaining the British decision to make their first use of chlorine gas prior to the opening assault[78] at Loos. In the event, the battle was so nearly a success but it was not properly exploited, with the result that three weeks of attacking advanced the line just over a mile either side of the town of Loos at a cost of 60,000 casualties. Most notably, Loos was the first real 'blooding' of some of Kitchener's 'New Army' divisions – in fact for many southern and midland battalions, the battle was a grim foretaste of the slaughter on the Somme in the summer of 1916.

When the Battle of Loos opened on 25th September, the infantry assault timed for 6:30 a.m. (Zero-hour) was preceded by a limited artillery barrage,

---

78   When the gas was released from its canisters at 5:50 a.m., it drifted towards the German lines but a shift in wind direction ensured that it did more damage to the British than to their enemies.

limited by a lack of big guns and by a persistent shortage of ammunition. Aware of these problems, the British decided to employ poison gas for the first time, partly justified as 'revenge' for the Ypres gas attack and partly on account of the relatively feeble artillery barrage that was available. 150 tons of chlorine gas were released from 5,000 heavy, iron cylinders installed on the front line in the course of three nights by the new Special Companies of the Royal Engineers – as usual, the grumbling infantrymen were used as labourers. The gas, in lower quantities than was requested, was released at sunrise, 5:50 a.m. – the wind, on which the success of the gas cloud depended, was light but fluky and in some places the chemical weapon was pushed back into the British front line and in others it 'stalled' in No Man's Land forcing the assault battalions to advance through chlorine. Despite wearing rudimentary 'smoke-hoods', a number of the attacking infantrymen suffered from the effects of gas.

As both 2nd and 7th Divisions featured in the initial assault, at least seven local lads in 1st and 2nd Battalions of the South Staffordshire went 'over the top' on 25th September. 2nd Division sat astride la Bassée Canal, towards the northern flank of the battlefield, with 2/South Staffordshire on the south bank of the canal to the east of Cuinchy. Despite the outstanding efforts of Captain A.F.G. Kilby, who earned a posthumous Victoria Cross[79] for his valour, the attack here failed. Among the attacking companies were at least five Elmore Green lads. The three experienced 'Old Contemptibles', **Jimmy Dawson, Ernie Lavender** and **Joe Bullock** had been joined by two locals in a draft of reinforcements on 25th May, **George Stych** (whose brother **Albert Stych** would later win the Military Medal) and **Alfred Main** (from the Regular reserve). Although the battalion sustained 269 casualties (including 130 victims of the British poison gas), all the local lads appear to have survived.

7th Division was towards the centre of the assault line, immediately to the north of the Vermelles to Hulluch Road. The division was to attack with 22nd Brigade on the left and 20th Brigade on the right; 22nd Brigade was to attack on a 600-yard front, leading with 2/Royal Warwickshire on the left and 1/South Staffordshire on the right, keeping 1/Royal Welch Fusiliers in support and holding 2/Queen's in reserve. The four-day bombardment that preceded the assault was apparently ineffective and was to cost the division many casualties at the uncut German wire. Among the divisional objectives were the German front line, then two strong defensive positions – The Pope's Nose and Spurn Head, The Quarries, on to the second line, north of Hulluch and finally into the village of Cité St. Elie – the latter stages were across open, level ground.

---

79 *"...Captain Kilby who, though wounded at the outset, continued to lead his men right up to the enemy wire under a devastating machine gun fire and a shower of bombs."* (Extract from the VC citation of Captain Kilby, VC, MC, 2/South Staffordshire).

Uncut wire at the German front line slowed the attackers, exposing them to intense fire that caused heavy casualties. Private Arthur 'Titch' Vickers of 2/RWR raced forward and, under fire, cut two gaps in the wire – an act of gallantry that rightly earned him a Victoria Cross[80] and allowed a badly-mauled 22nd Brigade to capture the German front line. 1/Royal Welch Fusiliers, the support battalion, was sent forward at the vital moment to help secure most of the German second line. When 2/Queen's was thrown forward from reserve to take The Quarries, the tiring, hard-hit troops of the brigade quickly moved on towards the edge of Cité St. Elie. Heavy fire and German reinforcements led to the sensible move back to The Quarries, where the Royal Engineers helped consolidate the defences for the expected counter-attack. The achievement of 22nd Brigade may be gauged by the casualties sustained during the first day – 1,689 of which 448 were from 1/South Staffordshire. Again the local boys had been fortunate in that Private **Arthur Kitson**, a pre-war miner at Wood Farm Colliery, and Private **Jim Jones**, also a mineworker, both survived the day's carnage. By coincidence, the two lads hailed from Marlborough Street.

The last of local lads to fight at Loos on 25th-26th September had only arrived in France with 21st Division on 9th and 10th of September and by 12th the division had concentrated at Tilques, to the west of St. Omer. **Private Sam Goodall**'s brother **Edgar** had joined the South Staffordshire regulars in France in late December of 1914; two months later he had transferred to one of the new Tunnelling Companies (173rd) of the Royal Engineers. Sam had volunteered for Lord Kitchener's 'New Army' in November 1914 and had enlisted in 13th Battalion of the Northumberland Fusiliers that was assigned to 62nd Brigade of 21st Division. In the same division but in 12/West Yorkshire Regiment (63rd Brigade), 25 year-old **Private George Smith** landed in France on 10th September from a different troop transport just a day after **Sam Goodall**. Their division was to receive a baptism of fire at Loos. By coincidence, George's 24 year-old brother, **Private Edward Smith**, landed in France on the same day as George but as a member of 10/West Yorkshire Regiment (50th Brigade, 17th 'Northern' Division) – Edward was bound for the Ypres Salient.

Though the 'Kitchener Men' were raw in terms of the Western Front, Sir John French was prepared to risk 21st Division, along with another inexperienced 'New Army' formation, 24th Division, that had been in France only a week longer than 21st, as the General Reserve. What is more, French kept that

---

80 *"Under very heavy enemy fire, he went out in front of his company and cut barbed wire....holding up the battalion's advance. It was broad daylight…he had to carry out this act standing up…but his gallant action contributed largely to the successful assault on German front-line trenches."* (Extract from the VC citation of Private Vickers).

reserve under his personal orders and located the two divisions near Lillers, sixteen miles back from Vermelles where the Corps Reserves were assembled under the control of First Army's commander, General Sir Douglas Haig. Haig told his superior that he wanted the General Reserve less than two miles west of Vermelles – he was overruled. As a result, the two unseasoned divisions were eventually brought forward at night in damp mist, arriving exhausted, hungry and unsure of their role beyond the fact that they were almost certain to go into battle for their first time. Poor staff work produced contradictory orders, rendering the outcome somewhat inevitable. On 26th September, a day that might have consolidated an encouraging opening attack, 21st Division suffered 3,941 casualties and 24th Division suffered 4,059. It was one reason among several that Sir John French was replaced as Commander-in-Chief of the BEF by General Sir Douglas Haig before the Yule logs were burning. As for **Sam Goodall** and 13/Northumberland Fusiliers, he had come through his first battle but 396 of his battalion had become casualties. **George Smith** of 12/West Yorkshire Regiment had also survived his 'blooding' but 314 of his new comrades had not been so lucky.

Between 25th September and 13th October, 1/South Staffordshire was out of the line for just five days and several times the battalion was fighting for its very existence. 2/South Staffordshire spent marginally less time in the front line but their losses were nearly as heavy. The fighting at Loos petered out following an unsuccessful German counter-attack on 8th October, most of the offensive having taken place under steady machine-gun and artillery fire; chlorine gas settled in many of the shell-holes while rain turned the ground to cloying mud. The Staffordshire Regiment's baton was soon to be passed to the Territorials.

Throughout the first two days' clashes at Loos, two local lads had been in General Reserve with the Guards Division, the same reserve from which 21st and 24th Divisions had left on their hard march to the battlefront. **Harry Willett** and **William Lawley** both volunteered for the Grenadier Guards following the declaration of war in August 1914; after training, Harry was posted to 3/Grenadier Guards but William was posted to 2/Grenadier Guards. Both had attended Elmore Green school, though Harry was three years older than William; their employment background could not have been more contrasting – prior to enlistment, **Harry** worked in a Gentlemen's outfitter in Wolverhampton while **William** was a miner at Huntington Colliery on the edge of Cannock Chase. One minor irony was that William's first job on leaving school was to work for the General Post Office as a telegraph messenger – popularly known as a 'telegram boy', the job carried responsibility, provided a uniform and a bicycle and was at the cutting edge of new technology. During the Great War, however, families dreaded receiving a telegram as the authorities used the system to impart bad news about loved ones in the forces. Two such telegrams would soon be on their way to Bloxwich families.

2/Grenadier Guards had been on the Western Front with 2nd Division since mid-August 1914 but **Guardsman Lawley** did not join his new comrades until soon after 26th July 1915 when he landed with a draft of Guards reinforcements at Le Havre, France. **Lance-Corporal Willett** arrived in France with 3/Grenadier Guards on 27th July 1915 just before the Guards Division[81] was created in August. The Battle of Loos was the first test for the new, elite division commanded by Lord Cavan.

On the opening day of the battle, the entire Guards Division had been located in final reserve at Allouagne, six miles west of Béthune. Late on 26th September (the second day), the division moved 'up the line', 3/Grenadier Guards (2nd Guards Brigade) facing the Loos Road Redoubt[82] on the Vermelles-Loos Road. The two divisions the Guards relieved, 21st and 24th Divisions, had between them suffered over 8,000 casualties in less than 48 hours. On 27th, the Guards attacked the German line to the north of Loos, two companies from 3/Grenadier suffering heavy casualties. As days passed, the fighting became more sporadic, though occasionally intense. On Sunday, 3rd October, 2/Grenadier Guards (1st Guards Brigade) moved into trenches just east of Vermelles in support of 2/Coldstream and 3/Coldstream who were in the old German trenches south of the Hohenzollern Redoubt. Shelling was heavy, two men being killed and five wounded. On Monday, 4th October, the Grenadiers spent the day digging communication trenches within thirty yards of the Germans – some change from ceremonial duties! The following day they moved into the front line trenches and on Thursday, 7th October 2/Grenadier moved into rest billets in Vermelles village – but only until late the next day when the battalion returned to the trenches to relieve 3/Coldstream. During the mid-afternoon of 8th October the Germans, piqued by their losses, launched a vigorous counter-attack, bombing (grenade) along the trenches and through the barricades.[83] This time 3/Grenadier in Big Willie trench (in front of the Hohenzollern Redoubt) was hardest hit and it took a fierce counter-attack by the Guards Division to force a German retirement. 2/Grenadier Guards battalion war diary records:

---

81 King George V approved the creation of a Guards Division in July 1915, bringing together all five guards regiments, Grenadier, Coldstream, Scots, Irish and Welsh. Some units transferred from existing divisions while others, like 3/Grenadier Guards, arrived straight from Britain.

82 A redoubt is a strongpoint in a line of defences. The Guards would be sorely tested at the Hohenzollern Redoubt later in the Battle of Loos.

83 Sometimes, both sides might occupy each end of the same trench-line, the men being separated only by temporary and dangerous barricades. In this vicious fighting, grenades, bayonets, knives and entrenching tools were the weapons of choice.

"8 October 1915 - Heavy artillery fire started at 11am and continued all day, a considerable number of shells falling in and around the village. Casualties – two men wounded."

William Lawley was one of these 'two men', severely wounded in the thigh by a piece of shrapnel during this fight and he was moved 'down the line' for treatment. From the Casualty Clearing Station in Béthune, William was evacuated by hospital train to Versailles and into No.4 General Hospital. During the heavy fighting for possession of the Hohenzollern Redoubt on 8th October, **Harry Willett** too was gravely wounded by shellfire and removed to No.33 Casualty Clearing Station behind the lines in Béthune. By the end of a hard-fought day, the Grenadiers still held their trench line in the Redoubt sector but both local Grenadier Guardsmen had been grievously wounded. In his hospital ward in Versailles, near the palace of Louis XIV, twenty year-old **William Lawley** clung on for five days until his strength gave out on **13th October**, just as his battalion was again attacking the Hohenzollern Redoubt – he was buried in Les Gonards Cemetery at Versailles, to the west of Paris. **Harry Willett** remained in No.33 C.C.S. in Béthune, possibly because it was judged too dangerous to move him; the young man finally lost his slim grip on life on **18th October** and was buried close by the hospital in the ever-expanding Béthune Town Cemetery. Neither of the young Grenadier Guardsmen had been in France for as long as three months.

Between 25th September and 8th October the conflict in the northern half of the Loos battlefield centred upon the powerful Hohenzollern Redoubt and the trench complex that enveloped it. Lads from Bloxwich were on the Loos battlefield, among the pit-heads, winding-gear, spoil heaps and miners' cottages (each with its separate cellar that required 'mopping up'), from start to finish of the battle. On 25th September a New Army unit, 9th 'Scottish' Division, was given the task of storming the Hohenzollern Redoubt; on their left flank was 2nd Division containing 2/South Staffordshire. On the Scots' right flank was 7th Division and 1/South Staffordshire. Though most of 9th Division was very badly mauled, its 26th Brigade took the Hohenzollern Redoubt at a cost in excess of 1,500 casualties on that day and a further 600 the following day. Mid-afternoon on 27th, 9th Division was relieved by the Regulars of 28th Division that had recently been at full stretch in the Ypres Salient – they held the Redoubt until 3rd October when German 'bombers'[84] stormed the adjacent trenches and control of the Redoubt was all but lost. When 28th Division was relieved by the Guards Division, the 28th had sustained more than 3,300

---

84 A grenade was known as a 'bomb', hence 'bombers' were grenade-throwers. At that time the German grenade was more effective than the British grenade, which was also in short supply.

Map 4:
13th to 18th October 1915
Hohenzollern Redoubt LOOS

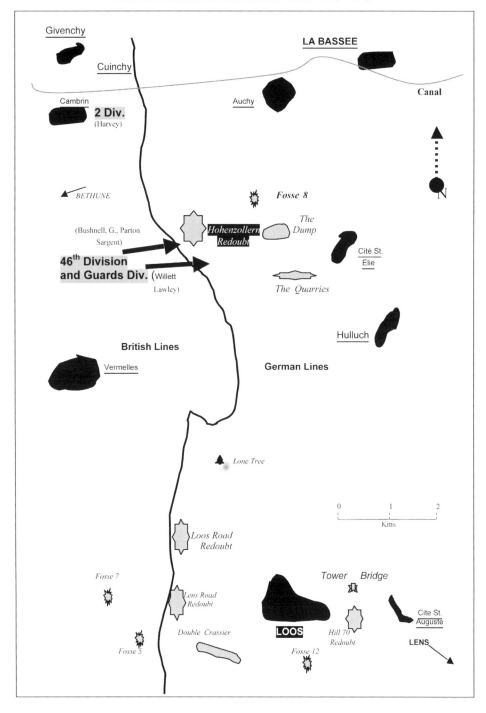

casualties in a week. The loss of the Hohenzollern Redoubt was vital and First Army commander, General Sir Douglas Haig, ordered all efforts around Loos to be concentrated upon retaking the strongpoint. As earlier recounted, the Guards Division was preparing an attempt to regain the Redoubt when, on 8th October, the German bombers of 57th Regiment struck and, although most attacks were repulsed, they did succeed in taking much of Little Willie Trench abutting the northern flank of the Hohenzollern Redoubt.

With the German assaults on 8th October, the main attacks at Loos ended but the subsequent postscript to the Battle of Loos was to leave an indelible mark upon the entire Walsall area. The results of the Actions of the Hohenzollern Redoubt from 13th to 18th October would eventually be the main topic of conversation at meal tables in the likes of Parker Street, at places of work and in the shops of Bloxwich High Street. At least fourteen Elmore Green Territorials,

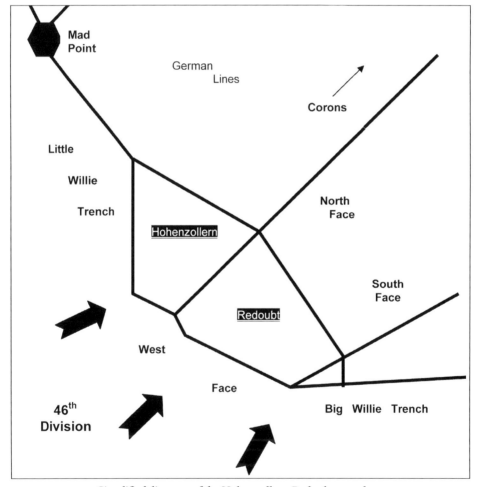

Simplified diagram of the Hohenzollern Redoubt complex

including five from 2nd Division's September attacks (and one lad new to the trenches), were thrust into the cauldron of the Redoubt – three of them would be killed and others wounded. 13th October 1915 was a date that in years to come would be spoken in awed, hushed tones in the locality. Most of the lads involved in these actions were Territorials in the 137th 'Staffordshire' Brigade[85] of the 46th '1st North Midland' Division. Waiting in the front line trenches were two lads from Parker Street, **George Sargent** and **Albert Stych**, Cope Street's **Jack Parton**, Bell Lane's **George Groves**, Marlborough Street's **Joe Handy**, May Street's **Arthur Parkes**, New Street's **Charles Bullock**, from the Leamore 'end' **George Bushnell** and from the 'posh' part of town, **Frank Lloyd** of Lichfield Road (who would earn a Military Medal).

There was little thought for Lord Kitchener's disparaging words of 1914 as company after company of local Territorials were hurled against the major German stronghold of the Hohenzollern Redoubt. The Redoubt had been constructed at the apex of a slightly raised, angled salient in the new German front line where it was closer to the British trenches than elsewhere in the immediate area. Across the point of the salient was a trench known as The Chord, and the trench facing No Man's Land was known as the West Face. At one end from The Chord, 'Little Willie' fire-trench extended almost due north; from other end of The Chord, 'Big Willie'[86] fire-trench extended almost due east. Roughly parallel to The Chord and linking the extremes of 'Big Willie' and 'Little Willie' fire-trenches was the old German front line (running from south-east to north-west) of Quarry Trench, Dump Trench and Fosse Trench. Linking The Chord to these three adjoining trenches were cut trenches known as the North Face and the South Face. This formidable German strongpoint situated north of Hulluch village had underground galleries, dugouts and trenches, all protected by thick belts of barbed wire.

Thus interlinked, laced with machine-guns and flanked by extra strong-points (such as Mad Point to the north-west) that could provide enfilading fire, the Hohenzollern Redoubt was a death-trap for attacking infantry. Successful assault was possible but it would always be at a high cost through hand-to-hand fighting. Beyond the seemingly impregnable Redoubt lay Fosse[87] No.8, in effect a mining community with its associated pit-head winding gear, offices, miners' cottages (known as 'corons' in the Loos area) and railway sidings; overlooking the buildings was the twenty-foot high (and thus important in a flat landscape) spoil heap known as The Dump. The prospect of battle here was bleak. Even

---

85 1/5th and 1/6th South Staffordshire, together with 1/5th and 1/6th North Staffordshire, made up the 137th 'Staffordshire' Brigade.

86 The two trenches were named by the British 'Tommy' after Kaiser Wilhelm and his son.

87 A 'fosse' was a mine.

so, much of the ground would in many respects have been rather familiar to the many miners among the local contingent – winding gear, spoil heaps and rows of miners' cottages but these offered precious little cover for advancing infantry. The 1/5th Battalion war diary retells the grim story:

> *"From 12 noon, Headquarters, 'A' and 'D' Companies were in the old front line trench between Hulluch Alley and Border Alley (this was the first line of attack); 'B' and 'C' Companies were in the first line of attack. At 2:10 p.m. the attack went in and 'B' Company was enfiladed and shelled. 'A' and 'D' Companies experienced machine gun and rifle fire from the left. All officers and most men were killed. At 2:20 p.m. the Germans counter-attacked Big Willie Trench but were driven back. A second counter-attack was also repulsed. Heavy losses among trained bombers led to a slight withdrawal. They were reinforced by a platoon of 1/6th South Staffordshire who, during the night, helped to bring in wounded men from No Man's Land."*

At the start of the attack, 1/6th South Staffordshire were in direct support to 1/5th South Staffordshire. The 1/6th Battalion war diary gives a view of the assault complementary to that of the 1/5th:

> *"…13th October 1915, Vermelles Sector, 46th Division was ordered to capture the Hohenzollern Redoubt and Fosse No.8; 137 Brigade was on the right flank. They formed up in four lines with 1/6th North Staffs. The attack was covered by a two-hour artillery bombardment from midday [gas at 1:00 p.m. and smoke shells to hide the points of attack]. At 1:30 p.m. and 1:45 p.m. enemy machine guns ranged on the assembly trenches. Ironically, smoke covered the first two lines but in the third line two companies suffered heavy casualties. The fourth line was hit by machine guns from the south face. Remnants of the third line reached the fire trench to assist the 1/5th South Staffs."*

Just as the 1/5th was halted by intense machine gun fire and effectively destroyed, so the leading companies of the 1/6th in reaching their sister battalion suffered an identical fate. Andrew Thornton, in his superbly researched (as yet unpublished) work[88] on the 137th 'Staffordshire' Brigade's Assault on the Hohenzollern Redoubt, summarises the situation thus:

---

88 Andrew's work on 137th Brigade is entitled, *'We had done all that was expected of us.'*

"By 4 o'clock, the fighting on the 137th Brigade front had virtually ceased, with both sides conducting an artillery duel over the area. In the space of about ten minutes, the Brigade had been decimated[89] and the remnants of the Staffordshire battalions had not made any significant progress against the defenders of the Hohenzollern Redoubt. The ground in front of the first line trenches was littered with dead, dying and wounded soldiers."

The Bloxwich lads had endured hell on Earth and, mercifully, their unit was subsequently moved north to a quieter sector around Neuve Chapelle to rest and recover. Colonel W.L. Vale in his, *'History of the South Staffordshire Regiment'*, commented:

"The flower of Staffordshire Territorials had largely perished (at Loos). The two battalions (1/5th and 1/6th South Staffordshire) had lost 32 officers, 533 other ranks killed or wounded and 157 missing…"

The artillery duel mentioned by Andrew Thornton explains why the bodies of so many of the casualties were never identified for burial. Every man who fought on the battlefield of Loos deserves respect yet our story will give special note to five of those lads. Following the German attack of 8th October, two Grenadier Guardsmen (both former pupils of Elmore Green) were already lying critically ill in hospital, **Harry Willett** in Béthune and **William Lawley** in Versailles; **Lawley** would not live beyond the 13th, Willett the 18th. Three more local lads, all of 1/5 South Staffordshire, were gravely wounded in the charge towards the West Face of the Hohenzollern Redoubt – the nature of their wounds will remain unknown but the torrent of artillery shells would ensure that none of them would be dragged to safety. Twenty-four year-old ex-miner, **George Sargent** of 'D' Company, eighteen year-old ex-miner, **George Bushnell** and eighteen year-old factory worker, **Jack Parton** of 'A' Company all perished on **13th October** among the jagged wire, flooded shell-holes, churned mud and shattered bodies in No Man's Land. None of the three was ever recovered and identified, so their names are commemorated on panels 73 to 76 of the Loos Memorial to the Missing that is located at the southern end of the battlefield. The only information that was reported to the battalion by survivors was that **Jack Parton** was seen to be mortally wounded by a German grenade. For John and Ruth **Bullock** of New Street the news of their son

---

89   The 46th Division lost 3,700 casualties in those ten minutes in front of the Hohenzollern Redoubt. Appropriately, there is a 46th Division memorial on the south side of the road from Vermelles to Hulluch.

Charles was slightly better – he had been wounded at Loos on 13th October and by the time of their notification Charles had been evacuated to hospital in England. He would not return to France until 1916. His parents had already lost a son John, serving with 1/South Staffordshire, to a German prisoner of war camp in November 1914 but at least he was alive. The news would not improve for them during 1916 and 1917. Even so, the final news to reach Bloxwich was at once pleasing and relieving. Elizabeth Lloyd heard that her son, **Sergeant Frank Lloyd**, had not only survived the Loos inferno but had earned the Military Medal on the eve of his twentieth birthday – it was officially announced in the Supplement to the *'London Gazette'* of 10th November 1916 (almost a year later), on page 10926:-

---

SUPPLEMENT

TO

The London Gazette

SATURDAY, 11 NOVEMBER, 1916

War Office,
11th November 1916

**His Majesty the KING has been graciously
pleased to award the Military Medal
for bravery in the field to the under-mentioned
Non-Commissioned Officers
and Men:—**

. . . .

16514 Cpl. C. A. Lloyd, R.E.
8424 Sjt. F. Lloyd, S. Staff. R.
5803 Pte. T. Lloyd, L'pool R.
7568 L./C. F. Lobel, Midd'x R….

It was not to be the last time that **Frank Lloyd**'s name would appear in the *'London Gazette'*. **George Sargent** was the first of the **'Parker Street Boys'** to be killed but he would certainly not be the last.

137th 'Staffordshire' Brigade casualty figures for 13th to 15th October 1915 were:

1/5 North Staffordshire	505	]
1/6 South Staffordshire	407	] killed, wounded or missing
1/5 South Staffordshire	**319**	]
1/6 North Staffordshire	315	]

46th Division suffered a total of 3,763 casualties over those three days. In a very unscientific survey of fifty-seven Territorials[90] from the Walsall area who died on 13th October or as a consequence of wounds sustained that day, all but six are commemorated on the Loos Memorial to the Missing – it speaks volumes for the bitter nature of the fighting at the Hohenzollern Redoubt. In Walsall Town Hall, on 21st February 1920, permanent tribute was paid to the brave lads who had taken part in the Assault on the Hohenzollern Redoubt at Loos on 13th October 1915, by the unveiling of two murals[91] that were painted (and presented) by Frank O. Salisbury.

Loos was the final major action of the year but there was still mixed news reaching Bloxwich families. **Private Edward Smith** of 10/West Yorkshire Regiment, who had arrived at the Ypres front on 10th September, was evacuated to hospital in Southall, West London, after suffering a gunshot wound to his right thigh on 2nd October – Edward's brother **George Smith** was still with the same regiment's 12th Battalion. At least two lads were involved in the 'new' warfare of tunneling with the Royal Engineers – **Edgar Goodall** had transferred to 173rd Tunnelling Company in February (served at Fauquissart, Aubers Ridge and Cuinchy in 1915) and **John Orgill** had transferred to 172nd Tunnelling Company in mid-October and served at the Bluff and Hill 60 south of Ypres; theirs was a precarious existence. **Gunner Bert Gill** of Parker Street had already served in Ireland for two weeks before his field gun battery was drafted to France on 21st June 1915 to be attached to the 3rd 'Lahore' Division of the Indian Corps. The division would leave France for Mesopotamia in December but the artillery, and thus Bertie, would remain in France.

November

Frank Harvey's part in the Great War was a time of contrasts. Prior to volunteering for the 4th 'Extra Reserve' Battalion of the South Staffordshire, Frank had worked for a blacksmith at Allen's Rough Colliery and was a well-known amateur boxer. His battalion trained on the Channel Island of Jersey,

---

90 5th South Staffordshire = 44 men; 6th South Staffordshire = 5; 5th North Staffordshire = 1; RE (North Midland) = 7.

91 The two murals are set either side of the stage and its tiered seating. The first mural depicts the Assault on the Hohenzollern Redoubt and the second mural depicts the local battalion's involvement in the Breaking of the Hindenburg Line on 29th September 1918.

where Frank spent most of his twelve months as an officer's servant. By mid-summer 1915 he was training for the hard-pressed regulars of 2/South Staffordshire and he joined the battalion in France on 29th September. His first action was related to the battalion's part in the Battle of Loos, which baptism of fire he managed to survive. During late October the battalion was taken out of the muddy trenches to rest and refit; on 28th of the month the men were inspected by King George V at Hesdigneul (by coincidence, 1/South Staffordshire was also selected for this parade). On Tuesday, 23rd November 1915 2/South Staffordshire took over trenches in the Cambrin sector, south of La Bassée Canal. The principal task of the battalion was to consolidate a huge crater known as 'Gibson's Crater' and incorporate it into the trench line. All day long the working party suspected that it might have been mined and at 4:30 p.m. on **24th November** their worst fears were confirmed when a massive explosion buried and killed the entire working party of two officers and twenty-four men, most of whose bodies were never recovered; moreover, in an effort to defend the crater three officers and ten other ranks were killed and thirty-three wounded. Among the dead was twenty-two year-old **Frank Harvey**. It is likely that Frank was killed defending the crater rather than in the explosion as his officer, Lieutenant Malpass (who was himself to die on 29th July 1916), wrote to Eli and Zillah Harvey of their son:

> "…he fell while taking part in a defence against a German attack. As his officer I very much regret his loss as he was a good soldier and always willing to do his duty. You have the consolation that he died for his country. I and his comrades wish to express our sympathy with you, for we miss him because he kept us all lively and in good spirits."

Frank had been at the front for just over six weeks. Like so many local lads he is commemorated on the Loos Memorial to the Missing.

December

During December 1915, three more lads reached the front line for the first time. On 8th of the month **David Goodall**, a cousin of tunneller **Edgar Goodall**, joined 1/South Staffordshire in France. On 10th December **Joseph Davies** arrived with a draft of replacements for 1/5 South Staffordshire and on New Year's Eve 1915, **John Goodall** reinforced 2/South Staffordshire. While the winter was cold and wet, it represented better than was to be their lot in 1916 and 1917. So, the second Christmas of the war had come and gone, the defensive trenches stretched from the Swiss border to the Channel coast of Belgium and the casualty lists grew longer with every battle that was fought. It had become more difficult to fill the gaps in the battalions and the time was at hand when new measures would have to be considered by the politicians.

By the end of 1915 many lads whose stories will be told were wearing khaki, as indicated in the following list (as far as may be ascertained from written records and family information). For many volunteers, it was to be a massive step into the unknown – patriotism, adventure, travel or simply a change of scenery were among the motivations for making the journey to the recruiting office:

Old Boys at the Front, 1915:

The local 'Old Contemptibles', surviving at the end of 1915:

James DAWSON	2nd (Reg) Battalion, South Staffordshire Regiment
Ernest Lavender	2nd (Reg) Battalion, South Staffordshire Regiment
John Bullock	1st (Reg) Battalion, S. Staffordshire Regiment [P.o.W.]
Joseph Bullock	2nd (Reg) Battalion, South Staffordshire Regiment

Other 1914 men surviving at the end of 1915:

Edgar GOODALL	173 Tunnelling Company, RE
James Jones	1st (Reg) Battalion, South Staffordshire Regiment

Men who arrived in theatre between 1st January and 31st December 1915:

William LAWLEY	2nd (Reg) Battalion, Grenadier Guards
Harry WILLETT	3rd (Reg) Battalion, Grenadier Guards
William GOODALL	2nd (Reg) Battalion, South Staffordshire Regiment
Frank HARVEY	2nd (Reg) Battalion, South Staffordshire Regiment
John GOODALL	2nd (Reg) Battalion, South Staffordshire Regiment
John YATES	2nd (Reg) Battalion, South Staffordshire Regiment
George Stych	2nd (Reg) Battalion, South Staffordshire Regiment
Alfred MAIN	2nd (Reg) Battalion, South Staffordshire Regiment
George SMITH	2nd (Reg) Battalion, South Staffordshire Regiment
Arthur KITSON	1st (Reg) Battalion, Royal Welch Fusiliers
David Goodall	1st (Reg) Battalion, South Staffordshire Regiment
Harry PERKS	15th Midland Brigade, TF, Royal Army Medical Corps
Thomas Dunn	89th Field Company, Royal Engineers
Edward SMITH	10th (Service) Battalion, West Yorkshire Regiment
Arthur Smith	10th Battery, 82nd Brigade, Royal Field Artillery
Horace FRANCE	14th Battalion, Motor Machine Gun Corps, RFA
Samuel GOODALL	13th (Service) Battalion, Northumberland Fusiliers

Alfred BUSHNELL	1st (Reg) Battalion, King's Own Scottish Borderers
Joseph ORGILL	2nd Field Ambulance, Canadian Army Medical Corps
Horace DOWNES	1/5th TF Battalion, South Staffordshire Regiment
Leonard MALPASS	1/5th TF Battalion, South Staffordshire Regiment
George BUSHNELL	1/5th TF Battalion, South Staffordshire Regiment
George SARGENT	1/5th TF Battalion, South Staffordshire Regiment
Jack PARTON	1/5th TF Battalion, South Staffordshire Regiment
George GROVES	1/5th TF Battalion, South Staffordshire Regiment
Joseph DAVIES	1/5th TF Battalion, South Staffordshire Regiment
Joseph HANDY	1/5th TF Battalion, South Staffordshire Regiment
Arthur LINNELL	1/5th TF Battalion, South Staffordshire Regiment
Albert STYCH	1/5th TF Battalion, South Staffordshire Regiment
Joseph Stych	1/5th TF Battalion, South Staffordshire Regiment
Charles BULLOCK	1/5th TF Battalion, South Staffordshire Regiment
Frank LLOYD	1/5th TF Battalion, South Staffordshire Regiment
John Orgill	1/5th TF Battalion, South Staffordshire Regiment
Simon Perks	1/5th TF Battalion, South Staffordshire Regiment
Robert Handy	South Staffordshire Regiment
Elijah Dunn	Tunnelling Company, Royal Engineers

UPPER CASE surnames indicate men whose names are commemorated on the Elmore Green school memorial.

Lower case surnames indicate men *related* to those who are commemorated on the Elmore Green school memorial.

(Reg)	indicates a Regular Army battalion.
TF	indicates a Territorial Force battalion.
(S)	indicates a Service or 'New Army' battalion.
(Sp. Res.)	indicates a Special Reserve or Extra Reserve battalion.

Where local volunteers might serve on the front line – theatres of war and garrison commitments in 1915:

Western Front	in France and Belgium against the German army.
West Africa	in Cameroon against German colonial troops.
East Africa	in N. Rhodesia, Nyasaland, Zanzibar, Geman East Africa against German troops and German colonial troops.

Mesopotamia (Iraq)   against Turkish troops.
Gallipoli   with ANZACs and French against Turks/
                         Germans.
Salonika/Macedonia   with French against Austrians/Germans/Bulgars.
Egypt/Suez Canal Zone against Turkish invaders.
Imperial Garrisons and RN coaling stations throughout the Empire –
Africa, India, West Indies, Gibraltar, Hong Kong and many others. Regular
troops gradually replaced by local 'native' and TF troops.
At sea   U-Boat war

Chronological Roll of Honour for 1915

March 10th	William	GOODALL	Neuve Chapelle
March 12th	John	YATES	Neuve Chapelle
May 16th	Timothy	Taylor **	Festubert
July 6th	Alfred	BUSHNELL	Gallipoli
July 17th	Horace	DOWNES	Ypres
August 30th	Leonard	MORRIS	Ypres
(served as	Leonard	MALPASS)	
September 20th	Horace	FRANCE	Estaires
October 13th	William	LAWLEY	Loos
October 13th	George	BUSHNELL	Hohenzollern Rdbt
October 13th	Jack	PARTON	Hohenzollern Rdbt
October 13th	George	SARGENT	Hohenzollern Rdbt
October 18th	Harry	WILLETT	Loos
November 24th	Frank	HARVEY	Loos sector

** Indicates a name related to those that appear on the Elmore Green School
Old Boys War Memorial.

Alphabetical Roll of Honour for 1915

Alfred James BUSHNELL

Born on 25th November 1893 in Bloxwich and lived at 42, May Street, Leamore
and later at 73, Leamore Lane, Bloxwich. Son of a blast furnace labourer,
Alfred James (who passed away between 1911 and 1915), and Ellen Bushnell
(née Sanders) who was 40 years old in 1911. Alfred was one of nine children

– two brothers (George Bernard and Ernest) and six sisters (Clara Jane, Ellen, Lucy, Beatrice Annie, Florrance and Gladys May). Educated at Elmore Green School (from 22/05/05). Single. In 1911, he was a metal-caster, employed by Cope's of Leamore. **Volunteered** in **August 1914** in Darlaston. 3645, Private, Highland Light Infantry and later transferred to…**19008, Private, 1st (Regular) Battalion, the King's Own Scottish Borderers (87th Brigade, 29th Division)**. *Unit History* – [1/KOSB] landed in the Gallipoli theatre on Tuesday, 25th May 1915. Gallipoli, 25-26/4/15 Landings at Cape Helles; 26/4/15 Capture of Sedd el Bahr; 28/4/15 1st Battle of Krithia; 1-2/5/15 Eski Hissarlik; 6-8/5/15 2nd Battle of Krithia; 4/6/15 3rd Battle of Krithia; 28/6-2/7/15 Gully Ravine (Saghir Dere). **Killed in action (age 21) near Krithia, Gallipoli on Tuesday, 6th July 1915** by a sniper while fetching tea from a 'dixie'. **Commemorated** as 'known to be buried' on Special Memorial A. 55 of **Twelve Tree Copse Cemetery,** south-west of Krithia, **Gallipoli**, Turkey. **Entitled** to the 1914-15 Star (Medal Roll – D/70B, p.24), British War Medal and Victory Medal (Medal Roll – D/105B8, p.783). Commemorated on the Elmore Green School Roll of Honour (formerly displayed in T.P. Riley School library), on the Bloxwich Roll of Honour and on the Walsall Roll of Honour. [Note: Although the index to the roll of honour and newspapers of the time spell his surname as *'Bushnall'*, all official documents, including the War Diary and census forms, have the spelling as *'Bushnell'*.] **Family** – a younger brother, 9440, Private George Bernard Bushnell of 1/5th South Staffordshire, was killed in action attacking the Hohenzollern Redoubt near Loos on 13th October 1915. A cousin, 9523, Private Timothy Taylor of 1st South Staffordshire, was killed in action (age 24) during the Battle of Festubert on 16th May 1915; an uncle, Fred Sanders, served as a sergeant in the Royal Engineers.

George Bernard BUSHNELL

Born between April and June of 1897 in Bloxwich and lived initially at 42, May Street, Leamore and later at 73, Leamore Lane, Bloxwich. Son of a blast furnace labourer, Alfred James (who passed away between 1911 and 1915), and Ellen Bushnell (née Sanders). One of nine children – two brothers (Alfred James and Ernest) and six sisters (Clara Jane, Ellen, Lucy, Beatrice Annie, Florrance and Gladys May). Educated at Elmore Green School. Single. Miner employed at Allen's Rough Colliery, Essington. Volunteered in October 1914 in Walsall.

9440, Private, 1/5th (Territorial Force) Battalion, the South Staffordshire Regiment, (137th Brigade, 46th '1st North Midland' Division). *Unit History* – 28th June 1915 landed at Le Havre, France. From 4/4/15 at Neuve Eglise/ Wulverghem. 7/15 to 2/10/15 Hill 60, Ypres. 13-15/10/15 Battle of Loos (Hohenzollern Redoubt and Hulluch Quarries). Killed in action (age 18), having been mortally wounded, on Wednesday, 13th October 1915 attacking the Hohenzollern Redoubt (posted missing in action at the time). Commemorated on panels 73-76 of the Loos Memorial to the Missing, near Lens, France. Entitled to the 1914-15 Star (Medal Roll – F/2B1, p.61), British War Medal and Victory Medal (Medal Roll – F/101B4, p.362). Commemorated on the Elmore Green School Roll of Honour (formerly located in the T.P. Riley School library), on the Bloxwich roll of honour and on the Walsall Roll of Honour. Family – his elder brother, 19008, Private Alfred James Bushnell of the 1st King's Own Scottish Borderers, was killed at Gallipoli on 6th July 1915. A cousin, 9523, Private Timothy Taylor of 1st South Staffordshire who was killed (age 24) in action during the Battle of Festubert on 16th May 1915, and nephew of Fred Sanders, a sergeant in the Royal Engineers. Both men are commemorated on the Bloxwich Roll of Honour and on the Walsall Roll of Honour.

Horace DOWNES

Born on 13th June 1896 in Bloxwich and lived at 23, Reeves Street, Bloxwich. Son of Hannah (née Dudley) and stepson of a coal-miner, Richard Lowbridge, of the same address. Horace's father, James Downes who predeceased his son, had served as a soldier and was subsequently employed as a coal miner (his mother, Hannah, then married Richard Lowbridge in 1909, also a coal miner, and continued residing at the home address.) Horace was the oldest of six children – two brothers (Frank James Downes and Leonard Downes) and three sisters (Ruth, Annie and Lily Downes). Educated at Elmore Green School (from 31/08/08). Single. Horace served in the Territorial Force in Bloxwich ('D' Company, 1/5th Battalion) from 1911 and in the meantime was employed as a horse driver at the Wyrley Plant Colliery. Volunteered in August 1914 in Bloxwich to serve overseas after serving more than

3 years with the local Territorial Force. 7993, Private, 'D' Company, 1/5th (Territorial Force) Battalion, South Staffordshire Regiment, (137th Brigade, 46th '1st North Midland' Division). *Unit History* – 5/3/15 landed at Le Havre, France. From 4/4/15 at Neuve Eglise/Wulverghem. 25/6/15 – moved to billets at Ouderdom in the Ypres Salient and manned the trenches at Hill 60. Died (age 19) of wounds on Saturday, 17th July 1915 sustained eight days earlier on regular trench duty on 11th July at Hill 60 in the Ypres Salient. Buried in plot III. B. 11A of Lijssenthoek Military Cemetery, near Poperinge, Belgium. Entitled to the 1914-15 Star (Medal Roll – F/2/B2, p.110), British War Medal and Victory Medal (Medal Roll – F/101B2, p.184). Commemorated on the Elmore Green School Roll of Honour (formerly located in the T.P. Riley School library), on the Walsall and Bloxwich Rolls of Honour and on the Roll of Honour in All Saints Church, Bloxwich.

Horace FRANCE

Born between April and June of 1894 in Bloxwich and lived at 65, Harrison Street, Bloxwich. Son of George (a coal-miner) and Martha France (née Simmons) of 4, New Street, Bloxwich (and later of 612, Bloxwich Road, Leamore). Educated at Elmore Green School. Horace was a single man who made his living as a spur maker for J. & J. Wiggin Limited, hardware manufacturers of Old Hill Works, Woodall Street, Bloxwich. Volunteered in May 1915 in Birmingham. 930, Gunner, 14th Battery, Motor Machine Gun Service, Royal Field Artillery, (20th 'Light' Division). *Unit History* – landed in France on 20th July 1915; no major actions. Died (age 21) on Monday, 20th September 1915 as a result of a motor accident near Estaires while testing a motor-cycle. Buried in plot III. G. 5 of Estaires Communal Cemetery, Merville, Nord, France. Entitled to the 1914-15 Star (Medal Roll – MGC/1B, p.18), British War Medal and Victory Medal (Medal Roll – MMG/103B, p.45). Commemorated on the Elmore Green School Roll of Honour (formerly located in the T.P. Riley School library) as well as on the Walsall and Bloxwich Rolls of Honour.

(James) William GOODALL

Born in 1891 in Bloxwich, the son of a colliery rock-blower, Edward, and the late Annie Goodall (née Poynor) of 15, Leamore Lane, then of 20a, Portland Street. Later, the family moved to 14, The Green, Bloxwich and at the time of William's death, dwelt at 18, Clarendon Street, Bloxwich. His mother, Annie, had died in 1891 and his father had remarried, to Emma in 1903.

William was educated at Elmore Green School. Single. Miner employed at the Leacroft Colliery. Served for four years in the Special Reserve of the South Staffordshire Regiment. Volunteered in August 1914 in Bloxwich as a special reservist. 8931, Private, 2nd (Regular) Battalion, South Staffordshire Regiment, (6th Brigade, 2nd Division). *Unit History* – landed in France on 26th January 1915. January 1915, battalion in front line, reserve trenches and rest billets north and east of Béthune. 1/2/15 and 6/2/15 Affairs of Cuinchy. Givenchy sector 4th February – trench duty; trench raid on 20th February. 10/3/15 Givenchy – diversionary attack near Neuve Chapelle. Killed in action (age 24) on Wednesday, 10th March 1915 attacking the 'Duck's Bill' in a diversionary action at Givenchy during the Battle of Neuve Chapelle. Commemorated on panels 21 or 22 of Le Touret Memorial to the Missing, Richebourg-L'Avoué, near Festubert, France. Entitled to the 1914-15 Star (Medal Roll – F/2/B2, p.153), British War Medal and Victory Medal (Medal Roll – F/101B3, p.277 or 297). Commemorated on the Elmore Green School Roll of Honour (formerly located in the T.P. Riley School library), on the Bloxwich Roll of Honour and on the Roll of Honour in All Saints Church, Bloxwich. Family – two of William's brothers served in the Army and survived the war. His elder brother, Edward of 47, Cobden Street, Walsall served with the South Staffordshire in Salonika whilst his younger brother, Edgar, was invalided home from Gallipoli with frostbite serving in the 7th Battalion, South Staffordshire Regiment and was later killed near Béthune. In addition, at least five of William's cousins were killed during the Great War.

Frank HARVEY

Born on 7th January 1893 in Bloxwich and lived at 50, Blakenall Lane. Son of Eli and Zillah Harvey (née Glover) of the same address; (at one time his father, Eli, had owned a greengrocery shop situated at 92, Parker Street, Bloxwich but was later employed as an insurance agent. Eli had, for about 20 years, been a checkweighman at Cannock Lodge Colliery). Frank was one of seven children – three older brothers (Oscar E., Bernard G. and Thomas Ralph) and three sisters (Wallena, Florence M. and Edith Billiah). Educated at Elmore Green School (from 21/08/05) and Bloxwich Primitive Methodist Sunday School. Frank was interested in all sports, boxing in particular – he was an amateur boxer of note. Single. A blacksmith's striker employed at Allens Rough Colliery. Volunteered in Lichfield, initially for the Territorial Force and then the Special Reserve. 8632, Private, 4th (Special Reserve) Battalion, the South

Staffordshire, until mid-1915, then posted to…, 8632, Private, 2nd (Regular Army) Battalion, South Staffordshire Regiment, (6th Brigade, 2nd Division). *Unit History* – trained with 4/South Staffordshire on Jersey for twelve months and spent most of this time as an officer's servant; he was then drafted into 2/South Staffordshire – landed in France on 29th September 1915. 25/9/15-4/10/15 Battle of Loos. 13-19/10/15 Actions of the Hohenzollern Redoubt. 24/11/15 Cambrin sector, south of La Bassée Canal. Killed in action (age 22) on Wednesday, 24th November 1915 on regular trench duty in the Cambrin sector near Loos. Commemorated on panels 73-76 of the Loos Memorial to the Missing, Dud Corner, near Lens, France. Entitled to the 1914-15 Star Medal Roll – (F/2/B3, p.178), British War Medal and Victory Medal (Medal Roll – F/101B3, p.140). Commemorated on the Elmore Green School Roll of Honour (formerly located in the T.P. Riley School library) and on the Walsall and Bloxwich Rolls of Honour. Family – a brother, Alfred, also served. His father, Eli, worked in a munitions factory.

William Henry LAWLEY

Born on 13th May 1895 in St. Mary's, Wolverhampton. Son of a coal-miner, George Henry, and Martha Lawley of 3 Court, Dudley Road, Blakenall and later at 33, West Street, Leamore. One of four children – two brothers (Fred and George) and one sister (Doris). Educated in Leamore and at Elmore Green School (from 20/08/06). Single. Employed by the General Post Office as a messenger; however, he was employed at the Huntington Colliery at the time of his enlistment in the Army. William was also associated with the Blakenall Congregational Sunday School. **Volunteered** in **1914** in Walsall. **20386, Private, 2 n d (Regular Army) Battalion, the Grenadier Guards, (1st Guards Brigade, Guards Division)**. *Unit History* – [4th Guards Brigade, 2nd Division] Landed in France on 2nd August 1915. [From 19th August 1915, 2/Grenadier Guards was transferred to the 1st Guards Brigade of the newly-created Guards Division] 26/9-8/10/15 Battle of Loos. **Died (age 20) in No.4 General Hospital, Versailles, on Wednesday, 13th October 1915 of wounds sustained five days earlier** during the Battle of Loos. **Buried** in plot 5. 28 of **Les Gonards Cemetery, Versailles**, near Paris, France. **Entitled** to the 1914-15 Star (Medal Roll – GG/1B, p.135), British War Medal and Victory Medal (Medal Roll – GG/103B9, p.747). Commemorated on the Elmore Green School Roll of Honour (formerly located in the T.P. Riley School library) and on the Walsall and Bloxwich Rolls of Honour.

Leonard MORRIS (served as Leonard MALPASS)

Born in 1894 or 1895 in Great Wyrley, son of Lydia Morris. One of six children (at least two brothers – John, a miner, and Thomas; at least one sister, Emily). In 1914 he resided with his married sister, Emily Malpass, at Pelsall Lane, Little Bloxwich. Single. Employed as a miner at Harrison's Colliery, Wyrley Grove, Pelsall. **Volunteered** in **1914** in Bloxwich, though probably served pre-war in the local TF. **7822, Private, 'D' Company, 1/5th (Territorial Force) Battalion, South Staffordshire Regiment, (137th Brigade, 46th '1st North Midland' Division)**. Unit History: Landed in France on 5/3/15 at Le Havre. From 4/4/15 to 7/15 at Neuve Eglise/Wulverghem. From 7/15 at Hill 60, Ypres. **Died (age 20 or 21) in 13th General Hospital at Boulogne, France on Monday, 30th August 1915 from shrapnel wounds** to his abdomen received nineteen days earlier on 11th July 1915, while in the trenches between St. Eloi and Hill 60, south of Ypres. **Buried** in Grave VIII.B.75 of **Boulogne Eastern Cemetery**, Pas de Calais, France. **Entitled** to the 1914-15 Star (Medal Roll, F/2B4, p.273), British War Medal and Victory Medal (Medal Roll F/101B2, p.170). Commemorated on the Walsall and Bloxwich rolls of honour and the roll of honour in All Saints Church, Bloxwich.

John 'Jack' E.W. PARTON

Born in 1897 or 1898 in Walsall and lived first at 50, Green Lane, Bloxwich and later at 33, Cope Street, Leamore. Son of a bridle-bit filer, Edwin Alfred, and Clara Parton (née Webb) of the same addresses. One of seven children of whom five were living at home in 1911 – at least four brothers (Stephen, Thomas Jonah, Edward [born 02/02/93; EGS from 28/08/05] and Frank [born 04/05/96; EGS from 01/08/07]). Educated at Elmore Green School. Single. Employed at the Talbot Stead Tube Works. **Volunteered** in **September 1914** in Walsall. **9441, Private, 'A' Company, 1/5th (Territorial Force) Battalion, South Staffordshire Regiment, (137th Brigade, 46th '1st North Midland' Division). Killed in action (age 18), mortally wounded by a bomb (grenade) on Wednesday, 13th October 1915** while attacking the Hohenzollern Redoubt during the Battle of Loos. **Commemorated** on panels 73-76 of the

Loos Memorial to the Missing, Dud Corner, near Lens, France. **Entitled** to the 1914-15 Star (Medal Roll – F/2B4, p.294), British War Medal and Victory Medal (Medal Roll – F/101B4, 363B).Commemorated on the Elmore Green School Roll of Honour (formerly located in the T.P. Riley School library) and on the Bloxwich Roll of Honour. **Family** – 30579, Private (Jonah) Thomas of 8th (Service) Battalion, the South Staffordshire Regiment was killed in action on 23rd April 1917 near Roeux during the Second Battle of the Scarpe. Stephen served as 59712, Corporal Stephen Parton in the Royal Welsh Fusiliers, surviving the war; Edward served as 43618, Private Edward Parton, the Lincolnshire Regiment and was discharged sick and awarded the Silver War Badge in December 1918. Frank served as 11637, Private Frank Parton, the Machine Gun Corps and survived the war.

George SARGENT

Born in 1892 or 1893 in Bloxwich, the son of William and Alice Sargent of 14, Tudor Place, Bloxwich and later of 60, Parker Street, Bloxwich. One of five children in 1911, George had at least two brothers, Harry and William, as well as two sisters, Susan and Alice. He was educated at Elmore Green School. Single. George, like his father, was employed as a miner at the Holly Bank Colliery, Essington prior to enlistment. He served eight years in the Bloxwich, 'D' Company, of the 1/5 South Staffordshire Territorials. **Volunteered** from the local Territorial Force in **August 1914** in Bloxwich. **6745, Private, 'D' Company, 1/5th (Territorial Force) Battalion, South Staffordshire Regiment, (137th Brigade, 46th 'North Midland' Division).** *Unit History* – 5th March 1915 landed at Le Havre, France. From 4/4/15 at Neuve Eglise/Wulverghem. 7/15 to 2/10/15 Hill 60, Ypres. 13-19/10/15 Battle of Loos (Hohenzollern Redoubt and Hulluch Quarries). **Killed in action (age 23) on Wednesday, 13th October 1915** attacking the Hohenzollern Redoubt during the Battle of Loos. **Commemorated** on panels 73-76 of the **Loos Memorial to the Missing**, Dud Corner, near Lens, France. **Entitled** to the 1914-15 Star (Medal Roll – F/2B4, p.342), British War Medal and Victory Medal (Medal Roll – F/ 101B, p.107). Commemorated on the Elmore Green School Roll of Honour (formerly located in the T.P. Riley School library), on the Walsall and Bloxwich Rolls of Honour and also on the Roll of Honour in All Saints Church, Bloxwich. **Family** – a brother, Harry Sargent served in the army.

Timothy TAYLOR⋆⋆ [not Elmore Green Memorial]

Born in 1890 or 1891 to Mrs. Mary Ann Titley, of 53, Alfred St., Bloxwich. Single. Employed as a miner at Holly Bank Colliery, just north of Bloxwich. **Volunteered** for the army pre-war, **February or March 1914**, possibly for the Special Reserve. Posted to 1/South Staffordshire as a replacement. **9523, Private, 1st Battalion, the South Staffordshire Regiment, (22nd Brigade, 7th Division).** Unit History: landed in France on 17th December 1914; Ypres area, 18/12/14 Attack on Well Farm, Rouges Bancs. 10-13/3/15 Battle of Neuve Chapelle. 9/5/15 Battle of Aubers (Fromelles). 15-19/5/15 Battle of Festubert. **Killed in action (age 24) on Tuesday, 16th May 1915** when shot in the head near La Ferme Cour d'Avoine during the Battle of Festubert. **Commemorated** on Panel 21 or 22 of **Le Touret Memorial to the Missing**, **Richebourg-L'Avoué**, near Festubert, Pas de Calais, France. **Entitled** to the 1914-15 Star (Medal Roll – F/2B.5, p. 382), the British War Medal and the Victory Medal (Medal Roll – F/101 B4, p.381). *'Walsall Observer'* report 26/6/15. **Family** – cousins 19008, Private Alf Bushnell of 1/KOSB and 9440, Private George Bushnell of 1/5 South Staffordshire were both also killed during 1915; an uncle, 8990, Sergeant John (Fred?) Sanders of Short Heath, was killed on 27/04/15 near Wulverghem, serving with 1/5 South Staffordshire.

John Henry 'Harry' WILLETT

Born in 1891 or 1892 in Walsall. Son of John Henry (a retired police sergeant; night-watchman at a colliery) and Amy Jane Willett (née Taylor) of 637, Bloxwich Road, Blakenall Heath and later of 45, Blakenall Lane, Leamore. Educated at Elmore Green School. One of five children in 1911 (two brothers at home in 1911 – Arthur Walter and William George; one sister, Lilian May – one child left home]. Single. Employed as an assistant in a Gentlemen's outfitter in Wolverhampton. **Volunteered** in **August 1914** in Stafford. **19038, Lance-Corporal, 3rd Battalion, the Grenadier Guards, (2nd Guards Brigade, Guards Division)**. *Unit History* – 27th July 1915, Harry landed at Le Havre, France. [Guards Division] 26/9-8/10/15 Battle of Loos. **Died (age 23) in hospital on Monday, 18th October 1915**

of wounds sustained ten days earlier while attacking the Hohenzollern Redoubt during the Battle of Loos on 8th October. **Buried** in plot IV. F. 44 of **Béthune Town Cemetery**, France. **Entitled** to the 1914-15 Star (Medal Roll – GG/1B, p.239), British War Medal and Victory Medal (Medal Roll – GG/103B15, p.1373). Commemorated on the Elmore Green School Roll of Honour (formerly located in the T.P. Riley School library) and on the Walsall and Bloxwich Rolls of Honour.

John YATES

John was born in Pelsall on Thursday 10th November 1892, the son of James and Jane (née Johnson) Yates of High Street, Pelsall and later of 28, Providence Lane, Bloxwich, his father being employed as a coal miner. John was educated at Leamore Boys School and then Elmore Green School (from 21/08/05). Single. A miner like his father, John **volunteered** for army service in **August 1914** in Walsall and was drafted on active service to France on Monday, 11th January 1915. At least 4 siblings. At least three brothers – James, George and Harry – and one sister, May. **Volunteered** in **August or September 1914** in Walsall. **12689, Private, 2nd (Regular) Battalion, the South Staffordshire Regiment, (6th Brigade, 2nd Division).** Unit History: Landed at Le Havre, France on 11th January 1915. Joined 2/South Staffordshire with a draft of replacements. January 1915, alternated between the front line, reserve trenches and rest billets north and east of Béthune. 4/2/15 Givenchy sector. 20/2/15 Trench raid. 10-13/3/15 Battle of Neuve Chapelle – diversionary attack at Givenchy. **Died (age 22) on Friday, 12th March 1915 of wounds sustained two days earlier** in a holding attack against the Duck's Bill at Givenchy (two miles west of La Bassée). **Buried** in plot IV.A.65 of **Béthune Town Cemetery**, France. **Entitled** to the 1914-15 Star (Medal Roll – F/2/B6, p.449), the British War Medal and the Victory Medal (Medal Roll – F/101B6, p.617). Commemorated on the Elmore Green School Roll of Honour (formerly located in the T.P. Riley School library and now re-located in Elmore Green School). Bloxwich Roll of Honour and on an addendum panel at Pelsall War Memorial.

Chapter Eleven

1916:

'Into the Cauldron of the Somme…'

December 1915
Allied Plans for Armageddon

Winter 1916
Winter warfare in the trenches

February
Together until war separates

March
Parker Street and May Street casualties

April
Parker Street again

May
A 'rookie' and a Tunneller

June
Illness then the Somme barrage

June/July
Plans on the Somme and a Military Medal

July
First Day Disaster on the Somme

August
Devil's Wood

September
The Guards at Morval

November
Death of an 'Old Contemptible.'

December 1915

Allied Plans for Armageddon

In December 1916 the Allied leaders met at Chantilly, near Paris, to discuss the military prospects for the coming year's campaigning. As a consequence of his apparent costly errors during the Battle of Loos, Sir John French had been replaced by Sir Douglas Haig as commander of the BEF. If a major British offensive were to develop, Haig favoured the area of Belgian Flanders around Ypres. However, Haig had been instructed by Lord Kitchener to offer full co-operation to 'Papa' Joffre and the French in order to maintain Allied unity, though technically Haig's command was independent of French control. Joffre favoured a two-stage campaign for 1916 – an 'opener' on the Somme during the spring to soften German resistance, after which he would then be prepared for Haig to execute his plans for Flanders later in the summer. For several reasons, not least

Thiepval Memorial

High on the old Somme battlefield of the Thiepval Ridge, Thiepval Memorial to the Missing bears on its many faces the names of more than 73,000 soldiers whose bodies were either never found for burial or were found and buried but never identified. It is a personal opinion but the Menin Gate Memorial to the Missing at Ypres bears one of the most fitting inscriptions to the 'missing' of any side, in any conflict: "Here are recorded names of officers and men who fell [in Ypres Salient] but to whom the fortune of war denied the known and honoured burial given to their comrades in death."

that of potentially damaging casualty figures from two battles rather than one, in mid-February Haig and Joffre agreed on a single joint offensive astride the River Somme in early July. However, in late February and far from the Somme the German army launched a major offensive against the iconic French fortress town of Verdun[92] and military plans for the summer had to be fundamentally re-organised.

---

92 Verdun was slightly nearer to Switzerland than to the Somme. Its bloody defence was to become an article of faith to the French – the cost in lives would be unimaginable.

Winter
Trench warfare

Meanwhile, 'Tommy' in the trenches knew nothing of plans for great offensives. His world was restricted to guarding the existing front-line, moving back to reserve lines when ordered and making the most of rare days of rest[93] back in billets. In winter, trench duty was generally harsh – the weather was frequently cold and wet, while duty was one continuous round of discomfort brought on by poor rations, rats and body lice in often-flooded dugouts and trenches where the senses were assailed by an all-pervading stink of sewage, unwashed human bodies and clothing, rotting corpses and gas-polluted earth. Winter coughs and colds seemed to be a normal state of affairs, occasionally developing into bronchitis or pneumonia; many soldiers suffered from 'trench foot', a condition brought on by feet and lower limbs that were constantly soaking wet and freezing cold – extreme cases, somewhat similar to the effects of frostbite, might result in amputation. And then there was the 'daily hate'. Although no major battles tended to be fought during the worst of the winter months, most days were marked by a few desultory guns or mortars exchanging a number of shells across No Man's Land, smashing in a few trenches and ending a few young lives. On such days, this reassuring message was passed up the line to Army Staffs:

"All quiet on the Western Front."

Or, on the other side of the wire:

"Im Westen nichts Neues."

Young Fritz and Tommy in their trench-bound existence might have disagreed!

Today, it is difficult for us to imagine a tour of duty[94] in the trenches in 1916. The typical British trench system then consisted of three main lines of trenches – firing line, close support and reserve, all running vaguely parallel to the German front line. Each main line was connected to the others by narrow communication trenches that were 'zig-zagged' to prevent being enfiladed by fire[95] from the enemy trenches. The main trenches themselves were divided into

---

93 'Rest' usually meant being used as available labour to deliver supplies to the front line or to re-build and re-wire damaged trenches.

94 A 'tour of duty' in the front-line trenches would normally last four days but might last from two to twenty or so days, depending on circumstances such as weather and enemy action.

95 That is, firing down the length of a trench and thus causing substantial casualties.

short bays known as traverses, each separated from the next by two reversed ninety-degree corners in order to reduce the effects upon infantrymen of shell blast. The firing line trench would be dug eight or so feet deep[96] with a notch or fire-step cut into the front edge while the top of the trench, known as the parapet, was reinforced by sandbags. A man might obtain a view towards the enemy lines by using a rudimentary periscope but otherwise he might spend months fighting, even dying, without actually seeing a German soldier. The rear edge of the trench, known as the parados, was also reinforced with sandbags while the bottom of the trench (known as the sump) was usually covered by a wooden duckboard walkway to reduce the strength-sapping effects of mud and water, though nature often won this particular battle.

Going 'up the line' to the fire-trench involved a wearying, heavily-laden approach march that would bring the relieving platoon, company or battalion to the narrow communication trench that was often thick with mud, deep in water or frozen solid. Men of the unit being relieved would be struggling in the opposite direction, frequently passing ribald comments towards their relief, safe in the knowledge that they themselves would be 'out of it' for a few short days. If the relieving unit was taking over a sector with which its men were familiar, they would already know the location of the best dugouts or 'funk holes', where the latrines were, which sections of trench were worst for sniper fire and so on. Twice a day, at first light and at dusk, the men would be 'stood to' on the firing step facing the enemy, as these were the most likely times for an attack to come in. Usually all was quiet so most of the men were stood down for breakfast, a meal that might consist of fried bacon, bread and strong sweet tea if they were lucky but more often breakfast was cold, apart from the mandatory strong, sweet brew known as 'gunfire'. The unlucky lads did a stint on 'sentry-go' where they were expected to be alert at all times – falling asleep on guard was, for obvious reasons, considered a very serious offence. The sentries would be relieved but most men would settle down to occupy long hours of boredom, reading letters and writing letters. Letters usually referred to how much the reluctant soldier was missing his family:

> *"This…is always the most touching part of my letters, when I mention you and my children. I can't help it…but a lump seems to come up into my throat which oft times is very hard to swallow and very often a tear drops on my paper as I am writing."* [Private Jim Elwell, 7/Suffolk, 1917.]

---

96 This was the norm except where the water table was high causing diggings to rapidly flood; in such locations, especially much of the Ypres Salient, digging would be shallow and the parapet built up by means of sandbags, timber and earth.

Time was also spent 'chatting' (hunting and killing body lice) or, during the winter months, more likely trying to sleep while keeping warm and dry.

> *"I should like to tell you what it is like in the firing line but can't, but I can tell you this, there's plenty of rats and plenty of chats, as we call them; you don't have to be long in the trenches before you get crummy[97] – we can't help it if we have to find room for them – but then all the while we were in (the line) we didn't get a wash, a shave or nothing else."*
>
> *"…And sleep, you have to get that when you can – when I get the chance, shots nor shells don't worry me (as) I am soon in Dreamland. Well, in fact, a soldier can sleep anywhere or anyhow, on sandbags, in dugouts or what-not – it matters not to Tommy Atkins, he's very glad to get the opportunity."* [Private Jim Elwell, 7/Suffolk, 1917.]

Keeping warm in open trenches in winter was nigh on impossible; lucky men might wear goat-fleece jerkins over their uniform and might have the benefit of woollen gloves or mittens and maybe a Balaclava-style helmet to help keep out the frost. Combatting the rain was even more difficult. All a soldier could do was to huddle into a small recess or 'funk hole' in the trench wall, pull his oilskin cape up to his neck and wait for the torrent to cease. When it did, the bottom of the trench would probably be awash with water and liquid mud that had nowhere to go but to seep into the men's boots to soak already cold feet; constant exposure to this treatment led to the condition known as 'trench foot'. Trench foot was so common that each platoon officer was later given with the task of regularly inspecting his men's feet and ensuring that they were treated with evil-smelling but quite effective whale oil; in addition, every man was expected to carry a change of socks, yet these were often as wet as those the man was already wearing. Another consequence of these conditions were colds, bronchitis and pneumonia, well known to the trench soldier as was an influenza-like infection known as 'trench fever'.

During the day sustenance was supposed to be brought up to the front line, hot rations (if the men were fortunate) in large containers known as 'dixies', while dry rations were delivered, often mixed together into an unrecognisable mess, in sacks. The perennial brew of 'gunfire', strong and sweet, was the Tommy's mainstay – lack of tea would lead to near-rebellious thoughts! Yet if the food was adequate and men were with their mates, their 'grousing' was not too serious – it was often said that if a soldier grumbled then there wasn't too much wrong with his morale!

---

97 'Crummy' was another term for 'lousy' or 'chatty.'

February

Our story now turns to the contrasting fortunes of a pair of brothers, eighteen year-old **John Cope** and twenty-one year-old **Ernest Cope**. Both lads were born in Hednesford where their father Isaac was a miner at one of the pits in the Cannock coalfield. While John was still of school age, the family moved to Bloxwich, residing first in Bell Lane and later at 33, The Flats; John was enrolled at Elmore Green school at the end of August 1909. By 1914 both brothers were employed at Huntington Colliery, also in the Cannock coalfield, and in August 1915 they decided to enlist together in one of the New Army battalions of the South Staffordshire Regiment – the lads' regimental numbers were consecutive. As miners, their skills were most useful in 9/South Staffordshire as it was a pioneer battalion with responsibilities similar to those of the Royal Engineers, being employed on improvements to trenches and on many other laborious but vital tasks, very often in the front line and within sight of the enemy. The lads went through basic training together and most likely joined their battalion in France just after New Year 1916, John being assigned to 'C' Company and thus separated from Ernest. From 1st February, 9/South Staffordshire was at Rue Marle, in the Armentières sector, a dozen miles south of Ypres. 'C' Company worked on various tasks in Queer Street Trench, 'White City', The Brewery (where the orchard was later converted into a military cemetery) and Moat Farm Avenue, not far from Bois Grenier. A comrade of John's, Lance Corporal Gough of Five Ways, Walsall, wrote to the Cope family with a detailed account of what happened to their youngest son. He explained that on Monday, 21st February 1916, John's company had changed locations in the Armentières sector. The battalion war diary states,

> *"Left Vieux Berquin at 8:30 this morning. Arrived La Belle Hôtesse 12:50 p.m. 21st February 1916 – fine day but very cold wind."*

Soon after arriving at La Belle Hôtesse, John was very badly wounded in the legs by a shrapnel burst and he was quickly removed to hospital near Bailleul where John Cope was treated in one of Nos. 2, 3, 8 or 53 (North Midland) Casualty Clearing Stations. However, the injury to his right leg was so severe that it necessitated amputation and John was so weakened by his wounds that he did not recover from the operation and passed away at 8:30 p.m. on Wednesday, **23rd February**. **Private John Cope** was buried nearby in Bailleul Communal Cemetery Extension. His brother Ernest, who was in another part of the line when John was wounded, survived the war in the same battalion but a much younger brother, 5057631, **Private Isaac Cope**, 5/Devonshire was killed in Germany during the Second World War.

March

Richard Henry and Agnes **Stych**, originally of Back Lane, Short Heath, moved to Parker Street, Bloxwich in the early years of the 20th Century. Of the couple's seven sons, at least four served in the army during the Great War, two of them never to return and two to be hospitalised in France. The two younger lads, **Albert** and **George**, signed up before the outbreak of war, Albert with the local Territorials on 22nd April 1913 and George with the regulars of 2/South Staffordshire in June 1914. Later in the summer the second oldest lad, **Joseph**, also volunteered for the Territorials and landed in France with young Albert at the beginning of March 1915. George was not sent to France until 25th May 1915, following the Battle of Festubert, probably on account of his age – he was not eighteen until 1915. Circumstances for the oldest brother, **Samuel**, were markedly different from his younger siblings. Sam was married and already had three children; he had moved to Pontefract in Yorkshire to obtain pit-work – like all the Stych males, Sam was a miner. The decision to volunteer was a difficult one, with financial support for his family being of prime concern; finally, Sam stepped over the threshold of the Pontefract recruiting office and volunteered for one of Kitchener's 'New Army' battalions, 17th West Yorkshire Regiment, known as the '2nd Leeds Pals', a Bantam[98] battalion. It was a decision his family would regret.

Following a now shortened basic training, 17/West Yorkshire crossed the Channel to Le Havre on 1st February 1916. Three weeks later, the battalion was attached to 19th 'Western' Division where 9/Welsh, 9/Royal Welch Fusiliers and 6/Wiltshire gave the Bantam companies training in trench life, fighting and survival. On 27th February the battalion returned to 35th Division and on 7th March, the division relieved its mentors, 19th 'Western', in the front line north-east of Festubert. 17/West Yorkshire took on its first trench duty in La Quinque Rue-Plum Street sector, in the left sub-sector known as Sign Post Lane – Erith Post. The relief was completed by 7:30 p.m. but the 'new boys' sent out no immediate patrols on account of heavy snow falls. The weather proved to be a mix of snowy and bitterly cold, frosty days. There were no attacks or trench raids but enemy snipers actively welcomed the newcomers and two-way rifle-grenade, mortar and artillery fire kept the Bantams on their mettle. This 'daily hate' accounted for the life of **Sam Stych** just two days into his first tour of trench duty. Twenty-six year-old Sam was killed on **9th March** and was buried in Rue-du-Bacquerot No.1 Military Cemetery at Laventie. The second of the 'Parker Street Boys' had 'gone west'.

---

98   In the early months of the war the official minimum height was five feet three inches but many taller men were not physically fit while many smaller men were frustrated by being refused. Alfred Bigland MP for Birkenhead, financed the first 'Bantam' battalion and soon the idea spread and was accepted. The first such battalion was 15/Cheshire. 17/WYR was not far behind.

Just three days after the death of Sam Stych, another soldier related to one of the Elmore Green lads was killed in a tragic accident. In 1903, **Thomas Dunn**, born in Leamore and a skilled bricklayer in the employ of Mr. Samuel Wootton of Bell Lane, had married a widow, Annie Haywood of May Street and had taken on the welfare of three boys aged eleven, nine and six years. The youngest of these, **Ernest Haywood** of 8/South Staffordshire, will play a part in the story of Elmore Green lads in the battles of Arras in 1917. In September 1914, Thomas Dunn gave up his job in Bell Lane and volunteered in Walsall, enlisting in the Royal Engineers. After six months of specialist training, Tom landed in France in May 1915 to join his new mates in 89th Field Company, R.E., that was part of 14th 'Light' Division. On **12th March** 1916 Sapper Dunn was working on the construction of a new gun-line in the Arras sector when he fell victim to the effects of late winter weather. His section Captain wrote in a sympathetic letter to the bereaved widow, Annie:

> *"He lost his life about 3 p.m. while doing some mining work in preparation for a gun emplacement. I was with him at the time and we were discussing the strength of the work when, without warning, the bank collapsed, bringing down the roof and burying us. Sapper Dunn was instantly killed. He was a good fellow."*

Thomas Dunn's unit had fought at Ypres at the end of July when the Germans employed 'liquid fire' for the first time and thus the flamethrower[99] was born. Apparently, 89th Field Company was attached to another unit for the preparations for the Battle of Loos in September and October 1915. The month after Loos, Tom was able to secure a week's home leave and so was able to visit his family for what proved to be the final time. One of Tom's colleagues, Corporal Shirley, wrote to Annie that,

> *"(Tom was)…liked by all who knew him and many of us feel his loss almost as a brother."*

Sapper **Thomas Dunn** was buried to the west of Arras in Dainville Communal Cemetery. His brother, **Elijah Dunn** who was employed as a miner in Yorkshire, enlisted in one of the Tunnelling Company of the Royal Engineers and served in France.

---

99   The German name for the flamethrower was *'flammenwerfer'*.

April

Bertie Gill was born in Short Heath in 1893 but by 1901 his parents, Jonah and Lydia Gill, had moved the family to Parker Street, Bloxwich and thus young Bertie went to Elmore Green School. Bertie followed his father into pit-work, finding employment at Holly Bank Colliery until his fateful decision to volunteer for the Royal Field Artillery on 11th January 1915. If Bertie was seeking a little colour in his life as a contrast to the daily blackening of coal dust he most definitely was to find it. Posted to 94th Battery of 18th Brigade RFA, Bertie found his unit briefly serving in Ireland for a fortnight prior to being attached to the 3rd 'Lahore' Indian Division in France where he arrived on 21st June 1915. The division had been in France since 26th September 1914, longer than all the British Territorial and New Army divisions and, despite the harsh weather, had fought at La Bassée, Givenchy, Neuve Chapelle, 2nd Ypres, Aubers Ridge and Festubert. Five months after Gunner Gill joined his battery in the 'Lahore' Division, it was decided to move the division to Mesopotamia (now Iraq) as it was proving impossible to replace their casualty losses in Europe.

The artillery and **Bertie Gill** remained in France. On 20th March 1916, the entire 'Lahore' Division artillery was temporarily attached to the newly-arrived 3rd Canadian Division, thus Gunner Gill had to accustom his ear to a third accent since the previous June. 18th Brigade RFA war diary says the gunners took over the Rue Flamande sector, Poperinghe, from the British 24th Division on 18th March and that they were still in that same sector of the Ypres Salient in early April. The war diary offers lucid detail:

> "*Eighty-five enemy shells of mixed calibre were fired at the trench system of the Right Group, distributed along the front line trenches. At 4:30 p.m. the enemy started shelling between…[trench co-ordinates here given]…and the road passing it. Firing continued until 5:15 p.m., in which time from 120 to 150 gas shells were fired. The battery shooting at us has been located as a 4.2" Howitzer battery…At 5 p.m. the 94th Battery was shelled by 4.2" Howitzers – a direct hit was recorded on one funk-pit [a large shelter for several men] and five men[100], including the sergeant-major and one sergeant were killed and seven wounded. The damage was done by a delay-action fuze, the shell penetrating the earthworks and bursting inside. Our batteries fired 81 rounds – 13 in retaliation to enemy activity, 19 at an earthwork reported to*

---

100   The other five men of 94th Battery, 18th Brigade who were killed in the shell blast were 14392 BSM E.J. Moore; 35638 Sgt. A. Clancy; 35728 Gnr. A. Brian; 76085 Gnr. W. Tarburn and 56469 Gnr. E. Myhill. All are buried in Railway Dugouts Burial Ground near Ypres.

be a strongpoint, the rest in dispersing enemy working parties and in registration (of gun ranges)…"

94th Battery RFA war diary reported for the day Bert Gill was wounded:

"10 April 1916 - an enemy aeroplane flew over Poperinghe at about 8 a.m. and was shelled and driven away. During the day between 50 and 60 4.2-inch howitzer dropped in [trench map reference…] Sq I.20.d and about 100 mixed calibre near the 59th Battery position and the ramparts of Ypres."

Private Gill, one of those wounded in the 'funk-pit', was buried by the explosion and suffered severe injuries; when extricated, he was unconscious. Nevertheless, he was treated in a local Casualty Clearing Station and then evacuated to one of 23rd, 24th, 26th General Hospitals and No.6 B.C.R.S. at Etaples - a major hospital base. His officer wrote to Bertie's parents that their son's wounds were:

"…severe but not considered dangerous."

However, despite prompt treatment following his rescue, twenty-two year-old **Bert Gill** never regained consciousness. He died seventeen days later on **27th April** and was buried close by in the huge Etaples Military Cemetery near the Channel coast. A third 'Parker Street Boy' would not return home.

May

Whereas Bertie Gill had served for over a year with a variety of nationalities in the gun line, our next 'memorial lad' was killed on his very first day in the firing line with 2/South Staffordshire. Eighteen year-old **Tom Bricknall** of Blakenall Lane was called up with his age group as one of the first lads enlisted under the new Military Service Act, what we would now call conscription, in February 1916. Although born into a coal-mining family, when Tom left Elmore Green School he was employed by J. &. J. Wiggin as a mopper and bobber at the Old Hall Works in Bloxwich. Having completed his basic infantry training, in late April Tom was sent across the Channel with a draft of mixed-age replacements for the distinguished 2/South Staffordshire whose 2nd Division had been transferred from the I Corps to the IV Corps and so had moved from La Bassée to south of Loos, taking over the Angres-Calonne-Souchez sector from the French 18th Division. From 23rd March to 19th April, 2nd Division was out of the line, resting, training in bombing techniques and providing working parties. When Tom Bricknall joined his unit in the front line on 14th May, 2/ South Staffordshire occupied Calonne South trench sector. That same day, a small, ultimately chaotic bombing raid on enemy trenches was aborted, possibly as a result of mistaking German whistles for British 'recall' whistles. The raid cost the life of a Sergeant[101] and, as a consequence of the raid, the Germans retaliated by bombarding the British lines with rifle grenades. It was probably during this barrage on **15th May** that **Private Tom Bricknall** lost his life at just eighteen years of age; 2/South Staffordshire battalion war diary (quoted below) suggests that it was his draft's first full day in the front line:

> "*14 May 1916 - Final preparations were made for the raid on the German trenches which had been fixed for this day. The raid was carried out at 12 midnight.*
>
> *A draft of 77 other ranks joined the battalion this day. About half these men had seen active service before in France or Gallipoli.*
>
> *15 May 1916 - There was considerable shelling of our lines probably in retaliation for the raid and we had several casualties from rifle grenades.*"

Killed in action, **Thomas Bricknall** was buried in Loos British Cemetery, just three plots away from Sergeant Ashlee who was killed on the same day.

The summer of 1916 would prove catastrophic for the wider Goodall family. **Edgar Goodall** of Leamore Lane had been 'out' since 18th December 1914, initially with the South Staffordshire Regiment. In early spring 1915 Edgar, a coal-miner, transferred to one of the new Tunnelling Companies (173rd) that were being established by the Royal Engineers in order to tunnel under the enemy front line, fill the resultant mine with explosives and detonate it to devastating effect. From mid-February 1915, miners were recruited directly into such companies, while miners already serving in the army were encouraged to transfer – the daily pay of between 2/2d and 6 shillings[102] (compared with the infantryman's one shilling) helped many miners to make their decision. 170th to 178th Companies were the first to be raised. While army discipline for the Tunnellers was very lax, life underground was tough. Excavating (known as 'clay-kicking') the tunnels was hot, hard work; worse, enemy miners occasionally exploded small, destructive charges, camouflets, close to the British workings or even broke into the tunnels and fought vicious, hand-to-hand battles with the British miners. **Edgar Goodall** was one of the first to join

---

101 9314, Sergeant T.W. Ashlee of Maidstone, Kent.

102 11 New Pence and 30 New Pence per day – worth much, much more in those days.

173rd Tunnelling Company. On its formation, the 173rd moved into the area north-east of Fauquissart, sinking its first mines on 3rd March 1915. Employed under the dual command of the I Corps and the Indian Corps on operations in preparation for attack at Aubers Ridge (9th May 1915), 173rd Tunnelling Company R.E. planted two 2000-pound mines under the German front lines in the northern sector of the proposed battlefield. To do this they drove two galleries, seventy yards apart, with tunnels 285 and 330 feet long respectively. Four other galleries, driven towards the enemy from the sector of 7th Division, became flooded and were abandoned. After Aubers Ridge, 173rd's sector extended to Red Lamp and Rue du Bois areas soon afterwards. Throughout the summer of 1915, the company was billeted at Noeux-les-Mines and employed under the command of 2nd Division on operations near Cuinchy. The following January, the tunnellers of 173rd moved to the Hulluch-Loos area where they remained throughout the spring and early summer, mining under the German positions at Hill 70. In May, Edgar's company was joined by the newly-formed 258th Tunnelling Company to share billets at Noeux-les-Mines and to receive front line experience. It is believed that twenty-nine year-old **Edgar Goodall** was killed when the Germans exploded a camouflet opposite Mine 23 killing several tunnellers[103] and their infantry guards on Wednesday, **24th May**. As with so many deaths underground, precious few details are known of Sapper Goodall's death but the nature of the work suggests that it was not a pleasant one. Unusually for a tunneller, Edgar's body was recovered from the site and buried nearby in Noeux-les-Mines Communal Cemetery. Back home in Bloxwich, Edgar left a widow, Mary Jane, and three young children, Florence May, Edgar and France. The latter never met his father. There were members of the Goodall clan other than Edgar then on the Western Front, including **John Goodall** (2/South Staffordshire), **Sam Goodall** (13/Northumberland Fusiliers), **David Goodall** (1/South Staffordshire) and **Fred Goodall** (also with one of the South Staffordshire battalions). None would provide a much happier ending to their army story.

June

The memorial story now takes us back to the Groves family. John and Annie Groves of Bell Lane had already lost their eldest son, John William Groves, in November 1914, whose uncle by marriage, William 'Coxy' Lavender, had also died just before his nephew. The honourable reputation of both soldiers being among the '*Old Contemptibles*' was scant consolation for a grieving family. In early summer of 1916 their plight worsened when news of eighteen

---

103 The only other tunneller casualty from 173rd Company traced is 86657, 2/Cpl James Gallagher from Yorkshire, who died from his wounds.

year-old son **George Groves**'s serious illness reached Bloxwich. Apparently enlisting underage, George had arrived in Flanders with 'D' Company of the local Territorials in March 1915; he had fought at the notorious Hill 60 near Ypres during 1915 and near Loos. From 19th March, 1/5 South Staffordshire moved south to Neuville St. Vaast/Ecoivres, just to the north of Arras, and during May and June of 1916, the battalion occupied the Fonquevillers sector of the northern Somme line, in preparation for playing its part on 1st July 1916 at Gommecourt. George Groves would not be with his comrades at Gommecourt. As a consequence of his time in the trenches, George had contracted what was then a serious illness, cellulitis[104] of the head and neck. **Private George Groves** was treated in either No.19 '2/1st Northumbrian' Casualty Clearing Station or No.41 Casualty Clearing Station in Doullens, a distance back from the front line. Having survived the rigours of front-line trench warfare for fifteen months, George was killed by severe illness contracted in the extreme conditions experienced in the trenches. He died in hospital in Doullens on Monday, **18th June** 1916, the 101st anniversary of the Battle of Waterloo and just two days before his nineteenth birthday. He is buried in Doullens Communal Cemetery Extension No.1, close to the hospital in which he was treated.

Six days after George Groves died in hospital, **Private Joseph Davies** of 1/5 South Staffordshire's 'A' Company was wounded at night near Foncquevillers[105]. Joe had been wounded in the back, most likely by shrapnel, at 12.15 a.m. on Saturday, 24th June whilst guarding the digging of a new front line trench. The 1/5 South Staffordshire battalion war diary records:

> "24 June 1916 - Seven covering parties (5 from 'C' Company, 2 from 'A') went out covering the digging off a new front line trench, in front of the centre sector. About 12.15 p.m., the enemy opened heavy shell and machine-gun fire on the covering and working parties. Our covering parties had 3 killed, 13 wounded. On our own sector the enemy was quiet."

Joe Davies was evacuated across the Channel to England and spent some time in hospital at Southampton, recovering sufficiently to return to his battalion by November 1916. His wound, just before 1st July on the Somme, might have saved his life – for the time being.

---

104 Cellulitis was then prevalent among concentrated populations sharing hygiene facilities and common living quarters, as did soldiers in trenches and billets.

105 To 'Tommy', Foncquevillers was always 'Funky Villas'.

June/July

Saturday, 1st July 1916, a day always remembered as the bloodiest in the long history of the British Army[106], witnessed the opening of a campaign that was to claim the lives of seven 'memorial' and related men and was to wound two others, one of whom would be killed later in the campaign. The Somme offensive had its origins in a proposal for a joint Anglo-French assault on the German lines in the previously 'quiet' Somme region, coinciding with a planned Russian offensive on Germany's Eastern Front. Careful military planning was overtaken by military necessity when the Germans launched a huge attack on the fortress town of Verdun on 21st February. The attack soon degenerated into an effort to 'bleed the French army to death'. In a campaign lasting from February to November 1916, losses to the French and German armies were roughly equal but still devastatingly high. From the British point of view, the massive French commitment at Verdun caused the Somme offensive to be reorganised – in the initial assault, fourteen British divisions would now attack on an eighteen-mile front while the French would attack on an eight-mile front instead of the planned twenty-five mile front using just five divisions, thus reversing the two Allies' roles. A greater problem for Haig was that the French insisted that they could not hold out much longer at Verdun and demanded that the Somme attack should begin in mid-June. Haig considered that his raw, 'unblooded', New Army divisions would not be fully prepared by then. Nonetheless, in the interests of inter-Allied co-operation, Haig agreed to open his attack on 25th June, though this was later deferred to 1st July on account of weather problems and a necessary extension to the preliminary, softening-up artillery bombardment. As a sweetener to the French, in late February Haig also agreed to the British taking over the front line around Arras from the French Tenth Army to allow more reinforcements to be fed into Verdun. The continuous front-line held by the British Army now stretched eighty miles from north of the Ypres Salient to the River Somme.

The basic plan for the Somme Offensive was relatively straightforward; General Haig considered simplicity as an essential as many of the New Army troops were unseasoned in battle. There would be a week-long artillery bombardment by over 1,500 guns that would cut the German barbed-wire and destroy their fire-trenches and dugouts. Two minutes before zero hour (7:30 a.m.) ten mine tunnels[107] packed with explosives[108] would be detonated under

---

106 On 1st July 1916, the attacking troops of the British Army suffered more than 57,000 casualties of whom in excess of 19,000 were killed. Many of these occurred within thirty minutes of zero hour, 7:30 a.m.

107 One massive mine, under Hawthorn Redoubt near Beaumont-Hamel, was detonated at 7:20 a.m., thus alerting the defenders to the imminent attack – a dreadful error of planning.

108 Ammonal and gun-cotton were most often used.

the German trenches enabling the leading waves of British troops to *walk* across No Man's Land carrying their rifles 'at the port'. The infantry would be weighed down by extra equipment such as wire-cutters, entrenching tools to 'reverse' captured trenches and hand grenades as well as spare magazines of ammunition. The idea was an old one – 'artillery would conquer, infantry would occupy', simply capturing and consolidating the undefended German front lines. Success depended on two crucial conditions – first, most of the German barbed-wire being cut by the artillery barrage preceding zero-hour and secondly, the German machine-gunners being either dead or trapped below ground in deep dugouts before the British infantry reached the enemy lines.

At the northern extreme of the eighteen-mile British sector, two of Third Army's Territorial Force divisions, 46th 'North Midland' and 56th '1st London', were tasked to engage enemy forces in a diversionary pincer attack[109] on the Gommecourt Salient, intended to draw German artillery and troops away from the main assault further south. As soon as the main assaulting infantry battalions to the south had broken into the German front-lines, three cavalry divisions commanded by Sir Hubert Gough would exploit the breakthrough to capture Bapaume and, when the infantry caught up, the exploitation would swing north towards Arras.

Most military assault plans depend on the enemy doing exactly what the planners expect – this rarely happens and the experience on the Somme on 1st July was to be no exception. Some of the problems might have been anticipated – the British had too low a proportion of heavy guns to destroy the strongly-built German trench system and up to a third of British 'heavy' shells were poorly manufactured. The shrapnel shells intended to cut the German wire were not up to the task, so too much of the wire remained uncut. Instead of employing the usual 'rush' tactics, the idea of walking across No Man's Land was intended to reassure 'green' troops and prevent loss of direction in the fog of battle. Sadly, slow-moving, heavily-laden infantry allowed the German machine-gunners sufficient time to race up the steps from their deep dugouts and set up their Maxim guns; in this respect, the difference between success and tragedy on 1st July was but a matter of seconds. Lastly, when most of the first waves of infantry had been cut down in the first minutes of the advance, lack of information[110] reaching battalion, brigade, division, corps and army headquarters led to misinformed decision-making in respect of subsequent infantry waves being sent forward into the whirlwind of machine-gun fire.

---

109 Only the men's senior commanders knew the diversionary nature of the Gommecourt attack.

110 Most methods, including flags, metal discs on soldiers' backs, telephone lines and runners, were destroyed by enemy fire or simply swallowed up by the 'fog of battle'.

Where successes did occur, obtaining intelligence was easier but most of the picture remained unknown to senior command or was distorted by 'optimistic interpretation'. The assault in the Somme sector would continue, in 'stop-start' fashion, until the weather dictated cessation on 18th November.

It was against this backdrop that the memorial lads' and their relatives played their part in a battle that was to enter the annals of military history on account of its sheer terror and bloodletting. That first day, 1st July 1916, witnessed the death of nearly 20,000 British soldiers but, perversely, none from our story was killed although five were wounded. One lad, a gunner in the South Midland TF Artillery, even earned the Military Medal during the massive, preliminary barrage – let his story be told first.

Posted to 242 Brigade RFA (previously 2nd 'South Midland' Brigade TF, RFA), **Gunner Thomas Eccleston** of Marlborough Street, Bloxwich, landed

in France between the start of 1916 and the opening battles of the Somme on 1st July 1916. His division, 48th '1st South Midland', had been in France since late March 1915 and had taken over a sector of the northern Somme front line from the French in July 1915, remaining there for almost twelve months. Twenty-four year-old Thomas Eccleston was awarded the Military Medal in June 1916 for his brave actions when a German shell hit a B/242 Battery gun-pit on 28th June during the thunderous seven-day artillery prelude to the first day of the Somme offensive. Locally, the *'Walsall Observer'* also carried recognition of Thomas Eccleston's acts of bravery:

> "The heroism of two more local soldiers has been recognised by the award of the Military Medal. One of them is Gunner Thomas Eccleston of the RFA whose wife resides at 90, New Street, Bloxwich and who was formerly a

Military Medal with ribbon

> member of the Walsall Police Force. He has received a congratulatory message from General Aylmer Hunter Weston[111]."

In a letter describing how he won the medal, **Gunner Eccleston** wrote:

---

111 Lieutenant-General Sir Aylmer G. Hunter-Weston was in command of the VIII Corps that was part of General Sir Henry Rawlinson's newly-established Fourth Army.

'*Well, the night I got it [the medal] we had a bit of bad luck in our battery. We had a shell come through the mouth of one of our pits and six were killed[112], and one severely wounded, but he died after he had been in hospital about four hours, and it set the pit all on fire, and I put the fire out and helped to get them out. I won't tell you everything I did, it's impossible to remember, and you don't think what you are doing when you have a chap shouting, 'For God's sake come and help us.' It's a sight I shall never forget as long as I live.'*'

THIRD SUPPLEMENT

to

The London Gazette

of

TUESDAY, the 8th of AUGUST, 1916

on

THURSDAY, 10 AUGUST, 1916

His Majesty the KING has been graciously pleased to award the **Military Medal** for bravery in the field to the undermentioned

Non-commissioned Officers and Men: —

2732 Pte. A. Eaglesham, York. R. (T.F.)
22765 Pte. W. K. Easton, R. Scots.
2337 Gunner T. F. Eccleston, R.F.A. (T.F.)
3730 Pte. A. Edgington, Lond. R. (T.F.)

2674 Pte. G. W. Edmonds, Lond. R. (T.F.)

The award was announced nationally in the '*London Gazette*' supplement edition of 10th August 1916, Issue 29701, page 7887 (shown above). Although Gunner Tom Eccleston's official recognition must have made his family proud, they must equally have been shocked by the circumstances in which Tom had 'cheated' death. Their worries would not have been assuaged by the fact that the 48th Divisional artillery went on to fight through five of the major battles

---

112 The authors have been able to trace only three of these casualties – 3079, Gnr. W.T. Leppard, aged 22; 2095, Bdr. P.G. Harber and 2503, Gnr. Andrew Hale.

on the Somme during the late summer and autumn of 1916. Sometimes it was better for those at home not to know too many details of life and death at the front.

July

At 7:15 a.m. on Saturday, 1st July the British artillery barrage in the Somme sector rose to a hurricane crescendo that the enemy knew as *'trommelfeuer'* or drumfire; in the British front-line trenches, battalion upon battalion of nervous young soldiers anticipated every tick of their wrist-watches. Every man's SMLE[113] rifle had its gleaming bayonet fixed in expectation of close combat; every couple of yards, rough wooden ladders leaned against the parapet – long-handled wire-cutter[114] carriers would be in the front of the first waves 'over the top'. At the foot of each ladder, an officer with revolver drawn and whistle between his lips was studying his watch and steadying his men. Underfoot, the trenches were still wet and muddy from the recent stormy weather; overhead, a damp summer mist was beginning to give way to a warm, midsummer morning. The air was filled with accented voices wishing each other 'good luck'; promises were made to send on personal letters if the 'worst' should happen; some lads, overcome by nerves or fear, gave way to the waves of nausea that they were feeling; 'old sweats' reassured the 'first-timers'. At 7:20 a.m., troops near the middle of the eighteen miles of British assault trenches felt the earth judder and rock as if shattered by a gigantic volcano – in reality, 40,000 pounds of ammonal had been detonated in a tunnel excavated under the German strongpoint of the Hawthorn Redoubt near Beaumont Hamel. Enemy trenches, men and equipment had been utterly destroyed beyond recognition. At 7:28 a.m., as the barrage rose, nine smaller mines were detonated under the German front line. The many remaining German machine-gunners, huddled deep in their dugouts, responded to hails from the brave lookouts of, "They're coming!", by rushing the stairways to set up their vital weapons at the parapet. In most sectors, the British were already too late by 7:30 a.m. – Zero Hour on the Somme.

Many of the local lads in our tale were serving with the 1/5th and 1/6th South Staffordshire battalions of 46th 'North Midland' Territorial Division whose task [in conjunction with 56th '1st London' Division] on 1st July was to co-ordinate and execute a diversionary attack on Gommecourt village and Gommecourt Park at the extreme northern end of the battle area. Their job was to prevent enemy forces from reinforcing units to their south and to

113 Short Magazine Lee Enfield was the standard British infantry rifle.
114 Most infantrymen had small wire-cutters attached to their rifles.

prevent German artillery at Gommecourt from enfilading 31st Division's assault on Serre village and 4th Division's assault on Redan Ridge, two major objectives to the south of Gommecourt. The two attacking Territorial divisions were tasked to 'pinch out' the Gommecourt salient by assaulting from north and south of it and joining forces behind the salient – it was a tough objective as the Gommecourt sector had been strongly fortified by the Germans. 46th Division attacked with two Brigades (137th 'Staffordshire' and 139th 'Sherwood Forester') and each brigade attacked with two battalions leading and two battalions in close support; the 'Staffordshire' Brigade was on the division's right flank, deploying 1/6th North Staffordshire (supported by 1/5th North Staffords) on the left and 1/6th South Staffordshire (supported by 1/5th South Staffords) on the right. In most places, 46th Division had to cross three hundred yards of open ground before reaching the German wire – it was to prove to be a killing ground.

In the ranks of 1/5 South Staffordshire were eight memorial lads or their close relatives – **Sergeant Arthur Linnell, Sergeant Frank Lloyd, Corporal Arthur Parkes, Private Charles Bullock, Private Joe Handy, Private Albert Stych, Private Sam Harrison** and **Private James Heeley**. It is not known for sure which lads were due to go 'over the top' with which of the nine waves of attackers but the only 1/5 South Staffords in the first four waves were 'bombers' – **Albert Stych** was the only local 'bomber'. The infantrymen of 1/5 South Staffords were in waves five to eight. The night spent waiting in the 'Staffordshire' assembly trenches had in places been spent knee-deep in mud and water left by the recent inclement weather, while frequent German shelling had killed or wounded several men and taxed the nerves of others. When the officers' whistles blew to send the battalions 'over the top', it released the tension. Yet there was to be no 'walkover' that the High Command had promised, as the waves of infantry fell to the hailstorm fire of Maxim machine guns. The few Staffords that reached the German lines were isolated, to be killed or captured. Considering that the battalion sustained 186 casualties (killed, missing or wounded) in its support attack on 1st July, it is remarkable that none of the lads in our story were killed and just two Elmore Green lads were wounded.

Richard Henry and Agnes **Stych** of Parker Street were no doubt still grieving for their oldest son, Sam Stych, who had been killed on 9th March that year serving with the West Yorkshires near Festubert. To receive a second telegram must have filled them with dread but it informed them that nineteen year-old son **Private Albert Stych** (1/5th South Staffordshire) had been wounded and evacuated to England. During the fighting at Gommecourt on 1st July 1916 he was wounded in both arms while bomb-throwing and it was necessary to

Map 5:
The Somme – 1st July 1916 (and to 18th November)

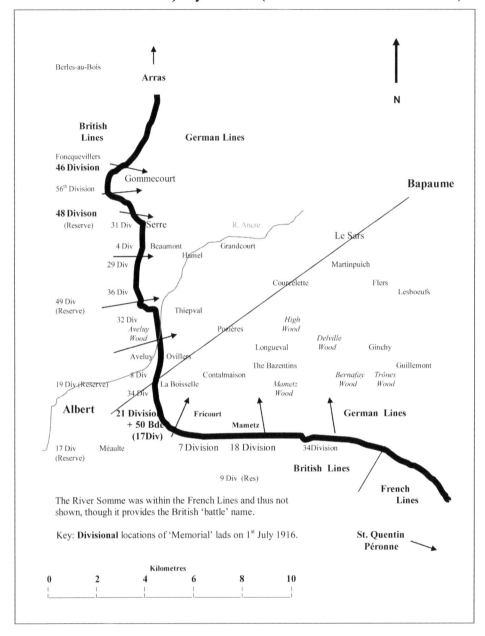

N

Berles-au-Bois

Arras

**British
Lines**

German Lines

Foncquevillers
46 Division

Gommecourt

56th Division

Bapaume

48 Divison
(Reserve)   31 Div   Serre

R. Ancre

Le Sars

4 Div   Beaumont   Grandcourt

Hamel

29 Div

Martinpuich

36 Div   Courcelette   Flers   Lesboeufs

49 Div
(Reserve)   Thiepval

32 Div   *High
Aveluy   Ponieres   Wood*
Wood

*Delville
Wood*   Ginchy

Longueval

Aveluy   Ovillers   The Bazentins   Guillemont

8 Div   Contalmaison   *Bernafay   Trônes
Wood   Wood*

19 Div (Reserve)   La Boisselle   *Mametz
Wood*

34 Div

Albert   **21 Division**   Fricourt   **German Lines**
+ 50 Bde
(17Div)   Mametz

17 Div   Méaulte   7 Division   18 Division   34Division
(Reserve)

British Lines

9 Div (Res)   **French
Lines**

The River Somme was within the French Lines and thus not
shown, though it provides the British 'battle' name.

St. Quentin
Péronne

Key: **Divisional** locations of 'Memorial' lads on 1st July 1916.

Kilometres

0   2   4   6   8   10

return him to England for treatment, thus he spent several weeks in hospital
at Birkenhead, near Liverpool. **Private James Heeley**, an infantryman with
the local 'D' Company of the same battalion, had been in France only since
late May 1916, so Gommecourt was his first taste of a major, set-piece attack.

216

James, the third son of John and Prudence **Heeley** of Cope Street, Leamore, was seriously injured by a gunshot wound in the 'walk' across No Man's Land into the teeth of the machine-gun storm. Like Albert Stych, nineteen year-old James Heeley was invalided to England for hospital treatment.

On the right flank of 56th Division there was no attack though this did not leave a gap in the British line as two brigades of 48th 'South Midland' Division were held there in reserve; two battalions of this division, 1/6th and 1/8th Royal Warwickshire, were attached to 4th Division for the assault on Redan Ridge to the south of Serre village. **Gunner Tom Eccleston** of 'B' Battery (242 Brigade, RFA), whose Military Medal would be confirmed by King George V in August, was with his 18-pounder Field-Gun team in 48th Divisional artillery. The artillery was tasked to furnish a week-long 'softening-up' of the enemy trenches, to destroy much of the German defensive barbed-wire and to keep the deadly German machine-gun teams deep in their dugouts until they had no time to reach their defensive parapet. The intention was for the artillery to destroy and for the British infantry, largely inexperienced as it was, to walk across and to occupy the German lines. There was a mix of divisional artillery (808 18-pounders and 202 4.5" Howitzers) and Army-controlled 'heavies' of various calibres, 32 4.7-inch; 128 60-pounders; 20 6-inch; one 9.2-inch; one 12-inch; 104 6-inch heavy howitzers; 64 8-inch howitzers; 60 9.2-inch heavy howitzers; 64 8-inch howitzers; 11 12-inch; 6 15-inch plus 100 borrowed French guns and howitzers. Unfortunately, along an eighteen-mile front, even this amount of artillery was inadequate; the result was that most of the German wire remained uncut and the relative shortage of super-heavy guns and howitzers led to many deep dugouts and their occupants surviving the barrage. In addition to these shortcomings, the German artillery did its best with counter-battery fire and also with shrapnel and High Explosive shells ranged at the British assembly trenches. Finally, the firing of the huge mine at Hawthorn Ridge ten minutes before Zero-Hour gave away the attack and encouraged many German machine-gunners to dash up to the fire-trench parapet to set up their Maxims.

31st Division at Serre, 4th Division at Redan Ridge and 29th Division at Beaumont-Hamel were all stopped in their tracks after suffering massive casualties. 36th 'Ulster' Division, straddling the Ancre Valley and up to Thiepval Wood towards Thiepval village, enjoyed early success breaking into the Schwaben Redoubt, taking 400 prisoners and heading on towards the crest of Thiepval Ridge. Follow-up battalions were caught in No Man's Land and the leading Ulstermen were isolated and besieged. On the right of the Ulster Division, 32nd Division on the Thiepval Ridge itself captured the Leipzig Redoubt but were beaten back from further advance. At Ovillers, 8th

Division had little success at huge cost; the story was similar across the Albert-Bapaume Road at La Boisselle, where the 'Tyneside Scottish' and 'Tyneside Irish' Brigades[115] of 34th Division were particularly badly mauled.

Beyond La Boisselle, Lieutenant-General Sir Henry Horne's XV Corps had the difficult and crucial task of assaulting two fortified villages, Fricourt and Mametz. To achieve this, Horne put into the line 21st 'New Army' Division (north of Fricourt) and 7th 'Regular Army' Division (south of Fricourt); the Kitchener division was further stiffened by 50th Brigade from 17th 'Northern' Division. **Private Sam Goodall** of 13/Northumberland Fusiliers (62nd Brigade) had been at the front since September 1915 and he was lucky on 1st July that his battalion was initially in support to 64th Brigade; in the afternoon 12th and 13th Battalions, N.F. went forward to relieve the 64th. Sam came through his experience relatively unscathed but his luck was running out. A short distance to the right of 13/N.F., near The Tambour where three mines had been detonated at 7:28 a.m., George Smith's younger brother, **Private Edward Smith**, had gone 'over the top' at Zero-Hour with 10/West Yorkshire (50th Brigade, 17th Division). The Official History (*'Military Operations, France & Belgium'*, 1916, volume 1) described 10/WYR's attack as follows:

> *"The attack was delivered on a frontage of six hundred yards. The two… leading companies crossed into the German front trench with little loss and pressed on…the Germans not emerging from their deep dug-outs quickly enough to stop them. [When]…the third and fourth companies [advanced]…the machine-guns…were in position. As a result [those] companies were practically annihilated. The leading companies… were isolated and…overcome later in the morning…[In their attack], the battalion lost twenty-two officers and six hundred and eighty-eight other ranks."*

Edward Smith was 'fortunate' in that he was 'only' wounded – he received a gunshot wound to his finger and was treated at 1st Australian General Hospital in Rouen. Edward had been wounded at Loos in October 1915 and in August 1918 he would receive a third wound stripe that would effectively end his war. But he would be alive to return home to his wife and daughter.

On 21st Division's right flank, 7th Division (containing three local lads) was tasked with capturing Mametz village. Even attacking with three brigades, the division had been handed a tough nut to crack. **Private Fred Goodall** and his cousin **Private David Goodall** were with 1/South Staffordshire that found

---

115 Tyneside 'Scottish' Brigade comprised 20, 21, 22 and 23/Northumberland Fusiliers. Tyneside 'Irish' Brigade comprised 24, 25, 26 and 27/Northumberland Fusiliers.

itself in the centre of the right-hand brigade (91st – 1/South Staffs had been transferred from 22nd Brigade in December 1915), facing Bulgar Point. On 7th Division's left flank, **Lance-Corporal Arthur Kitson** was among the ranks of 1/Royal Welch Fusiliers (22nd Brigade), facing Aeroplane Trench and the southern edge of Fricourt village. 1/South Staffordshire and 22/Manchester led the 91st Brigade attack and, despite the work of a few machine-guns in Danzig Alley (trench) and in Mametz, the Staffords were in the ruins of Mametz village by soon after 8 a.m. but had been brought to a halt. Reinforced by 21/Manchester, the 1/South Staffordshire captured first the southern and then the central areas of Mametz; by early evening, the Staffords were consolidating the day's gains. By that time, **David Goodall** who was still in one piece may well have heard on the battalion 'grapevine' that his nineteen year-old cousin, **Fred Goodall**, had sustained serious gunshot wounds between his eyes. Fred had been at the front since August 1915 – eleven months of worry for his parents William and Charlotte Goodall of Church Street, Bloxwich. On the left flank, **Arthur Kitson**'s 1/RWF and 20/Manchester were assaulting Fricourt village – by the end of the day Arthur was safe and Sunken Trench (just on the southern edge of the village) had been captured and consolidated.

The final two divisions in the British line, facing the village of Montauban, were 18th 'Eastern' Division on the left and 30th Division on the right – both were 'New Army' and both lacked the full confidence of the High Command. Yet on 1st July, in terms of territory gained, they were to prove the most successful. The two divisions took all their objectives but at a combined cost of more than 6,000 casualties. Much of their success was due to divisional artillery that recovered from a shaky start to lay down an effective 'creeping' or 'lifting' barrage (thirty-five 'lifts' of fifty yards every $1\frac{1}{2}$ minutes) that did much to protect their infantry. On the gun-line was twenty-five year-old **Arthur Smith**, elder brother of **James Smith** of Alfred Street who would join 2/South Staffordshire at the front in 1917. Arthur was already an experienced gunner with 10th Battery, 82nd Brigade of 18th 'Eastern' divisional artillery[116] and the success of the 18th was largely a consequence of the high standard of training demanded by the C.O., Major-General Ivor Maxse. While 30th Division was tasked to capture Montauban village, 18th Division was to assault the gap between the two villages of Mametz and Montauban, a task that required them to overcome several trench lines and strong-points such as The Castle, Glatz Redoubt and Pommiers Redoubt. Montauban village itself had been strongly fortified and, just on the reverse slope of the Montauban Ridge, the positions could be re-supplied from the long trench of Montauban Alley to the west of

---

116 Brigadier-General S.F. Metcalfe was the division's CRA – Commander Royal Artillery.

the village. In the light of the German defences, the subsequent success of the two New Army divisions was all the more remarkable.

On the right of 30th Division, the French attacks had been most successful; their troops, often veterans of Verdun, employed 'rush' tactics rather than 'walk over' and their artillery support contained a comparatively high proportion of 'heavies'. In summary of the first day of the British offensive, north of the Albert-Bapaume Road there had been much bravery, little territorial gain and at unbelievably high cost in casualties. South of the Albert-Bapaume Road there had also been much bravery but, though the cost had been high, Montauban, Mametz and Fricourt villages had been captured either in part or entirety. For their endeavours, Fourth Army (the main attack) and Third Army (the diversionary attack at Gommecourt) had paid the devil's price, in excess of 57,000 casualties of whom more than 19,000 had been killed – Regulars, Territorials and Pals' battalions had been devastated. Yet Elmore Green and Bloxwich had come through relatively lightly[117].

Although not on the Somme, **Private James Dawson** of 2/South Staffordshire was at that time wounded in the head while fighting with his battalion on Vimy Ridge. Out since August 1914, Dawson had fought at Mons and Loos; he had been wounded four times previously and was therefore entitled to five gold 'wound stripes' on his uniform's left cuff. He was treated in hospital in France. On 6th July back on the Somme an 'F. Lester' was wounded – it was not the Fred Lester of Sandbank whose name appears on the memorial (he did not arrive in France until November 1916) but his brother Frank, older by three years. **Private Frank Lester** had been in France since 21st May 1916 with 69th Company of the Machine Gun Corps (69th Brigade, 23rd Division); he suffered a gunshot wound to his right thigh in a successful night action near Contalmaison village. Frank was moved 'down the line' and his injuries were considered severe enough to warrant evacuation to England and hospital treatment in the city of Leeds. Frank recovered and even served in India after the war.

Despite the stunning losses, British High Command continued the initial attack and by 13th July they had been rewarded with the further capture of Contalmaison and La Boiselle villages, though by then they were little more than piles of rubble. On 14th July, in the area of Bazentin Ridge, a new plan was tested by the British. Troops were to assemble under the cover of darkness and the barrage, intense and supported by indirect machine-gun fire, commenced

---

117 Other than the lads in the Elmore Green story, four Bloxwich soldiers were killed on 1st July 1916 - Enoch William DAVIS of Alfred Street, Lance-Corporal Thomas Henry Reuben STACKHOUSE, Walter WILLIAMS of Providence Street (all 1/5 South Staffordshire) and Edward GUEST of High Street, Bloxwich (1/South Staffordshire).

at 3:20 a.m. and lasted just five minutes before the battalions went over the trench parapet. The infantrymen were preceded by a creeping barrage that was intended to keep enemy heads down and to hide the British from German observation. **Private George Smith** had volunteered for the West Yorkshire Regiment in the first month of the war, landing in France in September 1915. Having spent most of their duty in the Ypres Salient, on 8th July 1916 12/West Yorkshire (9th Brigade, 3rd Division) moved into the line, for the first time on the Somme, near Montauban. On 11th July the battalion was withdrawn to re-supply with stores, grenades and ammunition in preparation for the forthcoming attack on Bazentin Ridge. Two days later, on 13th, the troops assembled in Caterpillar Valley, between Mametz village and Mametz Wood, then moved up during the night (to be in place by 1:45 a.m.) and were due to attack at 3:25 a.m. 3rd Division was tasked to assault Bazentin-le-Grand village, with 9th Brigade on the left front and 8th Brigade on the right front; each brigade was to attack with two battalions – 12/West Yorkshire was ranged on the left of 9th Brigade while 13/King's (Liverpool) was on the right. The Brigade Major, K.A. Buchanan, ordered:

> *"Troops will advance to within charging distance in quick time. The assault will be delivered without cheering."*

The *'Official History, Military Operations in France & Belgium, 1916, volume II,'* comments:

> *"At 3:20 a.m. the whole sky behind the waiting infantry of the four attacking divisions seemed to open with a great roar of flame. For five minutes the ground in front was alive with bursting shell, whilst the machine guns…pumped streams of bullets to clear the way…When the barrage lifted at 3:25 a.m. the leading companies of the attack battalions…rose and advanced through the ground mist at a steady pace. There was just light enough to distinguish friend from foe."*

Although hindered by machine gun fire, 12/West Yorkshire succeeded in getting through the German barbed wire entanglements but became lost on account of the German trenches being obliterated by the preparatory barrage and consequently the troops ran into their own artillery fire. To their right, 13/King's was held up by heavy machine-gun and sniper fire. At 4:30 a.m. the two attacking battalions began to dig in where they thought the German line to be and they were hit by machine gun fire from both Bazentin-le-Grand village and the nearby wood. A call for reinforcements was made at 4:39 a.m., resulting in 1/Northumberland Fusiliers entering the battle. The village was not finally cleared of German troops until 9:30 a.m. That attack cost 12/West Yorkshire 253 casualties (killed or wounded), one of whom on **14th July** was twenty-six year-old **Private George Smith** formerly of Reeves Street, who had then served for 15 months in France. He is buried in Caterpillar Valley Cemetery, near Longueval. The battalion remained in the line until relieved by 2/Royal Warwickshire on 19th July 1916, by which time the battalion had lost a total of 342 officers and men killed, wounded or missing.

The summer of 1916 was cruel to the lads of the **Goodall** family. Edgar Goodall (173rd Tunnelling Company, Royal Engineers), had already been killed on 24th May, and Fred Goodall (1/South Staffordshire) had suffered a gunshot wound to the face on 1st July near Fricourt. The family was soon to lose two more of its soldier-sons, Sam and John, within eleven days of each other.

Sam Goodall landed in France on 9th September 1915 with 13/Northumberland Fusiliers (62nd Brigade, 21st Division) and took part in his first major battle sixteen days later at Loos. From 1st-3rd July his New Army battalion fought in the sector to the north-west of Fricourt village, suffering 158 casualties in three days and was then taken out of the line until 11th July but returned to action in Mametz Wood from 12th July until its relief on 18th July. During this time 13/NF suffered a further 272 casualties and it was in this wood that Sam was killed. Mametz Wood, in the southern section of the Somme battlefield, had largely been captured by 10th July, thanks to the remarkable efforts of 38th 'Welsh' Division. On Wednesday, 12th July, 62nd Brigade (Sam's battalion was part of this unit) of 21st Division, relieved the Welshmen and were ordered to clear the remaining 200 yards of woodland of the last German units. Sam's brigade, 62nd, dug in to consolidate possession of the wood and held fast until 18th July, by which time the brigade had suffered 950 casualties. Mametz Wood proved to be a 'killing ground' for both sides and a British soldier and author[118], Gerald Brenan, whose unit (48th Division) moved into the wood later in July, described the scene that then met his eyes:

"...After a little while we came to a large wood which the map told me was Mametz Wood. Its trees were torn and shattered, its leaves had turned brown and there was a shell-hole every three yards. This was a place where something almost unheard of in this war had taken place – fierce hand-to-hand fighting in the open (rather than in trenches) with grenades and bayonets. What seemed extraordinary was that all the

---

118 His war memoirs are recorded in his book, *'A Life of One's Own'*, published in 1962 (Jonathan Cape Ltd.).

dead bodies there lay just as they had fallen in their original places as though they were being kept as an exhibit for a war museum. Germans in their field-grey uniforms, British in their khaki lying side by side, their faces and their hands a pale, waxy green, the colour of a rare marble."

Brenan's description captures the horror and intensity of the fighting in Mametz Wood where twenty-six year-old **Private Sam Goodall** lost his life on **18th July**. Like so many of his comrades, Sam's body was never identified and he is thus commemorated on the Memorial to the Missing of the Somme at Thiepval.

John Goodall's battalion, 2/South Staffordshire, did not take part in the first assaults on Delville Wood but on 25th July it was attached to 3rd Division and moved up the line to take over the former German support trench line near Montauban. 2/South Staffordshire and 17/Middlesex, went forward under constant shellfire in support of 99th Brigade, relieving a unit of 23/Royal Fusiliers in the north-west front of the wood. 'C' Company extended a defensive flank on the west edge of the wood, 'A' Company held the northern edge, 'B' Company was in support and 'D' Company was held in reserve. 2/South Staffordshire held the most advanced position and consequently was in the greatest degree of danger. 99th Brigade fell back and the German artillery bombardment vented its fury on the wood's trench lines – 'B' Company was all but wiped out, though the few survivors drove off a German bombing assault. The other companies, in their turn, suffered grievously in the enfilading shellfire. Thus cut off, re-supply was hazardous by night and impossible by day; it was only an S.O.S. to the British artillery that saved the Staffords. John Buchan described those merciless days in Delville Wood:

"Hour after hour, day and night, with increasing intensity as the time went on, the enemy rained heavy shell into the area. Now he would send them crashing in on a line south of the road, eight heavy shells at a time, minute after minute, followed by a burst of shrapnel. Now he would place a curtain straight across this valley or that till the sky and landscape were blotted out, attack on except for fleeting glimpses seen as through a lift of fog."

When the battalion was finally relieved on 1st August, their replacement unit found that half of the Staffordshire men had become casualties; among their number, three of the company commanders were dead and so was eighteen year-old **Private John Goodall** (his death was officially dated **29th July**). John's body was never identified, so he too is commemorated on the huge

Memorial to the Missing on Thiepval Ridge. Two other local lads were on the same battlefield with the same battalion. **Private Alfred Main** of Bell Lane, a pre-war Special Reservist, was wounded for the first time near Montauban, in the bloody struggle for Delville Wood at the end of July. He was moved 'down the line' and the decision was taken to send him back to 'Blighty' for treatment. Following his recovery and convalescence, Alfred returned to France but was transferred to the 7/South Staffordshire, a battalion that itself had been heavily committed in the Somme fighting.

August

So, as July 1916 drew to a close, many members of the extended **Goodall** family were in mourning – such grief as was gripping many families throughout Britain. In May, Edgar had been killed underground near Loos; on 1st July Fred had been wounded near Fricourt; on 18th July Sam was killed in Mametz Wood and on 29th July John was killed in Delville Wood. It is a strange irony that Tunneller Edgar was the only one of the three Goodall brothers whose body was identified and buried, rather than being commemorated on a memorial to the missing in battle. Ten days after Sam Goodall had been killed in Mametz Wood the location claimed another Elmore Green victim, this time a severe wounding. John and Ruth Bullock of Church Street had already been through the trauma of opening an army telegram in November 1914 only to find that their eldest son, **Private John Bullock** of 1/South Staffordshire had been captured near Ypres – undoubtedly they had feared the worst. The next telegram brought worse news, though not *the* worst. They were informed that their fourth son, **Rifleman William Bullock**, had been wounded while serving with 16th 'Church Lads Brigade' Battalion, the King's Royal Rifle Corps. The unit had been in France since 14th April 1916 and fought on the Somme from 12th July in the southern sector near High Wood and Mametz Wood; it was near the latter on 8th August that **William Bullock** was hurt when he received a gas shell shrapnel wound to his back. He was initially treated by 104th Field Ambulance and later the same day was evacuated to No.61 '1st South Midland' Casualty Clearing Station. His wounds necessitated repatriation to 'Blighty' aboard Hospital Ship *'St. George'* on 14th August, to be treated at 3rd Scottish General Hospital, Royal Infirmary, Glasgow, until 23rd October 1916.

Our story returns to Delville Wood (known, for good reason, by 'Tommy' as 'Devil's Wood') but switches from the South Staffordshire Regiment to the Royal Welsh Fusiliers. When **Arthur Kitson**, a miner from Marlborough Street, volunteered for 1/RWF in November 1914, he probably expected to be in the thick of things earlier than July of 1915 but he was with the 'Welsh' in time for the Battle of Loos. What is more, he survived the experience, thus he was on the Somme with the Fusiliers of 7th Division's 22nd Brigade who helped capture Mametz village on 1st July and, after a brief spell of 'rest', took part in the successful Battle of Bazentin Ridge (14-17th July). On 20th July 1/RWF attacked High Wood (a tough 'nut' to crack) and was then taken out of the line for a fortnight's rest and refurbishment. The 'Old Sweats' among the RWF would have known that 'proper' rest meant a difficult task ahead and they were not wrong – it was to be Devil's Wood. On 26th August, when 22nd Brigade relieved part of 14th 'Light' Division on the eastern edge of Delville Wood, Arthur Kitson's battalion moved up to the north-eastern corner of the wood – 1/RWF was on the left of the line, with 20/Manchester on their right, 2/Royal Warwickshire in support and with 2/Royal Irish Regiment in reserve. Their task was to prepare the way for the main attack that was set for 5 a.m. on 28th August. In *'The Seventh Division, 1914-1918.'*, C.T. Atkinson notes:

> *"…early on the morning of 27th August, bombers of the RWF began fighting for possession of Ale Alley, which entered Delville Wood at its North-east corner, where the RWF's line formed a dangerous salient. A bitter struggle followed; after two hours the Fusiliers had gained about thirty yards but were held up by machine-gun fire from further along the Alley…Further efforts to gain ground in Ale Alley, however, were unsuccessful, even when assisted by a battalion (of Durham Light Infantry) from 14th Division on their left; a rush attack, supported by rifle-grenades, was equally unsuccessful."*

1/Royal Welsh Fusiliers' battalion war diary records:

> *"'B' Company suffered very heavily from enfilade shelling all day losing about 35 per cent casualties. Battalion casualties for the day:- Killed 15, wounded 56, missing one, sick two. Reinforcements:- one from hospital."*

The Germans retaliated with heavy artillery fire, causing many casualties and rendering the old trenches almost unrecognizable. During the course of four days, 1/Royal Welsh Fusiliers sustained in excess of 200 casualties – eloquent testimony to the severity of the fighting. Twenty-four year-old **Lance-Corporal Arthur Kitson** was posted missing, believed killed in action on Sunday, **27th August** 1916, thus his name is commemorated on the Thiepval Memorial to the Missing.

September

Through the late summer and early autumn, the campaign ground slowly onward – Delville Wood, High Wood, Pozières, Guillemont, Ginchy and Flers-Courcelette. British and Empire casualties mounted, German casualties mounted and a breakthrough seemed increasingly distant for both sides. The British had introduced their new 'wonder weapon', the tank[119], at Flers in mid-September and, while clearly shaking the enemy's infantry, the weapon initially proved unreliable.

By late September, the elite Guards Division had seen its first major action on the Somme in the successful Battle of Flers-Courcelette and on 21st of the month relieved 21st Division in the front-line west of Lesbeoufs. On 22nd September, **John Bate**'s battalion, 4/Grenadier Guards, made a bombing (grenade) attack up Gas Alley towards Gird Trench but gained little or no ground. Three days later, at 12:35 p.m. on 25th September, the Battle of Morval commenced under a creeping barrage, with John Bate's battalion tasked to assault the village of Lesboeufs. Located at the centre of the overall attack plan but situated on the extreme left front of the Guards Division, 4/Grenadier unexpectedly came under fire from forward of the enemy's Gird Trench, a strongly-held line strangely untouched by the artillery barrage:

> *"This they stormed with the bayonet, slaying over a hundred of the enemy." (Official History, 'Military Operations in France & Belgium, 1916, volume II').*

As the Guards progressed, employing bomb and bayonet, 4/Grenadier found its flank exposed to the enemy and so had to form a defensive barrier against enfilading fire. The C.O. of 4/Grenadier Guards, Lord Henry Seymour, who went forward some time later, commented:

> *"The Battalion [4/Grenadier Guards] did what they were told to do and I don't think they could have done better…Our dead lay in front of the first German trench but there were 100 to 150 German corpses there when I came up."*

4/Grenadier battalion war diary recorded the daylight assault thus:

> *"25 September 1916 – 11 p.m. The battalion took over its battle position last night. 2/Lt. Maine hit in the foot. A lot of shelling and bombing.*

---

119 Its official name was 'land battleship' but 'tank' was used to maintain secrecy.

The artillery bombarded the two lines in front of the battalion from 10 a.m. to 12 noon, but Capt. Britten in a message which reached Battalion Headquarters at 12.20 p.m. reported that the fire was weak and inaccurate.

At 12.35 p.m. the line advanced to the attack preceded by a creeping [artillery] barrage 150 yards in advance which moved at the rate of 50 yards a minute, and a stationary barrage on the second objective.

The battalion was met by a terrific machine gun and rifle fire which caused very heavy casualties but failed to stop them. The two left companies got into the German trench and killed many men there, numbering from 100 to 150; the two right companies, who had not met with such heavy opposition passed right on to the first objective, where later they were joined by the remnants of the two left companies. At 1.35 p.m. the attack on the second objective commenced, the brigade on our left had failed to reach the first objective, and our left was totally in the air. Consequently the right of the attack got forward and attained the second objective, while the left only partially got forward. Each unit then dug itself in facing the nearest enemy.

…The Welsh Guards now moved up and filled up gaps forming a continuous line facing north and north-east, and gradually all units became linked up. 1/ Grenadier on the right, on the third objective, facing east, 2/Scots Guards in the centre facing east and north-east, and Welsh Guards and 4/Grenadier on the left facing north.

The enemy made several half-hearted counter-attacks which were easily repulsed. 2nd Guards Brigade got into and through Lesboeufs and was in touch with 1/Grenadier."

Twenty-three year-old **Guardsman John Bate** died during that warm afternoon's assault on and capture of Lesboeufs – he had been in France for only six weeks before he was killed in action on **25th September** in the Battle of Morval. Sadly, John's body was never identified so he, like many of his comrades on the Somme, is commemorated on the Thiepval Memorial to the Missing, high on the Thiepval Ridge above the battlefields that claimed so many young lives.

The day after John Bate was killed in action pushing even further forward the British front line south of the Albert-Bapaume Road, on Thiepval Ridge the three Canadian and three British divisions were continuing the deadly struggle to secure what had been a first-day objective back at the start of July. Both sides knew that Thiepval Ridge was the key to the advance and the battle had proved bitter and costly. One of the three British divisions was 11th

'Northern' Division that had, in its 33rd Brigade, 7/South Staffordshire, the first of the regiment's 'Kitchener' battalions. The 'Seventh' had already served and suffered in the disastrous Gallipoli campaign from 6th August 1915 to the evacuation of the peninsula on 29th December that year. February to June 1916 had been spent serving in Egypt as part of the defence force of the vital Suez Canal Zone then, in July, to prepare for the Somme offensive, 11th Division sailed for France and by 6th September was in the front line in the Thiepval sector.

Edward Jones (known to all as 'Ted'), younger brother of **James Jones** who had been on the Western Front with 1/South Staffordshire since December 1914, had volunteered for the New Army in August 1914 but for reasons untraced he was not posted to 7/South Staffordshire in the front line until September 1916. He arrived on the Somme in time for the Battle of Flers-Courcelette and was then plunged into the Battle of Thiepval (26th-28th September). 33rd Brigade attack was led by 9/Sherwood Foresters and 6/Border; the Staffords' role was to 'mop-up' captured trenches and dugouts to ensure that units moving forward were not surprised by enemy survivors. The brigade captured and cleared their objectives, including Schwaben Trench, Zollern Trench and Hessian Trench – by 28th September the Thiepval Ridge would be under British control. **Ted Jones** came through unscathed but, sadly, the young man would not return home from the Somme.

November

Lance-Corporal James Dawson of 2/South Staffordshire was one of the few remaining *'Old Contemptibles'*. He had fought at Mons and foot-slogged the seemingly endless Retreat; he had fought in the Ypres Salient, among the spoil heaps of Loos and it was no accident that by September 1916 he had five gold 'wound stripes' on his left cuff. The most recent wound, to his head, was sustained on the Somme and he had only just returned to his battalion for early November. On 7th November, 2/South Staffordshire moved to Mailly Maillet to prepare for the planned offensive on Monday, 13th November that was intended to capture enemy strong-points north of the River Ancre, namely Serre village, the Redan Ridge and Beaumont-Hamel, all of which had been objectives on 1st July. Tasked to storm the Redan Ridge, 2nd Division attacked with 6th Brigade on the left and 5th Brigade on the right; in 6th Brigade, 2/South Staffordshire was left front with 13/Essex to its right. The battalions moved up to their assembly points during the night and at zero hour, 5.45 a.m., in the fog and darkness of the muddy jumping-off trenches, there was fortunately almost no shelling and so very few early casualties before the whistles blew. Struggling through a *"bluey mist"* and the cloying mud, with their officers having to use compasses to find their way, the Staffords lost contact with the creeping barrage and thus advanced into uncut wire and machine-gun fire from the German strongpoint of the Quadrilateral. In the teeth of such fierce resistance and despite the first German line having been taken, the attack stalled at the uncut wire in front of the second line, so the remnants of the battalion were quickly forced back to reoccupy the old defensive lines of Monk and Legend Trenches. Of the 2,500 men from 6th Brigade who had left their trenches at zero hour, all but seven hundred had become casualties – starkly reminiscent of Redan Ridge on 1st July! 2/South Staffordshire battalion war diary records the expensive action thus:

"13 November 1916 - The battalion successfully crossed the German front line and assaulted the second line wire, which was practically uncut. The battalions from the left divisions came across our front, breaking up our formations. Reorganisation was rendered difficult by the bluey mist. Casualties among officers and other ranks were very heavy. Among others, two company commanders are missing - one known to be wounded, two subalterns are missing and believed killed, several other subalterns were wounded; the four Company Sergeant Majors were wounded, C.S.M. Cox remained on duty till the battalion was relieved. The Chaplain joined Battalion H.Q. and acted as dresser. The old defensive lines in Monk and Legend were reoccupied."

Nevertheless, from 13th to 15th November, 2nd Division inched forward in howling wind and snow flurries to take Beaumont Trench; the battalion continued to lose men until it was deemed too weakened to remain in the line and was withdrawn to Louvencourt on the 16th November. Twenty-four year-old **Lance-Corporal James Dawson** was killed in the murderous actions of **13th November** – having previously survived numerous wounds, another of the *'Old Contemptibles'* of 1914 had rejoined his comrades. He is buried in Serre Road Cemetery No.2, a huge burial ground that seems to stretch forever. Two of Jimmy's older brothers, **George Dawson** and **Charles Dawson** served on in the South Staffordshire, while a younger brother, **Howard Dawson** would serve in the same regiment in 1918.

After four and a half months of bloody struggle, the battles on the Somme officially dragged to a wet, muddy close on 18th November but, after a brief respite, 7/South Staffordshire assumed trench-holding duties in the Ancre Valley, just to the north of the town of Albert. Having survived the horrors of the major battles on the Somme, it was here on **27th November** that **Ted Jones** of 'D' Company was killed on winter trench-holding duties north east of

Beaucourt-sur-Ancre. At the time of his death his battalion was endeavouring to dig a trench that was later known as 'Suvla Trench', its name reflecting 7/South Staffordshire's experiences on the beaches of Gallipoli in 1915. The battalion war diary records:

> *"27 November 1916 - The following telegram was received:-*
> *'Am much pleased with work done [digging trenches] by your battalion last night.' (GOC. RS)*
> *Considering that the battalion has now been under strain of constant shell fire for six days, this telegram affords an excellent commentary on the spirit of the battalion. Casualties 7 killed, 6 wounded."*

Twenty-one year-old **Ted Jones** of Marlborough Street is buried in Ancre British Cemetery, on the north bank of the river, a cemetery slightly raised above the valley in which flooding is still so regular a feature.

The Somme offensive had cost Elmore Green dear but the losses were being made good by new arrivals at the front. By the 'end' of the Somme battles upwards of a dozen local lads had entered the fray:

The local *'Old Contemptibles'*, surviving at the end of 1916:

Ernest Lavender   2nd (Reg) Battalion, South Staffordshire Regiment
John Bullock   1st (Reg) Battalion, S. Staffordshire Regiment [P.o.W.]
Joseph Bullock   2nd (Reg) Battalion, South Staffordshire Regiment

Other 1914 arrivals surviving at the end of 1916:

James Jones   1st (Reg) Battalion, South Staffordshire Regiment

Old Boys – arrivals at the Front, 1916:

Men who arrived in theatre between 1st January and 31st December 1916:

Archie HALL   1/5th TF Battalion, South Lancashire Regiment
Samuel HARRISON   1/6th TF Battalion, South Staffordshire Regiment
Arthur Parkes   1/5th or 1/6th TF Bn., South Staffordshire Regiment
George Stych   2nd (Reg) Battalion, South Staffordshire Regiment
Ernest HAYWOOD   8th (Service) Battalion, South Staffordshire Regt
Fred HARPER   15th (Service) Battalion, Sherwood Foresters
Robert SYLVESTER   8th (Service) Battalion, Gloucestershire Regiment
Fred LESTER   15th (Service) Highland Light Inf.
William Parkes   6th (Service) Battalion, Lincolnshire Regiment
Thomas EVANS   1st (Reg) Battalion, Leicestershire Regiment

Edward Rowbotham   71st Company, Machine Gun Corps
Thomas ROWBOTHAM S.S. *'Kilmaho'*, Royal Naval Volunteer Reserve
Samuel SMITH   Army Service Corps

In addition, the following *probably* arrived in theatre in 1916:-

Edward Parton   South Staffs & Lincolnshire Regiments
Frank Parton   Machine Gun Corps & South Staffs Regiment
(Jonah) Thomas Parton 8th (Service) Battalion, South Staffordshire Regt
Harold Pickin   South Staffs Regiment & Machine Gun Corps
Jonah Gill   2/5th TF Bn S. Staffs Regt & King's Liverpool Regt
Albert Sidney Hooper South Staffordshire Regiment
Stephen Parton   Royal Welsh Fusiliers
Charles Heeley   Army Service Corps

UPPER CASE surnames indicate men whose names are commemorated on the Elmore Green school memorial.

Lower case surnames indicate men *related* to those who are commemorated on the Elmore Green school memorial.

(Reg)   indicates a Regular Army battalion.
TF   indicates a Territorial Force battalion.
(S)   indicates a Service or 'New Army' battalion.
(Sp. Res.) indicates a Special Reserve or Extra Reserve battalion.

Where local volunteers might have to serve on the front line – theatres of war and garrison commitments in 1916:

Western Front   in France and Belgium against the German army.
East Africa   in Rhodesia, Nyasaland, Zanzibar, Tanga against German troops and German colonial troops.
Mesopotamia   in present-day Iraq against Turkish troops.
Salonika/Macedonia with French against Austrians/Germans/Bulgars.
Egypt/Suez Canal Zone against Turkish invaders.
Imperial Garrisons and RN coaling stations throughout the Empire – Africa, India, West Indies, Gibraltar, Hong Kong and many others. Regular troops gradually replaced by local 'native' and TF troops.
At sea   U-Boat war

1917 would prove no easier than 1916 for the lads in the front line.

Chronological Roll of Honour for 1916

February 23rd	John	COPE	Armentières
March 9th	Samuel	Stych**	Festubert sector
March 12th	Thomas	Dunn**	Arras sector
April 27th	Bertie	GILL	Ypres
May 15th	Thomas	BRICKNALL	Loos sector
May 24th	Edgar	GOODALL	Hulluch-Loos sector
June 18th	George	GROVES	Somme
July 14th	George	SMITH	Somme
July 18th	Samuel	Goodall**	Somme
July 29th	John	Goodall**	Somme
August 27th	Arthur	KITSON	Somme
September 25th	John	BATE	Somme
November 13th	James	DAWSON	Somme
November 27th	Ted	JONES	Somme

** Indicates a name related to those that appear on the Elmore Green School Old Boys War Memorial.

7th Division Christmas Card, 1916

Roll of Honour for 1916 (alphabetical order)

John BATE

Born on 24th May 1893 in Landywood, Staffordshire and lived at Cow Shed Row, Great Wyrley, then 231 Broad Lane prior to the family moving to 14, Elmore Green Road, Bloxwich. Son of James (a miner) and Ruth Bate (née Tranter) who married c.1891. The latter were 41 and 39 respectively in the 1911 Census. John was one of five children on the same Census – aged 16, John was the oldest of four brothers (James 12 [14/08/98, EG from 29/08/10] George 9 and Thomas 7); two further children died very young; he had one older sister, Fanny, 19, a chain-maker); all the children were born in Landywood except Thomas (born in Cheslyn Hay). John was educated at Elmore Green School (from 22/10/06). Single. John was a miner employed at Allen's Rough Colliery, Essington, (*"working on the rope"* according to the 1911 Census), possibly at the same pit as his father. **Volunteered** in **November 1915** in Walsall. **25095, Guardsman, 4th (Regular Army) Battalion, Grenadier Guards, (3rd Guards Brigade, Guards Division).** *Unit History* – Somme, 15-16/9 and 20-22/9/16 Battle of Flers-Courcelette; 25-28/9/16 Battle of Morval including the Capture of Lesboeufs (25/9/16) in the Battle of Morval. **Killed in action (age 23) on the Somme on Monday, 25th September 1916** during the Capture of Lesboeufs. He had been in France for only six weeks before he met his death. **Commemorated** on pier and face 8D of the **Thiepval Memorial to the Missing**, Somme, France. **Entitled** to the British War Medal and Victory Medal (Medal Roll – GG/103B2, p.82B). Commemorated on the Elmore Green School Roll of Honour (formerly displayed in T.P. Riley School library) and on the Walsall Roll of Honour.

Thomas Vaughan BRICKNALL

Born on 6th August 1897 in Blakenall (Bloxwich) and lived initially at 4, Northcote Street, Walsall and later at 200, Blakenall Lane, Bloxwich. Son of a coal-miner, Thomas Bricknall, 56 in 1911 Census, and Emma Bricknall (née Kirby), 54 of the same address. One of thirteen children, five living at home in 1911 – two brothers (Charles, a currier, 19, and Thomas 13, b. 1898) and two sisters (May, a harness-stitcher, 18, and Frances 11). Educated at Elmore

Green School (from 30/08/09). Single. Employed as a mopper and bobber by J. & J. Wiggin, Old Hall Works, Bloxwich. Enlisted in February 1916 in Walsall. 20667, Private, 2nd (Regular Army) Battalion, South Staffordshire Regiment, (6th Brigade, 2nd Division). *Unit History* – Loos-Lens sector. 2/South Staffordshire had been with the BEF since 13/8/14 and had fought at Mons, 1st Ypres, Festubert, Loos and the Hohenzollern Redoubt. Thomas was killed on his first day in the line with his battalion, in the Calonne South sector, south of Loos-Lens. Killed in action (age 18) on Monday, 15th May 1916 on regular trench duty near Loos. Buried in plot XVIII B. 24 of Loos British Cemetery, near Lens, France. Entitled to the British War Medal and Victory Medal (Medal Roll – F/101B9, page 1065). Commemorated on the Elmore Green School Roll of Honour (formerly displayed in T.P. Riley School library), on the Bloxwich Roll of Honour, on the Roll of Honour at All Saints Church, Bloxwich and on the Walsall Roll of Honour (on *all* as Thomas *Albert* Bricknall).

John Henry COPE

Born on 5th April 1897 in Hednesford, Staffordshire and lived at Belt Road, Chadsmoor, Cannock; the family later moved to Bloxwich, residing first in Bell Lane and later at 33, The Flats, Bloxwich. Son of a coal-miner, Isaac, and Mary Ann Cope (née Gaunt) of Bloxwich. One of seven children, six living at home in 1911 – one older brother (Ernest William) and four sisters (Lucy, Julia, Annie and Beatrice May). Educated at Elmore Green School (from 30/08/09, then living at 63, Bell Lane). Single. Miner employed at Huntington Colliery, near Cannock. **Volunteered** in **August 1915** in Hednesford, aged 17 years (underage), on the same day as his brother, Ernest William Cope – they served in 9/South Staffordshire together, having consecutive regimental numbers. **19803, Private, 'C' Company, 9th (Service) Battalion, South Staffordshire**

Regiment, (Pioneer Battalion, 23rd Division). *Unit History* – [9/South Staffordshire was a 'Pioneer' battalion and was used on improvements on trenches and so forth, very often in the front line and within sight of the enemy.] No major actions. The battalion shipped to Boulogne, France on 24th August 1915. Following his period of training, Private John Cope would probably have crossed the Channel to join his unit around the turn of the year 1915/1916. From 1st February, the battalion was at Rue Marle all month. Served in France for just eight weeks prior to his death. **Died (age 18) in hospital, on Wednesday, 23rd February 1916, from the effects of shrapnel wounds to his legs**, sustained in action near Armentières on 21st February 1916. **Buried** in plot II. C. 172 of **Bailleul Communal Cemetery Extension**, (Nord), France. **Entitled** to the British War Medal and Victory Medal (Medal Roll – F/101B9, p.1027). Commemorated on the Elmore Green School Roll of Honour (formerly located in the T.P. Riley School library) and on the Bloxwich and Walsall Rolls of Honour. **Family** – an elder brother, 19804, Private Ernest William Cope, enlisted in Hednesford at the same time as John and served in the same 9th Battalion of the South Staffordshire. He survived the war. Their younger brother, 5057631 Private Isaac Cope, 5/Devonshire was killed in Germany during the Second World War.

James DAWSON One of the *'Old Contemptibles'*

Born on 4th October 1892 in Blakenall and lived first at 35, Chapel Row, Blakenall Heath and later at 4, Blakenall Heath. Son of John and Hannah Dawson. One of eight children – five brothers (George, Charles, Howard, Leonard and Thomas) and two sisters (Elizabeth and Mary). Educated at Elmore Green School. Single. Previously employed as a miner at Aldridge Colliery. Then a professional soldier. **Volunteered** for the Regular Army in **August 1913** in Walsall. One of the *'Old Contemptibles'*. **9451, Lance-Corporal, 'C' Company, 2nd (Regular Army) Battalion, South Staffordshire Regiment, (6th Brigade, 2nd Division)**. *Unit*  *History* – 12th August 1914 landed at Le Havre, France. 23-24/8/14 Battle of Mons. Retreat from Mons. 1/2/15 and 6/2/15 Affairs of Cuinchy. 15-20/5/15 Battle of Festubert. 25/9/15-4/10/15 Battle of Loos. 13-19/10/15

Hohenzollern Redoubt (Loos). Somme, 25/7/16-9/8/16 Battle of Delville Wood including the Capture and Consolidation of the Wood (27-28/7/16); 8-9/8/16 Attack on Waterlot Farm near Guillemont; 13-16/11/16 Battle of the Ancre. **Wounded on** *five* **separate occasions**, first at St. Quentin in 1914 and the fifth time on the Somme in 1916, thus he would not have taken part in all of the named battles. Invalided to England with diptheria in September 1916. **Killed in action (age 24) on Monday, 13th November 1916** attacking the Quadrilateral strongpoint on Redan Ridge during the Battle of the Ancre on the Somme. **Buried** in plot II. D. 13 of **Serre Road Cemetery No.2, Somme**, France. **Entitled** to the 1914 'Mons' Star (Medal Roll – F/2/5, p.30), British War Medal and Victory Medal (Medal Roll – F/101B14, p.365). His left uniform sleeve would have borne five gold 'wound stripes. Commemorated on the Elmore Green School Roll of Honour (formerly located in the T.P. Riley School library as well as the Walsall and Bloxwich Rolls of Honour. **Family –** three brothers, George, Charles and Howard Dawson all served in battalions of the South Staffordshire Regiment. In addition, nine cousins served.

Thomas Henry DUNN** [not Elmore Green Memorial]

Born in Leamore. Married widow Annie Haywood in 1903 and lived at 32, May Street, Leamore. Worked for several years as a bricklayer in the employ of Mr. Samuel Wootton of Bell Lane, Bloxwich. **Volunteered** in Walsall in **September 1914**. **50614, Sapper, 89th Field Company, Royal Engineers (14th 'Light' Division).** *Unit History –* landed in France in May 1915. Ypres – 30-31/7/15 Actions of Hooge (First liquid fire attack); 25/9/15 2nd Attack on Bellewaarde. **Accidentally killed (age 35) on Sunday, 12th March 1916** by an earth slip whilst digging a gun-pit in the Arras sector. **Buried** in plot A. 4 of **Dainville Communal Cemetery, near Arras**, France. **Entitled** to the 1914-15 Star, the British War Medal and the Victory Medal. Commemorated on the Walsall Roll of Honour. **Family –** his youngest stepson, 30578, Private Ernest Haywood, of 8/South Staffordshire, was killed in action (age 20) on Tuesday, 17th April 1917 at Arras. Thomas Dunn's brother, Elijah, a miner in Yorkshire, enlisted in one of the Tunnelling Company of the Royal Engineers and served in France.

Bertie GILL

Born between October and December of 1893 in Short Heath, Willenhall, Staffordshire and lived at 100, Parker Street, Bloxwich. Son of a coal-miner, Jonah, and Lydia Gill (née Dean) of the same address. One of five children in 1911 – four brothers (Jonah Thomas, Norman Victor, Alexander and Arthur). Educated at Elmore Green School. Single. Miner/driver below ground employed at Holly Bank Colliery. **Volunteered** on **11th January 1915** in Walsall. **75940, Gunner, 94th Battery, 18th Brigade, Royal Field Artillery, (3rd 'Lahore' Indian Division>3rd Canadian Division).** *Unit History* – he served in Ireland for two weeks before being drafted to France on 21st June 1915. No major battles after Festubert (15th-25th May). The 3rd 'Lahore' Indian Division left France for Mesopotamia in early December 1915 but the artillery remained. On 20th March 1916 18th Brigade, RFA, joined 3rd Canadian Division. The brigade war diary says they took over the Rue Flamande sector, Poperinghe, from the British 24th Division from 18th March and they were still in that area in early April. **Died of wounds (age 22) on Thursday, 27th April 1916**, having been severely wounded near Poperinghe by counter-battery fire on 10th April 1916. **Buried** in plot V. B. 15A of **Etaples Military Cemetery**, France. **Entitled** to the 1914-15 Star (Medal Roll – RFA/7, p.5384), British War Medal and Victory Medal (Medal Roll – RFA/210B, p.21997). Commemorated on the Elmore Green School Roll of Honour (formerly located in the T.P. Riley School library) as well as on the Walsall and Bloxwich Rolls of Honour. **Family** – a younger brother, (Jonah) Thomas, enlisted at 16 years of age and he first saw service in the Irish rebellion with the 2/5th Battalion, the South Staffordshire Regiment. Drafted to France he transferred regiments and served as 260049, Corporal, in The King's (Liverpool) Regiment and survived the war, despite being badly gassed on Friday, 24th May 1918 during the German spring offensive of 1918. He was discharged from the Army on Wednesday, 27th November 1918.

Edgar GOODALL

Born between January and March of 1887 in Bloxwich to John Henry (a coal-miner) and Martha Goodall (née Wildman), living then at 79, Green Lane and later at 45, Leamore Lane (in 1901). Edgar had at least ten siblings, four brothers (Henry, Samuel, John and James William) and six sisters (Catherine, Jane, Martha, Elizabeth, Ada and Annie or Emma). Educated at Elmore Green

School. Married in 1905 to Mary Jane Darby, living at Binn's Yard, Park Road, Bloxwich and later at 36, Upper Green Lane, Birchills, Walsall; they had three children, Florence May, Edgar and France (the latter never met Edgar). Edgar, a coal-miner like so many of the Goodall men, was employed at Wood Farm Colliery. **Volunteered** in Walsall, probably in **August 1914**. 11456, Private, South Staffordshire Regiment. Transferred to... **86336, Sapper, 173rd Tunnelling Company, Royal Engineers.** *Unit History* – landed in France on 18th December 1914, almost certainly with the South Staffordshire Regiment – he had one narrow escape when a bullet hit him but was deflected by a knife he was carrying in his tunic. In response to the Germans exploding deadly mine tunnels under British trenches near Festubert and killing hundreds of men in December, the following February it was decided to respond in kind by forming Tunnelling Companies, under the control of the Royal Engineers. From mid-February 1915, miners were recruited directly into these companies, while miners already serving in the army were encouraged to transfer – the daily pay of between 2/2d and 6 shillings (compared with the infantryman's one shilling) helped many miners to make the decision. 170th to 178th Companies were the first to be raised. While army discipline for the Tunnellers was very lax, life underground was tough. Excavating (often known as 'clay-kicking') the tunnels was hot, hard work; worse, enemy miners occasionally exploded destructive charges (camouflets) close to the British workings or even broke into the tunnels and fought vicious battles with the British miners. **Killed in action (age 29) on Wednesday, 24th May 1916** in the Hulluch-Loos sector of the line. **Buried** in plot I. M. 27 of **Noeux-les-Mines Communal Cemetery**, south west of Béthune, France. **Entitled** to the 1914-15 Star (Medal Roll – RE/2C2, p.108), British War Medal and Victory Medal (Medal Roll, RE/101B139, p.30826). Commemorated on the Elmore Green School Roll of Honour (formerly located in the T.P. Riley School library) and also on the Walsall and Bloxwich Rolls of Honour. **Family** – left a widow, Mary Jane, and three children. A brother, 15590, Private Samuel Goodall of the 13th Northumberland Fusiliers, was killed in action on the Somme on 18th July 1916 (age 26); a second brother, John, was also killed and all three men are commemorated on the Walsall and Bloxwich Rolls of Honour (only Edgar was Elmore Green).

John GOODALL★★ [Not Elmore Green Memorial]

Born in Bloxwich in 1897 or 1898 to John Henry (a coal-miner) and Martha Goodall (née Wildman), living then at 79, Green Lane, later at 45, Leamore Lane (in 1901) and later still at 17, Blakenall Lane, Bloxwich. John had at least ten siblings, four brothers (Henry, Edgar, Sam and James William) and six sisters (Catherine, Jane, Martha, Elizabeth, Ada and Annie or Emma). Single. **Volunteered**, probably **early in 1915. 19972, Private, 2nd (Regular) Battalion, the South Staffordshire Regiment, (6th Brigade, 2nd Division).** Unit History: 2nd Battalion had been in France/Belgium since 13/8/14 and had been in action at Mons and on the Retreat to the Marne, and heavily engaged at 1st Ypres. John Goodall landed in France on New Year's Eve, 1915. 1/2/15 and 6/2/15 Affairs of Cuinchy. 15-20/5/15 Battle of Festubert. 25/9/15-4/10/15 Battle of Loos. 13-19/10/15 Hohenzollern Redoubt (Loos). Somme, 25/7/16-9/8/16 Battle of Delville Wood including the Capture and Consolidation of the Wood (27-28/7/16). **Killed in action (age 18 or 19) on 29th July 1916** in the terrible fighting for Delville Wood on the Somme. **Commemorated** on pier and face 7B of the **Thiepval Memorial to the Missing**, Somme, France. **Entitled** to the 1914-15 Star (Medal Roll – F/2B2, p.153), the British War Medal and the Victory Medal (Medal Roll – F/101B9, p.1033). His next-of-kin would have received a bronze Memorial Plaque (bearing John's name) and a scroll of thanks from King George V. **Family** – John and his two older brothers, Edgar(86336, Sapper, 173rd Tunnelling Company, R.E.) and Sam (15590, Private, 13/Northumberland Fusiliers) were all killed in action in France within a period of ten weeks in 1916. John was killed on 29th July 1916, just eleven days after his brother, Sam, who was killed on 18th July; both died within a relatively short distance of each other and both are commemorated on the same Memorial to the Missing at Thiepval Ridge. John's older brother, Edgar, was killed seven weeks previous to John, on 24th May. Edgar was killed underground near Loos – ironically, Tunneller Edgar is the only one of the three Goodall brothers whose body was identified and buried, rather than being commemorated on a memorial to the missing in battle. All three brothers are commemorated on the Walsall and Bloxwich Rolls of Honour. Edgar was the only one of the three to be educated at Elmore Green School and his name appears on the school's Roll of Honour, now back in pride of place in the main hall. The Goodall brothers were not the only ones in their wider family to be killed in the Great War – three Goodall cousins, Harold, William and David died. Harold and William Goodall are both commemorated on the Elmore Green School Roll of Honour.

Samuel GOODALL** [not Elmore Green Memorial]

Born in Bloxwich in 1889 or 1890 to John Henry (a coal-miner) and Martha (née Wildman) Goodall, living then at 79, Green Lane, later at 45, Leamore Lane (in 1901) and later still at 17, Blakenall Lane, Bloxwich. Sam had at least ten siblings, four brothers (Henry, Edgar, John and James William) and six sisters (Catherine, Jane, Martha, Elizabeth, Ada and Annie or Emma). Single. Sam, like so many of the Goodall men, was employed as a coal-miner. **Volunteered** in Walsall, probably in **1914. 15590, Private, 13th (Service) Battalion, the Northumberland Fusiliers, (62nd Brigade, 21st Division)**. Unit History: Sam landed in France on 9th September 1915 with 13/Northumberland Fusiliers and took part in his first major battle sixteen days later:- Battle of Loos (25th-26th September 1915 – the first two days of the battle, and these were the most successful.) He subsequently took part in the following battles on the Somme in the summer of 1916:- Battle of Albert (1st-3rd and 11th-13th July 1916) – the battalion fought in the sector to the north-west of Fricourt village and suffered 158 casualties in the first three days, and was then taken out of the line until 11th July. Battle of Bazentin Ridge (14th-17th July 1916) – the battalion returned to action in Mametz Wood from 12th July until its relief on 18th July, suffering a further 272 casualties. It was in this action that Sam was killed. **Killed in action (age 26) on 18th July 1916** in the fighting for Mametz Wood on the Somme. **Commemorated** on pier and face 10B, 11B and 12B of the **Thiepval Memorial to the Missing**, Somme, France. **Entitled** to the 1914-15 Star (Medal Roll – O/1/3B, p.400), the British War Medal and the Victory Medal (Medal Roll – O/1/105B13, p.2583). His next-of-kin would have received a bronze Memorial Plaque (bearing Sam's name) and a scroll of thanks from King George V. **Family** – Sam and his two brothers, Edgar (older) and John (younger), were all killed in action in France within a period of ten weeks in 1916. Sam was killed on 18th July, just eleven days before his younger brother, John (2nd South Staffordshire), who was killed on 29th July 1916; both died within a relatively short distance of each other and both are commemorated on the same Memorial to the Missing at Thiepval Ridge. Sam's older brother, Edgar (173rd Tunnelling Company, Royal Engineers), was killed seven weeks previous to Sam, on 24th May. Edgar was killed underground near Loos – ironically, Tunneller Edgar is the only one of the three Goodall brothers whose body was identified and buried, rather than being commemorated on a memorial to the missing in battle. All three brothers are commemorated on the Walsall and Bloxwich Rolls of Honour. Edgar was the only one of the three to be educated at Elmore Green School and his name appears on the school's Roll of Honour, now back in pride of place in the main hall. The Goodall brothers were not the only ones in their wider family to be killed in the Great War – three Goodall cousins, Harold, William and David died. Harold and William Goodall are both commemorated on the Elmore Green School Roll of Honour.

George Alexander GROVES

Born on Sunday, 20th June 1897 in Walsall and lived at 53, Park Road, Bloxwich (1911) and later at 72, Bell Lane, Bloxwich. Son of a brass caster, John William, and Annie (née Brown) Groves. One of six children, five of whom were living at home in 1911 – four brothers (John William, Alfie, Ernest and Charles) and one sister (Effie). Educated at Elmore Green School. Single. A baker employed by Mr. Jones of Broad Lane, Bloxwich. Single. **Volunteered** in Bloxwich **in 1914. 8605, Private, 'D' Company, 1/5th (Territorial Force) Battalion, South Staffordshire Regiment, (137th Brigade, 46th '1st North Midland' Division)**. *Unit History* – landed at Le Havre, France on Friday, 5th March 1915. From 4/4/15 at Neuve Eglise/Wulverghem to learn the methods of trench warfare. 7/15 to 2/10/15 Hill 60, Ypres – one of the most dangerous sectors of the Western Front at that time. From 19/3/16 the battalion moved south to Neuville St. Vaast/ Ecoivres, just to the north of Arras. During May and June of 1916, the battalion occupied the Fonquevillers sector of the northern Somme line – it was here that the South Staffordshire would play its part on 1st July 1916, though George Groves would not be with them. **Died (age 18) in hospital on Monday, 18th June 1916 from cellulitis** in the head and neck (contracted in the trenches). [Private Groves was treated in either No.19 '2/1st Northumbrian' Casualty Clearing Station or No.41 Casualty Clearing Station in Doullens, safely far back from the front line.] **Buried** in plot II. B. 11 of **Doullens Communal Cemetery Extension No.1**, France. **Entitled** to the 1914-15 Star (Medal Roll – F/2/B2, p.164 or 184), British War Medal and Victory Medal (Medal Roll – F/101B3, p.236). Commemorated on the Elmore Green School Roll of Honour (formerly located in the T.P. Riley School library) and on the Bloxwich Roll of Honour and the Roll of Honour in All Saints Church, Bloxwich. **Family** – a brother, 8605, Private John William Groves of 1/South Staffordshire, was killed in action at Ypres on 7th November 1914. An uncle, John Brown (Worcestershire Regiment), was twice wounded. George took his brother John's regimental number, 8605; both men are commemorated on the Walsall and Bloxwich Rolls of Honour.

Edward 'Ted' JONES

Born in 1895 or 1896 in Bloxwich. Son of a coal-miner, Thomas, and Ann Maria Jones of 21, Elmore Row, Bloxwich and later of 55, Marlborough Street, Bloxwich. One of eight children – four brothers (James, William, David and Thomas Edward) and three sisters (Flora, Mabel and Hetty). Single. Miner employed at Wood Farm Colliery. **Volunteered in August 1914** in Bloxwich. **40171, Private, 'D' Company, 7th (Service/New Army) Battalion, South Staffordshire Regiment, (33rd Brigade, 11th 'Northern' Division).** *Unit History* – September 1916 landed in France. Somme, 15-22/9/16 Battle of Flers-Courcelette; 26-28/9/16 Battle of Thiepval. **Killed in action**

(age 21) on Monday, 27th November 1916 in the Ancre Valley. **Buried** in plot VI. C. 45 of **Ancre British Cemetery**, **Beaumont Hamel**, Somme, France. **Entitled** to the British War Medal and Victory Medal (Medal Roll – F/101B12, p.1513). Commemorated on the Elmore Green School Roll of Honour (formerly located in the T.P. Riley School library), on the Walsall and Bloxwich Rolls of Honour and on the Roll of Honour in All Saints Church, Bloxwich. **Family** – an older brother, 9586, Private James 'Jimmy' Jones of 1/ South Staffordshire, was wounded at least once but survived the war.

Arthur KITSON

Born in 1891 or 1892 in Bloxwich. Son of Thomas (a coal-miner) and Martha (née Millington) Kitson of Front Lane, Short Heath, Willenhall. At some stage Martha passed away and in 1902 Thomas married Elizabeth Deakin, moving to 23, Marlborough Road, Bloxwich. One of six children – three brothers and a step-brother (Bertie Deakin, Frank, Fred and Harry Kitson) and one sister (Florence). Educated at Elmore Green Higher Elementary School. Single. Miner employed at Wood Farm Colliery. **Volunteered** in **November 1914** in Hednesford. **18399, Lance-Corporal, 1st (Regular Army) Battalion, Royal Welsh Fusiliers, (22nd**

Brigade, 7th Division). *Unit History* – landed in France on Wednesday, 7th July 1915. 25/9-8/10/15 Battle of Loos. Somme, 1-5/7/16 Battle of Albert including the Capture of Mametz (1/7/16); 5-10/7/16 – rest camps at Heilly and Citadel Camp. 14-17/7/16 Battle of Bazentin; 20/7/16 Attack on High Wood, right hand sector; 22/7/16-12/8/16 in rest at La Chaussée; 15/7-3/9/16 Battle of Delville Wood. **Killed in action (age 24) on Sunday, 27th August 1916** in Delville Wood on the Somme (the wood was known as 'Devil's Wood' to the Tommies). **Commemorated** on pier and face 4A of the **Thiepval Memorial to the Missing**, Somme, France. **Entitled** to the 1914-15 Star (Medal Roll – J/2/2B4, p.666), British War Medal and Victory Medal (Medal Roll – J/2/102B8, p.2253). Commemorated on the Elmore Green School Roll of Honour (formerly located in the T.P. Riley School library), on the Walsall and Bloxwich Rolls of Honour and on the Roll of Honour in All Saints Church, Bloxwich.

George SMITH

Born in Bloxwich in 1889 or 1890, George was the son of Edward and Elizabeth (née Newell) Smith of 94, Reeves Street, Bloxwich, his father being a stallman in a local colliery. George had two brothers (Edward and John) and four sisters (Frances, Eliza Ellen, Ruth and Elizabeth). Educated at Elmore Green School. Both parents having predeceased their son, (according to the 1911 Census that shows George as the head of the household), George moved to work in a colliery in Castleford, Yorkshire. Single. **Volunteered** in **August 1914** in Castleford, Yorkshire. **14757, Private, 12th (Service) Battalion, West Yorkshire Regiment, (9th Brigade, 3rd Division)**. *Unit History* – landed in France on 10th September 1915, joining his battalion in the Ypres Salient. Ypres Salient – 25/9/15 2nd Attack on Bellewaarde; 2/3/16 Recapture of The Bluff, in the south of the Salient; 27/3-4/5/16 Capture of the St. Eloi Craters; 30/4/16 Action of Wulverghem. Somme, 14-25/7/16 Battle of Bazentin. **Killed in action (age 26 years) on Friday, 14th July 1916** attacking Bazentin-le-Grand on the Somme. **Buried** in plot XV. C. 17 of **Caterpillar Valley Cemetery, Longueval**, Somme, France (this plot was added after the Armistice, from battlefield burials and smaller cemeteries.). Shown as 'C.' Smith not 'G.' Smith on headstone – other details correct on headstone and in cemetery register. **Entitled** to the 1914-15 Star (Medal Roll – O/2/1B, p.668), British War Medal and Victory Medal (Medal Roll – O/2/104B12, p.1359). Commemorated on the Elmore Green School Roll of Honour (formerly located in the T.P. Riley School library) and on the Walsall and Bloxwich Rolls of Honour. **Family** – a brother, 16510, Private Edward Smith, 10/West Yorkshire Regiment served on the Western Front. He was thee times wounded but survived the war to return Little Bloxwich to his wife Annie and daughter Lily.

Samuel Henry STYCH** [not Elmore Green Memorial]

Born in 1889 or 1890 in Short Heath, Willenhall to Richard Henry and Agnes Stych (née Simmons) of Back Lane, Short Heath. His father worked as a coal miner. Sam was one of nine children in 1911 – he had at least six brothers (Joseph, Albert, George, John, David and Harry) and at least two sisters (Martha and Maryann). The family moved to Bloxwich and lived at 78 then 102, Parker Street. Sam married and moved to Pontefract, Yorkshire, to obtain pit-work. Sam's father, Richard Henry, died during the war years. **Volunteered** in Pontefract in **late 1915**. **17/1041, Private, 17th (Service) '2nd Leeds Pals' Battalion, the West Yorkshire Regiment, (106th Brigade, 35th 'Bantam' Division)**. *Unit History* – 1/2/16 landed at Le Havre. No major actions. 7/3/16. First trench duty near Festubert. **Killed in action on Thursday, 9th March 1916 (age 26)** near Festubert. **Buried** in plot II. F. 1 of **Rue-du-Bacquerot No.1 Military Cemetery**, Laventie, France. **Entitled** to the British War Medal and the Victory Medal (Medal Roll – O/2/104.B4, p.398). **Family** – left a widow and three young children. Three of Sam's brothers served; a younger brother, 40593, Lance-Corporal Albert Stych of 7th Battalion, the Suffolk Regiment won the Military Medal and was killed in action (age 21) on Saturday, 28th April 1917 during the Battle of Arleux at Arras. Another younger brother, 242535, Private Joseph Stych of 1/6th Battalion, the South Staffordshire Regiment survived the war despite being twice wounded and also suffering a form of trench fever in 1917 (he was later discharged the army with the Silver War Badge on account of his wounds and sickness). A third younger brother, 242535, Private George Stych 2nd Battalion, the South Staffordshire Regiment and later of the King's Shropshire Light Infantry survived the war despite being wounded in his foot.

Chapter Twelve

1917:

Arras,Passchendaele and a World Bled Dry

January/February
Winter Trench Fighting

March
The German Retreat to the Hindenburg Line

April/May
Arras, Vimy Ridge and Bullecourt

May
The U-Boat Threat

June
Lens-Loos sector

June
Messines Ridge

July to November
Third Ypres, 'Passchendaele'

November & December
The Battles of Cambrai

December
The U-boat Threat

December
Beyond the Western Front

Ypres skyline as viewed from Hill 62 at dusk – a modern photograph with an eerily First World War 'feel'.

January & February: Winter Trench Fighting

To describe the 1916 fighting on the Somme merely in terms of numbers is to do grave disservice to the brave men who served there but the casualty figures would be seen as appalling in any war. By 18th November 1916, almost 420,000 British soldiers had become casualties on the Somme – many were still not accounted for but had 'died unremarked' in the heat of battle. The French Army had suffered even more shattering losses – 190,000 casualties on the Somme and perhaps 500,000 in the 'mincing-machine' of Verdun. For the French, 1917 would initially bring hope with a new military leader, General Robert Nivelle, but in the long term would bring the same old losses and, in consequence, an alliance-threatening mutiny by the ordinary 'Poilu'.[120] But the Somme was not yet done with the Elmore Green and Bloxwich lads. The prevailing weather and the consequent conditions in the trenches and across No Man's Land that separated the two sides explain why 1917 was ushered in by a relatively quiet January on the Western Front.

> *"Since mid-November [1916] constant rain and its effect upon the ground, pounded and lacerated by shell-fire and traffic, had made offensive operations impossible. The state of the ground of the Somme*

---

120 The term 'Poilu' was the French army's equivalent of 'Tommy'. It translates as 'hairy one' and reflects how a soldier appeared after long periods in the line.

battlefield during December was such as was probably never surpassed on the Western Front – hardly even in the Ypres Salient."
[Official History: *'Military Operations, France & Belgium, 1917'*, volume one]

The phrase, *'all quiet on the Western Front'* was a convenient method of expressing in reports to higher authority the absence of serious attacks or even trench raids but it did not mean that life for the trench-holding units was either quiet or comfortable. It meant that there had been, 'just the normal losses incurred during the normal tours of duty'. However, 'normal' during those abnormal times meant tours of duty in trenches deep in mud, sometimes liquid, sometimes frozen, with 'Tommy' grabbing 'forty winks' whenever possible in the open or in shallow 'funk-holes' scraped into the side of the trench. Rarely would a man have the opportunity to wash or shave in the fire-trenches and all soldiers, regardless of rank, were soon infested with body lice known as 'chats'. In fact, the modern term 'chatting' dates from when the resilient soldier turned emergency de-lousing into a communal pastime where army gossip was passed on and personal news discussed. In winter, weather and conditions underfoot made it often impossible to reach the front lines with hot rations and men would have to 'make do' with cold bully beef (now known as corned beef) and bread smeared with *'Tommy Tickler's'* plum and apple jam, giving rise to the perennial moan, '…when will it *ever* be strawberry?'. A man might put up with a few days of such privations but he would have grumbled loud and long if it he didn't get his brew of 'gunfire'. Moreover, failure to deliver the men's rum ration, especially in the coldest weather, would sap spirits rather than raise them! And all of this was endured under the constant expectation of the enemy artillery's 'daily hate' and never knowing when a skilled German sniper was watching your section of trench. One old hand who would no longer have to cope with the everyday problems of trench-life was **Private Ernie Lavender** (2/South Staffordshire) whose continuing medical difficulties had warranted a medical discharge from the army early in January 1917. He could wear his Silver War Badge with pride in the knowledge that, as an *'Old Contemptible'*, he had more than done his bit for King and Country.

Private Fred Lester of Sandbank, Bloxwich, had been called up for basic training with the South Staffordshire Regiment in April 1916 under the new Military Service Act[121]. However, because Scottish regiments were short of reinforcements and because no new recruit any longer had a say in the regiment to which he was posted, Fred found himself sent to 15/Highland Light Infantry,

---

121 This effectively introduced conscription to Great Britain for the first time. It was unpopular but necessary.

a New Army battalion that had been originally raised by Glasgow Tramways employees as a 'Pals' battalion known as the '1st Glasgow Pals'. How Fred took to his new comrades is not recorded but he had little time under fire to get to know any of them. 15/HLI landed at Boulogne in November 1916, at which time Fred was transferred to the Scots on their way to the front line. By the beginning of January 1917 15/HLI, as part of 14th Brigade, 32nd Division (under the V Corps) was in reserve in the northern sector of the Somme front. Six divisions were in the front line and twenty-two heavy artillery groups had been brought forward for the planned Operations on the Ancre. Fatefully for Fred Lester, the Army Commander decided to relieve the front line divisions and 'rotate' the reserve divisions into the line. After a successful operation on 10th January, 32nd Division's artillery supported further actions the following day; the division's infantry brigades had relieved 3rd Division on 9th January. Companies of Fred Lester's 15/Highland Light Infantry had been in and out of the line opposite the village of Serre, a first day objective on 1st July 1916 and still in German hands in the New Year. Fred met his death on **16th January** 1917 under a hail of shell fragments, not in battle but carrying rations up the line to his mates. Fred's Commanding Officer wrote in a letter to the parents:

> *"I have been in command only a short time and had not met your son personally but I have heard nothing but good about him since he joined."*

Private Fred Lester is buried in Euston Road Cemetery, Colincamps, in the northern sector of the Somme battlefields. Unlike his older brothers Edward and Frank (the latter was wounded earlier in the Somme campaign), Fred Lester would not return to Bloxwich and to his widowed father, Edward. At that time, the Lesters were out of the ordinary in that none of the four adult males in the family was a miner – father Edward and eldest son Edward were awl-blade makers, Frank was a needle-maker and Fred, the youngest, was employed first as a polisher at a Locksmith's, then as a 'bobber' for Abraham Wilkes Limited of Bloxwich.

In the same V Corps as 32nd Division, 46th 'North Midland' Division was a very experienced unit, having been in France or Belgium since March of 1915[122]. Following the disaster of 1st July in front of Gommecourt Wood, 46th Division had been moved three miles north to the quieter sector of Bailleulmont and Berles-au-Bois and the divisional commander, Major-General Stuart-Wortley, had been summarily sent home, effectively dismissed, for refusing to send more of 'his boys' to their deaths. The division felt that it still had a lot to

---

122 With exception of a very brief, quickly aborted trip to the Eastern Mediterranean.

prove and the chances came during the Operations on the Ancre and during the German Retreat to the Hindenburg Line (this 'retreat' was really a withdrawal to a stronger, shorter defensive line) in the Bucquoy sector.

March
Wounded during 1/5 South Staffordshire's attack on the Hohenzollern Redoubt in October 1915 and consequently invalided home, **Sergeant Arthur Linnell** had returned to his battalion in early March 1916. He appears to have been an inspiring leader as he was awarded the Military Medal for bravery in the field shortly before he was killed in action in March 1917. The citation read:

> *"This non-commissioned officer showed great gallantry and devotion to duty in rescuing wounded and buried officers and men during a heavy bombardment of our trenches on February 28, 1917 (near Monchy-Hébuterne). Regardless of personal risk from heavy trench mortar bombs, he dug out a wounded officer, although advised by the officer to go away. Two bombs fell within a few yards of him, leaving him untouched. During the whole work of rescue his conduct was worthy of the highest commendation."*

In March 1917, the Germans commenced their planned retreat to the recently-built, eighty-five mile long Siegfried Stellung[123]; this withdrawal shortened the German line by twenty-five miles and thus required ten fewer divisions to defend it. The importance of the latter to the German High Command was evidence that the British losses on the Somme had been effective in weakening the German army – in fact, apart from counter-attacks, the Germans launched no new major offensive until the spring of 1918 and meantime feared the British would launch another Somme-style offensive early in 1917. There were two other major variables in play in 1917 – the United States of America seemed ever likely to join the war on the Allied side, while as a counter-balance Russia was in political turmoil and might be ripe for defeat by Germany. This might release many German divisions sorely needed in the west. Well-prepared in the field, the German order in the West was, 'what we have, we hold'. And they held it with great courage, skill and determination.

This strategic withdrawal in 46th Division's sector involved the Germans executing a fighting retreat by 9th March to the village of Bucquoy, three miles east of the now-abandoned village of Gommecourt. The retreat, in short 'steps' from one defensive line to the next, was covered by heavy artillery

---

123 This was known to the British as the 'Hindenburg Line'.

fire, particularly around Monchy-au-Bois. Everything of use to the Germans was salvaged and removed to the Siegfried Stellung, after which the German engineers and pioneers applied the 'scorched earth' order issued by General von Kuhl. The devastated land was described by a German eye-witness, Ernst Jünger, an officer and the post-war author of 'Storm of Steel':

> *"Every village up to the Siegfried Stellung was a rubbish heap. Every tree felled, every road mined, every well fouled, every cellar blown up or made into a death-trap with concealed bombs, all rails ripped up and everything burnable burned."*

Worse still, the British could not work out exactly what the Germans intended and so the Allied reaction was measured, even slow. In short, the retreat was also a German tactical success. 1/5 South Staffordshire battalion war diary records the first indications of the German retreat, the incidents being those that led to the award to **Arthur Linnell** of the Military Medal:

> *"28 February 1917 - Z.2 Sector.*
> *Ravine, Farnborough Road and Nuts Lane [all trench locations] shelled with 77mm and 105mm shells from 10 a.m. to 12.30 p.m. Four or five salvoes of 77mm were fired into Nobody's Bottom at 6 p.m. Fifty heavy trench mortars were fired into Trench 112 support between 10 a.m. and 11 a.m. badly damaging the trench and inflicting casualties."*

When the decision was finally taken to advance, 137th 'Staffordshire' Brigade was tasked to attack Bucquoy village, thought to be lightly held, in order to cut off the retreating enemy. Confusion over orders for the night attack, some of which did not reach the battalions until it was too late[124], led to the assault turning into a disaster. Zero hour was set for 1:00 a.m. on **14th March**; yet seven hours prior to the attack, 1/5 South Staffordshire was in Souastre, five miles from their start point in Biez Wood. En route, the heavily-laden battalion was delayed by gas shelling in Foncquevillers and slowed further by the glutinous mud, resulting in arrival at assembly positions less than sixty minutes before Zero-Hour. Although exhausted, the battalion was immediately formed up for the attack – the order of the companies for the attack was 'A' on the right, 'C' in the centre and 'D' on the left. Night attacks are notoriously difficult and though the South Staffords advanced bravely they found the enemy wire uncut by the preliminary barrage, so German machine-

---

124   1/6 South Staffordshire received its orders too late to any take part in the assault.

guns consequently decimated troops bunching to access the few existing gaps. A few Staffords reached the enemy front trench but, lacking reinforcements, were soon ejected. Losses were heavy and one of them was twenty-four year-old **Sergeant Arthur Linnell, MM**, who must have been killed soon after leaving his own lines as his body was recovered for burial in Shrine Cemetery located in nearby Bucquoy village. The battalion retired at 6:30 a.m. to a trench system between Biez Wood and Square Wood, having sustained 160 casualties for no territorial gain.

Shrine Cemetery, Bucquoy

1/5 South Staffordshire battalion war diary (written by the battalion major) recalls:

"13/14 March 1917 - the battalion paraded at Souastre at 6 p.m. and proceeded to Fonquevillers, reaching Rossignol Wood at about 10 p.m. The south east corner of Biez Wood was reached about 12 midnight. The barrage was put on the front line German trench. At 1:00 a.m. the battalion advanced to the attack in waves.

The Radfehrer Graben proved to be a bad obstacle. All lines reached the German wire, and there were practically no casualties. The barrage was very satisfactory - there were no shorts (British shells landing 'short') and it was effective. At this point the whole was checked by German wire. At no point was it possible to penetrate to the German positions without cutting. Behind Radfehrer Graben the wire was swept by crossfire from machine guns. A large number of casualties were caused by officers and NCOs looking for gaps in this area. These machine guns were reported firing from behind the parados from the flanks, men having to bunch to get through the gaps in the outer wire, or gaps cut in the second belt. One gap in the third belt of wire, which runs up to the German parapet, was cut by one of our Lewis guns. Another Lewis gun got onto the German parapet and engaged two machine-guns firing from our right flank somewhere in Radfehrer Graben behind the front line. One gun was silenced entirely and another temporarily ceased fire.

Small parties of men succeeded in obtaining a foothold in the German trench, but this took some considerable time owing to lack of touch being kept, they were forced back by advancing Germans and lack of support.

I can give no information regarding the second line, although the Company Commander is known to have advanced in that direction but no-one came back.

The centre company found first and second belts of wire fairly well cut. 2/Lt. Frost and about 30 men gained a foothold in German trench. All the officers (except 2/Lt. Frost) and 13 NCOs were knocked out by bomb and machine-gun fire. 2/Lt. Frost reorganised the company in a sunken road and remained at this point for about two hours when recalled by me at daybreak.

The left company advanced on its objective. No gaps were found but the bulk of the company got into the trench without opposition. They were recalled by me at dawn."

In 'A' Company, **Private Joseph Davies** was posted 'missing in action' after the attack of **14th March**; his company had run into heavy machine-gun fire from the right flank and Joe Davies was probably one of its victims. The body of the twenty year-old miner from Elmore Green Road was never identified, thus he is commemorated on the impressive Thiepval Memorial to the Missing of the Somme. **Joseph Davies** is commemorated on the same South Staffordshire Regiment section of the Thiepval Memorial as Pelsall's Private James Croxall of 1/South Staffordshire who was killed near Delville Wood on 31st August 1916.

Losses were heavy on **14th March** and one of the fatalities in 'B' Company, in reserve, was **Corporal Joseph Handy**, a miner from Marlborough Street.

Thiepval Memorial,
Joseph Davies

Rossignol Wood Cemetery,
Hebuterne

It is most likely that he was killed by German artillery or indirect machine-gun fire as his body was recovered for burial at nearby Hébuterne in Rossignol Wood Cemetery. In a comforting letter to the lad's parents Edwin and Sarah, the Captain commanding 'B' Company said of Joseph Handy:

> *"We attacked the enemy in the early hours of the morning and it was while doing his duty like a gallant soldier that he met his end. He is buried in a soldier's grave near Hébuterne. The enemy has been driven back a long way and the guns cannot reach it."*

It was no great compensation but it showed that *someone* cared.

April & May

In comparison to his predecessors, the new French commander-in-chief, General Robert Nivelle was a junior and relatively inexperienced leader. He had made his name at Verdun in 1916 by carrying out an impressively effective counter-attack. However, his success at the iconic location of Verdun brought him to national attention and he tweaked the French desire for glory and revenge achieved with a degree of style and panache. It was irresistible. Nivelle claimed he could repeat the Verdun success in the Champagne region, attacking the Chemin des Dames in the Aisne Valley. A British attack further north would prevent the movement of German reinforcements towards the Aisne. Whether by intention or by chance, the Allied attack would commence at the two ends of the Siegfried Stellung – the British against Vimy Ridge/Arras at the northern extremity and the French against the Aisne in the south. There were good reasons for choosing the Arras region for the British attack – the city was a key transport centre where railway routes, major road routes and the Scarpe River coincided; moreover, a few miles to the north of the city lay the vital high ground of Vimy Ridge, the observation key for artillery facing either west over Allied lines or east over the German-held Douai Plain. From the ridge, German artillery fired shells into Arras with impunity; so, to protect a planned British advance along the Scarpe valley, Vimy Ridge must be taken. The Arras offensive, commencing at 5:30 a.m. on Easter Monday, 9th April (Z-Day), was preceded by a four-day artillery bombardment. The aim was for the Canadian Corps to wrest Vimy Ridge from its German defenders and thus cover the assault centred east of Arras whose objective was to break through the Hindenburg Line (Siegfried Stellung), use cavalry to exploit the gap and then to press on towards Cambrai. Military plans rarely survive contact with the enemy but by 12th April the Canadian Corps had captured the entire Vimy Ridge in one of the outstanding attacks of the Great War at a cost of 11,000

Map 6: Arras offensive, 9th March 1917 and beyond

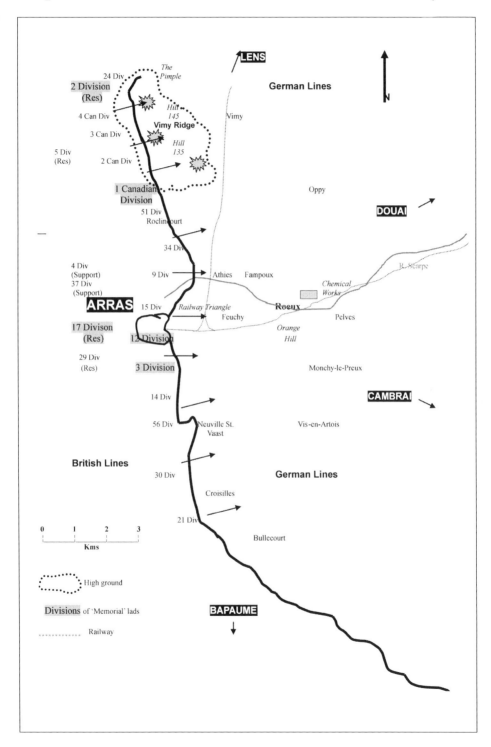

0   1   2   3
Kms

⋯⋯ High ground

Divisions of 'Memorial' lads

⋯⋯⋯ Railway

casualties. Over the five days of the opening battle in the Scarpe valley progress was patchy – impressive on the first day but somewhat squandered thereafter.

Several local lads were involved in those initial five days of the offensive. First into serious action, delivering part of the four-day preparatory artillery barrage, was **Gunner Alfred Sleigh** who worked on one of the 4.5-inch Howitzer teams of 129 (Heavy) Battery. Alf was one of the battery's 'new boys', having landed in France with the previous month's replacements. 42nd Brigade, RFA, to which Alf's battery belonged, was dug in at St. Sauveur, just to the south-east of Arras as part of 3rd Divisional Field Artillery (comprising three brigades of 18-pounder Quick-Firing field guns and one brigade of 4.5-inch Howitzers). The real… 'heavies', 60-pounders, 4.7-inch and 6-inch guns, 6-inch, 8-inch and 9.2-inch howitzers, were sited just to the west of Arras and would fire over the top of the various divisional artilleries. 3rd Divisional Artillery's targets included the German lines in front of the well-defended enemy village of Tilloy-les-Mofflaines. The barrage reached its crescendo seconds before the infantry began their charge across No Man's Land in the cold pre-dawn of 9th April 1917. Alf survived his first battle but the May assault on the Roeux chemical works ('Comical Works' to Tommy) was to be another matter entirely.

On 9th April, most of the locals were involved with 2/South Staffordshire as part of 2nd Division's 6th Brigade. There were two, possibly three local lads then serving in 2nd Battalion. The one name whose presence is in doubt was **George Stych** who had volunteered for the South Staffordshire pre-war but whose war service shows he was sometime transferred to King's Shropshire Light Infantry. Apparently George's transfer followed his recovery from a foot wound that necessitated removal to hospital back in 'Blighty'. One face that was definitely now missing from the ranks of 2nd Battalion was that of **Ernie Lavender**. Twenty-four year-old **Private Lavender** was an *'Old Contemptible'* who had been out since mid-August 1914, had been wounded three times and had lost a brother, **William 'Coxy' Lavender** (1/Lincolnshire), killed at Ypres in November 1914. His wounds had finally got the better of him in late 1916 and on 8th January 1917 he was discharged the service on the grounds of his wounds. As with most medical retirements, Ernie was awarded the Silver War Badge (number 212558) to show the public he had 'done his bit'. **Ernie Lavender** would be sorely missed. Though there was just five years difference in age between **Ernie Lavender** and **Harold Revitt** and both were married men, their army experiences could hardly have differed more – the old soldier and the young pup! Until April 1916, young **Harold Revitt** had been a shop assistant selling groceries in Mr. Stanley's store in Rushall. By May 1916 he had been called up with his age group and in January 1917 he had joined his battalion in France as **Private Harold Revitt** of 2/South Staffordshire. During March,

Harold helped in capturing Grevillers Trench near the village of Irles and then took part in the pursuit of the Germans towards the Hindenburg Line. On 9th April 1917, Harold was fully absorbed into the world that Ernie Lavender had left in his past. At Vimy Ridge, for 2/South Staffordshire it was a world of tense waiting as 2nd Division was held in reserve in the northern sector of the ridge, behind the British 24th and 4th Canadian divisions; ahead of these two assault divisions lay the daunting prospect of Hill 145[125] (the highest point on the ridge), covered by deadly machine-gun nests on a smaller hill just to the north and known as 'The Pimple'. Happily for the Staffords, their front-line compatriots did a wonderful job and on this occasion the Midlanders were not thrust into the maelstrom of battle.

The success of the Canadian Corps at the northern end of the Arras battlefield nevertheless left many wounded Canadians on Vimy Ridge needing the care of brave men such as **Lance-Corporal Joseph Orgill**, once of New Street, Bloxwich but since 1913 of Québec Province, Canada. The twenty-four year-old was serving with 'B' Company of 2nd Field Ambulance in 1st Canadian Division's Medical Corps, seeing at close quarters sights that no lad of his age should have to experience. Even so, Joseph survived for a few more months.

South of the Canadian Corps and away from Vimy Ridge the waiting ceased for thousands of British troops as the main infantry attack went in centred on Arras. Under the city of Arras during the months preceding Z-Day, engineers and tunnellers had developed the ancient catacombs into:

> *"…the most extensive underground network in British military history… In a matter of months they had created two inter-connected labyrinths, twelve miles long and capable of hiding 25,000 troops."*
> [Quoted from Robert Hardman's excellent article *'City under the Slaughter'* that appeared in the *'Daily Mail'* on 15th March 2008.]

This underground world, lit by electricity, enjoying running water and even housing a 700-bed hospital and a sixty-centimetre gauge light railway was constructed in order to spare the army such casualties as had been sustained on 1st July 1916. Tunnels stretched far into No Man's Land and troops could exit close to German lines. This was how 36th and 37th Brigades, the initial assault brigades of 12th Division, emerged into the sharp wind and snow showers of the early morning of 9th April. At 12:15 p.m., **Lance-Corporal Albert Stych, M.M.** of 7/Suffolk with 35th Brigade, similarly emerged onto the

---

125 Hills were *usually* named according to their height in metres above sea-level.

battlefield, his unit tasked with passing through the first brigades and capturing the Wancourt-Feuchy Line, the enemy's main trench at the foot of Orange Hill that rose from the south bank of the River Scarpe. This successful follow-up attack saw the capture of the Feuchy Road but advance to the final objective was frustrated by uncut wire and strong defences. Albert Stych, already a holder of the Military Medal from his days with 1/5 South Staffordshire, might not have remarked on the name 'Orange Hill'; however, towards the end of April he would fight again on that gently-sloping hillside.

Our final story of the part played by local lads in the first phase of the Arras battles takes us to 17th 'Northern' Division. Similar to 2nd Division facing Vimy Ridge, the 17th was in reserve for the opening of the offensive. By coincidence, 17th Division's reserve position was to the rear of **Albert Stych**'s 12th Division and to the rear of 3rd Division, in whose divisional artillery was the 129th Howitzer Battery of **Alfred Sleigh**. In the ranks of 10/ West Yorkshire Regiment (50th Brigade, 17th Division) was **Private Edward Smith**, who had already twice been wounded, at Loos in October 1915 and on the Somme on 1st July 1916 – however, Edward was luckier than his older brother, George Smith, who had been killed in action with 12/WYR on 14th July 1916 near Bazentin-le-Grand on the Somme. Also in the same division, with 8/South Staffordshire (51st Brigade), were twenty year-old **Private Ernest Haywood** of May Street, Leamore and twenty-five year-old **Private (Jonah) Thomas Parton** of Cope Street. **Haywood** had been called for army service on 28th August 1916, just two days after his twentieth birthday – by December, he was joining his battalion in France. Ernie's family had already suffered grievous loss in March 1916 when his step-father, **Sapper Thomas Dunn**, R.E., had been accidentally buried alive while 89th Field Company was constructing a new gun-line, ironically in the Arras sector. **Parton** probably also went to France in late 1916 and the two youngsters would be 'blooded' in the cauldron of Arras.

For Z-Day, 17th 'Northern' Division, unusually, was attached (from the VI Corps) to the Cavalry Corps that was designated the exploiting force to take advantage of any breakthrough. The three divisions of Cavalry and 17th Infantry Division were located south of the River Scarpe where success proved elusive, so they were not in action on 9th or 10th April. Next day, 17th Division was handed back to the VI (Infantry) Corps and was ordered to relieve the sorely-pressed 15th 'Scottish' Division the same night in Railway Triangle trenches, south of the railway running east from Arras. The relief was greatly slowed by heavy snowfall and consequent supply traffic congestion. 50th Brigade took over the front line in the sector on the line of the Monchy-le-Preux to Fampoux road and prepared to attack from Monchy towards Pelves

Mill on the Scarpe River. The attack was postponed until the bitterly cold but bright day of 14th April when 50th Brigade fought hard from their posts on the roads to Pelves Mill and Pelves village, firing with great effect into the flank of one section of a German counter-attack; at one point it was feared that the posts would be driven in but they held their ground against the odds. 10/WYR formed the left flank battalion during these operations while 51st Brigade with **Ernest Haywood** and **Tom Parton** was held in reserve. On 15th April, it was all change – 52nd Brigade relieved 50th Brigade in the front-line; 51st Brigade went into closer support and **Edward Smith** with the 50th again survived to go into reserve. Some of the German artillery could now reach the Staffords and, on Tuesday, 17th April, 8/South Staffordshire battalion war diary recorded:

> *"17 April 1917 - During the morning 'A' and 'C', 'B' and 'D' Companies change positions. 1.25 p.m. A few shells round the Railway Triangle. Two other ranks of 'B' Company killed. 6.30 p.m. – snow storm."*

Ernest Haywood was evidently one of the two lads killed on **17th April**. A letter written by the lad's officer to Ernie's mother, Annie, noted:

> *"He always did his duty cheerfully and well, and his loss is deeply felt by his comrades. He died a soldier's death…"*

Ernest had served just seventeen weeks in France. He is buried in Ste. Catherine British Cemetery on the northern outskirts of Arras. **Tom Parton**'s survival would be but a matter of days longer than Ernie.

British High Command would not abandon a job that had started so promisingly and thus planned a follow-up attack for 20th April[126]. However, it was judged more effective for the British to attack three days later – 23rd April, St. George's Day, 1917. The two-day battle was to become known as the 2nd Battle of the Scarpe. Again, **Private Edward Smith** of 10/WYR found himself in the thick of things. 17th Division was positioned on the right flank of 51st 'Highland' Division's attack on the Chemical Works at Roeux, a veritable fortress. 17th Division was just south of the Arras-Douai Railway and also on the south bank of the Scarpe. Yet again, **Edward Smith** came through the battle physically in one piece. On this occasion though, **Tom Parton**, 8/South Staffordshire and 51st Brigade played a vital but dangerous front-line role. Their initial objective was to 'pinch out' the German-held salient from the marshy south bank of the River Scarpe to just north of the village of Monchy-

---

126 The French attack had commenced on the Chemin des Dames on 16th April and General Nivelle reported it as a great success. Ultimately, he was economical with the truth.

le-Preux – if successful, the brigade was to push on to the village of Pelves. The Staffords were to attack on the left, nearer the river, while on the right would be 7/Border Regiment. As the clock ticked past midnight and on towards 2 a.m., the two assault battalions moved steadily into their assembly trenches near the Railway Triangle. By 3:30 a.m. the infantry was in place and waiting for the artillery bombardment that duly commenced at 4:45 a.m. However, it appears that the enemy had somehow spotted the front-line build up and, as the wire was largely uncut, they were easily able to train their heavy machine-guns on the few gaps. 8/South Staffordshire battalion war diary for 23rd April makes clear the ultimate hopelessness of their task:

> *"Two minutes after the barrage began, the first wave advanced under heavy machine gun fire from the left flank. 4:55 a.m., 'A' Company was in support but all officers had been killed or wounded, so the leaderless companies withdrew. They reorganised and two more attacks were made at 5:10 and 5:30, firing from the hip, yet machine-gun fire stopped the attack. At 5:40, the battalion was withdrawn. The remainder was reorganised into three companies to occupy the assembly trench and to dig in. 7:30 a.m., 7/Lincolnshire tried to attack but failed. For the remainder of the day the South Staffs and Lincolns reorganised and dug in under a barrage of 5.9's."*

The butcher's bill was horrific, as Jonathan Nicholls recounts in his excellent book on the Arras offensive, *'Cheerful Sacrifice'*:

> *"7/Border lost 15 out of 19 officers and 404 out of 505 other ranks. 8/S. Staffords' attack was also a bloody shambles. 7/Lincolns were sent in without artillery support and were slaughtered, losing 200 men in five minutes."*

Private Thomas Parton was one of the many from that terrible day, **23rd April**, that were never found – the enemy's artillery (5.9's) later in the day not only hampered the reorganisation of the survivors but also covered the remains of the dead. Twenty-six year-old **Private Tom Parton**, who had lost his younger brother Jack at the Hohenzollern Redoubt in October 1915, is commemorated on bay 6 of the beautiful Arras Memorial to the Missing. Tom's parents, Edwin and Clara, whose three other sons, **Stephen**, **Edward** and **Frank**, were serving in the army, must have wondered what more sadness might be in store for the family. In future, St. George's Day would not be celebrated in the Parton household.

Involved in the same attack on 23rd April but on the southern flank of the sector, around Croisilles, 33rd Division was able to make little headway. The fate of Elmore Green's **William Bullock** was about to bring his family back home in Church Street even more sadness. They had already lost an older son, **John** of 1/South Staffordshire, to a German prisoner of war camp while **Joseph Henry**, slightly younger, had experienced the worst of 2/South Staffordshire's battles. Their fourth son, **William Amos Bullock**, a twenty year-old rifleman serving with 1 Company, 16/King's Royal Rifle Corps (known as the 'Church Lads Brigade' Battalion) had suffered a shrapnel wound to his back on the Somme in the summer of 1916. His hospital stay in Glasgow was the last time he would return to 'Blighty'. The morning of 23rd April dawned with a heavy mist from the saturated ground and this was thickened by smoke shells and high explosive into a dense fog that lasted until around 8 a.m. when it was dispersed by wind and sun, revealing a rare warm and bright spring day. 33rd Division was allotted a dual task – first, a detachment was to capture and hold the section of the Hindenburg Line on the east bank of the River Sensée in order to prevent machine guns from firing across the stream on to the main attack (this task was allotted to **William Bullock**'s 100th Brigade); secondly, 98th Brigade was to make the main advance to the river. Each element of the assault was supported by two tanks. 100th Brigade's main force consisted of (in the words of the *Official History, 'Military Operations, France & Belgium, 1917 volume 1'*):

> *"1/Queen's (Royal West Surrey) with two companies of 16/KRRC acting as supports and carriers. It had a night march [of 1½ miles] from Croisilles [towards Fontaine] which was carried out in silence and good order. Unfortunately, both the tanks broke chains and took no part in the action. In front of the support line the wire was hardly damaged, so that very few men ever reached this trench and no permanent toehold in it was ever gained. About noon German bombers [grenadiers] developed counter-attacks from five separate points. With the aid of the KRRC companies the Queen's held out until 1:55 p.m. when the Germans rushed the trench-blocks under barrages of light trench-mortar bombs and the British detachment was expelled with heavy losses in casualties and prisoners."*

16/KRRC battalion war diary records:

> *"23 April 1917 - Croisilles - The attack was carried out by 100th Infantry Brigade on the right with the 98th Brigade on their left....*

The 100th Infantry Brigade objective being the Hindenburg Line, front and support trenches from Sensée River to Communication Trench on Contour 80. The 1/Queens supported by 'B' and 'C' Companies 16/ KRRC carried out the attack. 'A' and 'D' Companies were in reserve."

8.45 a.m. - One Platoon of 'D' Company under 2/Lt. Holloway went forward with 430 bombs.

11 a.m. - Report received from O.C. 1/Queens that more Lewis Gun ammunition was required. A party from 'D' Company under 2/Lt. Howatt was sent up with 54 buckets of ammunition.

12.15 p.m. - In response to further requests 40 boxes of bombs were taken up by a party of 'D' Company."

[The fight lasted from 4:45 a.m. to mid-afternoon, then....]

9 p.m. - The battalion moved back to Quarry and bivouacs west of St. Ledger.

Captains E.M. Gonner and A.B. Bernard, 2/Lt. Spreckley were reported wounded and missing, 2/Lt. Gerrard killed, 6 other officers were wounded, the casualties among Other Ranks were about 260. The German barrage was very heavy at times and our casualties were light considering the amount of open ground that had to be covered by the carrying parties."

According to Jonathan Nicholls in his landmark work, 'Cheerful Sacrifice – The Battle of Arras, 1917':

"After one bloody battle that day, the youngsters of the 16th (Church Lads) KRRC finally managed to capture Fontaine Trench, near Fontaine-les-Croisilles."

The diary entries show the typically desperate, close-quarter fighting of the day when **Rifleman William Bullock** was killed. His body was never identified, thus he is commemorated on the Arras Memorial to the Missing. The overall attack of **23rd April** cost 10,000 casualties in return for minor advances.

On 28th-29th April, the offensive at Arras was again drawn into the killing ground of the village of Roeux in the Scarpe valley. Although the next battle would become known as the Battle of Arleux, its objective was to win control of the Roeux chemical works that thus far had proved near-impossible to capture. However, Elmore Green's next casualty, **Albert Stych M.M.** of 7th Suffolk

Arras Memorial, William Bullock

(35th Brigade, 12th Division), was not killed in the attack on Roeux but as a consequence of 34th and 37th Divisions' failure to capture the village and its vital factory.

According to Scott and Brumwell in their divisional history, 12th 'Eastern' Division took position:

> "…on that portion of the front extending from the north east corner of Monchy (le Preux) to the River Scarpe."

In the attack, one that was dependent upon 34th and 37th Divisions north of the river capturing Roeux, the first objective of 35th Brigade was the northern section of Bayonet Trench and the section of Rifle Trench from the Monchy to Pelves Mill Road; the second objective was Pelves Mill itself, on the south bank of the River Scarpe east of Roeux. So the capture of Roeux was pivotal to the success of 7/Suffolk and 35th Brigade – without it, the attack would be doomed from the outset. The assault was to go in with 7th Norfolk on the right, 5th Royal Berkshire on the left and 7th Suffolk to pass through the Berkshires and capture the second objective of Pelves Mill. Zero hour was set for 4:25 a.m., thus it was still dark when Albert and his mates heard rather than saw the two lead battalions rise from their trenches to venture into No Man's Land. Immediately, 7th Norfolk's left wing companies were decimated by machine guns from Rifle Trench that had been almost untouched by the preparatory artillery barrage; however, their right wing companies courageously took the far end of Rifle Trench and made for their next objective at 5:45 a.m. but they too were stopped in their tracks by machine guns. To the left of the Norfolks, 5th Royal Berkshire stormed the whole of Bayonet Trench as far as the River Scarpe and also took a short section of Rifle Trench, preparing the way for Albert Stych and 7th Suffolk to pass through and strike for their final objective of Pelves Mill. In the rising light of a surprisingly mild day, 7th Suffolk left their trenches and, deploying into artillery formation[127], found and passed through the Berkshires. As the Suffolks breasted the ridge of Orange Hill and began a long, downhill trek with the River Scarpe flowing on their left, they walked into a heavy German defensive barrage rendered near impenetrable by murderous machine gun fire from the direction of the yet uncaptured village of Roeux and so were forced to take refuge in shell holes and dead ground. The surviving officers rallied the men for another '...*gallant effort*[128]...' to reach the distant Pelves Mill but the lack of cover and sheer weight of enemy fire kept them at bay as the butcher's bill rose alarmingly – by the end of the day, every one of 7th Suffolk's officers except the C.O. and the Adjutant had become casualties along with eighty-nine other ranks killed or missing with many more wounded. Despite its sterling efforts, the battalion had made little progress beyond Bayonet Trench and Rifle Trench. One survivor later said:

> *'The opposition was more than we expected and we lost heavily. The wounded and the dead were brought away as far as possible.'*

Other survivors spoke of:

> *'....many fatal wounds from shrapnel just in front of our trenches.'*

> *'....men caught by shells in the open, on top of the ridge (Orange Hill) and in the advance from the Sunken Road towards Monchy.'*

Such was the punishment taken by the battalion that it was withdrawn from the line on 29th April; at roll-call, so few men answered their names that the battalion was reorganised into just two very weak companies. One of those whose fate was not known but recorded as *'missing, believed killed in action'* on **28th April** was Military Medal holder, **Lance-Corporal Albert**

---

127 'Artillery formation' meant advancing in small units, such as platoons or sections, in narrow columns of fours or even in file, thus presenting a minimal target for enemy artillery.

128 Official History, 'Military Operations, France & Belgium, 1917 volume one'.

Stych – his courage is duly commemorated on the Arras Memorial to the Missing. Another of the 'Parker Street Boys' had gone west and Richard and Agnes Stych had lost a second son to the war.

[NOTE: *Albert Stych was not the only Walsall lad to be killed on Orange Hill attacking with 7th Suffolk on 28th April. Four lads who were transferred from 1/6th South Staffordshire to 7th Suffolks at the end of September 1916 were also killed, named as follows:-*

*40581, **Private Harry Birch** of Victor Street, Caldmore, Walsall.*

Commemorated on bay 4 of the Arras Memorial to the Missing.

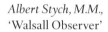
Albert Stych, M.M.,
'Walsall Observer'

*40596, **Private John Thomas Dickinson** of Frederick Street, Walsall.*

Buried in plot V. F. 9 of Feuchy Chapel British Cemetery, Wancourt.

*40652, **Private Arthur Ross** of Cemetery Road, Bloxwich.*

Commemorated on bay 4 of the Arras Memorial to the Missing.

*40659 **Private Jim Elwell** of 42, Blue Lane, West Walsall.*

Commemorated on bay 4 of the Arras Memorial to the Missing.]

Where the Battle of Arleux had concentrated on the narrow front at Roeux in the Scarpe valley, the final elements of the Arras offensive over-optimistically attacked on a broad, fifteen-mile front from the recently-captured Vimy village in the north to Bullecourt village in the south. The continuation of the British offensive was largely to disguise the fact that the armies of their French ally were enduring a series of mutinies in consequence of General Nivelle's disastrous, failed offensive on the Chemin des Dames. With the French temporarily out of the fray, Haig required a 'two or three week' extension of the fighting in the Arras sector to '…*strengthen the line*…' for future, as yet unplanned, attacks. It would cost Britain and her Empire dearly.

Drawn up in haste, the details of the attack-plan for Bullecourt were somewhat slipshod and the assault troops had to confront several fresh German divisions in the Siegfried Stellung (now known to the Tommies as the 'Hindenburg Line'). Communication of the plan to the troops was ineffective and the difficult, night attack on 3rd May, soon to be called the Third Battle of the Scarpe, was something of a fiasco. The sole notable success was in the north, where a number of local lads with 2/South Staffordshire (**Harold**

Revitt, **Joseph Bullock** and possibly **George Stych**) helped protect the Canadians' right flank in the capture of Fresnoy village. The by-now battered 2nd Division could muster just 1,800 men, where the peacetime establishment would have produced nearer 12,000. Mercifully, 2/South Staffordshire battalion's casualties would be relatively light that day. The battalion war diary observes,

> "*3rd May, in brilliant moonlight, the Germans lay down a violent bombardment on the front and support trenches. 2:45 a.m. German artillery caused casualties in the trenches but the first attack still went in at 2:45 and the first objective was taken. On the right flank, 31st Division's attack on Oppy Wood and Oppy village failed so the enemy was able to penetrate the left flank of the South Staffords' attack. Casualties on 3rd May were 7 killed, 1 died of wounds, 16 wounded and 8 missing.*"

Corporal Joseph Orgill was still with 2nd Field Ambulance of the 1st Canadian Division and had been frantically busy since before the Canadians' starting whistles sounded as the German artillery had poured a mixture of gas and high explosive shells into the assembly trenches. Joseph had been 'out there' since the spring of 1915 but even he must have been shocked at the scale of casualties so early in the assault plan.

Gunner Alfred Sleigh was firing the 3rd Divisional artillery barrage from the gun-line behind the ruins of Monchy-le-Preux village. However, the attackers soon lost the lifting barrage and were subjected to a fifteen-hour long bombardment from the other side of the wire – British suppressing counter-battery fire was largely ineffective. Many of the more inexperienced British infantry units were overwhelmed. Certainly, Gunner Sleigh was fortunate to survive the battle as none of the 3rd Division artillery forward observation officers and men in the village of Monchy lived to tell the tale.

In the southernmost sector of the line, centred on the village of Bullecourt where the Hindenburg Line was arguably at its strongest, the burden of a secondary offensive was carried by General Sir Hubert Gough's Fifth Army. On 11th April the First Battle[129] of Bullecourt was launched, spearheaded by 4th Australian Division and supported on their left by the British second-line Territorials of the 62nd '2nd West Riding' Division – within the ranks of the Territorials was Elmore Green's **James Bryan**, a private with 2/4th Battalion, Duke of Wellington's Regiment. Attacking two hours before first light, into a

---

129 The official record uses the term First 'attack' rather than 'battle'. I have used the terms 'First Battle' and 'Second Battle' for the sake of clarity and simplicity.

re-entrant,[130] and without the tanks[131] they had been promised, the 'Diggers' sustained nearly 3,500 casualties – they bitterly blamed lack of support from the tanks and from 62nd Division, though maybe they might have looked higher up the chain of command. General Gough believed that First Bullecourt had left the Hindenburg Line vulnerable to a second thrust to coincide with the 3rd May offensive at Arras. For the Second Battle of Bullecourt, 62nd Division remained on the left of the attack but the hard-hit Aussie 4th Division was replaced by the Australian 2nd Division; the objectives were much the same as on 11th April but this time the only tanks[132] were with 62nd Division. Again the 'Diggers' broke *into* the Hindenburg Line, though again there was to be no break*through*. The problems of stubborn German defence remained, as did the problem of 'flank fire' from the village of Quéant on the Aussies' right – this time, however, the Aussies retained a foothold in the Hindenburg Line. To their left, 62nd Division made better progress than before but was still driven back.

Thirty-nine year-old **Private David Goodall** of 1/South Staffordshire (91st Brigade, 7th Division) had been in reserve at Bullecourt since the second assault went in and no doubt had heard that the fortified village had become a death-trap – the troops' gallows humour had recently dubbed Bullecourt the 'blood tub'. 7th Division's 22nd Brigade was tasked to capture Bullecourt on 4th May but, despite losing over 750 men in little more than thirty hours, enjoyed minimal success. 20th Brigade replaced 22nd for the next attempt on 7th May and the tough Highlanders of 2/Gordons managed to break into Bullecourt and even to link with a few of 22nd Brigade's survivors and with the Australians. The success of 20th Brigade cost them similar casualties to their sister 22nd Brigade on 3rd May so, for the planned attempt finally to capture the whole of Bullecourt, 91st Brigade and thus 1/South Staffordshire were to take their turn. On 10th May, 1/South Staffordshire moved into the forward trenches under heavy shelling, losing a number of men on the way in. Their main assault commenced at 3:40 a.m. on 12th May, from trenches strewn with dead comrades from the previous days. The Staffords advanced with two companies on the left front of the attack; of these, the right-hand company made good headway but the left-hand company was halted by intense machine-gun and artillery fire. At 9 a.m., the reserves came up but they too could make no progress; at midday, three companies of 22/Manchester Regiment were similarly held up by German guns. The Staffords remained in the line until 16th May, no relief being able to take over under such intensity of

---

130 This is the opposite of a salient, resembling a 'pocket', and was thus fired on from three sides.

131 The Mark II tanks were expected to crush the enemy wire and silence strong-points. They arrived late and were soon put out of action, suffering more than fifty per cent casualties among the 91 crewmen.

132 This was at the Australians' own insistence after their first bad experience of tank 'support'.

fire. Sometime during that first assault of **12th May**, **Private David Goodall** was killed, the fourth member of that family to die within twelve months. That his body was never identified is explained by the heavy artillery bombardment pinning down his unit for those ensuing three days – David, a former brickyard worker who landed in France in December 1915, is another of the brave lads commemorated on the Arras Memorial to the Missing.

Meanwhile, **Private James Bryan,** with 2/4 DWR of 62nd Division, was in either support or, more likely, reserve while 2/7 DWR was making an abortive attempt to capture the 'Crucifix', the key to the supply line to the Germans' isolated south-west corner of Bullecourt village. This vicious fight for Bullecourt continued until 17th May when units from 58th '2/1st London' Division finally took the last corner of the village. General Gough had his wish, General Haig had kept the spotlight off his mutinous and thus vulnerable French allies but the 'Diggers' and the 'Tommies' had paid an horrific price in casualties:-

62nd Division	– 4,233
7th Division	– 2,722
58th Division	– 1,938
1st, 2nd Aus Divisions	– 3,300 (1st Bullecourt)
1st, 2nd & 5th Aus Divisions	– 7,482 (2nd Bullecourt)

With Vimy Ridge, Monchy-le-Preux and finally Bullecourt in Allied hands, there remained only Roeux and Oppy Wood to be taken. It would cost another Elmore Green lad dearly. Twenty-four year-old **Gunner Alfred Sleigh** landed in France in March 1917 and his war, though limited to a matter of a few weeks, coincided with the remarkably intense battles of Arras and it cost him his young life. During the night of 14th-15th May, 51st 'Highland' Division relieved 4th Division that had taken the shattered Chemical Works and the Scots went on to capture the whole of the village of Roeux, an objective that had defied the British from the opening of the Arras offensive on 9th April and through several subsequent unsuccessful attacks in April and May. The Germans, however, were unwilling to accept Roeux's eventual loss and throughout 15th May put down what Brigadier-General H.P. Burn (C.O. 152nd Brigade) described as:

> *"…the heaviest hostile bombardment he had experienced in two and a half years on the Western Front."*

In so doing, the enemy employed all calibres of artillery up to 21 cm. (8-inch) and much of their barrage was counter-battery work aimed to destroy the Royal

Artillery's ability to oppose the expected infantry follow-up attack. **Gunner Alfred Sleigh**'s 129th (Heavy) Battery, part of 3rd Division's artillery, was in the eye of the storm and sometime during that intense day of **15th May** he was killed in action, just two days short of his twenty-fifth birthday. Alf lies buried in the nearby village cemetery of Tilloy-les-Moufflaines – at 8, Clarendon Street in Bloxwich he left a young widow, Annie Theresa. He would spend no more time with his home pals, nor would he again make the daily trek to his work as a currier with Boak Limited of Station Street, Walsall.

Alf is shown in the centre of the seven men pictured.

There was a deadly postscript to the May battles around Arras. **Sergeant Arthur Smith** had been with the divisional artillery of 18th 'Eastern' Division since he landed in France towards the end of August 1915. With his 10th Battery, 82nd Brigade, Arthur had fought through the long, difficult days of the Somme, had moved with the pursuit of the enemy in their withdrawal to the Hindenburg Line and had stood in the gun-line at Arras (even though 18th Division's infantry was formally involved only in 3rd Battle of the Scarpe on 3rd and 4th May). As with so many deaths that occurred in the daily grind of trench warfare, it is not easy to establish precisely how Arthur Smith lost his life but it is known that in the week after 2nd Bullecourt ended, 18th Division's guns were still in the area just to the north-west of the ruins of Bullecourt village. The struggle for Bullecourt had often been reduced to an artillery duel in which the British guns had finally managed to prevail – but at a cost. Twenty-six year-old **Arthur Smith** was killed in action on **28th May**, most likely beneath a random artillery barrage – he was buried in St. Martin

Calvaire British Cemetery in the village of St. Martin-sur-Cojeul, south-east of Neuville-Vitasse. He left behind in Bloxwich a young widow, Lilly, and three children. Parker Street and Holly Bank Colliery had both lost another familiar face. Arthur Smith's younger brother James of 2/South Staffordshire would be killed during the following winter.

May

Just two days after the death of **Alfred Sleigh** on the Western Front, news was winging its way to Bloxwich of the demise of yet another former pupil of Elmore Green School. One of fourteen children, **Tom Rowbotham** was born in February 1894, the son of a coal miner, Edward, and Eliza Jane Rowbotham of Church Street, Bloxwich. Tom's mother died in October 1913, nearly three years before Tom enlisted in the RNVR (September 1916). At the time of his enlistment, Tom was employed as a bobber at J. & J. Wiggin Limited, hardware manufacturers of Old Hill Works, Woodall Street, Bloxwich. In February 1917 the German government announced it intended to use unrestricted submarine warfare in order to cut off Britain's vital supply routes across the Atlantic Ocean

Emblem: Royal Naval Volunteer Reserve

and across the English Channel. During April, U-Boats sank 155 British merchant ships (representing over 500,000 tons of shipping) and in May another 106 (300,000 tons). Gradually, counter-measures[133] were introduced but 1917 proved to be the low-point for the British merchant fleet. The decision was taken to arm merchant ships, creating a need for trained sailors to fire the deck-gun and this was how **Able Seaman Tom Rowbotham** of the Royal Naval Volunteer Reserve came to be serving aboard a merchant vessel that was sunk off the Cornish coast. The S.S. *'Kilmaho'*, of 2,155 gross tonnage, was a defensively-armed (one 12-pounder gun) steamship cargo vessel built in 1898 by John Priestman and Company of Sunderland. On Thursday, 17th May, ten miles west-north-west from the Lizard (Cornwall) and carrying a cargo of railway materials between Cardiff and Dunkirk, the *'Kilmaho'* was torpedoed and sunk without warning by a German submarine, UB-20. The ship's last known position, just after 11 p.m.,

---

133 These included organising escorted convoys and using lone 'Q-ships' to sink surfaced U-boats.

was 49° 58' north by 05° 28' west. Twenty-one lives were lost including the ship's Master and at least two reservists, A/2325, Leading Seaman John Main, RNR, and Bristol Z/9639, **AB John Thomas Rowbotham**, RNVR. Only one of the ship's complement of 21 men was saved, an Arab fireman who was picked up by a patrol boat six hours later. UB-20 was a German Type UB[134] II submarine or *'Unterseeboot'* of the German Imperial Navy (*'Kaiserliche Marine'*). The U-boat, built by Blöhm & Voss of Hamburg, was launched on 26th September 1915 and was commissioned into the German Imperial Navy in February 1916. UB-20 sank twelve ships (totalling 9863 tons) in the course of fifteen patrols but on 28th July 1917, just two months after sinking the S.S. *'Kilmaho'*, UB-20 hit a mine and sank with its commander Kapitänleutnant Hermann Glimpf and all twelve hands while on a diving trial off Zeebrugge (Belgium). S.S. *'Kilmaho'* was the fifth ship sunk by UB-20 under Glimpf's command. Twenty-three year-old **Thomas Rowbotham** of Church Street, Bloxwich was presumed drowned at sea on Thursday, **17th May** 1917 – he is commemorated on panel 24 of the Royal Naval Memorial on Plymouth Hoe. One of Tom's older brothers, Edward 'Ted' Rowbotham whose memoirs[135] have been published, served in the Machine Gun Corps and survived the war. On hearing the news of his younger brother Tom's death at sea in May 1917, Ted pledged to kill seven German soldiers in revenge. He kept his promise the very same night but regretted it on later reflection.

June

Another Elmore Green lad with good reason to want to avenge a brother's death was **Private Charles Bullock** who was serving with the Bloxwich-based 'D' Company of 1/5 South Staffordshire (46th Division) in the Lens-Loos sector of the front line. His younger brother, **Private William Bullock** of the Church Lads' Brigade, 16/KRRC, had been killed in action at Arras on 23rd April, 1917. Both lads had suffered previous wounds that necessitated being invalided to England (Charles at Loos in 1915 and William on the Somme in 1916). What was more, a third member of the family, **Private John Bullock** of 1/South Staffordshire, had been captured in November 1914 in the Ypres Salient. The fourth member of this fighting family and one of the '*Old Contemptibles*', **Private Joseph Bullock**, was still serving with 2/ South Staffordshire – parents John and Ruth Bullock of New Street, Bloxwich had certainly 'done their bit' for King and Country. **Charles Bullock** had volunteered in October 1914 and had been in France since early March 1915;

---

134 The UB Type was a smaller submarine originally designed to operate in coastal waters.

135 '*Mud, Blood and Bullets – Memoirs of a Machine Gunner on the Western Front*' (History Press, 2010) edited by his grand-daughter, Janet Tucker. It is a very good read.

the former miner at Holly Bank Colliery had fought in all his battalion's engagements, had been wounded in the cauldron of the Hohenzollern Redoubt at Loos, had survived Gommecourt on the first day of the Somme and had had the satisfaction of occupying the Gommecourt Defences when the Germans retreated in March 1917. Ironically, it was back in the Loos-Lens sector that Charles met his death. On 28th May, 1/5 South Staffordshire was on trench-holding duty in the front line of the Lièven-Angres sector, south-west of Lens. According to the battalion war diary, the day was 'normal' for those weeks:

> "28/5/17, Loos sector. It was fairly quiet during the day but the enemy was constantly using trench mortars on our right ('A' Company) front. All work during the night, except for Novel Alley (front-line), was stopped by gas shells. The work to be done in this sector is enormous!"

This diary entry was typical of the conditions under which the battalion operated – no great battles but the constant, wearing grind of trench warfare. **Charles Bullock** was wounded on 8th June in the Lens sector, possibly in a minor trench raid on Nash Alley; the 1/5 South Staffordshire war diary records:

> "8 June 1917 - Very quiet day. At 7 p.m. 'C' and 'D' Companies took up positions in assembly trenches and at 8.30 p.m. went over (the top).
>
> 9 June 1917 - Quiet day. Enemy rather subdued, shelling considerably less than usual. Pineapples [grenades] again put over by enemy on to left posts at 7.30 p.m. but soon stopped by our own. Relieved during the night by 1/6 North Staffordshire."

Private Charles Bullock was moved down the line to Bracquencourt but died from his wounds two days later, on Sunday, **10th June**, in No. 7 Casualty Clearing Station and was buried nearby in Noeux-les-Mines Communal Cemetery.

June

During the summer and autumn of 1917 attention would be drawn to Flanders and the Ypres salient. General Sir Douglas Haig had long harboured the inclination to pursue a major offensive centred on the town of Ypres in the low-lying Flanders Plain; he cherished the idea of advancing the front-line to both north and south of the Salient in order to reduce the shelling on the town. Securing the area would stabilise British lines of communication to the vital Channel ports and any Allied advance north-eastwards along the Channel coast would necessarily threaten enemy U-boat bases at Zeebrugge and Ostend, further securing supply routes from southern England. Following the collapse of General Nivelle's offensive in April 1917, the French army had been beset by mutiny and consequently took no part in offensive operations. Unsurprisingly, Robert Nivelle was sacked in mid-May and his replacement, General Henri Philippe Pétain, concentrated his efforts on repairing morale in the French military. Thus there was no French plan to which Haig had to conform and he took the opportunity to look to his favoured sector of the line – Flanders in general and the Ypres Salient in particular. Given the low-lying character of Flanders, it follows that possession of any slightly higher ground, especially ridges, would be of great advantage. Messines Ridge, the highest land in the area, is but six miles south of Ypres and afforded the Germans excellent observation into the Salient.

There is compelling evidence that General Sir Hubert Plumer's attack[136] at Messines, a vital prelude to the 3rd Ypres offensive (later to gain notoriety as 'Passchendaele'), was one of the better-planned and more successful schemes. Control of the ridge that overlooked the Ypres Salient from the south was a pre-requisite of the coming offensive (to commence late in July 1917) in the Salient itself. Just as the area around Ypres, known to the Tommies as 'Wipers', was an Allied-held salient bulging into the German lines, so the ridge at Messines lay at the heart of a German-held salient pressing into Allied lines – on the map and from the air, the front line from north to south described a huge, reversed capital 'S'. As the Germans held the higher ground, a plan based on an artillery bombardment followed by a frontal infantry assault might prove disastrous, so General Plumer's inventive scheme used the topography to advantage by employing Royal Engineer 'Tunnellers' to drive galleries beneath the enemy's trenches, packing the resultant nineteen mines with nearly one million pounds of high explosive, namely ammonal primed with gun-cotton and blasting gelatine. The consequent man-made 'earthquake', timed for 3:10 a.m. on 7th June 1917 (Zero-Hour), was to shatter the German fire-trenches and thus suppress the deadly Maxim machine-guns. The British barrage had, in effect, commenced in late May and continued, rising in intensity until Zero-Hour on 7th June. British counter-battery fire destroyed almost half of the German artillery's guns prior to the infantry going 'over the top', suppressing much of the German gunners' threat. As with most battles, lowly infantrymen like **Private William Parkes** had been told little in advance about the tunnels and on the day many would have been terrified by the mines exploded by their own side, a sound, sight and tremor compounded by the barrage of a thousand artillery pieces.

---

136 Plumer was commander of 2nd Army and had spent two years in the sector of the Ypres Salient – it was logical that he should draw up the plan of the attack on Messines Ridge.

William Parkes had landed in France in November 1916, joining 6/Lincolnshire (33rd Brigade, 11th 'Northern' Division) in the flooded Ancre Valley. Although it was a New Army battalion, the 'Sixth' had already fought at Gallipoli and Egypt (in the Suez Canal Zone) before returning to France and the struggle on the Somme front. Cold and wet though his arrival on the Somme might have been, during early 1917, a relatively quiet few months enabled **William Parkes** to settle in with his new mates, many of whom had been with the battalion on the ill-fated Gallipoli expedition. In mid-March, the battalion was out of the trenches, providing heavy labour for improvements to the vital railway line in the Authie Valley – a task the men did not relish but one for which their efforts earned their brigadier's praise. The winter was long, cold and frequently snow-bound, lasting through April and the offensive at Arras. On 28th March, the battalion was moved to Orville (still out of the line) and not until 12th April did they go back into the fire-trenches at Haplincourt (a ruined village, eight miles east of Bapaume) on the eastern edge of the 1916 Somme battlefield; it was by then a rather quiet sector, and on 17th May they entrained at Albert, heading for Caestre in Flanders. There, on 22nd May, 11th 'Northern' Division (or more precisely, 33rd Brigade under the control of 16th 'Irish' Division) was put on notice for the planned operations on the Messines Ridge. It was to be William's first major battle.

On 24th May, 6/Lincolnshire was ordered to march to a training area six miles back from the front line at Wytschaete (known to the Tommies as 'Whitesheet') where the assault was practised in detail. Meanwhile, the massed British artillery pounded the German lines for nearly a week, denying the enemy respite, food and reinforcement. Then, at 11:00 p.m. on Wednesday, 6th June, William's battalion was ordered to move from their training camp to Butterfly Farm, located on the northern edge of Kemmel Hill, for the forthcoming attack on Messines and Wytschaete. At 11:00 a.m. on the morning of 7th June, the battalion moved up to a trench line named Vierstraat Switch. 6/Lincolnshire were to await 16th Division's capture of the third objective, then move forward through the Irish lads and push ahead covered by another artillery barrage timed for 3:00 p.m. Unfortunately, at that time the Lincolns were spread over 1,000 yards of trench and only 'D' Company was in position to advance, which it did. Amazingly, the battalion lost but two or three men in the advance; at 5:00 p.m., a German counter-attack was broken with the assistance of tanks, after which the senior company C.O. brought forward the remaining three companies of 6/Lincolnshire. On 8th June, 'A' Company broke up a dangerous counter-attack while yet another, on the evening of 9th June, was halted with serious losses. In all, 6/Lincolnshire lost six officers and 160 Other Ranks during their four-day role in the Battle of Messines Ridge. Positions were held until the night of

Sunday, 10th June 1917 when the battalion was relieved to a camp near the village of Kemmel. Thirty-one year-old **Private William Parkes** was one of many men reported 'missing, believed killed in action' on **10th June**, dead after just eight months' active service. His body was never identified so William is commemorated on the Menin Gate Memorial to the Missing in Ypres. He left behind a young widow, Clara, and three children under the age of six years – it was not only the soldiers who paid a high price in the war. Shattering as was William's death for his parents, John and Matilda, it was not the last grievous news that they would receive of their four sons in khaki.

By coincidence, two more Elmore Green lads, **Robert Sylvester**, a Holly Bank collier who had lived in Parker Street and **Bernard Hooper**, a baker from Bloxwich Road, Leamore, were serving together in 8th (Service) Battalion, the Gloucestershire Regiment (57th Brigade, 19th 'Western' Division) and both took part in the Battle of Messines Ridge. Only one of the two would survive it. In all, nine assault divisions (with three more in support) were ranged in front of Messines and Wytschaete, from Mount Sorrel in the north to Ploegsteert[137] Wood in the south. 19th 'Western' Division (part of the IX Corps) was located just to the east of Vierstraat village, facing Oosttaverne Wood and village; 41st Division was on their left flank and 16th 'Irish' Division was on their right flank. 56th Brigade was on the left divisional front and 58th Brigade was on the right divisional front of the assault with **Sylvester** and **Hooper**'s 57th Brigade initially in reserve – 57th Brigade was tasked to 'leapfrog' the assault brigades, capture the fourth objective and establish a strong line of outposts. Soon after 3 a.m., nineteen mines packed with a total of more than 900,000lbs of ammonal and gun cotton, were detonated beneath the Messines Ridge in tunnels that had taken upwards of two years to excavate. The *'Daily Chronicle's'* war correspondent (and eye-witness), Philip Gibbs, described the man-made earthquake thus,

> "[From]…*the dark ridges of Messines and Wytschaete…there gushed out and up enormous volumes of scarlet flame from the exploding mines, and of earth and smoke all lighted by the flame spilling over into mountains of fierce colour…the ground trembled and surged violently to and fro. Truly the earth quaked…"*

As the infantry attack developed, 56th and 58th Brigades took the first three objectives and 57th Brigade moved through to take the line from Wytschaete village to Oosttaverne Wood. Soon after midday, 57th Brigade went on and, with minimal support, took their sector of the Oosttaverne (trench) Line in

---

137 This was known to the Tommies as 'Plugstreet' Wood, just as Wytschaete was 'Whitesheet'.

just twenty minutes. During the course of this, Druid's Farm was captured and, in recognition of the skill, bravery and initiative shown, the Divisional Commander (Major-General C.D. Shute) gave the battalion the right to wear the Divisional sign, a butterfly, on the sleeve of their service jackets. Although overall casualties were light, twenty year-old **Private Robert Sylvester** was badly wounded on 7th June and removed from the battlefield to one of the Field Ambulances stationed in the Convent of St. Antoine at Locre, south west of Ypres (a convent that was also occupied by Nuns) but he died from his injuries three days later, on **10th June**. Robert, who had volunteered in September 1914 and had seen service in Ireland with 2/5 South Staffordshire, had been posted to 8/Gloucestershire when he arrived in France in August 1916. He would never return to the coal-face at Holly Bank Colliery.

Lance-Corporal Bernard Hooper, who had volunteered in August 1915 and served with 2/5 South Staffordshire in suppressing the Irish 'Easter 1916' Rebellion, survived the main event on Messines Ridge though it would be but a short respite. His battalion remained in the same sector of the ridge, securing and strengthening their section of the Oosttaverne Line by 'reversing' German trenches and digging new ones. Prior to 31st July, the British artillery bombarded the German lines for more than a week, while intelligence-gathering raids went back and forth across No Man's Land. Occasionally the enemy replied in kind and at 1:25 a.m. on 28th July, with 8/Gloucestershire beginning the last day of a tour of duty in the front line, their advance posts came under attack from a determined German raid that was carried out by men of the 31st Reserve Infantry Regiment and Fourth Army Storm Troops. They assaulted 8/Gloucestershire with the object of blowing up Well Farm but were repulsed with considerable losses among the attackers. A few of the enemy obtained a footing in one of the posts but were quickly ejected by a well-led counter-attack in which all the Gloucesters were accounted for.

8/Gloucestershire battalion war diary records:

> "28 July 1917 - Battalion in the line. Enemy made a determined raid on front line posts, at 1.25 a.m. with 'Stürm Truppen' and were repulsed with considerable loss."

In repelling the main raid the battalion suffered casualties to the tune of two officers and about sixty-five other ranks. Twenty-one year-old **Lance-Corporal Bernard Hooper** was killed in action by a bursting enemy shell during the **28th July** raid and his body was never subsequently identified, thus he is commemorated on the Tyne Cot Memorial to the Missing, north-east of Ypres. He was the third Elmore Green lad to be killed as a result of the Messines Ridge action. Bernard's two brothers, **Albert Sidney Hooper** and **Leonard John Hooper**, both served in the army and fortunately survived their experiences.

July to November

The success of the assault on Messines Ridge boded well for the follow-up offensive that would become Third Ypres, more commonly known as 'Passchendaele'. The principal objective was to capture the higher ground of the Gheluvelt Plateau to the east of Ypres and ultimately to eject the enemy from the Passchendaele Ridge that overlooked the Salient. Passchendaele would become synonymous with battles fought in deep, glutinous mud, and with casualty lists on the scale of the Somme offensive of 1916. Initially, the High Command could not agree on whether 3rd Ypres was intended as a breakthrough offensive or whether it should have limited objectives and gradually overcome the enemy in 'bite and hold' attacks. During the six weeks that had passed since taking Messines Ridge, the British had been busy moving their field artillery and 'heavies' to their allotted gun-lines for the preparatory bombardment for the Ypres offensive – though less than ten miles, it was a massive logistical problem and a major obstacle to a rapid exploitation of General Plumer's remarkable

Still daunting ninety years later…A concrete German blockhouse (MEBU) at Hill 60, near Ypres. It would have been manned by machine-gunners and would have been vulnerable only to a direct hit by heavy artillery shells.

advance. Unfortunately, the delay wasted more than a month of good weather that would prove pivotal. The German defenders east of Ypres had used the six-week respite to complete and strengthen numerous concrete pillboxes or blockhouses (known as 'MEBUs' from their longer German name) that provided interlocking fields of fire for their machine-guns. The weather, favourable for the best part of six weeks, produced one of the wettest late summers Belgium had seen for many years – 31st July, the date the offensive commenced, endured nearly an inch of rain and this set the pattern for much of the campaign.

Eventually, more than 3,000 artillery pieces launched a ten-day preliminary bombardment but the guns' most significant but unintended effect was to destroy the drainage system that in peacetime made local agriculture both possible and productive. Instead of the rainfall running into drainage ditches, water now remained on the surface, turning soil into deep, muddy swamps. Movement of man, beast or artillery was difficult and sometimes impossible; fighting in such conditions was a nightmare and the longer the offensive went on, the more these conditions deteriorated.

Given the conditions and the intensity of the fighting around the Salient, it is remarkable that just four Elmore Green lads died in the struggles of 3rd Ypres, although several more experienced the deadly, flooded battlefields of 'Passchendaele'. One, possibly two, local lads, took part in Fifth Army's opening assaults on Pilckem Ridge from 31st July to 2nd August – **Private Isaac Andrews** of Church Street, who had been posted to 1/9 Royal Scots (51st 'Highland' Division) and possibly **Private Harry Perks** of Harrison Street, who was transferred to 1/Worcestershire (8th Division) around the time of 3rd Ypres. Both survived the battle, which initially was successful, despite the assault costing 31,000 casualties. Pilckem Ridge was fought in heavy rain and this unseasonable deluge continued through much of August. On 16th August, German counter-attacks and minor engagements gave way to a major assault towards Langemarck – **Harry Perks** was again involved though while **Frank Lester**'s 69th Machine Gun Company attacked as part of 23rd Division, Frank was not there. He had been invalided to England aboard S.S. '*St. David*', suffering a severe bout of trench fever. Again, **Harry Perks** came through but the main offensive had stalled in the Flanders mud.

General Sir Douglas Haig now handed General Plumer's Second Army a lead role and the attack focus shifted to the Gheluvelt Plateau, east of Ypres. While Plumer's plans were drawn up, there was a lull in the fighting and even the weather relented. Neither would last for long. On 20th September, the principal assaults went in astride the Menin Road while Fifth Army secured the left flank; seven local lads were present in four of the divisions engaged.

In 23rd Division, **Private Ernest Cope** (9/South Staffordshire, Pioneers) had enlisted with his elder brother, **Private John Cope** in August 1915 (they even had consecutive regimental numbers, 19804 and 19803 respectively) and had joined their unit in France early in 1916. Nineteen year-old John died on 23rd February 1916 from serious shrapnel wounds to the legs in the line near Armentières. Ernest would survive the war. Close to Langemarck and under Fifth Army control, **Private Isaac Andrews** was in the heat of 154th Brigade's assault on Pheasant Trench – despite stiff resistance and a counter-attack, 1/9 Royal Scots took and held their objectives. A short distance south of the Highlanders, **Sapper Ambrose Squire** of 55th 'West Lancashire' Division witnessed their infantry take most of its objectives and then the work of Squire's 419th Field Company began in earnest, reversing captured trenches and establishing dugouts for immediate use. The three local lads in 59th '2nd North Midland' Division, **Private Fred Harper** (2/6 Sherwood Foresters), **Private Wm Edw Pickin** (2/5 South Staffordshire) and **Private Albert Simmons** (2/6 South Staffordshire), were not moved up the line until 23rd September and their units played but a minor role in the battle – their luck would not last much longer.

The advance along the Menin Road encouraged successive, concentrated, narrow-front battles to be launched; the cost remained high and Elmore Green paid part of the price. On 26th September a follow-up attack was initiated in the area of Polygon Wood, north of the Menin Road. On the left flank of the attack were the Londoners of 58th Division and on their right, north of the Ypres to Roulers railway and facing Gravenstafel were three Elmore Green lads in 59th '2nd North Midland' Division, each in separate battalions. On a warm morning, heavy with mist and drizzle, the well-trained 59th attacked on a divisional front of 2,000 yards using two brigades, 177th on the right and **Private Fred Harper**'s 2/6 Sherwood Foresters in 178th Brigade on the left, while 176th 'Staffordshire' Brigade was held in reserve. At 5:50 a.m. and beneath an effective artillery barrage, 2/6th and 2/7th Battalions of the Sherwood Foresters led the assault, capturing strong, concrete blockhouses at Schuler Farm, Kansas House, Cross Cottages, Martha House, Green House, Road House, Kansas Cross, Focker, Riverside, Toronto and Deuce House. Despite vigorous German counter-attacks between 5:30 and 6:50 p.m., the advance had been consolidated by midnight. However, the attack cost 59th Division 1,110 casualties and the capture of one of the blockhouses towards Gravenstafel cost twenty-three year-old **Fred Harper** his young life on **26th September**; he was reported as 'missing in action' and his body was never identified, thus his name is commemorated on the Tyne Cot Memorial to the Missing, to the north-east of Ypres. Fred had been among the last of the volunteers in December 1915, largely because height requirements had prevented his enlisting earlier in the war; when the lower limit was reduced to five feet, Fred at 5' 1¾" was accepted into the army, eventually joining 15/ Sherwood Foresters, one of the new 'Bantam' battalions. At the front, **Private Harper** endured his share of 'scrapes', on one occasion he survived being buried alive during a battalion retirement and on another (in early January 1917) he contracted a severe bout of trench fever and was invalided home to be treated in No.2 Western General Hospital, Manchester until May 1917. He returned to France on 9th June and at the end of that month was posted to 2/6 Sherwood Foresters – it was not to be Fred's luckiest break.

Thursday, **27th September** dawned muggy but free from rain. It was to be a day of German attempts to regain lost ground, though the main counter-attacks tended to be centred on 3rd Division's front, immediately to the south of 59th Division. In the absence of a direct assault, German artillery maintained harassing fire on the line of outposts established the previous day by 177th and 178th Brigades and it was this shellfire that accounted for **Private Wm Edw Pickin**. 2/5 South Staffordshire battalion war diary records that day as follows:

> *"27 September 1917 - Shell hole east of Primrose Cottage…very heavy enemy shelling experienced during the day…heavy enemy barrage from 6:00 p.m. till 7.45p.m. At 9:00 p.m. the battalion withdrew to Cambrai Reserve Trench, east of Wieltje."*

During the day the battalion suffered casualties to the tune of 15 men killed, 40 wounded and 4 missing in action. Edward's body was one of those never identified. His Company Commander later kindly wrote to Edward's mother:

> *"As you are no doubt aware, he was killed during a very recent advance and met his death about 7 p.m. on the 27th of last month. He was killed whilst doing an act of great kindness to a wounded enemy soldier. His death was instantaneous, the result of a shell which burst very close to him. His loss will be felt by all his comrades, and no-one more so than myself, his company commander. He was always a very willing and cheerful man and was extremely popular throughout the battalion among both the officers and the men."*

Twenty-one year-old **Private Wm Edw Pickin** is commemorated on the Tyne Cot Memorial to the Missing. His brother, **Harold Pickin**, who was a year younger than Edward, served in both the South Staffordshire Regiment and the Machine Gun Corps and would survive the war though not without injury. Present in the same 176th Brigade but in 2/6 South Staffordshire was **Private Albert Simmons** of Park Road. He came safely through the Battle of Polygon Wood and would survive the mud of Passchendaele only to fall later in 1917 at Cambrai.

At least four more local lads fought in the Polygon Wood engagement, all of them in General Plumer's Second Army to the east of Ypres. Here, 5th Australian Division was tasked to a direct assault on Polygon Wood[138] itself. Initially, 33rd Division supported the Aussies' right flank and it was this British division that **Ernie Cope**'s 23rd Division relieved during the night of 27th September. For this privilege, the division was subjected to an unsuccessful but terrifying counter-attack at dawn on Sunday the 30th, the enemy employing a dense smoke barrage north of the Menin Road that allowed their flamethrowers to advance within effective distance. 23rd Division was itself relieved on 2nd October by 5th Division, whose 1/Bedfordshire contained nineteen year-old **Arthur Parkes** of May Street – it was just three days before his twentieth birthday. His best present was to be his survival.

On 30th September, the day that the German *'flammenwerfer'* attacked 23rd Division, two more Elmore Green Old Boys numbered among the ranks that relieved the tough Aussie 5th Division. **Jimmy Jones** and **Bill Haycock** of 1/ South Staffordshire were soldiers of the 'old' type. Jimmy had been out with the battalion since December 1914. Bill, on the other hand, had seen pre-war service with 'D' Company of the regiment's Territorials, earning his corporal's stripes – he was wounded early in the war and discharged but Bill Haycock re-enlisted and was posted to 1st Battalion. A married man with a young family, his bravery would cost him dearly. In the meantime, both lads survived the German dawn raid on 1st October and fought on, as did **Arthur Parkes** of 1/Bedfordshire (5th Division) through the subsequent Battles of Broodseinde (4th October) and Poelcapelle (9th October).

On 12th October, the first real push to reach Passchendaele Ridge and village was made but stiff enemy resistance and worsening weather conspired to frustrate the attempt. 17th 'Northern' Division attacked just to the north of Poelcapelle though their success was one among few on that day. **Edward Smith** of 10/West Yorkshire was lucky in that his 50th Brigade was not in front line action. 23rd Division and **Ernie Cope** had relieved 7th Division in front of Polygon Wood where ground conditions were dreadful; in his excellent 23rd Divisional History, Lt.-Col. H.R. Sandilands commented:

---

138 Locally known as the 'Polygone de Zonnebeke'.

"Rain and incessant shellfire had produced a quagmire…a wilderness of shell-holes, surrounded by all the hideous wreckage of war and filled with slimy water which failed to hide the dead bodies of men and mules, which it had not been possible to clear from the field of battle. Men would sink so deep and fast in the mud that it would take…an hour or two…to drag them out; laden mules would sometimes be drowned."

When the division was relieved after eleven days in the line, 23rd Division had sustained in excess of 1,200 casualties – **Ernie Cope** was not among them.

Fifty miles south of the Ypres Salient, **Isaac Andrews** of Church Street might have been ruing his insistence on enlisting in the army – it was a far cry from making motor locks next to his brother Ernie at the Old Hall Works for J. & J. Wiggin of Bloxwich. He volunteered soon after the war's outbreak but was rejected by a medical Board on account of his poor hearing; however, he persevered and was eventually accepted in October 1916. It appears that he originally joined the South Staffordshire second-line Territorials and was sent to Ireland in the aftermath of the 1916 Easter Rebellion. By 1917, on account of the small population north of the border, Scottish regiments were finding it difficult to attract new Scots recruits, so many English 'conscripts' were posted to Highland and Lowland battalions. Such was the reason Isaac Andrews came to be serving in the 1/9 Royal Scots, the senior British army regiment. After his battalion joined 51st 'Highland' Division in March 1917, the Royal Scots served with distinction in the snow of Arras and in the mud of 3rd Ypres, from Pilckem Ridge on 31st July to Poelcapelle in late September. The division was relieved on 25th September and subsequently **Isaac Andrews** and his mates were transferred from the dreaded Ypres Salient south to the Arras sector. The 'Highland' Division had impressed the commander of Fifth Army, General Sir Hubert Gough, who commented:

"In bidding farewell to the 'Highland' Division, the Army Commander wishes to express his great admiration for and his appreciation of their splendid record during the fighting of the past two months."

Even so, by 5th October, 1/9 Royal Scots (154th Brigade) were back in the trenches, this time in the Héninel-Wancourt, Fontaine-les-Croisilles and Guémappe sectors, south-east of Arras, areas in front of the Hindenburg Line described in a German newspaper, *'The Local Anzeiger'*, thus:

"…great stretches…have been turned into a dead country…No village or farm was left standing, no road was left passable, no railway track or

embankment was left in being. Where once were woods, there are gaunt rows of stumps; the wells have been blown up."

During the month of October, 1/9 Royal Scots was not involved in any major actions but a hefty share of trench-holding took its perennial toll upon the troops. In the divisional history, Major F.W. Bewsher DSO, MC commented:

"…even the quiet periods were often eventful enough for those in immediate contact with the enemy."

It is most likely that twenty-four year-old **Isaac Andrews**, a Midlander in a Scottish battalion, was killed on such regular trench duty on **23rd October**. The Scots' German opponents might well have recorded that it was,

"All quiet on that sector of the Western Front."

Private Isaac Andrews is buried in Wancourt British Cemetery, on a sunny hillside to the south-east of Arras.

In the Salient, the struggle for Passchendaele Ridge dragged on, made increasingly problematic by several factors. The surface of the battlefield was already deep in liquid mud and flood water; further bombardment would make it even worse, as would any further rainfall. Movement of men, animals and artillery was a slow, near-impossible process. Any movement up the long, glutinous slope towards Passchendaele was easily overlooked by enemy observers who could quickly call up an artillery or infantry reinforcements. Before and during the struggle for the ridge, the Germans were making more effective tactical use of gas. Initial use of Blue Cross gas (a sneezing agent) made wearing respirators very difficult; the follow-up gas shells contained Yellow Cross (mustard gas) that severely blistered skin, eyes and respiratory system, disabling rather than killing its victims. Worse still, while many gases dispersed after a few hours, mustard gas remained in the mud and the mustard oil remained effective for weeks. Finally, every night when flying was possible, German bombers peppered the rear areas (various headquarters, ammunition and other supply dumps, rest camps and important routes, railways and junctions) with high explosive and incendiary bombs.

Local lads were in three of the divisions that were involved in the opening attacks on 26th October (known as the Second Battle of Passchendaele). The main offensive was in the Second Army sector, east of Ypres, where 7th Division was facing Gheluvelt; on that division's left flank was 5th Division facing the remains of Polderhoek Chateau. To the north-east of Ypres, Fifth

Army was to create the impression of a major, wide-front offensive, though the real objective was the capture of the Passchendaele Ridge. Immediately north of the remains of Poelcapelle village, 57th '2nd West Lancashire' Division was to employ a single brigade, 170th, with three battalions attacking and with one in support and one (from 171st Brigade) in reserve. On a dully overcast and very rainy morning, **Sam Smith**'s 170th Brigade attacked with his 2/4th Battalion of the Loyal North Lancashire accompanied by 2/5th and 4/5th Battalions, L.N.L. The attack was launched at 5:40 a.m. and immediately encountered an impassable morass of knee-deep mud that caused the assault to come to a halt only a short distance from the 'start' line. Against all odds, however, two posts were established, at Rubens Farm and Memling Farm, 350 yards and 200 yards respectively in front of the original trench line. During this abortive advance, 57th Division suffered 1,634 casualties on **26th October**, one of the fatalities being twenty-two year-old **Private Samuel Smith** of Sandbank who was killed in action – surprisingly, given the battlefield conditions, Sam was found, identified and subsequently buried in Poelcapelle British Cemetery. The news of the loss of their eldest son must have been hard for parents Joe and Edith to accept – they could but hope that the war would end before younger son, Joseph, was old enough to be called up for service.

7th Division contained **Jimmy Jones** and **Bill Haycock**, both of 1/South Staffordshire (91st Brigade). At zero-hour, 5:40 a.m., their battalion was one of the three assault units intending to make progress onto the Gheluvelt Plateau on the eastern edge of the Salient. Initially, the lie of the land shielded the South Staffords from enemy machine-guns but the attempt on Hamp Farm and Berry Cottage exposed 'C' and 'D' companies to murderous fire and the advance was stopped in its tracks. Although their battalion suffered 278 casualties on that day, Jones and Haycock lived to fight again. 7th Division's losses totalled 2,724 – the shattered division was relieved from the front line by 39th Division and was ordered to refit and reinforce.

On the left flank of 7th Division, **Arthur Parkes** of 1/Bedfordshire witnessed his 5th Division comrades capture Polderhoek Chateau then lose it to a counter-attack. On 28th October, 14th Division relieved 5th Division but on a damp, overcast 1st November the relief was reversed. Yet as the Second Battle of Passchedaele tailed into November, the persistent rain that had dogged the initial days of the battle all but ceased. Even so the mud, churned by thousands of high explosive shells that had long-since destroyed the drainage system around Ypres, grew deeper and more unforgiving by the day. The job of the stretcher-bearers, extracting grievously-wounded men from the morass, became nigh on impossible. One such bearer, **Corporal Joseph Orgill**, had followed a circuitous route from Bloxwich to the 2nd Canadian Field Ambulance post at Luna Farm on the outskirts of the shell-torn town of Ypres. Born in the nearby village of Pelsall in 1892, Joe soon moved to Bloxwich and in 1913 took the momentous step of emigrating to Canada. No sooner had he settled than war was declared and by September 1914 Joe found himself at Valcartier volunteering for the 2nd Field Ambulance of the Canadian Army Medical Corps (with the 1st Canadian Contingent, later to become 1st Canadian Division). Following a cold winter in England the Canadians embarked in February at Avonmouth and landed at St. Nazaire in France. Their baptism of fire was to be the Second Battle of Ypres in April 1915, then on to Festubert and Givenchy. 1916 saw the division in action at Mount Sorrel near Ypres and on the Somme in some of the bloodiest fighting of that fearful campaign. Into 1917 and the division played a major part in the Battles of Arras, notably at Vimy Ridge; and so once more to Ypres. Thus far into a long war Joe Orgill had survived despite being injured and gassed on several occasions during his service. He must have come to the Second Battle of Passchendaele (ironically 1st Canadian Division's only major engagement in the whole of the 3rd Ypres offensive) with mixed feelings – grateful for his hitherto good fortune but, equally, wondering when that luck might run out. He did not have long to wait. According to the war diary of 2nd Canadian Field Ambulance, the unit took over the tented hospital at Luna Farm on 27th October, the second day of the battle, inheriting fifty sick patients from their predecessors. On 31st October, 'C' section moved to Moated Farm (near Vlamertinghe, just outside the western limits of Ypres) where their role was to deal with the sick rather than the wounded. The ensuing two days proved to be relatively quiet but Saturday, 3rd November witnessed a steady trickle of Canadian wounded into the Moated Farm post. 2nd Field Amulance, CAMC, war diary asserts:

> "3 November 1917 – Moated Farm. Six other ranks killed in action and one wounded and evacuated (on) this date."

It takes little imagination to work out that twenty-five year-old stretcher-bearer **Corporal James Orgill** was killed while bringing in wounded men from the battlefront to the 2nd Field Ambulance's Regimental Aid Post (RAP) or to its Advanced Dressing Station (ADS). His party of stretcher-bearers was most probably hit by a shell. However, a report by the Graves Registration Commission (GRC) gives a trench-map location (28.c28.a.7.2) for his grave and states:

> "The cross found without remains and bearing the name of this soldier with five others has been re-erected in the Memorial Plot of White House British Cemetery." [The original place of burial is recorded as]…

"Bilge Dump, north of St. Jean-Wieltje Road, 1½ Miles N.E. of Ypres. Actual graves cannot be found on research. These reports refer to a Memorial Cross only."

The GRC report also refers to Joe's unit as, *"working in the Passchendaele area,"* at the time of his death. The war diary for the Assistant Director of Medical Services, 1st Canadian Division, nevertheless records:

*"**3 November** 1917 – the Officers Commanding the 1st, 2nd and 3rd Canadian Field Ambulances were each detailed to supply four, two and three motor ambulance cars respectively to work with the C.O. 14th Motor Ambulance Convoy. Six other ranks killed and one wounded of the 2nd Canadian Field Ambulance bearers near Waterloo* [a small habitation at the roadside just beyond Gravenstafel] *this morning."*

Joe's body was never identified and thus he is one of the many lads commemorated on the Menin Gate Memorial to the Missing in Ypres. His long journey was at an end. Two of his brothers, George Orgill and John Orgill were still serving in the British army.

From 8th November, **Edward Smith** of 17th 'Northern' Division also had a brief taste of Passchendaele's mud but luckily there were no attacks. **Arthur Parkes** and **Edward Smith** remained in the sector until the 3rd Ypres offensive was abandoned for the year on 10th November.

Already out of the line for five days, on 28th October 23rd Division was warned to be ready to move for an 'unknown destination'. It turned out to be Italy. On 14th November, 7th Division was also given orders to move to the Italian Front where the junior ally was in danger of defeat by Austrian and German units. A few local lads would be travelling further afield than they could ever have dreamed.

November & December
Cambrai was another of the 'nearly' battles when early success was followed by hard-hitting enemy counter-attacks. The battlefield chosen was between Arras and the Somme where the firm, open ground was ideal for the first mass use of tanks and the British set almost five hundred of them against the powerful Hindenburg Line. Cambrai developed into a three-phase battle. The Tank Attack (20-21st November) encouraged the British high command to think of possible breakthrough and this was reinforced by the Capture of Bourlon Wood (23-28th November). Three Elmore Green lads were involved in the first two stages of the battle. The last time that our story touched on **James**

Heeley of Cope Street, he had suffered a serious gunshot wound to his right thigh at Gommecourt with the local Territorials on the first day of the Somme offensive in July 1916. As his battalion had left their trenches that morning they were struck by a German artillery barrage, resulting in most of the day's casualties. James was returned to England on Monday, 3rd July 1916 for hospital treatment. On recovery in England, James was transferred to the Durham Light Infantry, being posted to 18/DLI on 18th November 1916, though James did not join his battalion in France until 17th May 1917 when it returned from Egypt. On 2nd June he was again posted, this time to 14/DLI in 18th Brigade, 6th Division, a unit that had been fortunate to miss in its entirety the horrors of 'Passchendaele' – at the time of James's arrival, 14/DLI was in the quieter Loos-Lens sector. 6th Division was to take part in all three engagements of the Cambrai Battle. When the offensive opened on 20th November, **Heeley**'s 18th Brigade, in the centre of the battlefront and facing Marcoing, advanced successfully to occupy the Prémy Chapel Ridge. Next day, 21st November, 14/DLI took part in the capture of the ground in front of Cantaing, to the east of Bourlon Hill. Beyond 51st Division on Heeley's left, 62nd '2nd West Riding' Division was in the line facing Havrincourt and among the men of 2/4 Duke of Wellington's Regiment was **Private James Bryan**, a former ironworker of Providence Lane. He had fought at Arras and at Bullecourt – in short, he was lucky still to be alive! On the right wing of the assault, facing the village of Bantouzelle, **Sapper Ambrose Squire** waited with 419 Field Company of 55th Division – as usual, the Sappers' part in the battle depended largely upon the success of the infantry. The tanks and the infantry were successful in their attacks that day and the Engineers duly moved onto the battlefield to improve trench-lines and clear tracks and roads. In places, the line had been moved forward four miles and many prisoners and guns had been captured. However, the initial advance and the taking of Bourlon Wood had created a vulnerable British salient; there were few reinforcements by way of fresh troops and extra artillery so it seemed that the success was almost unexpected and a price was to be paid when enemy counter-attacks commenced on 30th November.

By then, 6th Division (**James Heeley**) and 55th Division (**Ambrose Squire**) were still in the line but 62nd Division had been relieved, so **James Bryan** would live to see 1918. 2nd Division had taken over the Bourlon Wood front on 27th November, so four more local lads with 2/South Staffordshire re-entered the fray – amazingly, all four, **Harold Revitt**, **Joe Bullock**, **James Smith** and **Alfred Main** would come through despite the successful German counter-attacks. Two more local lads were with the North Midland second-line Territorials, **Albert Simmons** in 2/6 South Staffordshire and **Leonard Beech** in 2/5 South Staffordshire, whose 59th Division had relieved the

Guards Division in the line opposite Fontaine, a large village five miles west of Cambrai.

On 30th November, the German counter-attack overran Gouzeaucourt and 6th Division's 16th Brigade was sent to shore up the front line. Later that day 14/DLI, until then in reserve, was sent up to Highland Ridge in the Hindenburg support system. Next day, 1st December, the enemy attempted to recapture Cantaing but was driven off by British machine-guns. During the night of Sunday, 2nd December 1917 the battalion moved from Highland Ridge to trenches east of the canal at Marcoing. There were three companies in the line, 'A' Company's trench being only two or three feet deep in places and badly-sited, forcing the company to start digging a new trench. Shortly after 10 a.m. on **3rd December**, 14/DLI battalion lines in the bend of the St. Quentin Canal came under a heavy enemy barrage but an attack in the area of 'A' Company was repelled by intense retaliation with rifle and Lewis-gun fire. A second German attack caused the DLI first to give ground and then counter-attack; at 11.30 a.m. a third enemy effort, covered by another barrage, saw savage fighting in which the DLI, using rifle, Lewis-gun, bomb and bayonet, again fought the enemy to a standstill. 14/DLI, despite suffering grievously in losing fourteen officers and 262 other ranks from their strength of just 450, were forced back by weight of numbers alone and managed to re-cross the canal by means of the railway bridge to a defensive line south west of Marcoing. At 4 p.m. the decimated Durhams bravely counter-attacked, utilising a barge to cross the canal. Fierce fighting again took place before the battalion recaptured their old reserve trench and beyond. The line was held until about 10.15 p.m. when the battalion made a tactical withdrawal to the Hindenburg support line, north east of Ribécourt. Sometime during this day of vicious fighting, twenty year-old **Lance-Corporal James Heeley** was killed in action; his body was never identified. At the front for just six weeks, James is commemorated on the Cambrai Memorial to the Missing, at Louverval, between Cambrai and Bapaume.

On 30th November, **Albert Simmons**' 176th Brigade was holding the sector Cantaing village to Bourlon Wood when German artillery set ablaze Cantaing Mill and drenched the wood in gas from 10 p.m. to 4 a.m., causing 350 casualties to Albert's battalion, and 318 more to 2/6 North Staffordshire; the two battalions were immediately relieved. Casualties were so high because the enemy employed mustard gas shells against which British respirators were totally inadequate. Two German attacks next morning, at 9 a.m. and 11 a.m., were broken up by accurate artillery fire. By 4th December the situation had changed for the worse; many British units were forced to pull back, albeit in good order. The *'Official History, Military Operations in France & Belgium, 1917, volume III'*, records the organised and defended withdrawal:

"Normal night firing was maintained and the enemy's response seemed to show that he had no inkling of any unusual movement within the British lines. The main bodies of infantry moved at 11 p.m. when platoon after platoon of heavily-laden men (carrying tools, small arms ammunition, bombs, rifle grenades, S.O.S. rockets and flares, and even Stokes mortar shells) began to dribble back from the front."

Each division left a lightly-held Covering Position and the 59th efficiently withdrew down the slope from Bourlon Wood to man the defences in the Flesquières Salient. 2/6 South Staffordshire battalion war diary records only one man injured that day:

"4/5 December 1917 – Moved to Havrincourt by march route, cross country, leaving Ribécourt at 12 midnight. Battalion accommodated in a dug out, from 5 a.m. till 12 noon. Bombing raid by enemy aircraft, one man injured. Moved by route march across country to Ytres arriving at 4 p.m. Billeted in huts in Little Wood Camp."

Sometime during the eventful day and night of 4th/5th December, twenty year-old former locksmith, **Private Albert Simmons** was severely wounded and moved down the line to Abbeville where he subsequently died on **6th December** in No.2 or No.5 Stationary Hospital. Albert was buried near the hospital in Abbeville Communal Cemetery Extension.

December

During February 1917, in a desperate gamble to strangle Britain's food and war supplies, Germany announced it would carry out unrestricted submarine warfare. For several months in 1917 the number of merchant ships sunk and the total tonnage lost peaked as never previously during the war:

January	49	ships sunk	153,000	gross tonnage
February	105	"	313,000	"
March	127	"	353,000	"
April	169	"	545,000	"
May	122	"	352,000	"
June	122	"	417,000	"
July	99	"	364,000	"
August	91	"	329,000	"
September	78	"	196,000	"
October	86	"	276,000	"

| November | 64 | " | 173,000 | " |
| December | 85 | " | 253,000 | " |

[Source: Official History: *'Merchant Navy, volume III'*, by Archibald Hurd.]

While food shortages affected most families in Britain, the U-boat threat directly affected two families whose sons were in some way connected to Elmore Green School. Our story has already recounted the loss in May 1917 of **Tom Rowbotham**, RNVR, aboard the merchant vessel S.S. *'Kilmaho'*. Now, Charlotte Goodall of Church Street, who had not long been widowed, received the harsh news around Christmas of the death of one of her younger sons. After leaving school **Harold Goodall**, one of twenty children, found employment as a grocery assistant in the Bloxwich branch of the Walsall and District Co-operative Society. From 1915 to early 1917, the wider Goodall family had lost four lads killed and another badly wounded (on the first day of the Somme). Harold did not turn 18 years of age until 7th July 1916 and so was called up with his age group, enlisting in the Royal Naval Volunteer Reserve[139] on 3rd October 1916. **Able Seaman Harold Goodall** (part of the Bristol Division, like Tom Rowbotham before him) was not tall (5' 3¼"), had light brown hair, blue eyes and a fresh complexion; his service record also described a small scar on his forehead. His record also spoke of *'satisfactory ability and very good character'*. Harold served in shore (training) establishments until 31st October 1917 when he was posted as a gunner to a merchant vessel, the S.S. *'Ottokar'*:

> *'The Admiralty…..provided, for each gun which they mounted in a merchant ship, a trained gunlayer, a second and, for certain guns, a third hand, bearing all the expense of paying and of victualling these men, who were to be carried in addition to the normal ship's complement.'*
>
> [Official History: *'Merchant Navy, volume III'*, by Archibald Hurd.]

Harold's ship was an armed merchantman, the 957-ton iron steamer *'Ottokar'* built in Germany by Elbing in 1884, owned by Marcus Cohn of Königsberg in East Prussia and managed by Messrs. Everett and Newbiggin for the British Admiralty by whom she was requisitioned at Plymouth in August 1914 – the requisition was somewhat ironic, given the ship's early history.

The S.S. *'Ottokar'* sailed from Newcastle on Tuesday, 11th December 1917 bound for London with a cargo of coal but was not heard from again. It is thought that the UB-75 (a type III diesel submarine built in 1916) sank the S.S.

---

139 The RNVR accepted men from all walks of life *except* maritime trades – the latter joined the Royal Naval Reserve (RNR).

'Ottokar' off the Yorkshire coast near Whitby on **11th December** 1917. The UB-75, commanded by Oberleutnant Franz Walther, left Borkum (an island U-Boat base off the mouth of the River Ems) on the 29th November 1917 and headed for its patrol area, the North Sea coast of England. After sinking five merchant ships (one of which was the S.S. 'Ottokar'), it is assumed that UB-75 would then have set a course for home, scheduled to arrive there on 13th December. All that is known for certain is that she never made it back to Borkum and her last resting place was discovered off Robin Hood's Bay near Scarborough in September 2002 by Carl Racey and Andy Jackson; UB-75 was upright and intact, showing mine damage at the stern end and missing about five metres of the hull. It seems that hunter and prey shared a similar fate.

As for **Harold Goodall** and the S.S. 'Ottaker', his vessel was listed as 'missing' by Lloyds of London, with public notification published in 'The Times' newspaper of 21st February 1918. Harold and two more of the crew of twenty were RNVR and are thus commemorated on the Plymouth Naval Memorial on Plymouth Hoe – the other sailors were Mercantile Marine and they are commemorated on the Tower Hill Memorial. In addition, **Harold**, **Edgar** and **William Goodall** are all commemorated on the Elmore Green school roll of honour.

Beyond the Western Front

December

At the time that 23rd Division, containing 69th Brigade and was en route for Italy, **Frank Lester** of 69th Machine Gun Company (69th Brigade) was in England recovering from a virulent dose of trench fever, an illness that displayed most of the symptoms of severe influenza. Thus parted from his mates, Frank was subsequently posted to Egypt on 9th December 1917 and disembarked at the port of Alexandria on 3rd January 1918 where he was posted to 155th Company, Machine Gun Corps. His time in the African sun lasted but a few short weeks as he returned to France and the BEF on 17th April 1918.

The local *'Old Contemptibles'*, surviving at the end of 1917:

Ernest Lavender   discharged 8/1/17 due to wounds
John Bullock   1st (Reg) Battalion, S. Staffordshire Regiment [P.o.W.]
Joseph Bullock   2nd (Reg) Battalion, South Staffordshire Regiment

Other 1914 men surviving at the end of 1917:

James Jones   1st (Reg) Battalion, South Staffordshire Regiment

Old Boys – arrivals at the Front, 1917:

Men who arrived in theatre between 1st January and 31st December 1917:

Harold REVITT	2nd (Reg) Battalion, South Staffordshire Regiment
James SMITH	2nd (Reg) Battalion, South Staffordshire Regiment
Alfred SLEIGH	129th (Heavy) Battery, RFA, 3rd Divisional Artillery
William HAYCOCK	1st (Reg) Battalion, South Staffordshire Regiment
Bernard HOOPER	8th (Service) Battalion, Gloucestershire Regiment
Albert COOPER	12th (Service) Battalion, Durham Light Infantry
Horace JORDAN	4th (Extra Reserve) Bn, South Staffordshire Regiment
William GRIMSLEY	4th (Extra Reserve) Bn, South Staffordshire Regiment
Bertie ELKS	4th (Extra Reserve) Bn, South Staffordshire Regiment
Albert WILKES	1/5th TF Battalion, Sherwood Foresters
Horace HILL	1/6th TF Battalion, South Staffordshire Regiment
Harold BAUGH	1/4th TF Battalion, Leicestershire Regiment
Isaac ANDREWS	1/9th TF Battalion, Royal Scots Regiment
Ambrose SQUIRE	419th Field Company, Royal Engineers
Wm Edw PICKIN	2/5th TF Battalion, South Staffordshire Regiment
Albert SIMMONS	2/6th TF Battalion, South Staffordshire Regiment
Leonard BEECH	2/5th TF Battalion, South Staffordshire Regiment
James BRYAN	2/4th TF Battalion, Duke of Wellington's Regiment
Harold GOODALL	S.S. *'Ottokar'*, Royal Naval Volunteer Reserve

UPPER CASE surnames indicate men *whose* names are commemorated on the Elmore Green school memorial.

Lower case surnames indicate men *related* to those who are commemorated on the Elmore Green school memorial.

(Reg)	indicates a Regular Army battalion.
TF	indicates a Territorial Force battalion.
(S)	indicates a Service or 'New Army' battalion.
(Sp. Res.)	indicates a Special Reserve or Extra Reserve battalion

Where local volunteers might serve on the front line – theatres of war and garrison commitments in 1917:

Western Front	in France and Belgium against the German army.
Southern Front	(v. Austrians/Germans) – North Italy from Autumn 1917 to autumn 1918. Start of November 1918, Hungary out of war.
East Africa	in Rhodesia, Nyasaland, Zanzibar, Tanga against German troops and German colonial troops.
Salonika/Macedonia	with French against Austrians/Germans/Bulgars.
Egypt/Suez Canal Zone	against Turkish invaders.
Mesopotamia	in present-day Iraq against Turkish troops.
Palestine	(v. Turkish troops) From March 1917.

Imperial Garrisons and RN coaling stations throughout the Empire – Africa, India, West Indies, Gibraltar, Hong Kong and many others. Regular troops gradually replaced by local 'native' and TF troops.

At sea	U-Boat war

Chronological Roll of Honour for 1917

January 16th	Fred	LESTER	Somme
March	14th	Joseph DAVIES	Somme
March	14th	Joseph HANDY	Somme
March 14th	Arthur	LINNELL, MM	Somme
April 17th	Ernest	HAYWOOD	Arras
April 23rd	William	BULLOCK	Arras
April 23rd	(J) Thomas	Parton**	Arras
April 28th	Albert	STYCH, MM	Arras
May 12th	David	Goodall**	Bullecourt
May 15th	Alfred	SLEIGH	Arras
May 17th	Tom	ROWBOTHAM	Western Approaches
May 28th	Arthur	Smith**	Arras/Bullecourt
June 10th	Charles	BULLOCK	Lens
June 10th	William	Parkes**	Ypres
June 10th	Robert	SYLVESTER	Ypres
July 28th	Bernard	HOOPER	Ypres
September 26th	Fred	HARPER	Ypres
September 27th	Wm Edw	PICKIN	Ypres
October 23rd	Isaac	ANDREWS	Arras sector
October 26th	Samuel	SMITH	Ypres
November 3rd	Joseph	ORGILL	Ypres

December 11th	Harold	GOODALL	North Sea
December 12th	Albert	SIMMONS	Cambrai
December 17th	James	HEELEY	Cambrai

** Indicates a name related to those that appear on the Elmore Green School Old Boys War Memorial.

Roll of Honour for 1917 (alphabetical order)

Isaac ANDREWS

Born between June and September 1893. Lived at 77, Church Street, Bloxwich. Son of Isaac (a coalminer) and Mary Ann Andrews (née Cartwright) of the same address, who were married in 1882. One of at least eight children in 1901 – John 18, Ernest 14, Isaac 7, Archibald 3, Florence 16, Harriet 12, Edith 10. Educated at Elmore Green School. Single. Toolmaker employed by J. & J. Wiggin of Old Hall Works, Woodall Street, Bloxwich, alongside his elder brother, Ernest Andrews, making 'motor locks'. **Enlisted**, eventually, in **October 1916** in Walsall having previously been rejected on grounds of deafness). **352832, Private, 1/9th (Territorial Force) 'Highlanders' Battalion, Royal Scots Regiment, (154th '3rd Highland' Brigade, 51st 'Highland' Division)**. *Unit History* – Served initially in Ireland. Landed in France in May 1917. Arras, 9-11/4/17 1st Battle of the Scarpe; 23-24/4/17 2nd Battle of the Scarpe; 13-16/5/17 Capture and Defence of Roeux. 3rd Ypres ('Passchendaele'), 31/7-7/8/17 Battle of Pilckem; 20-24/9/17 Battle of the Menin Road. **Killed in action (age 24) on Tuesday, 23rd October 1917**, on regular trench duty in the Arras sector. **Buried** in plot I. B. 53 of **Wancourt British Cemetery**, south east of Arras, France. **Entitled** to the British War Medal and Victory Medal (Medal Roll – D/101B35, p.3635). Commemorated on the Elmore Green School Roll of Honour (formerly displayed in T.P. Riley School library), on the Roll of Honour in All Saints Church, Bloxwich and on both the Bloxwich and Walsall Rolls of Honour.

(Alfred) Charles BULLOCK

Born between October and December of 1893 in Blakenall and lived at 28, New Street, Bloxwich. Son of John (a bricklayer's labourer) and Ruth Bullock (née Henden) of the same address. Educated at Elmore Green School. One of eleven children – nine brothers (John, Joseph Henry, William Amos, Frank, Lilias, George Edward, Leonard, Herbert, Harold) and one sister (Amy Gladys). Single. Employed in 1911 as a coal mine labourer (above ground) at Holly Bank Colliery, Essington. **Volunteered** in **October 1914** in Walsall. **9725>200822, Private, 1/5th (Territorial Force) Battalion, the South Staffordshire Regiment, (137th Brigade, 46th '1st North Midland' Division)**. *Unit History* – landed in France on 5th March 1915. 7/15 to 2/10/15 Hill 60, Ypres. 13-15/10/15 Battle of Loos (Hohenzollern Redoubt and Hulluch Quarries). Wounded on Wednesday, 13th October 1915 attacking the notorious Hohenzollern Redoubt and was invalided to England. Returned to France in January 1916. January 1916 the battalion sailed to Egypt but in February 1916 returned to France. From 19/3/16 Neuville St. Vaast/ Ecoivres. May/June 1916 Fonquevillers sector of the Somme. Somme, 1/7/16 Battle of Gommecourt. 3/7/16 to 28/10/16 Berles-au-Bois and Bailleulmont sector on the Somme. 1-13/3/17 Operations on the Ancre including the Occupation of the Gommecourt Defences (4/3/17) and the Attack on Rettemoy Graben (12/3/17). 14/3/17-22/3/17 German Retreat to the Hindenburg Line. 18/4/17 to 15/6/17 Lens sector (Cité St. Pierre). 3/6/17-26/8/17 Lens sector. **Died (age 23) on 10th June 1917 in No.7 Casualty Clearing Station of wounds sustained two days earlier,** near Lens. **Buried** in plot II. A. 3 of **Noeux-les-Mines Communal Cemetery, south of Béthune,** France. **Entitled** to the 1914-15 Star (Medal Roll – F/2B1, p.58), British War Medal and Victory Medal (Medal Roll – F/101B18, p.2285). Commemorated on the Elmore Green School Roll of Honour (formerly displayed in T.P. Riley School library) as well as on the Bloxwich Roll of Honour, the roll of honour at All Saints Church, Bloxwich and on the Walsall Roll of Honour. **Family** – A brother, R/16384, Rifleman William Amos Bullock of 16/KRRC was killed in action on 23rd April 1917 and is commemorated on the Elmore Green roll of honour; a second brother, 7745, Private John Bullock of 1/South Staffordshire was held prisoner in Germany from November 1914; a third brother, 6285, Private Joseph Henry Bullock of 2/South Staffordshire served on the Western Front and survived the war.

William Amos BULLOCK

Born between June and September of 1895 in Blakenall and lived at 105, Church Street, Bloxwich. Son of John (a bricklayer's labourer) and Ruth Bullock (née

Henden) of 105, Church Street. Educated at Elmore Green School. One of eleven children – nine brothers (John, Joseph Henry, Alfred Charles, Frank, Lilias, George Edward, Leonard, Herbert, Harold) and one sister (Amy Gladys). Single. Employed as a painter by Mr. G. Bentley of Bloxwich. **Volunteered on 6th December 1915** in Walsall (aged 20 years and 3 months; 5' 7½", 133lbs). **R/16384, Rifleman, 1 Company, 16th (Service/New Army) 'Church Lads Brigade' Battalion, King's Royal Rifle Corps, (100th Brigade, 33rd Division)**. *Unit History* – [16/KRRC was formed at Denham, Buckinghamshire, on 19th September 1914 by Field-Marshal Lord Grenfell, Commandant of the Church Lads Brigade, from current and previous members of that organisation.] Embarked at Folkestone on 14th April 1916 aboard S.S. *'Invicta'*. Reached Etaples (France) Base Depot on 15/4/16. Joined 16/Battalion on 26/5/16. Somme, 12-13/7/16 Battle of Albert; 14-17/7/16 Battle of Bazentin; 18-21/7/16 Attacks on High Wood; William was wounded on Tuesday 8th August 1916 when he received a gas shell shrapnel wound in his back. He was initially treated by 104th Field Ambulance on 8/8/16 and later the same day was evacuated to No. 61 (1st 'South Midland') Casualty Clearing Station. His wounds necessitated repatriation to the UK aboard Hospital Ship *'St. George'* on 14/8/16. Invalided to the 3rd Scottish General Hospital, Royal Infirmary, Glasgow, until 23/10/16. 4/2/17 embarked Southampton and landed at Le Havre, France on 5/2/17; 28/2/17 rejoined battalion. Arras, 14/4/17 1st Battle of the Scarpe; 16/4/17 Operations on the Hindenburg Line around the Wancourt Tower; 23-24/4/17 2nd Battle of the Scarpe. **Killed in action (age 21) on Monday, 23rd April 1917** on the first day of the 2nd Battle of the Scarpe. **Commemorated** on bay 7 of the **Arras Memorial to the Missing**, France. **Entitled** to the British War Medal and Victory Medal (Medal Roll – M/101B26, p.3282). Commemorated on the Elmore Green School Roll of Honour (formerly displayed in T.P. Riley School library), on the Bloxwich Roll of Honour, the Roll of Honour in All Saints Church, Bloxwich and on the Walsall Roll of Honour. **Family** – an older brother, 200822, Private Charles Bullock of 1/5 South Staffordshire was killed in action on 23rd April 1917 at Arras; a second brother, 7745, Private John Bullock of 1/South Staffordshire was held prisoner in Germany from November 1914; a third brother, 6285, Private Joseph Henry Bullock of 2/South Staffordshire served on the Western Front and survived the war.

Joseph James DAVIES

Born on 27th February 1897 in Bloxwich, Joseph was a single man living with his parents at 68, Elmore Green Road, Bloxwich. Educated at Elmore Green School (from 15/02/09). A miner by trade at Holly Bank Colliery. **Volunteered** in **September 1914** in Walsall. **9240>200630, Private**, '**A**' **Company, 1/5th (Territorial Force) Battalion, South Staffordshire Regiment, (137th Brigade, 46th '1st North Midland' Division)**. *Unit History* – drafted to France on Friday, 10th December 1915. January 1916 to Egypt. February 1916 to France. From 19/3/16 Neuville St. Vaast/Ecoivres. May/June 1916 Fonquevillers sector of the Somme; 24/6/16 wounded and evacuated to England. Somme, November 1916 returned to duty in France. 1-13/3/17 Operations on the Ancre including the Occupation of the Gommecourt Defences (4/3/17) and the Attack on Rettemoy Graben (12/3/17). 14/3/17-22/3/17 German Retreat to the Hindenburg Line. **Killed in action (age 20) on Wednesday, 14th March 1917 near Bucquoy** (three miles to the east of Gommecourt) at the start of the German retreat to the Hindenburg Line. **Commemorated** on pier and face 7B of the **Thiepval Memorial to the Missing**, Somme, France. **Entitled** to the 1914-15 Star (Medal Roll – F/2/B2, p.103), British War Medal and Victory Medal (Medal Roll – F/101B18, p.2267). Commemorated on the Elmore Green School Roll of Honour (formerly located in the T.P. Riley School library), on the Walsall and Bloxwich Rolls of Honour and on the Roll of Honour at All Saints Church, Bloxwich (surname is incorrectly spelt as '*Davis*').

David GOODALL** [Not Elmore Green memorial]

Born in Bloxwich in 1877 or 1878, the son of David and Mary Goodall of 64, New Street, Bloxwich. The family later moved to Chesterton, on the outskirts of Newcastle-under-Lyme, where they lived at 53, Heath Street. David had at least five siblings including two brothers Joseph and Frederick, and three sisters Fanny, Gertie and Jane. In 1901, David was a labourer in a brickyard in Chesterton but it appears that he returned to Bloxwich prior to the outbreak of the Great War in August 1914. **Volunteered** in Walsall, probably in **early 1915**. **16677, Private, 1st Battalion, the South Staffordshire Regiment, (91st Brigade, 7th Division)**. Unit History: landed in France on 8th December 1915. Somme, 1-5/7/16 Battle of Albert including the Capture of Mametz (1/7/16); 14-17/7/16 Battle of Bazentin; 20/7/16 Attack on High Wood; 21/7-3/9/16 Battle of Delville Wood. 3-7/9/16 Battle of Guillemont.

11-15/1 and 21/2- 5/3/17 Operations on the Ancre. 14/3-5/4/17 German Retreat to The Hindenburg Line. Arras, 11/4-16/6/17 Flanking Operations around Bullecourt including 3-17/5/17 Battle of Bullecourt. **Killed in action (age 39) on 12th May 1917** to the south-east of Arras during the Battle of Bullecourt. **Commemorated** on bay 6 of the **Arras Memorial to the Missing**. **Entitled** to the 1914-15 Star (Medal Roll – F/2B2, p.153), British War Medal and Victory Medal (Medal Roll – F/101 B8, p.849). **Family** – Five of David's 'Goodall' cousins were killed during the Great War; all six of the lads were born in Bloxwich. Three of the cousins were brothers – Edgar, Samuel and John; the two other cousins were Harold and William.

Harold GOODALL

Harold was one of twenty children. He was born on Tuesday, 5th July 1898 (from RNVR records - though the 1901 census records him as being 9 months old, that is to say, born in July 1900), the son of William and Charlotte Goodall (née Hall) of 51, Reeve Street, Bloxwich and later of 13, Church Street, Bloxwich. Harold's father, a coal miner, predeceased him. Prior to enlisting in the Royal Navy, he was employed as a grocery assistant in the Bloxwich branch of the Walsall and District Co-operative Society. Single. **Enlisted** in the **Royal Naval Volunteer Reserve** on 3rd October 1916. **Division: Bristol. Z/10064, Able Seaman, S.S. 'Ottokar',** **RNVR.** Information from RNVR service record – height 5' 3¼"; chest = 33"; light brown hair, blue eyes, fresh complexion. Small scar on forehead. 'Character = Very good; Ability = satisfactory.' Served on shore establishments until 31/10/17. Joined S.S. 'Ottokar' on 31st October 1917. Harold, as a member of the Royal Navy Volunteer Reserve, served as a gunner aboard the S.S. 'Ottokar', a 957-ton iron steamer built by in Germany by Elbing in 1884, owned by Marcus Cohn of Königsberg in East Prussia and managed by Messrs. Everett and Newbiggin for the British Admiralty by whom she was requisitioned at Plymouth in August 1914. **Presumed drowned at sea (age 19) on Tuesday, 11th December 1917** when his ship, the S.S.'Ottokar', was sunk by UB-75 off the coast of Whitby, Yorkshire. **Commemorated** on Panel 24 of the **Plymouth Naval Memorial**, situated on Plymouth Hoe in Devon. **Entitled** to the British War Medal and Victory Medal. Commemorated on the Elmore Green School Roll of Honour (formerly located in the T.P. Riley School library), on the Walsall and Bloxwich Rolls of Honour and on the Roll of Honour of All Saints Church, Bloxwich. **Family** – Five of Harold's 'Goodall' cousins were killed during the Great War; all six of the lads were born in Bloxwich. Three of the cousins were brothers – Edgar, Samuel and John; the two other cousins were David and William. Harold, Edgar and William Goodall are all commemorated on the Elmore Green school roll of honour.

Joseph Henry HANDY

Born between October and December 1894 in Walsall to Edwin and Sarah Emma (née Smith) Handy and initially lived at 21, Alma Street, Darlaston, his father being a Police Constable. Edwin left the Police Force prior to the turn of the century and opened a greengrocery shop at 49, Marlborough Street, Bloxwich where the family also resided. Joseph was one of three children – one brother (Edwin Arthur) and one sister (Bertha Annie). Educated at Elmore Green Church of England School. Single. Miner employed at Wyrley Plant Colliery (having previously been employed in the motor trade). **Volunteered** in **February 1912** in Bloxwich for the Territorial Force. **7821>200088, Corporal, 'B' Company, 1/5th (Territorial Force) Battalion, South Staffordshire Regiment, (137th Brigade, 46th '1st North Midland' Division)**. *Unit History* – Volunteered for overseas service. 5th March 1915 landed at Le Havre, France. From 4/4/15 at Neuve Eglise/Wulverghem. 7/15 to 2/10/15 Hill 60, Ypres. 13-15/10/15 Battle of Loos (Hohenzollern Redoubt and Hulluch Quarries). January 1916 to Egypt. February 1916 to France. From 19/3/16 Neuville St. Vaast/Ecoivres. May/June 1916 Fonquevillers sector of the Somme. Somme, 1/7/16 Battle of Gommecourt. 3/7/16 to 28/10/16 Berles-au-Bois and Bailleulmont sector on the Somme. 1-13/3/17 Operations on the Ancre including the Occupation of the Gommecourt Defences (4/3/17) and the Attack on Rettemoy Graben (12/3/17). 14/3/17-22/3/17 German Retreat to the Hindenburg Line. **Killed in action (age 22) on Wednesday, 14th March 1917** near Bucquoy in a night attack during the German Retreat to the Hindenburg Line. **Buried** in plot B. III of **Rossignol Wood Cemetery**, **Hébuterne**, Somme, France. **Entitled** to the 1914-15 Star (Medal Roll – F/2/B2, p.171), British War Medal and Victory Medal (Medal Roll – F/101B17, p.2218). Commemorated on the Elmore Green School Roll of Honour (formerly located in the T.P. Riley School library), on the Walsall and Bloxwich Rolls of Honour, where his rank is incorrectly recorded as 'Sergeant', and on the Roll of Honour in All Saints Church, Bloxwich. **Family** – A cousin was wounded and an uncle, 13628, A/CSM Robert Handy DCM, served in 8/South Staffordshire.

Fred HARPER

Born on 10th July 1896 in Bloxwich and lived at 8, Elmore, Green Road, Bloxwich. Son of a bricklayer's labourer (and was later a colliery boilerman) Frederick William, and Eliza Harper (née Stokes) of 6, Elmore Green Road. One of nine children – six brothers (William, Charles, George, Harry, Philip and Ernest) and two sisters (Louie and Harriet). Educated at Elmore Green School (from 03/04/05). Tilemaker employed by G.W. Lewis Tileries, Essington. Height: 5' 1¾". Attested in Walsall on Saturday, 11th December 1915. **Enlisted on 14th April 1916** in Walsall. **42192, Private,** Posted to the 19th (Reserve) Battalion, SF, from 4/4/16 then to France – 15/SF 'Bantams'. Ill with trench fever and invalided to UK. **2/6th (Territorial Force) Battalion,** [from 30/6/17], **Sherwood Foresters Regiment, (178th Brigade, 59th '2nd North Midland' Division).** *Unit History* – 18/7/16 landed in France. On one occasion he was buried alive during a battalion retirement. Invalided home in early January 1917 suffering from trench fever and was in No.2 Western General Hospital, Manchester between Tuesday, 23rd January 1917 and Thursday, 3rd May 1917. Returned to France on Saturday, 9 June 1917 was posted to the 2/6th Battalion on Saturday, 30th June 1917. 3rd Ypres ('Passchendaele'), 20-25/9/17 Battle of the Menin Road; 26/9-3/10/17 Battle of Polygon Wood. **Killed in action (age 21) on Wednesday, 26th September 1917** when the battalion captured several German blockhouses near Gravenstafel on the first day of the Battle of Polygon Wood during 3rd Ypres ('Passchendaele'). **Commemorated** on panels 99-102 and 162, 162A of the **Tyne Cot Memorial to the Missing**, near Ypres, Belgium. **Entitled** to the British War Medal and Victory Medal (Medal Roll – F/103B13, p.2430). Commemorated on the Elmore Green School Roll of Honour (formerly located in the T.P. Riley School library), on the Walsall and Bloxwich Rolls of Honour and on the Roll of Honour in All Saints Church, Bloxwich. **Family** – a brother, identity unknown, served for at least three years, sometime in the Gibraltar garrison.

Ernest HAYWOOD

Born on 26th August 1896 in Walsall. Son of widow Annie Elizabeth Haywood (née Moores), a self employed grocer of 17, Providence Street, Blakenall. Ernest was thus stepson to bricklayer, Thomas Dunn (whom Annie married in Walsall in 1903) of 32, May Street, Leamore. One of three children in 1911 – two older brothers (Clifford and George Wilfred). Educated at Elmore Green

School. Single. Bit and stirrup filer employed by B. Cope & Sons. **Enlisted** on **28th August 1916** in Walsall.

30578, Private, 'B' Company, 8th (Service) Battalion, South Staffordshire Regiment, (51st Brigade, 17th 'Northern' Division). *Unit History* – landed in France in December 1916. Arras, 12-14/4/17 1st Battle of the Scarpe. **Killed in action (age 20) on Tuesday, 17th April 1917** at Arras. **Buried** in plot J. 21 of **St. Catherine British Cemetery**, **Arras**, France (this plot was formed after the Armistice from battlefield burials and the amalgamation of smaller cemeteries.) **Entitled** to the British War Medal and Victory Medal (Medal Roll – F/101B10, p.1205). Commemorated on the Elmore Green School Roll of Honour (formerly located in the T.P. Riley School library) and on the Walsall and Bloxwich Rolls of Honour. **Family** – his step-father, 50614, Sapper Thomas Dunn of 89th Field Company, the Royal Engineers, who volunteered in September 1914, was killed in action and is commemorated on the Walsall Roll of Honour. Tragically, Thomas Dunn was killed just five weeks prior to the death of his stepson Ernest Haywood. Thomas Dunn's brother, Elijah, served in the RE Tunnelling branch.

James HEELEY

Born on 25th April 1897 in Blakenall and lived at 23, Cope Street, Leamore. Son of a coal-miner, John, and Prudence Heeley (née Simmons). One of twelve children, of whom ten were living at home in 1911 – at least four brothers (John, Arthur, Victor H. and Norman) and at least five sisters (Lily, Ethel, Emma, Agnes and Florrence M.). His mother passed away on Tuesday, 5th March 1912. Educated at Elmore Green School (from 31/08/09). Single. Employed as a labourer at the Talbot Stead Tube Works in Green Lane, Walsall.

Enlisted on **Wednesday, 5th May 1916** in Walsall. 422 >35073, Private, 'B' Company, 3/5th (TF) Battalion, South Staffordshire Regiment. Transferred to..., **'D' Company, 1/5th (TF) Battalion, South Staffordshire Regiment**. On 18th November 1916 transferred to..., **56837, Lance-Corporal**, **18th (Service) '1st County' Battalion, Durham Light Infantry,** (93rd Brigade, 31st Division). On Saturday, 2nd June 1917 posted to..., **14th (Service) Battalion, Durham Light Infantry, (18th Brigade, 6th Division)**. *Unit History* – [5/South Staffordshire] Landed in France on

Wednesday, 24th May 1916. Wounded in July 1916, invalided to England. [18/Durham Light Infantry] returned to France on Thursday, 17th May 1917. [14/Durham Light Infantry] Cambrai, 20-21/11/17 British Tank Attack; 23-28/11/17 British Capture of Bourlon Wood; 30/11-3/12/17 German Counter-Attacks. **Killed in action (age 20) on Monday, 3rd December 1917** in the German Counter Attacks at Cambrai. **Commemorated** on panel 10 of the **Cambrai Memorial to the Missing**, Louverval, France. **Entitled** to the British War Medal and Victory Medal (Medal Roll – D/1/103B22, p.4262). Commemorated on the Elmore Green School Roll of Honour (formerly located in the T.P. Riley School library) and on the Walsall and Bloxwich Rolls of Honour. Note: he is incorrectly shown on the records of the Soldiers Died in the Great War as having the surname of 'Steeley'. **Family** – A brother, T/344176, Private, Charles Henry, served in France with the Army Service Corps from 1916.

Bernard Clarence HOOPER

Born on 17th May 1896 and lived in Bloxwich. Son of a coal miner, George, and Louisa Elizabeth (née Fellows) Hooper of 7, Reeve Street, Leamore and later of 670, Bloxwich Road, Leamore. Educated at Elmore Green School. He was employed locally as a baker in New Street, Bloxwich although he had previously been employed as a 'butcher's traveller'. Single. One of seven children -had at least two brothers, Sidney Hooper and Leonard Hooper (7 years older). **Volunteered** in **August 1915** in Walsall. 719, Private, 2/5th Battalion, South Staffordshire Regiment. Transferred to…**37061, Lance-Corporal**, **8th (Service) Battalion, Gloucestershire Regiment, (57th Brigade, 19th 'Western' Division)**. *Unit History* – [2/5 South Staffordshire] served in Ireland during the rebellion. Landed in France in February 1917. [8/Gloucestershire] 7-14/6/17 Battle of Messines. 28th July – Oosttaverne sector of the Messines Ridge.

    Killed in action (age 21) on Saturday, 28th July 1917 by a shell burst at Oosttaverne near Ypres. **Commemorated** on panels 72-75 of the **Tyne Cot Memorial to the Missing**, near Ypres, Belgium. **Entitled** to the British War Medal and Victory Medal (Medal Roll – L/101B14, p.2454). Commemorated on the Elmore Green School Roll of Honour (formerly located in the T.P. Riley School library) and on the Walsall and Bloxwich Rolls of Honour. **Family** – He was the brother of Sidney Hooper and Leonard John Hooper, also commemorated on the Roll of Honour. Details are difficult to trace as Census information for 1891, 1901 and 1911 shows that the given names of the Hooper boys are not consistently recorded.

Fred LESTER

Born in 1894 or 1895 in Bloxwich and lived at 11, Sand Bank, Bloxwich. Son of an awl-blade maker, Edward, and the late Elizabeth Lester (née Handy) of the same address. One of eight children, six of whom were living at home in 1911 – three brothers (Edward 'Ted', Frank and Charles Henry) and two sisters (Olive and Nellie). Educated at Elmore Green School. Single. A polisher employed at a locksmith's in 1911, Fred, by the time of his enlistment in 1916 had taken work as a bobber employed by Abraham Wilkes Limited of Bloxwich. **Enlisted** in **April 1916** in Walsall. 23707, Private, South Staffordshire Regiment Then to…, **41279, Private, 15th (Service) '1st Glasgow Pals' Battalion (also called 'Glasgow Tramways'), Highland Light Infantry, (14th Brigade, 32nd Division)**. *Unit History* – November 1916 landed in France. (15/HLI) Somme, 23/10-11/11/16 Battle of the Ancre Heights; 17-19/11/16 Battle of the Ancre. 11/1-15/2/17 Operations on the Ancre. **Killed in action (age 22) on Tuesday, 16th January 1917** by shell fragments while carrying rations up the line in the Serre sector of the Somme. **Buried** in plot I. H. 27 of **Euston Road, Cemetery**, **Colincamps**, Somme, France. **Entitled** to the British War Medal and Victory Medal (Medal Roll – D/104B17, p.1386). Commemorated on the Elmore Green School Roll of Honour (formerly located in the T.P. Riley School library) on the Walsall and Bloxwich Rolls of Honour and on the Roll of Honour in All Saints Church, Bloxwich. **Family** – An older brother, Frank (a needle-maker by trade), served as 9814, Private, 69th Machine Gun Company, (69th Infantry Brigade) the Machine Gun Corps and suffered a gunshot wound to his right thigh in July 1916 on the Somme and was treated in hospital in Leeds – Frank's Service Records exist and indicate that he also served post-war in India, attached to the Royal Welch Fusiliers. Another older brother, 30921, Private Edward ('Ted') Lester, served in the South Staffordshire in France.

Arthur LINNELL, MM

Born in 1892 or 1893 in Bloxwich. Son of a boat-builder, Joseph, and Mary Linnell (née Woolley) of 119, Green Lane, Walsall and later of 89, Hatherton

Lane, Leamore. One of eleven children, of whom six were living at home in 1911 – at least four brothers (John, Joseph, Alfred and Ernest) and at least one sister (Amy). Educated at Leamore Board School and at Elmore Green School. Single. Employed as a general labourer at the Birchills Blast Furnaces Limited, Green Lane, Birchills. **Volunteered** in **August 1914** in Walsall. **8706>200373, Sergeant, 1/5th (Territorial Force) Battalion, South Staffordshire Regiment, (137th Brigade, 46th '1st North Midland' Division)**. *Unit History* – landed in France on 26th June 1915. From 4/4/15 to 7/15 at Neuve Eglise/Wulverghem. 7/15 to 2/10/15 Hill 60, Ypres. 13-15/10/15 Battle of Loos (Hohenzollern Redoubt and Hulluch Quarries). October – invalided home to England. From 19/3/16 Neuville St. Vaast/Ecoivres. May/June 1916 Fonquevillers sector of the Somme. Somme, 1/7/16 Battle of Gommecourt. 3/7/16 to 28/10/16 Berles-au-Bois and Bailleulmont sector on the Somme. 1-13/3/17 Operations on the Ancre including the Occupation of the Gommecourt Defences (4/3/17) and the Attack on Rettemoy Graben (12/3/17). 14/3/17-22/3/17 German Retreat to the Hindenburg Line. **Killed in action (age 24) on Wednesday, 14th March 1917** at Bucquoy in a night attack during the German Retreat to the Hindenburg Line. **Buried** in plot I. A. 23 of **Shrine Cemetery**, Bucquoy, France. **Entitled** to the Military Medal (for gallant actions in early March 1917. Posted in the *'London Gazette'*, Supplement to 17th April 1917, page 3698); recommended for, but not awarded the DCM; 1914-15 Star (Medal Roll – F/2/B5, p.353), British War Medal and Victory Medal (Medal Roll – F/101B18, p.2244). Commemorated on the Elmore Green School Roll of Honour (formerly located in the T.P. Riley School library) and on the Walsall and Bloxwich Rolls of Honour. **Family** – A brother and a brother-in-law served in France. There are no details of which brother served, thus no surviving military record apart from the fact that he served in France and would have qualified for the British War Medal and the Victory Medal.

Joseph ORGILL

Born on 6th July 1892 in Pelsall and baptised on 27th July same year. Son of John and Letitia Orgill (née Bramwell) of 62, New Street, Bloxwich; his father, a stationary engine driver, predeceased him. Lived in Bloxwich as a child then in 1913 emigrated to Canada. Educated at Bloxwich Council School and at Elmore Green School. Had at least six siblings - one sister, Gladys Maude, was living at home in 1911 – his 'next-of-kin' was listed as 'Miss G.M. Orgill of 107,

Station Street, Bloxwich. Emigrated to Canada in 1913. 5' 6" tall; grey eyes; light brown hair; Church of England. Single. Engineer (formerly employed by the Talbot Stead Tube Works, Walsall). **Volunteered** on **23rd September 1914** in Valcartier, Canada. Previously served 3 years in the South Staffordshire Territorials or Special Reserve. **33146, Corporal, 'B' Company, 2nd Field Ambulance, Canadian Army Medical Corps, (1st Canadian Division, Canadian Expeditionary Force).** *Unit History* – 2nd Ypres, 22-23/4/15 Battle of Gravenstafel; 24/4-4/5/15 Battle of St. Julien including the First as Attack. 15-25/5/15 Battle of Festubert. 15-16/6/15 2nd Action of Givenchy. 2-13/6/16 Battle of Mount Sorrel. Somme, 15-22/9/16 Battle of Flers-Courcelette; 26-28/9/16 Battle of Thiepval; 1-18/10/16 Battle of Le Transloy; 1/10-11/11/16 Battle of the Ancre Heights. Arras, 9-14/4/17 Battle of Vimy Ridge; 28-29/4/17 Battle of Arleux; 3-4/5/17 3rd Battle of the Scarpe; Capture of Fresnoy. 3/6-26/8/17 Operations Towards Lens including 15-25/8/17 Operations Towards Lens. 3rd Ypres ('Passchendaele'), 26-29/10/17, 2nd Battle of Passchendaele. *Was both wounded and gassed.* **Killed in action (age 25) on Saturday, 3rd November 1917** in the Ypres Salient. **Commemorated** on panel 32 of the **Menin Gate Memorial to the Missing**, Ypres, Belgium. **Entitled** to the 1914-15 Star, British War Medal and Victory Medal. Commemorated on the Elmore Green School Roll of Honour (formerly located in the T.P. Riley School library), on the Bloxwich Roll of Honour, the Roll of Honour in All Saints Church, Bloxwich and on a new panel at the foot of Pelsall War Memorial. **Family** – Two brothers, George Henry and John, served in France. John Orgill, served actively in 'D' Company, 1/5th Battalion, South Staffordshire Regiment with service number 9009. He landed in France on Wednesday 3 March 1915 with 46th '1st North Midland' Division but transferred to the 172nd Tunnelling Company, Royal Engineers with service number 137606 on Friday, 15 October 1915. He survived the war and was discharged from the Army on Tuesday, 28th January 1919.

William PARKES✶✶ [Not Elmore Green memorial]

William was born in Hednesford to John and Matilda Parkes (née Turner) of 40, Providence Lane, Blakenall Heath and later of 4, May Street, Leamore, his father being employed as a coal miner. One of nine children in 1901, William had four brothers and four sisters. His youngest brother, Arthur, was killed in France in September 1918. William married Clara Maud, with whom he had three children; in 1911, William resided with his family at 17, Providence

Street, Leamore and was employed as a bridle bit polisher by J. and J. Wiggin Limited, Old Hall Works, Woodall Street, Bloxwich. Enlisted during August 1916 in Lichfield. 6650 > 40801, Private, 6th (New Army/Service) Battalion, Lincolnshire Regiment, (33rd Brigade, 11th 'Northern' Division). *Unit History* – [Before William Parkes arrived, the battalion served on Gallipoli, from 6/8/15 to 20/12/15. From 19/2/16-17/6/16 the battalion served in Egypt in the Defence of the Suez Canal. Returned to France in July 1916. Somme, 15-22/9/16 Battle of Flers-Courcelette; 26-28/9/16 Battle of Thiepval.] William Parkes landed in France during November 1916. 11-19/1/17 Operations on the Ancre. 9-14/6/17 Battle of Messines. Killed in action (age 31) on Sunday, 10th June 1917 near Wytschaete during the Battle of Messines. Commemorated on panel 21 (The Lincolnshire Regiment) of the Menin Gate Memorial to the Missing, Ypres. Entitled to the British War Medal and the Victory Medal (F/105B14, page 1855). Commemorated on the Bloxwich roll of honour but not on the Elmore Green Memorial. Mis-spelt on *'Soldiers Died in the Great War'* as William Parker but correctly spelt on the Commonwealth War Graves Commission Casualty database as William Parkes. Family – Left a 27 year-old widow, Clara Maud, and three children under the age of six years. William had four brothers, all of whom served during the war; among them, his youngest brother, Arthur, died in battle during September 1918.

(Jonah) Thomas PARTON★★ [Not Elmore Green Memorial]
Born between January-March 1891 in Walsall to parents Edwin (a bridle-bit filer) and Clara Parton (née Webb) first of 50, Green Lane, Bloxwich and later of 33, Cope Street, Leamore. One of seven children, of whom five were living at home in 1911 – at least four brothers (Stephen, John, Edward and Frank. Employed as a bridle-cutter. **Enlisted** in Walsall, **probably in 1916**. **30579, Private, 8th (Service) Battalion, the South Staffordshire Regiment, (51st Brigade, 17th 'Northern' Division).** *Unit History –* (Depending on when arrived in France) **1916** 14/2/16 and 2/3/16 Actions of the Bluff (Ypres). Somme, 1-10/7/16 Battle of Albert including the Capture of Fricourt (2/7/16); 1-12/8/16 Battle of Delville Wood. **1917** Arras, 12-14/4/17 1st Battle of the Scarpe; 23-24/4/17 2nd Battle of the Scarpe. **Killed in action on 23rd April 1917** near Roeux during the Second Battle of the Scarpe. **Commemorated** on Bay 6 of the **Arras Memorial to the Missing**, Faubourg d'Amiens, Arras. **Entitled** to the British War Medal and the Victory Medal (Medal Roll – F/101B10, p.1205). **Family** – four brothers served in the army. 18 year-old John (Jack), 9441, Private, 'A' Company, 1/5th Battalion, South Staffordshire Regiment was killed in action on 13th October 1915 attacking the Hohenzollern Redoubt during the Battle of Loos. Stephen served

as a Corporal in the Royal Welsh Fusiliers, surviving the war; Frank served as a Private in the Machine Gun Corps and survived the war; Edward served as a Private in the Lincolnshire Regiment and was discharged sick and awarded the Silver War Badge in December 1918.

Wm Edw PICKIN

Born in 1894 or 1895 in Bloxwich and lived at 88, Field Street, Blakenall Heath and later of 57, Marlborough Street, Bloxwich and at Back 158, High Street, Bloxwich (back of the old picture house). Son of a coal-miner, Richard, and Martha Alice Picken (née Johnson) of the same address. Educated at Elmore Green School. Single. Miner employed at Holly Bank Colliery, Essington. Member of the Wesleyan Old Boys Sunday School. **Volunteered** in **October 1914** in Walsall. **200823, Private, 2/5th (Territorial Force) Battalion, South Staffordshire Regiment, (176th Brigade, 59th '2nd North Midland' Division)**. *Unit History* – Formed at Walsall in September 1914 as a home service ('second line') unit. Became part of 2nd Staffordshire Brigade in 2nd North Midland Division. Moved to Luton area by January 1915 and in July went on to St. Albans. Moved to Ireland in April 1916 to quell disturbances. Ireland - Both the 2/5th and 2/6th Battalions were involved in hostilities in Dublin during the 1916 Easter Rising. Soldiers from the regiment are alleged to have murdered a number of civilians in the North King Street area. These actions inflamed the Irish public's hostility towards the British, alienating even the most moderate of nationalists. [Wounded in the thigh in 1916, possibly in Ireland.] In January 1917, 59th Division moved to Fovant in Wiltshire and landed in France at Le Havre on 25th February 1917. 14/3-55/4/17 German Retreat to the Hindenburg Line. 3rd Ypres ('Passchendaele'), 20-25/9/17 Battle of the Menin Road; 26/9-3/10/17 Battle of Polygon Wood. **Killed in action (age 21) at 7 p.m. on Thursday, 27th September 1917** by shellfire in front of Gravenstafel on the second day of the Battle of Polygon Wood. **Commemorated** on panels 90-92 and 162, 162A of the **Tyne Cot Memorial to the Missing**, near Ypres, Belgium. **Entitled** to the British War Medal and Victory Medal (Medal Roll – F/101B18, p.2285). Commemorated on the Elmore Green School Roll of Honour (formerly located in the T.P. Riley School library) on the Walsall and Bloxwich Rolls of Honour and also on the Roll of Honour in All Saints Church, Bloxwich. He is named on the rolls of honour and on his birth certificate as being Edward Pickin. The 1891 and 1901 census returns, the Medal Index Card and in *'Soldiers Died in the Great*

War', all record his surname as Picken. **Family** – His brother, Harold, served in the South Staffordshire Regiment with service number 38312 and in the Machine Gun Corps with service number 172144; he was wounded by a gas shell in January 1918.

(John) Thomas 'Tom' ROWBOTHAM

One of fourteen children, Tom was born on Wednesday, 7th February 1894, the son of Edward and Eliza Jane Rowbotham (née Starkey) of 60, Church Street, Bloxwich, his mother predeceasing him in October 1913. His father was a coal miner by trade. Tom was educated at Elmore Green School and later was employed as a bobber at J. & J. Wiggin Limited, hardware manufacturers of Old Hill Works, Woodall Street, Bloxwich. **Enlisted** in the RNVR on **7th September 1916**. **Division: Bristol. Z/9639, Able Seaman, S.S. *'Kilmaho'*, Royal Naval Volunteer Reserve.** Information from RNVR service record – height 5' 4¾"; chest = 33"; brown hair, gray eyes, fair complexion. 'Character' = V.G; 'Ability' = Satisfactory. *Unit History* – shore establishments (Victory & Excellent) until 12/2/17; joined S.S. *'Kilmaho'* on 15th February 1917. **Drowned at sea (age 23) on Thursday, 17th May 1917** when his ship was torpedoed by a submarine, UB-20, off the Cornish Coast. **Commemorated** on panel 24 of the **Royal Naval Memorial, Plymouth**. **Entitled** to the British War Medal and Victory Medal. Locally commemorated on the Elmore Green School Roll of Honour (formerly located in the T.P. Riley School library) and on the Bloxwich Roll of Honour. **Family** – At least one brother, Edward Rowbotham, served in the Machine Gun Corps and survived the war (see his book/diary, *'Mud, Blood and Bullets – Memoirs of a Machine Gunner on the Western Front',* Edited by his grand-daughter, Janet Tucker, 2010). Edward pledged to kill seven German soldiers in revenge for his brother Tom's death at sea in May 1917. He kept his promise.

Albert James SIMMONS

Born in 1895 or 1896 in Bloxwich and lived at 55, Park Road, Bloxwich. Son of Thomas and Annie Simmons of the same address; his father, who predeceased him, was a brush-maker. One of six children in 1911 – Albert had at least two brothers (William Thomas and Victor Hiram) and at least two sisters (Lily and Rose Annie). Albert was educated at Elmore Green School and was a member of the Wesleyan Sunday School. Single. Locksmith employed by Sanders of Field

Street, Bloxwich and attended the Wesleyan Sunday School. **Enlisted in April 1917** in Bloxwich. **38357, Private, 2/6th (Territorial Force) Battalion, South Staffordshire Regiment, (176th Brigade, 59th '2nd North Midland' Division).** *Unit History* – Landed in France in July 1917. 3rd Ypres ('Passchendaele'), 20-25/9/17 Battle of the Menin Road; 26/9-3/10/17 Battle of Polygon Wood. Cambrai, 30/11-6/12/17 German Counter-Attacks. **Died (age 21) on Thursday, 6th December 1917 of wounds** sustained on 4th December in the wake of the German Counter Attacks at Cambrai. **Buried** in plot III. F. 3 of **Abbeville Communal Cemetery Extension**, Somme, France. **Entitled** to the British War Medal and Victory Medal (Medal Roll – F/101B12, p.1437). Commemorated on the Elmore Green School Roll of Honour (formerly located in the T.P. Riley School library), on the Walsall and Bloxwich Rolls of Honour and also on the Roll of Honour in All Saints Church, Bloxwich.

Alfred SLEIGH

Born in 1892 or 1893 in Bloxwich. Son of Alfred and Annie Maria Sleigh (née Wilkes) of 9, Reeve Street, Leamore; Alfred's father made his living as a coal miner. The family later moved to 89, Sneyd Lane, Bloxwich, his father then being a self employed 'beer retailer'. Young Alfred was educated at Elmore Green School. Married to Annie Theresa Whitehouse at Wolverhampton in 1915 and then resided at at 8, Clarendon Street, Bloxwich. Employed by Boak Limited of Station Street, Walsall. **Enlisted** on **14th October 1916** in Walsall. **185228, Gunner, 129th (Heavy) Battery, 42nd Brigade, Royal Field Artillery, (3rd Division).** *Unit History* – Landed in France in March 1917. Arras, 9-14/4/17 1st Battle of the Scarpe; 23-24/4/17 2nd Battle of the Scarpe; 28-29/4/17 Battle of Arleux; 3-4/5/17 3rd Battle of the Scarpe; 13-14/5/17 Capture and Consolidation of Roeux. **Killed in action (age 24) on Tuesday, 15th May 1917** near Roeux. **Buried** in plot I. B. 3 of **Tilloy British Cemetery**, Tilloy-les-Mofflaines, France. **Entitled** to the British War Medal and Victory Medal (Medal Roll – RFA/282B, p.36407). Commemorated on the Elmore Green School Roll of Honour (formerly located in the T.P. Riley School library) on the Walsall and Bloxwich Rolls of Honour and on the Roll of Honour in All Saints Church, Bloxwich. **Family** – Left a widow, Annie Theresa, who married George Griffiths at Wolverhampton in late 1919 and moved to 10, Upper Sneyd Road, Essington.

Arthur SMITH** [not Elmore Green Memorial]

Born in Essington in 1890 or 1891, the son of coal miner Arthur (died in 1905) and Florence Smith of 14, Elmore Green Road (1901), Bloxwich. Mother remarried by 1906 – Charles Cash. Arthur Lived at 86, Parker Street, Bloxwich. Married (Mrs. Lilly H. Smith, and three children). Miner employed at Holly Bank Colliery. Volunteered in **December 1914** in Wolverhampton. **Sergeant, 31332, 10th Battery, 82nd Brigade, Royal Field Artillery (18th 'Eastern' Division).** *Unit History* – Landed in France on 22nd August 1915. Somme, 1-8/7/16 Battle of Albert; 14-17/7/16 Battle of Bazentin including the Capture of Trônes Wood (14/7/16); 19-21/7/16 Battle of Delville Wood; 26-28/9/16 Battle of Thiepval; 1-5/10 and 17/10-11/11/16 Battle of the Ancre Heights; 13-18/11/16 Battle of the Ancre. 16/1-13/3/17 Operations on the Ancre including the Actions of Miraumont (17-18/2/17) and the Capture of Irles (10/3/17). 14-20/3/17 German Retreat to the Hindenburg Line. Arras, 3-4/5/17 3rd Battle of the Scarpe. **Killed in action (age 26) on Monday, 28th May 1917**, just north of Bullecourt in the aftermath of the Arras Offensive. **Buried** in plot I. B. 4 of **St. Martin Calvaire British Cemetery**, St. Martin-sur-Cojeul, **SE of Arras**, beyond Neuville-Vitasse. **Entitled** to the 1914-15 Star (Medal Roll – RFA/2AB, p.2904), British War Medal and the Victory Medal (RFA152B, p.10340). **Family** – left a widow, Mrs. Lilly H. Smith, and three children. Three brothers served; Alfred was a pioneer in the 9/South Staffordshire and was gassed in September 1918 but survived; he was a miner at Holly Bank Colliery. Edward was a private in 1/South Staffordshire in Italy, 1917-18. 201540 Private James Smith was then in training, later to join 2/South Staffordshire in France.

Samuel SMITH

Born in 1894 or 1895 in Blakenall and lived at 76, Sandbank, Bloxwich. Son of Joseph and Edith Hannah Smith of the same address. One of three children in 1911 (one brother, Joseph and one sister, Edith). Educated at Elmore Green School. Single. Machinist employed by Haywards

of Bloxwich. Member of the Walsall YMCA. **Volunteered** in **December 1915** in Willenhall. T/37306, Driver, Army Service Corps. To…, **28503, Private, 2/4th (Territorial Force) Battalion, Loyal North Lancashire Regiment, (170th Brigade, 57th '2nd West Lancashire' Division)**. *Unit History* – May 1916 – landed in France. 3rd Ypres ('Passchendaele'), 26/10-10/11/17 – 2nd Battle of Passchendaele. **Killed in action (age 22) on Friday, 26th October 1917** attacking Memling Farm in a muddy morass near Poelcapelle on the first day of the 2nd Battle of Passchendaele. **Buried** in plot XLII. D. 5 of **Poelcapelle British Cemetery**, near Ypres, Belgium. **Entitled** to the British War Medal and Victory Medal (Medal Roll – H/2/101B13, p.1812). Commemorated on the Elmore Green School Roll of Honour (formerly located in the T.P. Riley School library).

Albert STYCH, MM

Born in 1895 or 1896 in Short Heath, Willenhall to Richard Henry and Agnes Stych (née Simmons) of Back Lane, Short Heath, his father working as a coal miner. The family later resided at 102, Parker Street, Bloxwich. Albert was one of nine children in 1911 – he had at least six brothers (Samuel Henry, Joseph George, John, David and Harry) and at least two sisters (Martha and Maryann). Educated at Elmore Green School. Single. Like all the Stych men of working-age, Albert was a miner – in his case, employed at the Fair Lady pit, Coppice Colliery, Cannock. **Volunteered** on **Tuesday, 22nd April 1913** in Bloxwich (and agreed to serve overseas from August 1914). **8281, Private, 1/5th (Territorial Force) Battalion, South Staffordshire Regiment. Transferred to..., 40593, Lance-Corporal, 7th (Service) Battalion, Suffolk Regiment, (35th Brigade, 12th 'Eastern' Division)**. *Unit History* – [1/5th South Staffordshire] 5th March 1915 landed in France, From 4/4/15 to 7/15 at Neuve Eglise/Wulverghem. 7/15 to 2/10/15 Hill 60, Ypres. 13-15/10/15 Battle of Loos (Hohenzollern Redoubt and Hulluch Quarries). January 1916 to Egypt. February 1916 to France. From 19/3/16 Neuville St. Vaast/Ecoivres. May/June 1916 Fonquevillers sector of the Somme. Somme, 1/7/16 Battle of Gommecourt (wounded in both arms). [7th Suffolk] 22/10/16 Arras sector. Battles of Arras, 9-12/4/17 1st Battle of the Scarpe; 29-29/4/17 Battle of Arlcux. **Killed in action (age 21) on Saturday, 28th April 1917** during the Battle of Arleux at Arras**. Commemorated** on bay 4 of the **Arras Memorial to the Missing**, France. **Awarded** the Military Medal (earned with the South Staffordshire Regiment; posted in the *'London Gazette'* supplement to the edition of 11th November 1916, page 10931 – name recorded as *'Styche'*). **Entitled** to the 1914-15 Star (Medal Roll – K/1/6B2, p.311), British War Medal and Victory Medal Medal Roll – (K/1/103B23, p.4611). Commemorated on the Elmore Green School Roll of Honour (formerly located in the T.P. Riley School library) on the Walsall and Bloxwich Rolls of Honour and on the Roll of Honour in All Saints

Church, Bloxwich. (Albert Stych was also recommended for the Distinguished Conduct Medal). **Family** – Three brothers served; the eldest brother, 17/1041, Private Samuel Henry Stych (a former worker at Hollybank Colliery, aged 26 and married with three children; Samuel enlisted in Pontefract, Yorkshire) was killed in action with 17/West Yorkshire on 9th March 1916 near Festubert; another brother, 9486, Private George Stych – a former worker at Allens Rough Colliery who enlisted in 2/South Staffordshire two months before the war – was wounded in the foot (and later was posted to the KSLI with the number 48753); a third brother, 25 year-old Joseph of the South Staffordshire, was hospitalised with an undiagnosed illness at the time of Albert's death.

Robert SYLVESTER

Born in 1896 in Bloxwich and lived first at 42, Parker Street, Bloxwich and later lived at 4, The Green, Bloxwich. Son of a miner, William, and Mary Ann Sylvester (née Argyle, deceased) of Bloxwich. Educated at Elmore Green School. One of six children in 1911 – three sisters at home (MaryAnn, Lucy and May). Single. Miner employed (as was his father) at Holly Bank Colliery, Essington. **Volunteered** in **September 1914** in Walsall. 9543, Private, 2/5th (Territorial Force) Battalion, South Staffordshire Regiment. Transferred to…**37046, Private, 8th (Service/New Army) Battalion, Gloucestershire Regiment, (57th Brigade, 19th 'Western' Division)**.

Unit History – early service in Ireland during the Easter Uprising. [19th Division] Landed in France in August 1916, at which time he most likely transferred to 8/ Gloucestershire. 7-14/6/17 Battle of Messines. **Died (age 21) on Tuesday, 10th June 1917 of wounds** sustained near Wytschaete during the Battle of Messines. **Buried** in plot I. A. 23 of **Locre Hospice Cemetery**, just east of Loker, south of Ypres, France. [This cemetery was begun after the Battle of Messines and contains the body of a deserter from Robert Sylvester's 57th Brigade, who left his battalion, 8th North Staffordshire, on the eve of the Battle of Messines]. **Entitled** to the British War Medal and Victory Medal (Medal Roll – L/101B26, p.4591). Commemorated on the Elmore Green School Roll of Honour (formerly located in the T.P. Riley School library), on the Walsall and Bloxwich Rolls of Honour and on the Roll of Honour in All Saints Church, Bloxwich.

Chapter Thirteen

1918:

'Through Hell to an Expensive Victory…'

The changing imperative for 1918

**January/February
Calm before the storm**

**March/early April
Somme spring offensive – *'Die Kaiserschlacht'***

**April
The German offensive on the Lys**

**May
Trench raiding**

**June to August
Italian Front – Asiago Plateau**

**May/June
The German offensive on the Aisne**

**July
Allied counter-attack in Champagne**

**August/September
2nd Battles of the Somme**

**September/October
Battles of the Hindenburg Line**

**September/October
Bellenglise – Crossing the St. Quentin Canal**

**October/November
The final advance in Artois**

**November 1918
The Armistice – Eleventh hour, day and month**

**November 1918
Victorious but never to return**

Breaching the Hindenburg Line, 1918
*British troops cross the Ricqueval Bridge after 46th Division's remarkable storming of the St.
Quentin Canal on 29th September 1918.*

The changing imperative for 1918

Once the German invasion of Belgium and France had been brought to a muddy halt in the trench warfare of 1914-1915, the German army tended to fight a well-sited defensive war. On the other hand, the French army could never rest until the invader had been ejected from *'La Patrie'*. Time was then on the side of the Germans. As the Western Front juddered under the weight of three years of tactical stalemate and industrial-scale killing, so the balance of external factors changed.

During the Allied offensives on the Somme in 1916, at Arras, 3rd Ypres and Cambrai in 1917, German manpower losses had all but matched those of the Allies such as had moved British Prime Minister David Lloyd-George to view General Sir Douglas Haig's conduct of the BEF as unnecessarily wasteful of human life. In France, General Robert Nivelle's costly offensive on the Chemin des Dames had led to widespread mutiny in the ranks[140], to Nivelle's dismissal and to the temporary 'hamstringing' of the French army. 1917 also witnessed the exit of Russia from the war, on account of revolutions that toppled the old regime and ultimately ushered in the Bolsheviks, and the entry of the United States of America to the war – apparently in consequence of Germany's implementation of unrestricted submarine warfare. These adjustments changed the balance of time and numbers – if the USA had the time to train a large army that would flood the Western Front with men and *matériel*, Germany was doomed to defeat. However, if Germany could transfer the divisions released from the Eastern Front to the west before the Americans arrived in effective numbers, perhaps the Germans might yet be victorious. Time was thus now on the side of the Allies.

This change was never more apparent than on the German home front. German civilians were suffering terrible privations as a result of the Allied naval blockade of German ports; unrest was not far below the surface and the quality and numbers of the young recruits reaching the trenches fell month on month.

Even so, there were other factors in play. Despite his later claims to the contrary, the British Prime Minister, David Lloyd-George, a fierce critic of his military commander, was severely restricting the flow of trained reinforcements to Haig's army. In February 1918, Haig responded by reorganising the structure of brigades. Instead of four below-strength battalions per brigade, the Commander-in-Chief reduced this to three battalions, disbanding a number of battalions and redistributing the soldiers among the remaining units. Whatever the process, it did not strengthen the British army facing the Germans.

---

140 Surprisingly, this situation appears to have escaped German attention.

In the light of these factors and with the benefit of sixty extra divisions from the Russian front, the German army commander, General Erich Ludendorff, decided to plan and launch a last-ditch offensive in early spring 1918. Ludendorff needed to strike hard and strike quickly. The location for the first offensive – *die Kaiserschlacht* (The Emperor's Battle) was a fifty mile front straddling the old Somme battlefields. It would prove to be a death sentence for three of the Elmore Green Old Boys.

January & February

Beyond the normal round of 'daily hate', the German trenches remained unusually quiet throughout the first two and a half months of 1918. As the weeks passed, so the British began to suspect a steady enemy build-up of troops and supplies. A new defensive system, defence in depth, was being introduced on the British Somme front but the Fifth Army, in the southern sector, had had insufficient time to complete the new set-up. Apart from the winter weather, in the calm that preceded the subsequent storm, local lads appear to have suffered few problems – with the unfortunate exception of nineteen year-old **James Smith** of Elmore Green Road. From Elmore Green School, James found employment at Holly Bank Colliery and enlisted in the army with his age group late in 1916. James trained with the South Staffordshire Regiment and was eventually posted to Second Battalion that had been serving on the Western front with the BEF since August 1914. He was most likely posted to France in time for the engagements at Arras and certainly for the battles at Cambrai later in the year. On 24th January 1918, 6th Brigade moved up into Divisional Reserve near Equancourt and on 28th of the month 2/South Staffordshire became support battalion near La Vacquerie; on 31st, the battalion relieved 13/Essex and finally moved into the firing line. The trenches were very wet and muddy, in places merely isolated outposts, which the working parties laboured to improve; an infrequently-mentioned aspect of their work, as explained in the Official History for 1918 (volume I), was the recovery of useable salvage, in this case to the valuable tune of £30,000. During the quiet month of January, reinforcements raised the battalion roll to 22 officers and 672 other ranks but James Smith had little opportunity to help settle in the new lads as, on 3rd February when 2/South Staffordshire was moving to a training and refit camp in Havrincourt Wood, German artillery peppered the wood with high explosive and trench mortars. **Private Smith** was killed under one such bombardment on **3rd February** and he lies buried in Metz-en-Couture Communal Cemetery British Extension. His death came just nine months after that of his older brother, **Sergeant Arthur Smith** of the Royal Field Artillery, who was killed at Arras.

March & early April

Then the gathering storm broke on a fifty-mile front that stretched from near Vimy Ridge in the north to the River Oise in the south. At 4:40 a.m. on 21st March, an intense German barrage opened, battering mercilessly to a depth of almost a mile the entire length of the British Third and Fifth Armies. Orchestrated by *Oberstleutnant*[141] Georg Bruchmüller, a German artillery 'legend', shells filled with high explosive, shrapnel, mustard gas[142] and lachrymatory gas engulfed trenches and battalion headquarters alike for five mind-numbing hours. Then, as synchronised watches reached 9:40 a.m. the tense, British front-line troops at their battle stations were shaken to see wave upon wave of dull grey shapes emerging from the fog that blanketed No Man's Land. Spearheaded by elite Storm Troops, Operation *'Michael'* (21st March to 5th April), the first phase of Ludendorff's great spring offensive known as *'die Kaiserschlacht'* was under way and would drive back the British almost forty miles to the outskirts of the city of Amiens. On that first day five local lads were in the firing line, in four divisions in the salient around Flesquières and just to its north. In 47th '2nd London' Division's gun-line, **Gunner Bill Sharratt** experienced a torrid time throughout the opening bombardment but he lived to fight again. On the left edge of the salient was 17th 'Northern' Division; with 10/West Yorkshire, **Private Edward Smith** had been wounded twice previously and considered himself fortunate to survive the German spring offensive on the Somme. A short distance north of the 17th, close to the ruined town of Bapaume, **Lance-Corporal Tom Evans** of Bloxwich Road and **Lance-Corporal Bill Cockayne** of Bentley Lane together with their mates in 1/Leicestershire (6th Division), nervously awaited the German infantry – a delay that must have seemed interminable. On the left flank of 6th Division was 59th '2nd North Midland' Division, a unit that had already seen the loss of three Elmore Green lads (**Fred Harper**, **Wm Edw Pickin** and **Albert Simmons**). There, **2nd Lieutenant Leonard Beech** of 2/5 South Staffordshire, was expected to show his men an example of calm resilience – it must have been difficult given the intensity of the German barrage and its resultant gas cloud.

1/Leicestershire (part of 6th Division's 71st Brigade), having deployed near to Maricourt Wood and close to the Allied-held town of Bapaume, sent out two raiding parties in the days before 21st March. The first raid encountered empty German trenches, so no prisoners were taken for interrogation; the second raid, on the Magpies Nest Post, was also a failure. As a result, intelligence was extremely patchy and the question remained about an enemy attack. The

---

141 The rank of '*Oberstleutnant*' is the equivalent of Lieutenant-Colonel.

142 Mustard gas, whose terrible effects were long-lasting, was used only against the Flesquières Salient that the Germans did not immediately intend to assault head-on.

Map 7: Operation *'Michael'*, 21st March 1918

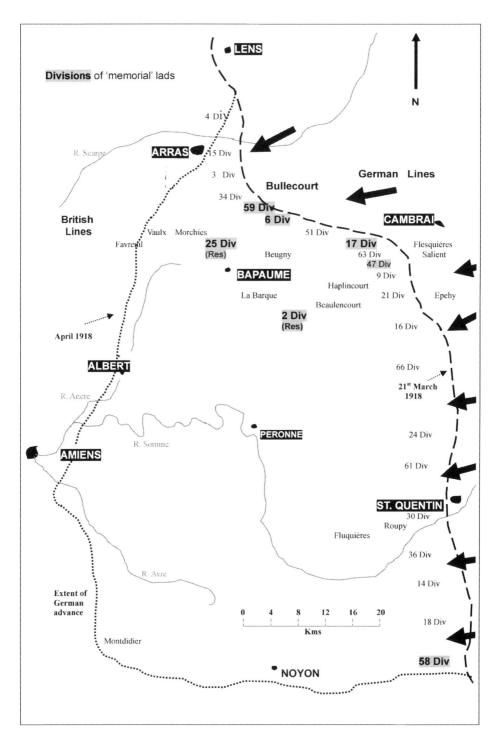

question was answered at 4:40 a.m. on **21st March** when a massive artillery bombardment of high explosive laced with gas shell hit the British lines. Exactly five hours later the shelling ceased and the German infantry, led by Storm Troops and shielded by fog and smoke, surged forward through the thinly-held British forward areas. Adding to the confusion, telephone cables had been effectively cut and the weather meant that air observation sorties were greatly restricted. The enemy quickly infiltrated 6th Division's front and then swept through the reserve lines. 71st Brigade was hard pressed but held tight until 11:15 a.m. – **Corporal Tom Evans** and his battalion, 1/Leicestershire, were held in brigade reserve. After the Germans took the village of Lagnicourt, the first companies of the Leicestershire were moved into the line and, though surrounded on three sides, held fast during a perilous afternoon. 1/Leicestershire stood firm until darkness fell, when their commander made the decision to withdraw to positions north of Beugny so that the battalion no longer held a vulnerable salient. The retreat was well organised so that all the wounded could be removed. During this torrid day's fighting, twenty-two year-old former brass caster **Tom Evans** was killed in action and his body was never identified, so he is commemorated on the Arras Memorial to the Missing – he left a widow, Hannah, and a young child. When the roll was called, it was found that the unwounded survivors of the battalion amounted to just 40 men – **Bill Cockayne** was one of the few.

Elmore Green's next casualty was not far from **Tom Evans** when the German offensive burst upon the British infantry lines. **Corporal Horace Jordan** of the unlucky 4/South Staffordshire was in 7th Brigade of 25th Division, a unit that was to suffer grievously during the desperate German offensives from March to June. Part of the IV Corps with 6th Division (and thus with Tom Evans' 1/Leicestershire), 25th Division was relatively fortunate to be initially in Corps reserve when General Ludendorff's Operation *'Michael'* commenced on 21st March. Gradually, all three of 25th Division's infantry brigades and two artillery brigades were moved forward in support of 6th Division and 51st 'Highland' Division. As a result, 4/South Staffordshire and 7th Brigade was moved up the short distance from their camp at Achiet-le-Grand to the village of Frémicourt, just to the east of Bapaume, where they were placed in IV Corps reserve. By the evening of 21st March, 7th Brigade was holding part of the Third or 'Army' Line and worked through the night to strengthen the trenches; stragglers from the forward lines were added to the brigade's three battalions, with 10/Cheshire on the left, 1/Wiltshire in the centre and **Horace Jordan** with 4/South Staffordshire on the right. Apart from light shelling, the following night (22nd-23rd) was relatively quiet. On the morning of 23rd March the enemy attacked on the brigade's left but was repulsed; early afternoon saw a heavy artillery barrage along the whole brigade front and this was the prelude to an infantry assault upon the three battalions. 4/South Staffordshire battalion war diary records these days as follows:

"21 March 1918 – 11.30 p.m. Battalion went up and dug in behind the Army Line on left of the road between Beugny and Frémicourt.

22 March 1918 – Remained in this line during the day.

23 March 1918 – 3 p.m. 'C' and 'D' Companies formed a defensive flank on the left, 'A' and 'B' Companies remaining in their position. At night 'C' and 'D' returned to support 'A' and 'B' who were still in the Army Line, which had now become the front line."

Although the day's second German assault was also beaten back, **Corporal Jordan** suffered serious wounds and was evacuated to the town of Doullens where he was initially treated in a Canadian Casualty Clearing Station (either No.18 or No.48) and later in the No.3 Canadian Stationary Hospital in Doullens. Sadly, two days later, on **25th March**, his twentieth birthday, **Horace Jordan** of Green Lane died of his wounds and was buried nearby. Horace was the oldest of Sam and Sarah Jordan's six children and the only one of an age to serve in the Great War; he was educated at Elmore Green and at Queen Mary's School, obtaining skilled employment as a pattern-maker with J. Birch & Sons of Brook Steet, Walsall. Horace was also assistant secretary of the Bloxwich Primitive Methodist Sunday School and a member of that Church. He enlisted in February 1917 and landed in France with his battalion on 10th October that year. He was at the front for just three months and he died on the same day that his battalion's commanding officer, Lieutenant-Colonel C.W. Blackall was killed in action near Biefvillers. During the retreat overall, 4/South Staffordshire lost 259 men killed, wounded or missing. Among them, **Horace Jordan**, is buried in Doullens Communal Cemetery Extension No.1, near the site of the hospital in which he died of his wounds.

Another 'local' battalion given a brief reprieve by being in divisional reserve on 21st March was twenty-year-old **Harold Revitt**'s 2/South Staffordshire, a unit that had been 'out' since 13th August 1914. On 20th March, according to the 2/South Staffordshire war diary:

"…[the]..battalion moved to Rocquigny sector, 4 miles south-east of Bapaume."

…where they spent 21st March, the first day of Operation *'Michael'*, in divisional reserve:

> *"….standing to, on 5 minutes' notice* [to move]. *Remainder of day was spent resting."*

The lads of the battalion didn't know just how much they were to need that day's rest. Harold, the youngest of Richard and Elizabeth Revitt's eight children, had been called up with his age group in May 1916. Previously employed as a shop assistant by a grocer, Mr. Stanley of Rushall, Harold joined his battalion in France in January 1917 and, before the year was out, took part in the Pursuit of the Germans to the Hindenburg Line, several battles at Arras and two of the battles at Cambrai. Early in February 1918, Harold became the envy of his mates in the battalion when he was granted home leave to marry his fiancée, Rose Ward. They commenced their very brief married life at 42, Mary Street, Walsall. **Harold Revitt** had only just returned to his battalion following his marriage when the Germans launched their major spring offensive in the Somme sector – he would never see his young bride again.

> *"…*[On 21st March]*..the battalion moved to north-west of Haplincourt; in reserve until 4:30 p.m. Then took position in the Green Line."*

The 23rd saw intermittent shelling, some of it from the RFA whose rounds were falling short, and at 7 p.m. the enemy was noticed:

> *"…massing behind Vélu Wood."*

The tide was about to surge over 2/South Staffordshire. The battalion war diary describes the day's desperate defence:

> *"24th March, Haplincourt-Boulencourt-La Barque. 8:50 a.m., enemy barrage as troops massed behind ridge. 9:35, barrage lifted and attack came in on the Cheshires to the left. At 10:30, the Cheshires were driven back but they counter-attacked with help of 'C' Company of 2/South Staffs. 2:00 p.m.; we were attacked on our entire front; troops on right seen retiring; then the Cheshires fell back so our left flank was 'in the air'; 'C' Company retired, was cut off and lost. Battalion retired to line of Sunken Road and then back to the ridge. Enemy moved up machine guns and snipers to hinder retirement. [The battalion C.O.]… Lieutenant-Colonel Alban seriously wounded. Held ridge then retired*

to Beaulencourt; enemy reported to be holding Le Transloy. Order soon came to evacuate; remnants of the battalion went back through Gueudecourt to Flers. Then pushed back across country to Eaucourt L'Abbaye to take up position south east of La Barque (10 a.m. to 5 p.m.). 25th March, retired to line of Pys-Courcelette; held on for most of the day and then retired to Miraumont."

The field-grey, enemy divisions rolled remorselessly forward. 2/South Staffordshire's roll-call the following day showed a battalion complement of just four officers and about 80 men. In two days, 2/South Staffordshire had been pushed back nine miles – it was happening along the entire Somme front. Sometime during this desperate, fighting retreat on **24th March**, **Private Harold Revitt** was killed – his body was never identified so Harold is commemorated on the regimental panel of the Arras Memorial to the Missing. He was exactly a month short of his 21st birthday.

April

As the story of **Horace Jordan**'s death shows, 4/South Staffordshire and 25th Division were fighting off the German Somme offensive in late March – the Division having lost half its strength in the Battle of Bapaume (24th-25th March), five days later it was moved north to the Ploegsteert Wood sector, just to the south of the Ypres Salient. In a brief respite from the fighting, the weary Staffords were reinforced and refitted and then moved on to Neuve Eglise where the battalion was promptly put in the front line at Ploegsteert Wood. 25th Division improved the 'Plugstreet' defences and received many replacements, the line being held by **Bill Grimsley** and **Bert Elks'** 7th Brigade on the left and 75th Brigade on the right.

The subsequent German offensive towards the Lys was intended to break through to the vital town of Hazebrouck, thus disrupting British supply routes, transport and communications. On 9th April Operation *'Georgette'*, the second strike of the German Spring Offensive, hit the British line immediately south of 25th Division's position so 75th Brigade was moved slightly south to reinforce 34th Division and to take part in counter-attacks. 7th Brigade's sector remained relatively quiet until the early hours of 10th April when gas shelling and an artillery barrage proved to be the prelude to an infantry attack under thick morning fog at 5:40 a.m. 7th Brigade managed to repel these initial assaults, although 1/5th Battalion, the King's Shropshire Light Infantry had to be attached to 7th Brigade to help strengthen the line. Despite the Germans penetrating the southern edge of Ploegsteert Wood, they were held back by the howitzers of 2nd Brigade, New Zealand R.F.A. Just to the north of the wood, 4/

South Staffordshire held the line stubbornly throughout a day's bitter fighting – their battalion war diary recorded:

> *"10 April 1918 – Enemy attack opened about 3.30 a.m. by heavy shelling of back area with gas shell. At 5.30 a.m. he opened his barrage on front and support lines last about an hour, then lengthened to Reserve on about line of Grey Farm. 'C' Company in front line wiped out. 2/Lts. S.K. Morey and A.P. Walker were missing. Number 6 Platoon 'B' Company withdrew to Watchful Post owing to severity of shelling, ordered to re-occupy Useful Spot at all costs, platoon moved forward but was unable to re-occupy position. Lieutenant Laver wounded and missing. The Gloucestershire on left, 10/Cheshire on right having withdrawn, orders issued to withdraw from Watchful Post. Battalion withdrew to catacombs at 2 p.m. order to re-occupy old positions, re-occupied 5 p.m. The Boche attacked 7 p.m., Grey Farm garrison stood fast, remainder of battalion withdrew to Hill 63, position isolated. Battalion withdrew to Neuve Eglise."*

Ploegsteert Memorial to the Missing

Twenty-two year-old **Lance-Corporal Bill Grimsley** of Reeve Street was killed during this action – his body was never identified and so he is commemorated on the circular Ploegsteert Memorial to the Missing. Bill was one of Frederick, and Mary Jane Grimsley's ten children, was educated at

Elmore Green School and subsequently took a skilled job as a wood-turner. He enlisted in the South Staffordshire during 1916 and went to France with 4th Battalion in October 1917. He was killed in action on **10th April** 1918 during what was later officially termed the Battle of Messines. 7th Brigade held their line throughout the day but in an early evening attack on 10th April the Germans skilfully infiltrated British lines and opened up on 4/South Staffordshire from the rear, wiping out 'C' Company completely; from there, attacks were then made on the other companies. By the 11th April, 75th Brigade had been forced back and 7th Brigade was ordered back to the high ground west of Neuve Eglise and the tunnels of the 'Catacombs' in Hill 63. As the Germans enveloped Hill 63, the withdrawal became most hazardous and all three of 7th Brigade's battalions took severe casualties, though **Private Bertie Elks** was among those who escaped. During the night of 11th-12th April the sector was quiet but at 8 a.m. a heavy assault hit the entire front line in 25th Division's area and further withdrawal was necessary. Reports came through that the enemy had broken through to the town of Bailleul from the south, so at 4 p.m. 7th Brigade with its twelve machine-guns was tasked to secure the area of the Asylum, to the north of Bailleul town centre; when that report proved to be false, the brigade moved forward to a position near Crucifix Corner. By then, the divisional line was held by a composite force of infantry battalion survivors and men from three field companies of Royal Engineers. Sometime on Friday, 12th April, during the confused fighting around Bailleul in the lines towards Ploegsteert Wood, **Bertie Elks** was badly wounded by a gunshot wound to the abdomen and quickly evacuated towards Poperinghe where he was treated in a Casualty Clearing Station. Despite his treatment, Bertie died from his injuries 24 hours later on **13th April**, a mere five days after his twenty-third birthday. Elmore Green School had lost another of its Old Boys. A valuable miner at Great Wyrley Colliery, Bertie had been dissuaded from enlisting until April 1917 but had finally crossed the Channel to Le Havre in October 1917 with 4/South Staffordshire, fighting in all the engagements until his downfall in the Battle of Bailleul. Back home in Wallington Heath, Bloxwich, William and Elizabeth Elks would have been devastated when the bad news arrived by official telegram.

Around Bailleul, the battalion fought on. For the next few days the Germans constantly attacked until 4/South Staffordshire was forced to retire on 15th April 1918. The battalion's war diary recorded these complex days and identifies where **Private Elks** was probably wounded on 12th April:

"10 April 1918 - Boche attacked 7 p.m. Grey Farm garrison stood fast, remainder of battalion withdrew to Hill 63, position isolated. Battalion withdrew to Neuve Eglise.

11 April 1918 - Battalion reorganised and took up outpost duty. Afternoon marched to Bailleul and took up outpost position.

12 April 1918 - 12.30 a.m. marched to Crucifix Corner, occupied line of trenches. Enemy attacked about 7 a.m. and at 7 p.m., unsuccessfully in both cases."

Bertie Elks is buried in the huge Lijssenthoek Military Cemetery on the southern outskirts of Poperinghe in Belgium[143]. However, Operation *'Georgette'* was not yet finished with the lads from Elmore Green.

When Operation *'Georgette'*, the second element of the German spring offensive, struck in French and Belgian Flanders on 9th April 1918, 55th 'West Lancashire' Division, as part of the XI Corps, was deployed in the line in the Festubert to Givenchy sector, immediately to the east of Béthune. 55th Division, with 2nd Portuguese Division on its left, found itself in the eye of the storm. The 55th Divisional front was part of the 'Line of Resistance' that had been identified by Lieutenant-General Haking to be:

"…denied to the enemy at all costs."

55th Division had been able to set up strong-points by the employment of barbed-wire so as to 'funnel' the enemy attackers into the deadly field of fire of the British machine-guns; each platoon was also expected to counter-attack on its own initiative. The Royal Engineers, of which **Sapper Ambrose Squire**'s 419th Field Company was one of three in 55th Division, were tasked to attend to the demolition (if necessary) of permanent and temporary bridges and to the swinging of emergency bridges.

The division's front was hit by phosgene gas and high explosive, a destructive prelude to the infantry assault at 8:45 a.m. that advanced under a heavy creeping barrage. The brigades of the 55th held their positions under great pressure (two men were awarded posthumous Victoria Crosses), however the 2nd Portuguese Division quit the battlefield, creating a huge gap to the left of the 55th. The Germans tried to 'envelop' the 55th from the left and so the R.E. Field Companies of the division, 419th, 422nd and 423rd, bolstered by a company of tunnellers (251st), two pioneer companies and a single, weakened battalion of 51st Division, were thrust into the fray to plug the gap as makeshift infantry. Despite heavy fighting all afternoon, the hastily-formed unit held the line. The story of the 55th Division was one of the few successes on 9th April.

---

143 Bailleul, where Private Elks was mortally wounded, is very close to the Franco-Belgian border and to Poperinghe, where he was treated.

Though under continued heavy pressure, next day the division again held the line; the process was repeated on 11th April, as the German assault found itself:

"…stuck in front of Givenchy and Festubert."

On 12th April, 55th Division was transferred to the I Corps, though this did not affect the division's actual deployment in the field. Apart from frequent, heavy shelling, the enemy again made no progress in this sector. The 13th dawned grey and cold, with mist thickening near watercourses; again the activity on 55th Division's front was limited to shelling but the engineers were constantly involved in strengthening defences, repairing or demolishing bridges and ensuring that the division maintained its strong grip around Festubert and Givenchy. Sometime during the day of **13th April**, twenty-three year-old **Sapper Ambrose Squire** of Blakenall Lane was killed in action near Gorre, most likely by enemy artillery fire. His body was never identified and thus he is commemorated on the Loos Memorial to the Missing. Having given up his job as a currier[144] with Walsall's largest firm in that animal hide business, Boak Limited of Station Street, Ambrose had enlisted in the Yorkshire Regiment during the battles on the Somme in September 1916. He transferred to the Royal Engineers and landed in France in September 1917, being involved in every engagement of 55th Division until he was killed in the Battle of Hazebrouck.

Three more Elmore Green lads took part in and survived the defence on the Lys in April 1918: **Lance-Corporal Bill Cockayne** of 1/Leicestershire (6th Division), **Private Archie Hall** of 1/4 King's Shropshire Light Infantry (19th 'Western' Division) and **Second Lieutenant Len Beech** of 2/5 South Staffordshire (59th '2nd North Midland' Division). 6th Division and thus 1/ Leicestershire was almost continuously engaged from 13th April to the end of that month, taking part in the Battles of Bailleul, Kemmel (twice) and the Scherpenberg – **Bill Cockayne** did well to come through those encounters. **Archie Hall** and 1/4 KSLI fought in three of the engagements: Messines, Bailleul and 1st Kemmel – and he lived to fight beside the French on the River Aisne in June.

Len Beech had been in France with 2/5 South Staffordshire since late February 1917 and had fought at 3rd Ypres and Cambrai; his battalion saw more service on the Lys in April 1918, at Bailleul and 1st Kemmel. Though Len would survive the war, he would not live long beyond the peace.

---

144 A currier prepared tanned hides for specialist usage.

May

Albert Wilkes arrived in France in February 1917 and, having served for three months in the ranks of 2/5 South Staffordshire, Albert was returned to England in order to train as an officer, obtaining his commission in the same regiment on 30th October 1917. He returned to the front in early January 1918, having been transferred as a 2nd Lieutenant to 1/7th Sherwood Foresters.

His return coincided with his battalion absorbing 2/7th Sherwoods on 31st January, together being renamed 7/Sherwood Foresters. The action Albert Wilkes had seen as a private did not compare in intensity to that he experienced as an officer with the Sherwood Foresters in the spring of 1918. In March, his battalion was on the Somme when the first strike of the *'Kaiserschlacht'* punched a huge hole in British lines. In April, the battalion was moved to a relatively quiet sector south of Ypres – then the second strike of the spring offensive hit home astride the River Lys. Again Albert survived but the battalion was so weakened that it was temporarily withdrawn from its division (7th May 1918). It appears that Second Lieutenant Wilkes was subsequently attached to 1/5 Battalion, Sherwood Foresters (139th Brigade, 46th '1st North Midland' Division), serving in the Locon sector close to Le Quesnoy, to the north of Béthune. It was during action with this unit on **24th May** that he was killed on patrol in No Man's Land getting information in advance of a trench raid. The war diary of 1/5 Battalion, Sherwood Foresters recorded the days either side of Albert's death:

> *"18 May 1918 – Essars section. Relieved 1/8th Battalion, Sherwood Foresters in right sub-sector* [of the front line].

> *19 to 22 May 1918 – Enemy raided left company post on 18th and 19th. Repulsed each time without casualties to us. A number of rifles and bombs were afterwards found. Enemy gas shelling abounds during tour.*

> *22 May 1918 – Relief postponed. 138th Brigade which should have relieved 139th Brigade relieved 137th Brigade in Gorre sector owing to the large number of casualties caused by gas shelling.*

> *23 to 24 May 1918 – Right sub-sector. Artillery active on both sides.*

> *25 May 1918 – Relieved by the 1/6 South Staffords and moved into Divisional Reserve in bivouacs at Vaudricourt Wood."*

Twenty-one year-old **Albert Wilkes** was the sole fatality and his body was never recovered. News of his demise was relayed home in a letter from a fellow officer:

> *"He was going out with his Company Commander to reconnoitre the post which his platoon was to raid, but unfortunately encountered the enemy post, when the first shots hit him and one of his men. His Company Commander endeavoured to get him away, but as many other Germans attempted to surround him, he was compelled to leave your son."*

Lieutenant Wilkes' Commanding Officer said of him in a letter to Albert's parents:

> *"He has done such excellent work since he joined the battalion and I should most certainly have recommended him for a Military Cross for a very daring patrol he carried out the day before we lost him.'* [Note: Wilkes did not receive the Military Cross as it could not be awarded posthumously at that time].

Major-General W. Thwaites, commanding 46th '1st North Midland' Division, wrote of his junior officer:

> *"Your son has earned for himself the reputation of a very gallant and capable young officer. He has done some valuable reconnaissance work and on this occasion was in the act of obtaining information for a special purpose when he met his death, bravely and fearlessly, as was to be expected of him..."*

[Much of the above information derives from an extract from Lt. W.H. Waterhouse's diary and is taken from the 1/5th Sherwood Foresters, Battalion History].

As **Albert Wilkes**' body was never identified, he is commemorated on the Loos Memorial to the Missing. Albert, of New Street, was the oldest of six children and had worked in his father's brass-casting business; he was also a noted member of the Walsall and Birchfield Harrriers. Albert's parents erected an alabaster memorial to their son's life and death; it remains to this day in All Saints Church, Bloxwich.

Albert Wilkes memorial, All Saints Church, Bloxwich

June to August THE ITALIAN FRONT – ASIAGO PLATEAU

Early in the Great War, Italy had changed to the Allied side in the expectation of capturing the long-coveted port of Trieste (on Italy's north-east border beyond the River Isonzo) from the Austrians. The Austrians were fighting a war on two fronts (against Italy and Russia) and the Italians hoped for easy pickings but were frustrated as battle after battle around the Isonzo River produced no decision. In October 1917 a combined Austrian and German force struck against the Italians, delivering a crushing blow at the Battle of Caporetto, on the upper reaches of the Isonzo. The Italians had to relinquish all their gains thus far and were forced back seventy miles, almost to Venice. Moreover, the Italians lost 340,000 fighting troops, mostly captured – without subsequent military support Italy might have been swept out of the war, allowing more troops to be transferred to the Western Front at a pivotal moment. By the end of 1917, six French and five British divisions had been transported to Italy – the British contingent comprised 5th Division (returned to France in April 1918), 7th, 23rd, 41st (returned to France in April 1918) and 48th '1st South Midland' Divisions. In all, four local lads served in Italy, though in just two of the divisions, 7th and 23rd. In 23rd Division were **Private Ernest Cope** (9/South Staffordshire, Pioneers) and **Private Albert Cooper** (12/Durham Light Infantry, 68th Brigade) – Cooper would never return to his home in Sandbank, Bloxwich. There were two lads in 7th Division, **Sergeant Bill Haycock** and **Corporal Jimmy Jones**, both served with 1/South Staffordshire and both wore at least one gold wound stripe on the left uniform cuff.

23rd Division was in the Montello sector (behind the River Piave) from 4th December 1917 to 14th March 1918 when it was moved westward to take over the right sector of the line near Monte Kaberlaba on the Asiago Plateau. 23rd Division was in the line on 15th June when the Austrians launched their offensive against a mixture of Italian, British and French divisions. Following at least three hours of preparatory artillery work, using gas, shrapnel and high explosive shells, Austrian infantry hit the 23rd Division lines at about 7 a.m. where the division was holding the right hand sector of the British front. The 23rd's two forward brigades were 68th Brigade on the left and 70th Brigade on the right; 12/Durham Light Infantry (Albert Cooper) was the centre battalion of 68th Brigade, with 11/Northumberland Fusiliers to its left and 13/DLI to its right. One battalion (8/York & Lancaster) was in support and two battalions (10/NF and 8/King's Own Yorkshire Light Infantry) in reserve. The main assault targeted 48th Division to the 23rd's left but soon the attack veered into 11/NF and broke into the front line but was soon ejected. The 11/NF held the line all day at a cost of 104 casualties. **Albert Cooper**'s battalion, 12/DLI, like the whole of the 23rd Division front, came under attack but the heaviest attack fell upon the right of the British, hitting 11/Sherwood Foresters, a battalion that had already been grievously damaged by the Austrian artillery. Desperately heroic defence by the Sherwoods' C.O., Lieutenant-Colonel Hudson, saved the position and earned the colonel a well-merited Victoria Cross: he had already earned the Distinguished Service Order and bar, as well as the Military Cross. For the rest of the day, small parties of enemy infantry sought to return to their own lines but vigorous sniper fire was maintained throughout, which resulted in further enemy casualties. At dusk, about two hundred enemy infantry attempted to return to their original positions but by showing themselves the majority were either killed or wounded. A defensive patrol that had earlier in the day been sent out by the battalion was in 'No Man's Land' during the enemy bombardment, and it did good work in helping to repel the later infantry attack. When the patrol returned to battalion lines, all of its wounded men were brought back.

By the end of 16th June the Austrian assault was completely defeated, 23rd Division having lost 555 officers and men killed, missing or wounded. Twenty year-old **Private Albert Cooper** was one of the 35 officers and men from 12/DLI to be killed or wounded during the two days of the Austrian offensive; he suffered severe wounds during the Battle of the Piave on 15th June and was evacuated to either No.24 or No.39 Casualty Clearing Station at Montecchio Precalcino, north of Vicenza. Albert's injuries were such that he died the following day, **16th June**, and he is buried nearby, in Montecchio Precalcino Communal Cemetery Extension. He had served for just eight months at the front in Italy. One of ten children and only five feet tall, Albert Cooper had surely 'done his bit' for King and Country.

Also present with 23rd Division when the Austrian offensive commenced was **Private Ernest Cope** of 9/South Staffordshire who had enlisted in the battalion with his younger brother, eighteen year-old **John Cope** in August 1915 – John died of wounds near Armentières on 23rd February 1916. 9/South Staffordshire, pioneer battalion of the 23rd Division, had reached the Mantua area of North Italy on 16th November 1917. Less than three weeks later the division took over the Montello sector of the front line on the River Piave where, apart from eight days, it remained until mid-March 1918. After a short period in rest, the unit took over a front line sector on the Asiago Plateau and in June fought in the defensive Battle of the Piave. With the division's 69th Brigade was 69th Machine Gun Company, one of four MG Companies in the newly-created 23rd MG Battalion that contained sixty-four machine guns. From the two MGs per battalion in August 1914, by June 1918 the MG battalion had developed into a major battle weapon.

Sergeant Bill Haycock and **Corporal Jimmy Jones** of 1/South Staffordshire (91st Brigade, 7th Division) were both experienced soldiers who had seen most things that could happen on a field of battle. Jimmy had himself been wounded and evacuated to England; his younger brother, **Private Ted Jones** of 7/South Staffordshire, had been killed on the Somme in November 1916. Bill Haycock had been wounded early in the war and had been discharged but he insisted on re-enlisting in the South Staffordshire – he was duly accepted as 'Old Soldiers' like Bill were in short supply. His brother **Private Ben Haycock**, younger by five years, had also volunteered in 1914 and had been in France for two years with the South Staffordshire. He was severely gassed during the German spring offensive and his war service ended prematurely.

Since 7th Division's arrival on 25th November 1917 near Mantua, no opportunity of crossing swords with the Austrians on a large scale had presented itself. While 1/South Staffordshire had been on the Asiago Plateau (north of Vicenza and Verona), raiding had become a favoured pastime and the enemy had been given no rest. The South Staffordshire carried out a successful raid on the Austrian lines at Canove on the night of August 8th/9th. Canove was a large village on the Asiago, less than a mile in front of the Val d'Assa, a deep and rugged defile. It formed a very strong position with heavy belts of wire to its front. The enemy was alert as Canove had previously been raided on several occasions. The idea of the August raid was to seize the village, advance to the Val d'Assa, and capture or kill parties of the enemy who lived in dug-outs there. The experienced **Sergeant Haycock** was a natural choice for the night raid. On its advance towards the enemy wire at zero-hour (12 midnight) the battalion was met by very heavy machine-gun fire but still forced its way into the village, where many of the enemy were shot in the streets but any further advance was prevented by a pillbox at the far end of the village. The enemy's fire was continuous until 2 a.m. and all ranks in the raiding party displayed great determination under pressure. The very heavy fire rendered impossible the second part of the task (advancing on the Val d'Assa) and prevented the raiding party from deploying further. So, having thoroughly cleared and searched Canove village, they withdrew, taking with them 27 Austrian prisoners, including two officers. In two dashing raids (15th April on Vaister and 9th August on Canove) troops of 1/South Staffordshire had distinguished themselves, taking a total of 54 prisoners. British casualties were five killed (4 dying of their wounds), 54 wounded and four missing. The success of the raid was confirmed in the battalion war diary:

"8/9 August 1918 - The battalion in conjunction with raids of other battalions of the division raided Canove on night 8/9th. Zero hour

was 12 midnight. They succeeded in getting into the village, inflicting considerable losses on the enemy who refused to leave dugouts. Heavy machine gun fire prevented the raiding party deploying from the village, and raiding the Cemetery as was the original intention. The raiding party returned at 2 a.m. Number of prisoners 27 (including two officers)."

Twenty-six year-old **Bill Haycock** was one of the lads who were posted missing, presumed killed on **9th August**. His body was never identified, so he is commemorated on the Giavera Memorial to the Missing, near Treviso. Back at the family home in Station Gates, Bloxwich, Bill left a young widow, Mabel, and their baby with his parents Albert and Elizabeth.

May & June

To return to the Western Front our story also takes us back several weeks from Bill Haycock's death in action in Italy. On 27th May Ludendorff launched Operation *'Blucher'* against the French-held Chemin des Dames, overlooking the River Aisne, in a final push towards Paris. Once again, the German offensive opened with a massive barrage planned by Colonel Georg Brüchmuller; once again the Allied line was pushed back. By 6th June, several British divisions that had originally been transferred to the Aisne for 'rest and refitting' had been incorporated into the French front line. One of those divisions was 19th 'Western', in which **Private Archie Hall** of Wolverhampton Road served. Archie had been present on the Somme on 1st July and soon after was transferred to the Hampshire Regiment for eighteen months (though his battalion is not known). In April 1918 he was again transferred, this time to the 1/4th Battalion, the King's Shropshire Light Infantry (56th Brigade, 19th 'Western' Division).

The battalion, already badly mauled, began 6th June in brigade support but was called forward after the enemy had captured the village of Bligny and the Montagne[145] de Bligny. The KSLI and a few elements of 8/North Staffordshire and 9/Cheshire quickly retook the vital hill and bravely defended it until early evening when French reinforcements recaptured the village and made good the front line. For the battalion's courage in recapturing the Montagne de Bligny and holding it while the French re-grouped, 1/4 King's Shropshire Light Infantry were awarded the French decoration of the **Croix de Guerre** in June 1918, an accolade of which **Private Archie Hall** would rightly have been immensely proud.

---

145 In reality it was little more than a hill.

July

The fifth and final German attempt to force a breach in the Allied line was made in the Champagne region from 15th to 17th July, known as the Second Battle of the Marne; it was foiled by an Allied counter-attack led by the French and supported by British, American and Italian divisions with a large number of tanks and lasted until 31st July. The British XXII Corps was sent south to aid the French – 15th 'Scottish' and 34th Divisions went to the western edge of the salient driven into the French line, while 51st 'Highland' and 62nd '2nd West Riding' Divisions went to the eastern edge. In the ranks of the latter division's 2/4 Duke of Wellington's Regiment was Providence Lane's **James Bryan**, who had enlisted in April 1916 and had been in France since the Arras offensive in the spring of 1917. By 18th July, 62nd Division was concentrating its units to the east and south-east of Epernay, where it was allocated to the reserve of the French Fifth Army. During the night of 18th/19th July and the following early morning, 62nd and 51st Divisions left Germaine, crossed the River Marne and re-grouped in Forêt de la Montagne de Reims. On 19th July, the Italian Corps that was then in the front line lost 9,334 officers and men out of a total fighting strength of about 24,000. Berthelot, the French commander, rushed his two newly-arrived British infantry divisions through the Italians straight into the attack down the Ardre Valley, into what became the Battle of the Tardenois, with 62nd Division deploying to the sector opposite Chambrécy and Bligny. In action at 8 a.m. next day, 20th July, having received its orders very late, the Division found the fighting severe and, unlike recent experience for the British, in open woodland. The undergrowth was dense and their front was raked by machine-gun fire from the Bois de Courtron across the Ardre Valley, thus the odds were heavily in the enemy's favour. 185th and 187th Brigades were in front, with James Bryan's 186th Brigade in close support. Despite coming under artillery fire they continued the advance through the village of Pourcy from where, though hampered by taking fifty per cent casualties, 2/4 DWR then attacked Marfaux. The northern edge of the village was breached but the attackers were forced to retire. After a promising start, the advance came to a halt in mid-afternoon and by late that evening the line had to be consolidated just half a mile forward of the start line. Twenty-three year-old **Private James Bryan** was one of sixty-six men killed in action during the battalion's testing day's fighting outside Marfaux on Saturday, **20th July**. James is buried in Marfaux British Cemetery, near Reims. Another of the Elmore Green lads had 'gone west'.

On 20th July Ludendorff ordered a withdrawal to the positions from which they had started their final spring offensive, taking up a line from the upper (River) Ourcq to Marfaux. By 27th July, the Germans had withdrawn their centre behind Fère-en-Tardenois and had retained the town of Soissons in the west. 1st August saw General Mangin's Tenth French Army renewing the assault, advancing to a depth of nearly 5 miles; the attack petered out on 6th August. This two week period of fighting is known as the Second Battle of the Marne and represented a significant Allied victory after the many reverses since 21st March. During 2nd Marne, the Allies took 29,367 prisoners, 793 guns and 3,000 machine guns and inflicted 168,000 casualties on the Germans. This was followed up between 8th and 11th August when the Battle of Amiens witnessed the true turning of the tide in favour of the Allies – and thus commenced the later-named '100 Day Advance to Victory'.

August & September

Two local lads, **Edward Smith** of 17th 'Northern' Division and **Bill Sharratt** of 47th '2nd London' Division, fought in the turning-point Battle of Amiens and thus contributed their small bit to what Ludendorff would describe as the 'Black Day of the German Army'. As the Allies began their forward press, 2nd Battle of the Somme commenced, as had its predecessor in 1916, with the Battle of Albert (21st-23rd August) – among the troops of the twenty-three Allied divisions involved were nine local lads. In 2nd Division were four lads with 2/ South Staffordshire, while there were individuals in 5th, 17th, 47th, 58th and 59th Divisions. Good initial progress was made and the Germans were forced to retreat towards Bapaume, the Allied advance being much more rapid than in 1916. One of the divisions that had fought at Albert and was driving the enemy eastwards was 58th '2/1st London' Division, a Territorial unit that contained 7th Battalion, the London Regiment – nicknamed the 'Shiny Seventh'. Posted to the battalion in the late summer of 1918 were several nineteen year-old lads from the area north of Walsall – **Frank Groom** of Bloxwich and four Pelsall lads, C. Lydall, Sid Jones, Joe Stackhouse and Walter Brown. All the lads were in their late teens, though Walter Brown had enlisted underage and was thus a veteran of the Western Front fighting since 19th August 1915, initially with the South Staffordshire Territorials, then later with the Londons. **Frank Groom** and the three Pelsall 'novices' had all enlisted in the army at Lichfield in 1918 and were all assigned to the same battalion of the North Staffordshire Regiment where their regimental numbers were very close. Once in France, the lads were transferred to 7/London, a battalion desperate for reinforcements. All five came safely through the epic Battle of Amiens and by 24th August the battalion was to the south-west of Morlancourt, though on 23rd August, nineteen year-old 'veteran' Walter Brown, had been in action near Billon Wood and had been reported 'missing in action' – his fate was to end the conflict in a German prisoner of war camp.

The story of the Second Battle of Bapaume in late August is related by 7/London battalion war diary:

"25th August, advanced to occupy captured ground east of Billon Wood. A violent thunderstorm made progress slow as it was very dark. 26th August, an advance was made under machine guns with heavy casualties but two field guns were captured. 27th August, 4:55 a.m., the operation was continued with 7/London on right and 6/London on left and 8/London in support; the Australians covered the right flank and 173rd Brigade the left. Following a six-minute (opening) barrage, we attacked under a 'lifting' barrage, having to overcome several machine guns in capturing and consolidating the old British front line, although exploitation was not attempted as the enemy was still strong. One field gun was captured. 25th-29th August, casualties were 13 officers and 280 other ranks."

The final sentence relating to casualty figures is by far the most revealing – the enemy was on the run but was still fighting a desperately effective rearguard action. 7/London battalion war diary continued:

"31 August 1918 - At 2 a.m. orders were received that the brigade would attack Marrières Wood under a barrage starting at 5.10 a.m. and lifting forward at 5.30 a.m. 6/London on the right and 8/London on the left and 7/London in support.

At 3.30 a.m. the battalion moved from Junction Wood to their assembly positions and were placed in position by the Adjutant, Captain K.O. Peppiatt. 'C' and 'D' Companies leading companies, 'A' and 'B' Companies in support. Their orders were not to enter Marrières Wood till it had been cleared by the assaulting battalions or unless assistance was necessary and in any event 'A' and 'B' Companies were to remain in brigade reserve west of the wood, but there had been no time to explain orders fully and when the assault took place, Numbers 9 and 10 Platoons under 2/Lt. Cooke followed through with the 6/London, worked right through the wood and across the valley and along the far slope to the Old Quarry cutting off a number of enemy who were retiring down the eastern slope of Marrières Wood and making them prisoners.

They established themselves in the Old Quarry with elements of the 6/London and 8/London, this was 500 yards beyond the objective laid down and its capture and retention was of the greatest assistance in securing the left flank of the Australian troops operating on our right and assuring the position was east of Marrières Wood.

> *Small parties of the enemy filtered back through Bouchavesnes village but were held in check by Lewis gun fire from the Old Quarry.*
> *1 September 1918 - 173rd Brigade passed through 174th to carry on the attack. At night 174th Brigade was relieved and marched back to bivouacs near Battery Copse."*

Private Lydall walked away from 2nd Bapaume physically unhurt. His two Pelsall mates, Sid Jones and Joe Stackhouse, were dead. Nineteen year-old **Private Frank Groom** had been wounded and was critically ill; he was treated in one of the six Casualty Clearing Stations (5th, 37th, 41st, 53rd, 55th and 61st) that had been established near Daours, six miles east of Amiens, during the German Spring advance of 1918. Frank was too severely wounded to survive and he died on Sunday, **1st September** 1918. He was subsequently buried close by, in Daours Communal Cemetery Extension. Another of the 'Parker Street Boys' would never see his home again.

Gunner William Sharratt worked the guns of C/235 Battery (they were 18-pounder field guns) through the whole of the German spring offensive on the Somme from 21st March to 5th April. His unit rejoined the fray in August and found itself in the 47th Division gun-line (and supporting that of the adjacent 18th 'Eastern' Division) on the left flank of the British Fourth Army in front of the village of Moislains during the 2nd Battle of Bapaume. The guns laid down a 'creeping' barrage[146] under which the infantry of 47th Division attacked at 5:30 a.m. on 31st August.

At 11 a.m. a fresh German battalion counter-attacked and was repulsed only after heavy fighting – this was repeated three more times during the afternoon, each occasion producing a similar result. On the following day, again at 5:30 a.m., the entire III Corps advanced under the protection of the artillery's creeping barrage – of 47th Division's battalions, one reached Moislain Wood, a second failed to take St. Pierre Vaast Wood, while a follow-up battalion took the village of Rancourt. The Germans at this time had an abundance of ammunition which was put to good effect by laying down gas and high explosive shells on the guns of the British artillery. So on **2nd September,** when 47th divisional artillery once more provided the barrage for the advance of the III Corps, German counter-battery fire led to nineteen year-old **Bill Sharratt** of Blakenall Lane being killed in action at his gun. William's family had working ties to the saddlery and lorinery industries – his father, Josiah, was a stirrup forger while Bill himself had worked as a currier for T.B. Buxton & Company of Queen Street, Walsall. He had enlisted in January 1917 with his age group

---

146 The steady, 'creeping' barrage was intended to protect advancing infantry.

and had landed in France exactly a year later. Gunner Sharratt is buried in Combles Communal Cemetery Extension.

September & October

Throughout the several phases of the German spring offensives, the front line had moved up to forty miles west of where it had been in 1916 and 1917. In the spring of 1917, the German High Command had completed the construction of the Siegfried Stellung (Hindenburg Line) and had ordered German forces to carry out an orderly withdrawal to the new defensive line. Their front line was made considerably shorter, requiring fewer divisions to man it; it was also a formidable defence that would be difficult to breach. Several unsuccessful attempts were made to breach it in 1917 but the main effort came after the tide of war had turned in the Allies' favour in the late summer of 1918. Having stemmed the German advance all along the front line, during September the Allied counter-attack encountered the lengthy, concrete fortification that had proved so daunting in 1917. However, there were in total six lines of defence facing the advance – three former British lines that had been 'reversed' after capture in the spring of 1918 and three elements of the Hindenburg Line (Advanced, Main and Reserve lines). Of the four losses suffered by the Elmore Green Old Boys during September 1918, the first two were involved in preparing the approach to the Hindenburg Line and the second two were involved in breaching it in one of the most remarkable feats of arms in the Great War. As the British Third and Fourth Armies pushed forward over the old Somme battlefields of 1916 and 1917, so the advance became a war of movement interspersed by occasional and difficult assaults on strong-points and powerful trench-lines. On 12th September, when the New Zealanders captured the village of Havrincourt, Joseph Bullock and Alfred Main of 2/South Staffordshire (2nd Division) were making progress just to the north towards Flesquières; just to the south of Havrincourt, Edward Smith advanced with 10/West Yorkshire in 17th Division. Although the second phase of the advance on 18th September was known as the Battle of Epehy, Lance-Corporal William Cockayne of 1/Leicestershire (71st Brigade, 6th Division), was fighting ten miles to the south of that blood-soaked village. 71st Brigade was initially in reserve and so did not take the full force of the enemy defence but later in the day the brigade was brought forward and suffered considerable losses to accurate German artillery fire.

Having come through that ordeal, hostile engagements came thick and fast for 1/Leicestershire as the British line remorselessly advanced. Following the costly successes of 18th September, 6th Division's flank was very exposed and plans were made to remedy this by a combined attack on the 24th. During the intervening days, artillery duels and machine-gun fire made life hazardous and on 22nd the Germans attempted to break into the British line but were repulsed. For the attack on the 24th, 1/Leicestershire was temporarily attached to 18th Brigade, one of the two assault brigades that advanced at zero hour, 5 a.m. The principal objective was the Quadrilateral, one of the most powerful sectors of the Hindenburg Line. Of the four tanks of 13th Tank Battalion allocated to the task, one was quickly knocked out and the remaining three reached the objective but they too were soon neutralised. 2/Durham Light Infantry and 1/West Yorkshire (18th Brigade) encountered thick, uncut wire and were severely delayed; one company of 11/Essex reached one trench face of the Quadrilateral and the ensuing bombing fight at lasted into the night. It was at that point, near 11 p.m., that 1/Leicestershire was tasked to assault the western face of the Quadrilateral from their positions Holnon Village, in bright moonlight and under a heavy preparatory artillery barrage. After a sharp fight, 1/Leicestershire took the strong-point that had caused so many casualties throughout a day and night – their success was due mainly to the fact that the attacking companies bravely followed the creeping barrage so closely that they arrived at the trench at the same time as the barrage giving the Germans no time to regroup. The battalion killed 25 Germans and took a number of prisoners for the loss of one officer and 47 men. During the intense fighting on **24th**

Vis-en-Artois Memorial to the Missing

September, having served for just seven months at the front, twenty year-old **William Cockayne** of 1/Leicestershire was killed in action assaulting the Quadrilateral and Selency, two areas of high ground east of St. Quentin. His body was never identified, so Lance-Corporal Cockayne is commemorated on the Vis-en-Artois Memorial to the Missing (shown on page 338).

Initially serving with the South Staffordshire Territorials (1/5th or 1/6th Battalion) in the 46th '1st North Midland' Division, **Arthur Parkes** transferred to the Bedfordshire Regiment, most likely in April 1918 when 1/Bedfordshire (15th Brigade, 5th Division) returned to France from service in Italy. 5th Division then served on the Lys battlefield as a welcome and vital reinforcement and when, by August, the German army was on the back foot, the division was part of the advance through the old Somme battlefields. On 27th September 5th Division faced its sternest test to date – the heavily-defended Canal du Nord. If the Hindenburg Line was to be breached then obstacles such as the canal had to be overcome. During a five-day battle, seventeen divisions were launched against the German defenders (**Edward Smith** of 10/WYR fought in this action, as did the two remaining local lads in 2/South Staffordshire). 5th Division was located on a ridge overlooking the Couillet Valley, where the village of Beaucamp (1/Bedfordshire's prime objective) nestled just north-west of Villers-Plouich. 1/Bedfordshire battalion war diary records the following:

"26 Sept 1918 - Battalion received orders to move up to assembly positions ready for forthcoming operations.

27 Sept 1918 - Beaucamp. Battalion advanced over the top to the attack at 7.52 am and captured part of Beaucamp Village, all objectives taken. During the afternoon German bombing party attacked which caused Battalion to draw back to Sunken Road and evacuate the village.

28 Sept 1918 - Germans evacuated Beaucamp. Cheshires and Norfolks advanced with Bedfords and Warwicks in support."

Nineteen year-old **Corporal Arthur Parkes** of May Street was killed in action on **27th September** in the attack on the village of Beaucamp during the Battle of the Canal du Nord. The village was successfully taken on 28th September but at a cost of 8 officers and 135 men killed or wounded. Arthur was the second of the Parkes brothers to be killed on the Western Front – the oldest, **Private William Parkes** of 6/Lincolnshire was killed on Messines Ridge in June 1917; three other brothers served and survived. Arthur was originally buried in a small battlefield cemetery but his grave was relocated after the war in Fifteen Ravine British Cemetery, just to the east of Villers-Plouich.

September & October

At the end of September, the Allies (in this case British, Australian and American units) were in place to attempt to breach the Hindenburg Line by crossing the St. Quentin Canal. The men of 46th '1st North Midland' Division had been used sparingly during the summer and early autumn of 1918 and they soon discovered why – the division was to be deployed as the spearhead unit for the assault upon the Hindenburg Line that, near Bellenglise, was sited just behind the eastern lip of the St. Quentin Canal. The waterway, 35 feet wide and up to 15 feet deep, was located in a steep-sided cutting nearly 50 feet deep. The German defences bristled with machine-guns that had 'registered' all possible approaches and sheltered up to 3,000 men in secure trenches and concrete emplacements. One soldier from 46th Division described it as:

> '…a most unpromising position to attack – indeed, we thought it impregnable.'

  Private Harold Baugh (1/4 Leicestershire, 138th 'Lincoln & Leicester' Brigade) and **Private Samuel Harrison** (1/6 South Staffordshire, 137th 'Staffordshire' Brigade) were both involved in the historic assault at Bellenglise and both would pay with their lives. **Private Horace Hill**, also of 1/6 South Staffordshire, would survive the day but would be a victim of the battalion's next battle, at the Beaurevoir Line. Two more local lads came through the assault Bellenglise relatively unscathed – **Private Joseph Stych** and **Private Simon Perks** both crossed the St. Quentin canal with the boys of 1/5 South Staffordshire. The British assault, with their left flank protected by the American 30th Division, was preceded by a forty-eight hour Allied bombardment that included a heavy lacing of mustard gas. The actual assault was be accompanied by a creeping barrage of smoke and High Explosive (H.E.) while dozens of machine-guns would fire over the heads of the advancing infantry at pre-registered defensive targets. At 5:30 a.m. on **29th September**, in thick fog and under an ear-splitting barrage, 137th Brigade (with 1/6 South Staffordshire on the right brigade flank) went forward, many men swimming the cold canal to secure the east bank; a party of 46th Division's Royal Engineers (466th Field Company, RE) stormed Riqueval Bridge and thus secured a vital crossing point for the follow-up attacks. **Sam Harrison** and 137th Brigade had secured a near-impossible objective just one hour after zero! At 9:30 a.m. **Harold Baugh**'s 138th Brigade was ordered to advance on the left while 139th

'Sherwood Foresters' Brigade advanced on the right; the support battalions, each aided by eight tanks of 9th Tank Battalion, crossed the canal by wooden bridges, passed through the Staffords and headed for Bellenglise village to deal with its pill-boxes and machine-guns. For the infantry, the fighting in Bellenglise was often hand-to-hand while the Royal Engineers and pioneers followed up to clear obstructions. 138th Brigade was faced by a strong trench system in front of the village of Magny-la-Fosse, beyond which was a sunken road defended by numerous machine-gun posts. In the capture of this line the tanks played an important part, cutting swathes through the wire entanglements. By 3 p.m., all three brigades of 46th Division had secured all their objectives beyond Magny-la-Fosse in the north (138th Brigade) and Léhaucourt in the south (139th Brigade). By 5:30 p.m., the first companies of 32nd Division were passing through to take over the line. After only five hours fighting, 46th Division had gained all its objectives and captured over 4,000 prisoners and 70 guns – in view of the strength of the German defences, the success was described as one of the greatest feats of arms in the entire war. The cost to 1/6 South Staffordshire was 225 men killed, wounded or missing and sometime during this remarkable, frenetic infantry advance, nineteen year-old **Private Harold Baugh** of Cope Street was killed in action – he is buried in La Baraque British Cemetery, Bellenglise. The cemetery is sited, fittingly, on the northern side of the St. Quentin Canal and just a short distance from the vital Riqueval Bridge. It is not known how or exactly when twenty year-old **Private Sam Harrison** of Field Street was killed in action but as 32nd Division advanced beyond 1/4 Leicestershire, Sam's body was identified and he was subsequently buried in a marked grave in Bellicourt British Cemetery. However, the marked grave can no longer be located so Sam is commemorated on a Special Memorial in the same cemetery, indicating that he is known to be buried there. Sam, previously a miner employed at Hawkins Colliery, volunteered in October 1915 and was unlucky not to survive the final three months of the war.

Despite 46th Division's remarkable exertions on 29th September, it remained in the line that night and was continually in action – it would not be until the following evening that it was withdrawn from the line for a brief but well-merited rest. Just three days later, near Rémicourt on 3rd October, 46th Division met in open battle four German divisions (even though two were much weakened) and defeated them in a tough fight. The enemy front consisted of two lines of trenches, heavily wired, overlooked by artillery and enfiladed by machine-guns. 139th Brigade was on the front left 137th 'Staffordshire' Brigade on the front right when the assault began at 6.05 a.m. in rapidly thinning fog; behind the infantry again rumbled the much-improved tanks. On the front right of 137th Brigade, **Horace Hill** and 1/6th South Staffordshire ran into heavy fire from Chataignies Wood; then the battalion was held up by machine-guns but, despite heavy casualties, reached its objective of Mannequin Hill. 6/South Staffordshire battalion war diary records the contact:

> *"The battalion met with very strong opposition from the enemy, his machine gunners being especially troublesome. After some very hard fighting during which many of the enemy were killed and many captured the battalion reached its objectives by about 10 a.m.*
>
> *Outposts were pushed forward on to Mannequin Hill but later had to be withdrawn owing to the intense enfilade machine gun fire. Unsuccessful counter-attacks on both flanks were made by the enemy. Shelling and machine-gun fire was severe throughout the day."*

Although the entire engagement was close-fought, all the division's objectives were attained yet the open nature of the ground ahead and the Germans' control of the heights meant that further immediate progress was impossible. Twenty-one year-old **Private Horace Hill** of 1/6th South Staffordshire was badly wounded during the assault of 3rd October and, despite being evacuated to either No.47 or No.48 Casualty Clearing Station, he died the following day, **4th October**, and was buried in the nearby Brie British Cemetery. Overall casualties amounted to 225 men killed, wounded or missing.

October & November
During the vital month of August 1918, Harry Perks' battalion, 1/Worcestershire, was with 24th Brigade, 8th Division as part of the British First Army, fighting in the Battle of the Scarpe (26th-30th August). By the start of October, 8th Division was still in the broad sector to the east of the city of Arras though the Germans were now in full retreat but still fighting. On 10th October the division advanced a mile, capturing Rouvroy; a day later the division, though not using **Harry Perks'** 24th Brigade until evening, captured their sector of the Drocourt-Quéant Line with little or no opposition. The 12th brought advances to the outlying buildings of the town of Douai and the 13th saw an approach to the Haute-Deule Canal, though 8th Division was somewhat held up by the enemy cutting the banks of the Scarpe Deviation Canal to increase the local floods. At 2 p.m. on Sunday, 13th October 1918 1/Worcestershire relieved 2/Northamptonshire along the Planques-Cité Ouvrière road and that night an attack was ordered on two villages in the 8th Division sector, Wagnonville and Flers. Harry Perks' 24th Brigade took Flers without difficulty but then one company of his 1/Worcestershire went on to explore a wood south of Auby, capturing two machine-guns. However, as the water-table was high, defensive

trenches only a foot deep could be dug and before dawn a German counter-attack on both flanks from Auby village drove the company to retreat, having suffered heavy casualties from German machine gun and mortar fire. It is very likely that **Private Harry Perks** was in 'C' Company that advanced into the wood and that the twenty-three year-old from Harrison Street was one of those killed by the German counter-strike on **14th October**, the 852nd anniversary of the Battle of Hastings. The battalion's casualties are recorded as being 11 killed, 33 wounded and 57 missing. **Harry Perks** is buried in Orchard Dump Cemetery, near Arleux-en-Gohelle, north-east of Arras, between the villages of Vimy and Oppy.

Mercifully, Harry Perks' death in mid-October, was Elmore Green School's final fatality of the war years – he volunteered for service in early September 1914 and had been in France and Flanders since March 1915. The guns may have fallen silent but the effects of war would claim five more victims in the two years that followed the 1918 Armistice.

THE ARMISTICE – 11a.m., 11th November 1918

By 11th November, the German army was taking unsustainable punishment, the civilian population back home was close to starvation, Kaiser Wilhelm II had abdicated and fled to the neutral Netherlands; Bolshevik revolution was not far beyond the realms of possibility and the country was suffering rampant inflation. The German government took the logical step of suing for peace and the Allies put forward their terms for an Armistice.

Outline of the 11th November Armistice with Germany:

The Armistice simply represented a ceasefire agreement – it was far from a peace treaty or settlement. Its terms reflected the Allies' cautious understanding that the conflict might yet re-ignite. The Armistice was, however, the first necessary step towards peace. In brief, the following major demands were placed before the German delegation in a railway carriage in a siding near Compiègne in the Forest of Rethondes, north-east of Paris:

- German forces were to pull back behind pre-war frontiers.
- The Allies would occupy the Rhineland, with control of several major bridgeheads (notably Köln, Bonn, Koblenz and Mainz) to ensure German compliance.
- The German army would hand over 5,000 artillery pieces, 25,000 machine-guns, 3,000 *Minenwerfer* and 1,700 military aircraft.
- The German navy would surrender all 150 of its submarines along with 74 of its powerful surface fleet.
- All prisoners of war were to be released by Germany.

Failure on the part of Germany to comply with the terms would result in the immediate resumption of hostilities. The German delegation of four comprising two civilian politicians (Matthias Erzberger and Count Alfred von Obersdorff), one navy representative (Captain Ernst Vanselow) and one army representative (Major-General Detlev von Winterfeldt) duly signed this harsh document. The hard-line Maréchal Ferdinand Foch and Admiral Sir Rosslyn Wemyss signed on behalf of the French and British Allies.

> Note: The full Peace Settlement was drawn up in Paris in the Palace of Versailles during the summer of 1919. By then, the few known survivors among the Elmore Green Old Boys and their families had, for the most part, returned home. However, there were two Elmore Green lads who had fought through the latter years of the war, had witnessed the Armistice but were destined to be buried near the now-quiet Western Front where so many of their mates lay at final rest.

November 1918: Victorious but never to return

When hostilities ended on 11th November, there remained in hospital near the Western Front many soldiers recently wounded or whose wounds were too grave to allow their evacuation across the Channel. Two Elmore Green lads fell into this category, **Corporal Thomas Eccleston M.M.** and **Private Archie Hall C.de G.**

Thomas Eccleston landed in France between early January 1916 and the opening of the battles of the Somme on 1st July 1916. Tom's 48th '1st South Midland' Division had been in France since March 1915 and took over a sector of the northern Somme front line from the French in July 1915, remaining there for twelve months. **Thomas Eccleston** was awarded the Military Medal in June 1916 for his bravery when a German shell hit a B/242 Battery gun-pit during the week-long artillery prelude to the first day on the Somme [see the 1916 stories for details of the award]. 48th Divisional artillery fought through five of the major battles on the Somme (including Bazentin Ridge, Pozières and the Ancre) and in January 1917 242nd Brigade was transferred to a new role as an Army Field Artillery Brigade. This meant that the brigade would be used wherever it was needed at a particular time and would no longer be attached to a specific 'parent' division. In this role the brigade first saw action in April 1917 at Vimy Ridge in support of the Canadian Corps, although the brigade's engagement over the subsequent eighteen months is difficult to trace. What is known is that twenty-six year-old **Thomas Eccleston**, a married man of New Street, survived the horrors of front line action only to fall victim to the virulent Spanish 'Flu pandemic that was ravaging Western Europe in October and November 1918. Treatment in either 39th Stationary Hospital or the 1st Australian Casualty Clearing Station was unable to save him as the 'flu was complicated by pneumonia. Tom died on **17th November** and was buried in Lille Southern Cemetery – one that contained many British lads who had died as prisoners of war between 1914 and 1918. Though Tom left a widow, Ethel, they were together as a married couple for just one day – they married on Saturday, Tom left for his regiment on Sunday and they never saw each other again. Ethel never re-married. Life could be very harsh. In his short life Tom Eccleston had worked as a coal-miner, fourteen months as a police officer in Walsall and three and a half years in the Royal Field Artillery. He had surely 'done his bit'.

Just four days after the untimely death of Tom Eccleston in Lille, another Elmore Green Old Boy fell victim to the scourge of post-war Europe, Spanish 'Flu. Twenty-one year-old **Private Archie Hall** of Wolverhampton Road, his body weakened by nearly three years of trench life, developed pneumonia and, despite prompt treatment in No.4 or No.34 Casualty Clearing Station in Solesmes, died on **21st November** 1918. In civilian life Archie, the only son of George and Eleanor Hall, had worked as an assistant operator at the Imperial Picture House in Darwall Street, Walsall. He volunteered for army service in October 1915 and served in the 1/5 South Lancashire and the Hampshire Regiment before being transferred to 1/4 KSLI (19th 'Western' Division) in April 1918. His unit fought beside the French at the Battle of the River Aisne for which Archie's battalion was awarded the French decoration of the Croix de Guerre in June 1918. From 12th October 1918, 19th 'Western' Division was pushing forward north-westwards from Cambrai as a part of XVII Corps, 3rd Army towards Marasches and Jenlain (south of Valenciennes). Fighting was almost continual, though German resistance varied in intensity. When the Armistice was announced on 11th November, **Private Hall**'s battalion was in the French town of Bry, to the west of Bavai, though by that time the young man was almost certainly in hospital. Archie is buried to the south of Valenciennes, in Solesmes British Cemetery, near to the hospital in which he died.

As the front line troops accustomed themselves to a daily round not dominated by random danger, so thoughts turned to those who had not lived to tell the tale. Few families were untouched by the war and few villages would, in years to come, lack a centrally-located memorial to their lost sons.

The local 'Old Contemptibles', surviving at the end of 1918:

Ernest Lavender   discharged 8/1/17 due to wounds
John Bullock   1st (Reg) Battalion, S. Staffordshire Regiment [P.o.W.]
Joseph Bullock   2nd (Reg) Battalion, South Staffordshire Regiment

Other 1914 men surviving at the end of 1918:

James Jones   1st (Reg) Battalion, South Staffordshire Regiment

Old Boys – arrivals at the Front, 1917 and 1918:

Men who arrived in theatre between 1st January and 1st November 1918:

William COCKAYNE   1st (Reg) Battalion, Leicestershire Regiment
William SHARRATT   C/235 Brigade, RFA, 47th Div. Artillery
Frank GROOM   7th TF Battalion, London Regiment
Howard Dawson   South Staffordshire Regiment

The following men's arrival date in theatre is unknown but thought to be between 1st January 1917 and 1st November 1918:

James Hayward   Royal Army Medical Corps (RAMC)
Henry Lavender   Royal Military Police (RMP)
Joseph Stych   1st (Reg) Battalion, Royal Warwickshire Regiment
Edward Lester   South Staffordshire Regiment>RAMC
Joseph Harrison   Unit unknown
Alfred Harvey   Unit unknown
Frederick Sanders   Unit unknown
George Main   Unit unknown
Linnell (brother)   Unit unknown
Parkes (brother)   Unit unknown
Sharratt (brother)   Unit unknown
Revitt (brother)   Unit unknown

UPPER CASE surnames indicate men whose names are commemorated on the Elmore Green school memorial.

Lower case surnames indicate men *related* to those who are commemorated on the Elmore Green school memorial.

(Reg)   indicates a Regular Army battalion.
TF   indicates a Territorial Force battalion.
(S)   indicates a Service or 'New Army' battalion.
(Sp. Res.)   indicates a Special Reserve or Extra Reserve battalion

Where local volunteers might serve on the front line – theatres of war and garrison commitments in 1918:

Western Front	in France and Belgium against the German army.
Southern Front	(v. Austrians/Germans) – North Italy from Autumn 1917 to autumn 1918.
East Africa	in Rhodesia, Nyasaland, Zanzibar, Tanga against German troops and German colonial troops.
Mesopotamia (Iraq)	against Turkish threat.
Salonika/Macedonia	with French against Austrians/Germans/Bulgars.
Egypt/Suez Canal Zone	against Turkish threat.
Palestine	(v. Turkish threat) From March 1917.

Imperial Garrisons and RN coaling stations throughout the Empire – Africa, India, West Indies, Gibraltar, Hong Kong and many others. Regular troops gradually replaced by local 'native' and TF troops.

[December 1917 – Russia out of war BUT... Russia – from June 1918; support for the 'White' Russians against the Bolsheviks.

Occupation of the Rhineland - November 1918 onward.

At sea	U-Boat war

Chronological Roll of Honour for 1918

February 3rd	James	SMITH	Rest camp, Bapaume
March 21st	Tom	EVANS	Kaiserschlacht/Somme
March 24th	Harold	REVITT	Kaiserschlacht/Somme
March 25th	Horace	JORDAN	Kaiserschlacht/Somme
April 10th	Bill	GRIMSLEY	Messines/Lys
April 13th	Bertie	ELKS	Bailleul/Lys
April 13th	Ambrose	SQUIRE	Hazebrouck/Lys
May 24th	Albert	WILKES	Bailleul/Lys
June 16th	Albert	COOPER	Asiago Plateau, Italy
July 20th	James	BRYAN	Tardenois/Aisne
August 9th	Bill	HAYCOCK	Asiago Plateau, Italy
September 1st	Frank	GROOM	Bapaume/ 2nd Somme
September 2nd	Bill	SHARRATT	Bapaume/ 2nd Somme
September 24th	Bill	COCKAYNE	St. Quentin/2nd Somme
September 27th	Arthur	Parkes**	Hindenburg Line
September 29th	Harold	BAUGH	Hindenburg Line
September 29th	Samuel	HARRISON	Hindenburg Line
October 4th	Horace	HILL	Hindenburg Line
October 14th	Harry	PERKS	Advance/Artois

1918 Post-war in France

November 17th	Tom	ECCLESTON	Spanish 'flu - France
November 21st	Archie	HALL	Spanish 'flu - France

** Indicates a name related to those that appear on the Elmore Green School Old Boys War Memorial.

Roll of Honour for 1918 (alphabetical order)

Harold BAUGH

Harold was born in 1898 or 1899 in Leamore (Bloxwich) to Enoch and Ellen Baugh (née Nolan) of 13, Crossland Street, Blakenall Heath and later of 67, Cope Street, Leamore (in the 1911 Census). His father was initially employed as a bridle-polisher however later changed his occupation, by 1911, to that of miner (below ground). In the 1901 Census (when his parents were 33 and 32 respectively), two year-old Harold had two older sisters (Mary J. 12 and Harriet 10), three older brothers (John 8, Alfred 6 and Joseph 4) and one younger brother (Enoch 2 months) – all the children, up to 1901, were born in Leamore. By 1911, three more sisters had been born – May 8, Ellen 6 and Evelyn 4 – then the births recorded as 'Bloxwich' for all the Baugh children on 1911 Census. By 1911, Joseph was an errand-boy, Alfred was an (iron-) caster's helper and John worked in a factory. John was married to Clara Jane. **Enlisted in Darlaston during or after 1916. 18363, Private, 1/4th (Territorial Force) Battalion, Leicestershire Regiment, (138th Brigade, 46th '1st North Midland' Division).** *Unit History* – 3/6/17-26/8/17 Lens sector including the attack on Liévin (1/7/17); 15-25/8/17 Battle of Hill 70. March 1918 Cuinchy (near Béthune). Battles of The Hindenburg Line, 29/9-2/10/18 Battle of St. Quentin Canal including the Passage at Bellenglise (29/9/18). **Killed in action (age 20) on Sunday, 29th September 1918** during the Passage at Bellenglise of the St. Quentin Canal. **Buried** in plot B. 11 of **La Baraque British Cemetery**, **Bellenglise**, near St. Quentin, France. **Entitled** to the British War Medal and Victory Medal (Medal Roll – F/ 102B8, p.926). Commemorated on the Elmore Green School Roll of Honour (formerly displayed in T.P. Riley School library) and on both the Bloxwich and Walsall Rolls of Honour. **Family** – Left a widow, Clara Jane.

James BRYAN

Born in 1892 or 1893 at Pratts Bridge, Bloxwich and lived initially at 307, Bloxich Road, Blakenall and later at 31, Providence Lane, Leamore. Son of Joseph (a puddler in an ironworks but deceased prior to 1911) and Elizabeth Bryan (née Sanders) of the same address. The second son of five children –

one sister (Edith) living at home in 1911. James was educated at Elmore Green School. Worked initially as a horseman on a farm but at the time of his enlistment in 1916 was employed by J.W. Marshall and Company of Staffordshire Ironworks, Green Lane, Walsall. Single. **Enlisted in April 1916** in Walsall. **202609, Private, 2/4th (Territorial Force) Battalion, Duke of Wellington's West Riding Regiment, (186th Brigade, 62nd '2nd West Riding' Division).** *Unit History* – Arras, 11/4/17 1st Attack on Bullecourt; 15/4/17 German Attack on Lagnicourt; 3-17/5/17 Battle of Bullecourt; 20/5-16/6/17 Actions on the Hindenburg Line. Cambrai, 20-21/11/17 Tank Attack; 23-28/11/17 Capture of Bourlon Wood. Kaiserschlacht – Somme, 24-25/3/18 1st Battle of Bapaume; 28/3/18 1st Battle of Arras. Counter-Attack in Champagne, 20-31/7/18 Battle of the Tardenois. **Killed in action (age 23) near Chambrécy on Saturday, 20th July 1918** during the Battle of the Tardenois. **Buried** in plot VII. I. 7/9 of **Marfaux British Cemetery**, near **Reims**, France. Medals & Commemorations – **Entitled** to the British War Medal and Victory Medal (Medal Roll – O/2?101B17, p.2469). Commemorated on the Elmore Green School Roll of Honour (formerly displayed in T.P. Riley School library), on the Bloxwich Roll of Honour and on the Walsall Roll of Honour. **Family** – A brother served in the army.

William Charles COCKAYNE

Born in 1899 in Bloxwich and lived in Bentley Lane, Bloxwich with his widowed grandmother Sarah Cockayne and with his parents Charles (a stationary engine driver at a local colliery) and Annie Cockayne (née Stibbs). One of six children in 1911 – two younger brothers (Harold H. and Howard J.W.) and three sisters (Beatrice A., Doris J. and Daisy). Educated at Elmore Green School. Single. Grocery assistant employed by Atkins and Son of Park Street, Walsall. **Enlisted in March 1917** in Walsall. **47918, Lance-Corporal, 1st (Regular Army) Battalion, Leicestershire Regiment, (71st Brigade, 6th Division).** *Unit History* – Battles of the Hindenburg Line, 18/9/18 Battle of Epehy. **Killed in action (age 19) at Epehy on the Somme on Tuesday, 24th September 1918. Commemorated** on panel 5 of the **Vis-en-Artois Memorial to the Missing**, Haucourt, France. **Entitled** to the British War Medal and Victory Medal (Medal Roll – F/102B18, p.2187).

Commemorated on the Elmore Green School Roll of Honour (formerly located in the T.P. Riley library) on the Bloxwich Roll of Honour, on the Roll of Honour at All Saints Church, Bloxwich and on the Walsall Roll of Honour. **Family** – Two cousins served, of whom one was wounded at Loos.

Albert Ernest COOPER

Born in 1898 in Bloxwich and lived at 1, Sandbank, Bloxwich. Son of a miner, Ernest, and Hannah Cooper (née Higgitt) of the same address. One of ten children – five brothers (Charles James, William, Arthur, Horace and Thomas) and four sisters (Nellie, Annie, Doris and Ethel) who lived at the same address in 1911. Educated at Elmore Green School. Single. Employed as a Carter by Thomas Edwards of Sandbank, Bloxwich. **Enlisted on 26th February 1917** in Walsall (aged 18 years and 5 months. 5' 0½", 108lbs). 35429, Private, South Staffordshire Regiment. Transferred to…, TR/5/13991, Private, 4th Training Reserve Battalion. Transferred to…, Northumberland Fusiliers from July 1917. Transferred to, in November 1917… **78533, Private, 12th (Service/New Army) Battalion, Durham Light Infantry, (68th Brigade, 23rd Division).** *Unit History* – Sent abroad on Tuesday, 20th November 1917, joining his unit in Italy. 12/ DLI had been sent to Italy in November 1917, arriving near Mantua on the 16th. Italy, Battle of the Piave – 15-16/6/18 Fighting on the Asiago Plateau. **Died of wounds (age 20), in either No.24 or No.39 Casualty Clearing Station at Montecchio Precalcino, north of Vicenza on Sunday, 16th June 1918 of wounds** sustained on the Asiago Plateau the previous day. **Buried** in plot 4. B. 5 of **Montecchio Precalcino Communal Cemetery Extension**, South of Sanango, Vicenza, Italy. **Entitled** to the British War Medal and Victory Medal (Medal Roll – O/1/103B44, p.8647). Commemorated on the Elmore Green School Roll of Honour (formerly located in the T.P. Riley School library), on the Walsall and Bloxwich Rolls of Honour and on the Roll of Honour at All Saints Church, Bloxwich. Several personal items were returned to his parents on 28th September 1918 – his identity disc, a purse, cap badge, belt, wallet, note-book cover, several letters, photos and cards. A Memorial Plaque and Scroll were received by his parents on 22nd May 1920.

Thomas Frederick ECCLESTON, M.M

Born on 21st January 1892 in Cheslyn Hay, Staffordshire. Son of a coal-miner, Charles, and Agnes Zillah Eccleston (née Winfer) of 97, New Street,

Bloxwich and later of 12, Marlborough Street, Bloxwich. One of six children, of whom three were living at home in 1911 – one brother (George) and one sister (Edith Agnes). Educated at Elmore Green School. Married (to Ethel) and then lived at 90, New Street, Bloxwich. Thomas was employed first as a coal-miner and later enrolled as an officer in Walsall Borough Police Force (for fourteen months prior to his army enlistment). **Volunteered on 15th April 1915** in Birmingham. **2337>836120, Corporal,** (2nd Warwick Battery, III 'South Midland' Brigade) that later became…, **'B' Battery, 242nd (Territorial Force) Brigade, Royal Field Artillery,** (48th '1st South Midland' Division) the brigade transferred to…, **Army Field Artillery** (from 20/1/17). *Unit History* – [48th '1st South Midland' Division] Somme, 1/7/16 Battle of Albert; 15-17/7/16 Battle of Bazentin including the Capture of Ovillers (17/7/16); 23-27/7 and 13-28/8/16 Battle of Pozières; 3-11/11/16 Battle of the Ancre Heights; 13-18/11/16 Battle of the Ancre. [From 20/1/17 242nd Brigade became 242 Army Field Artillery Brigade – WO95/205]. April-May 1917, Battle of Vimy Ridge; subsequent service record untraced. **Died (age 26) from the effects of influenza and pneumonia on Sunday, 17th November 1918**. **Buried** in plot I. B. 21 of **Lille Southern Cemetery,** France. **Entitled** to the Military Medal, awarded in June 1916 for brave action when a shell hit a gun-pit (posted in the *'London Gazette'* supplement edition of 10th August 1916, page 7887), British War Medal and Victory Medal (Medal Roll – TF/RFA/147B, p.9561). Commemorated on the Elmore Green School Roll of Honour (formerly located in the T.P. Riley School library), on the Walsall and Bloxwich Rolls of Honour and the Roll of Honour at All Saints Church, Bloxwich. **Family** – left a widow, Ethel, who never re-married after the war.

Bertram Laurence ELKS

Born between April and June of 1895 in Bloxwich and lived at 32, Wallington Heath, Bloxwich. Son of a coal dealer, William Edward, and Elizabeth Elks (née Martin) of the same address. His parents had married in Pelsall on Sunday, 2nd June 1878, his father being employed as a 'checkweighman' at a local colliery. Bertram was one of eleven children of whom seven were living at home in 1911 – three brothers (Leonard Levi, Ernest Gladstone and Edward William) and three sisters (Alice Elizabeth, Doris May and Ivy

Alexandra). Educated at Elmore Green School. Single. Miner and stoker employed at Great Wyrley Colliery. **Enlisted in April 1917 in Walsall**. **37996, Private, 4th (Extra Reserve) Battalion, South Staffordshire Regiment, (7th Brigade, 25th Division).** *Unit History* – 10/10/17 landed at Le Havre, France. Kaiserschlacht – Somme, 21-23/3/18 Battle of St. Quentin; 24-25/3/18 1st Battle of Bapaume. [25/3/18 Biefvillers – Lt-Col. C.W. Blackall killed]. 1/4/18 to Neuve Eglise, inspected by General Plumer. Then to Ploegsteert Wood. Kaiserschlacht – Lys, 10-11/4/18 Battle of Messines; 11/4/18 Loss of Hill 63; 13-15/4/18 Battle of Bailleul. **Died (age 23) on Saturday, 13th April 1918** of gunshot wounds to the abdomen sustained the previous day near Bailleul. **Buried** in plot XXVI. HH. 2 of **Lijssenthoek Military Cemetery**, near Poperinge, Belgium. **Entitled** to the British War Medal and Victory Medal (Medal Roll – F/ 101B12, p.1427). Commemorated on the Elmore Green School Roll of Honour (formerly located in the T.P. Riley School library), on the Walsall (incorrectly spelt as 'Elkes') and Bloxwich Rolls of Honour and the Roll of Honour at All Saints Church, Bloxwich.

Thomas EVANS

Born between April and June of 1896 in Bloxwich to Thomas and Elizabeth Evans of 62, Reeves Street, Bloxwich; his father worked as a coal miner. Educated at Elmore Green School. Worked as a brass caster, employed by Wilkes and Company of Pargeter Street, Walsall. Thomas married Hannah (Rosehannah) at Walsall Register Office on Wednesday, 14th July 1915 and later resided at 546, Bloxwich Road, Leamore with her and their child. **Enlisted on 3rd July 1916** in Lichfield. **28737, Lance-Corporal, 1st (Regular) Battalion, Leicestershire Regiment, (71st Brigade, 6th Division).** *Unit History* – Landed in France on 21st December 1916. He was promoted Lance-Corporal on Tuesday, 24th April 1917. Cambrai, 20-21/11/17 Tank Attack; 23-28/11/17 Capture of Bourlon Wood; 30/11-3/12/17 German Counter-Attacks. Kaiserschlacht – Somme, 21-22/3/18 Battle of St. Quentin. **Killed in action (age 22) on Thursday, 21st March 1918** on the first day of the German Spring Offensive (*'die Kaiserschlacht'* or 'Emperor's Battle'). **Commemorated** on bay 5 of the **Arras Memorial to the Missing**, France. **Entitled** to the British War Medal and Victory Medal (Medal Roll – F/101B12, p.1334). Commemorated on the Elmore Green School Roll of Honour (formerly located in the T.P. Riley School library), on the Walsall and Bloxwich Rolls of Honour and on the Roll of Honour at All Saints Church, Bloxwich. **Family** – Left a widow, Hannah, and one child. A brother served.

William Ernest GRIMSLEY

Born between July and September of 1895 in Bloxwich and lived at 43, Reeves Street, Bloxwich. Son of a self-employed house painter, Frederick, and Mary Jane Grimsley of the same address. One of ten children, of whom eight were living at home in 1911 – at least three brothers (Baden Christopher, Jesse and Frederick Robert) and at least four sisters (Florence Elizabeth, Margaret, Emily Louisa and Edith Laura). Educated at Elmore Green School. Single. Employed as a wood-turner. **Enlisted in Bloxwich. 36920, Lance-Corporal, 4th (Extra Reserve) Battalion, South Staffordshire Regiment, (7th Brigade, 25th Division).** *Unit History* – 10/10/17 landed at Le Havre, France. Kaiserschlacht – Somme, 21-23/3/18 Battle of St. Quentin; 24-25/3/18 1st Battle of Bapaume. [25/3/18 Biefvillers – Lt-Col. C.W. Blackall killed]. 1/4/18 to Neuve Eglise, inspected by General Plumer. Then to Ploegsteert Wood. Kaiserschlacht – Lys, 10-11/4/18 Battle of Messines.

   Killed in action (age 22) on Wednesday, 10th April 1918 in the Battle of Messines during the second phase of the German Spring Offensive (*'die Kaiserschlacht'* or *'Emperor's Battle'*). **Commemorated** on panel 6 of the **Ploegsteert Memorial to the Missing**, near Ypres, Belgium. **Entitled** to the British War Medal and Victory Medal. Commemorated on the Elmore Green School Roll of Honour (formerly located in the T.P. Riley School library), on the Walsall and Bloxwich Rolls of Honour and on the Roll of Honour at All Saints Church, Bloxwich.

Frank James GROOM

Born between October and December of 1898 in Bloxwich and lived first at 64, Church Street, Bloxwich then later at 92, Parker Street, Bloxwich. Son of a coal-miner (a 'stallman' at a local colliery), Thomas, and Florence Groom (née Alden) of the same address. One of four children – one brother (Alfred Thomas) and two sisters (Florence Emma and Rose). Educated at Elmore Green School. Single. **Enlisted in April 1918** in Walsall. 61223, Private, North Staffordshire Regiment. Transferred to…, **G/62991, Private, 7th (Territorial Force) Battalion, London Regiment, (174th Brigade, 58th '2/1st London' Division).** *Unit History* – Advance in Picardy, 8-11/8/18 Battle of Amiens. 2nd Somme, 21-23/8/18 Battle of Albert; 27/8/18 near Billon Wood, Morlancourt. 31/8-3/9/18 2nd Battle of Bapaume. **Died (age 19) on Sunday, 1st September 1918 of wounds** sustained during the 2nd Battle of Bapaume. **Buried** in plot VIII. B. 39 of **Daours Communal Cemetery Extension**, east of Amiens, France. **Entitled** to the British War Medal and Victory Medal (Medal Roll – E/1/102B/31, p.5266). Commemorated on the Elmore Green School Roll of Honour (formerly located in the T.P. Riley School library) and commemorated on the Bloxwich Roll of Honour and the Roll of Honour in All Saints Church, Bloxwich.

Archie George HALL, Croix de Guerre (Bn)

Born between June and September of 1897 in Bloxwich and lived at 78, Bell Lane, Bloxwich, 14, Aston Villas, Sandbank, Bloxwich and later at 3, Wolverhampton Road, Bloxwich. Only son of a bricklayer, George, and Eleanor Jane Hall (née Judd) of 5, Wolverhampton Road, Bloxwich. One of two children – had an older sister, Annie Kathleen. [Archie's father, George, had previously been married to Anne Wootton of 8, The Green, Bloxwich in 1882 and they had three children. Anne passed away in 1887, aged just 23 years.] Educated at Elmore Green School. Single. Assistant operator, Imperial Picture House, Darwall Street. **Volunteered on 11th October 1915.** 1205, Private, South Lancashire Regiment. In August 1916 to…, 26772, Private, Hampshire Regiment. In April 1918 transferred to…, **205143, Private, 1/4th (Territorial Force) Battalion, King's Shropshire Light Infantry, (56th Brigade, 19th 'Western' Division).** *Unit History* – To France in February 1916. record untraced as battalion not known. [Hampshire Regiment from 8/16] record untraced as battalion not known. [KSLI from 4/18] Kaiserschlacht – Champagne, 29/5-6/6/18 Battle of the Aisne. Final Advance in Picardy, 18-23/10/18 Battle of the Selle; 4/11/18 Battle of the Sambre; 5-7/11/18 Passage of the Grande Honelle; present at Mons when the armistice was signed.

   Died (age 21) from 'Spanish' influenza complicated by pneumonia on Thursday, 21st November 1918. Buried in plot I. C. 13 of **Solesmes British Cemetery**, south of Valenciennes, France. **Entitled** to the Croix de Guerre (battalion award, June 1918), British War Medal and Victory Medal (Medal Roll – J/1/102B16, p.5115). Commemorated on the Elmore Green School Roll of Honour (formerly located in the T.P. Riley School library), on the Walsall and Bloxwich Rolls of Honour and on the Roll of Honour in All Saints Church, Bloxwich.

Samuel George HARRISON

Born between October and December of 1897 in Bloxwich and lived with his parents at 6, Bullock's Fold, Bloxwich and later at 85 and 19, Field Street, Bloxwich. Son of a coal-miner (at Hawkins Colliery), Samuel George, and Sarah Louisa Harrison (née Dean) of the same address. One of five children – one older brother (Joseph) and three sisters (Fanny, Elizabeth and Lydia). Educated at Elmore Green School. Single. Miner employed at Hawkins Colliery. **Volunteered on 5th October 1915** in Walsall. **1201>>20124>242568, Private, 1/6th (Territorial Force) Battalion, South Staffordshire Regiment, (137th Brigade, 46th '1st North Midland' Division).** *Unit History* – May/June 1916 Fonquevillers sector of the Somme. Somme, 1/7/16 Battle of Gommecourt. 3/7/16 to 28/10/16 Berles-au-Bois and Bailleulmont sector on the Somme. 1-13/3/17 Operations on the Ancre including the Occupation of the Gommecourt Defences (4/3/17) and the Attack on Rettemoy Graben (12/3/17). 14/3/17-22/3/17 German Retreat to the Hindenburg Line. 18/4/17 to 15/6/17 Lens sector (Cité St. Pierre). 3/6/17-26/8/17 Lens (Battle of Hill 70) including the attack on Liévin (1/7/17). March 1918 Cuinchy (near Béthune). Battles of The Hindenburg Line, 29/9-2/10/18 Battle of St. Quentin Canal including the Passage at Bellenglise (29/9/18). **Killed in action (age 20) on Sunday, 29th September 1918** attacking the Hindenburg Line during the Battle of the St. Quentin Canal. **Commemorated** on Special Memorial A. 4 of **Bellicourt British Cemetery, east of Péronne**, France. [Samuel Harrison was one of 21 casualties known or believed to be buried in the cemetery and thus recorded by Special Memorial. He was originally buried in a marked grave in Bellicourt British Cemetery, Aisne but is now commemorated on Special Memorial A.4 in the same cemetery as his grave can no longer be located.] **Entitled** to the British War Medal and Victory Medal (Medal Roll – F/101B22, p.2832). Commemorated on the Elmore Green School Roll of Honour (formerly located in the T.P. Riley School library); he is also commemorated on the Walsall and Bloxwich Rolls of Honour. **Family** – An older brother, Joseph, and a brother-in-law served.

William Albert HAYCOCK

Born between January and March of 1892 in Rugeley and lived at 92, Bescot Street, Walsall. Son of an London & North-Western Railway platelayer, Albert Israel, and Elizabeth (née Powis) Haycock of 38, Bell Lane, Bloxwich and later of Station Gates, Bloxwich. One of five children, of whom four were living at home in 1911 – two brothers (Benjamin A.C.F. and Jasper J.H.) and one sister (Celia A.H.). Educated at Elmore Green School. Married in Walsall in 1913 to Mabel (coincidentally née Haycock), had one child, and lived with Bill's parents at Station Gates, Bloxwich. Employed as a bricklayer at the Spelter Works, Bloxwich. **Volunteered for the Territorial Force in 1914** in Walsall;

discharged wounded but rejoined, hence the unusual number for a 1st Battalion soldier. **203479, Sergeant, 1st (Regular Army) Battalion, South Staffordshire Regiment, (91st Brigade, 7th Division)**. *Unit History* – much of the service record is untraced on account of the discharge on an unspecified date. Italy, 28/11/17 arrived at Legnago on the Adige. 15-16/6/18 Fighting on the Asiago Plateau. **Killed in action (age 26) on Friday, 9th August 1918** during a raid on the village of Canove in Northern Italy. **Commemorated** on the **Giavera Memorial** to the Missing, Treviso, Italy. **Entitled** to the British War Medal and Victory Medal (Medal Roll – F/101B19, p.2496). Commemorated on the Elmore Green School Roll of Honour (formerly located in the T.P. Riley School library) and on the Walsall and Bloxwich Rolls of Honour. **Family** – Left a widow, Mabel, who moved to 92, Bescot Street, Walsall.

Horace HILL

Born on 29th October 1896 in Blakenall. Son of David and Alice Hill of 38, Regent Street, Birchills, Walsall. Educated at Elmore Green School (from 31/08/08). Living with his grandmother, Jane Hill, at 10, Stafford Road, Bloxwich (1911 Census). **Enlisted** in Bloxwich, **date unknown**. **201723, Private, 1/6th (Territorial Force) Battalion, the South Staffordshire Regiment, (137th Brigade, 46th '1st North Midland' Division)**. *Unit History* – Front line after 1/1/16. Battles of The Hindenburg Line, 29/9-2/10/18 Battle of St. Quentin Canal including the Passage at Bellenglise (29/9/18); 3-5/10/18 Battle of Beaurevoir. **Died (age 21) on Friday, 4tH October 1918 of wounds** sustained the previous day (3rd October) attacking Rémicourt during the Battle of Beaurevoir. **Buried** in plot V. B. 12 of **Brie British Cemetery**, **south of Péronne**, France. **Entitled** to the British War Medal and Victory Medal (Medal Roll – F/101B18, p.2350). Commemorated on the Elmore Green School Roll of Honour (formerly located in the T.P. Riley School library) and on the Walsall and Bloxwich Rolls of Honour and on the Roll of Honour in All Saints Church, Bloxwich.

Horace JORDAN

Born in 1897 or 1898 in Bloxwich. Son of a coal-miner, Samuel, and Sarah Ann Jordan (née Jennings) of 116, Field Street, Blakenall Heath and later of 14, Green Lane, Bloxwich. One of six children in 1911 – three brothers (Samuel Grant, Sidney and Cecil Norman) and two sisters (Sarah Millicent and Dorothy). Educated at Elmore Green School and Queen Mary's School. Single. Pattern-maker employed by J. Birch & Sons of Brook Steet, Walsall. Assistant secretary at the Bloxwich Primitive Methodist Sunday School and a member of the Church. **Enlisted in February 1917** in Walsall. **35447, Corporal, 4th (Extra Reserve) Battalion, South Staffordshire Regiment, (7th Brigade, 25th Division).** *Unit History* – 10/10/17 landed at Le Havre, France. Kaiserschlacht – Somme, 21-23/3/18 Battles of St. Quentin; 24-25/3/18 1st Battle of Bapaume. [25/3/18 Biefvillers – Lt-Col. C.W. Blackall killed]. **Died of wounds (age 20) in Doullens in No.3 Canadian Stationary Hospital on Monday, 25th March 1918** during the German Spring Offensive (*'die Kaiserschlacht'* or *'Emperor's Battle'*). **Buried** in plot V. A. 75 of **Doullens Communal Cemetery Extension No.1**, France. **Entitled** to the British War Medal and Victory Medal (Medal Roll – F/101B11, p.1372). Commemorated on the Elmore Green School Roll of Honour (formerly located in the T.P. Riley School library) and on the Walsall, Bloxwich, Queen Mary's School and All Saints Church (Bloxwich) Rolls of Honour.

Arthur PARKES** [*should* be on Elmore Green Memorial]

Born in 1897 or 1898 in Walsall to John (a coal miner) and Matilda Parkes (née Turner) of 40, Providence Lane, Blakenall Heath and later of 4, May Street, Leamore, Educated at Elmore Green High School. One of nine children in 1901, (four brothers and four sisters) – his oldest brother, William, was killed in Belgium, on Messines Ridge, in June 1917. Single. Arthur was employed at the Leamore Currying Company, Leamore. **Volunteered in November 1915** in Wolverhampton. 202694, Corporal, 1/5th or 1/6th (Territorial Force) Battalion, the South Staffordshire Regiment, (137th Brigade, 46th '1st North Midland' Division), transferred to....**205934, Corporal, 1st (Regular) Battalion, Bedfordshire Regiment, (15th Brigade, 5th Division).** *Unit History* – Arthur Parkes probably transferred to 1/Bedfordshire as an experienced N.C.O. after 5th Division returned from Italy. During April 1918, they fought on The Lys in the Battle of Hazebrouck (12-15/4/18); in the Advance to Victory at Albert (21-23/8/18), 2nd Bapaume (31/8 to 3/9/18); in the 2nd Battles of the Hindenburg Line – Epehy (18/9/18), Battle of the Canal du Nord (27-30/9/18). **Killed in action (age 20) on Friday, 27th September 1918** near Beaucamp during the Battle of the Canal du Nord on the Hindenburg Line. **Buried** in plot II.G.20 of **Fifteen Ravine British Cemetery,** Villers-Plouich, (his body was relocated after the Armistice by concentrating nearby battlefield and cemetery graves into Fifteen Ravine Cemetery), a village about 13 kilometres south-west of Cambrai. **Entitled** to the British War Medal and the Victory Medal (both K/2/101B2, page 194). Commemorated on the Walsall and Bloxwich rolls of honour. Although educated at Elmore Green School, Arthur's name does not appear on the school's war memorial. **Family** – Arthur was the brother of William Parkes, also killed during the war.

Harry Virginus PERKS

Born in 1896 or 1897 in Old Hill, Staffordshire and lived with his parents at of 80, Revival Street, Bloxwich and later at 199, High Street, Bloxwich, and at 99, Harrison Street, Bloxwich. Son of colliery stallman Henry, and Gertrude Jane Perks (née Burgess) of the same address; at least one brother, Simeon Frank. Educated at Elmore Green School. Single. Mine worker employed at Allens Rough Colliery. **Volunteered on Monday, 14th September 1914** in Birmingham. 1952, Private, Royal Army Medical Corps. To…, 248693, Private, Army Service Corps. To…, 47821, Private, Royal Welch Fusiliers. To…**238021, Private, (probably) 'C' Company, 1st (Regular Army) Battalion, Worcestershire Regiment, (24th Brigade, 8th Division).** *Unit History* – trained for field ambulance work with the 15th Midland Brigade at Witham, Essex; landed in France on 29th March 1915. 2nd Arras, 26-30/8/18 Battle of the Scarpe. Final Advance in Artois, 7-8/10/18 Forcing the Rouvroy-Fresnes Line. **Killed in action (age 23) on Monday, 14th October 1918. Buried** in plot VI. C. 42 of **Orchard Dump Cemetery, Arleux-en-Gohelle**, France. (Harry was originally buried in Quiery-La-Motte British Cemetery, north west of La Motte, but was re-buried in Orchard Dump Cemetery.). **Entitled** to the 1914-15 Star (Medal Roll – L/5C, p.66), British War Medal and Victory Medal (Medal Roll – L/102B33, p.7270). Commemorated on the Elmore Green School Roll of Honour (formerly located in the T.P. Riley School library) and on the Bloxwich Roll of Honour. **Family** – A brother, Simeon Frank Perks, served in 'A' Company, 1/5th Battalion, the South Staffordshire Regiment.

Harold REVITT

Born in 1896 or 1897 in Bloxwich, Harold was the son of Richard and Elizabeth Revitt (née Allen) of 58, Reeves Street, Bloxwich, his father making his living as a bricklayer. Harold was educated at Elmore Green School and, prior to enlisting, he was employed as a shop assistant to Mr. Stanley, a grocer of Rushall. Harold married Rose Ward at Walsall on Monday, 11th February 1918 whilst he was home on leave and they resided at 42, Mary Street, Walsall. **Enlisted in May 1916** in Walsall. **25383, Private, 2nd (Regular Army) Battalion, South Staffordshire Regiment, (6th Brigade, 2nd Division).** *Unit History* – Landed in France in January 1917. Capture of Grevillers Trench near Irles (10/3/17). 14-19/3/17 German Retreat to the Hindenburg Line. Arras, 12-14/4/17 Battle of Vimy Ridge (1st Battle of the Scarpe); 28-29/4/17 Battle of Arleux; 3/5/17 3rd Battle of the Scarpe. Cambrai, 27-28/11/17 Capture of Bourlon Wood; 30/11-3/12/17 German Counter-Attacks. Kaiserschlacht – Somme, 21-23/3/18 Battle of St. Quentin; 24-25/3/18 1st Battle of Bapaume (Flesquières Salient). **Killed in action (age 21) on Sunday, 24th March 1918** in the Flesquières Salient sector of the 1st Battle of Bapaume during the German Spring Offensive (*'die Kaiserschlacht' or 'Emperor's Battle'*). **Commemorated** on bay 6 of the **Arras Memorial to the Missing**, France. **Entitled** to the British War Medal and Victory Medal (Medal Roll – F/101B10, p.1143). Commemorated on the Elmore Green School Roll of Honour (formerly located in the T.P. Riley School library) on the Walsall and Bloxwich Rolls of Honour and also on the Roll of Honour in All Saints Church, Bloxwich. **Family** – left a widow, Rose who, four years after Harold's death, married George Lynex and moved to 122, Green Lane, Walsall. One brother and three brothers-in-law served.

William SHARRATT

Born in 1898 or 1899 in Bloxwich and lived at 23, Blakenall Lane, Leamore. Son of Josiah (a stirrup forger) and Sarah Jane Sharratt (née Morris), who lived at 63, Leamore Lane, Blakenall Heath and later at 23, Blakenall Lane, Bloxwich. One of eight children in 1911 – four brothers (John Thomas, Josiah, Samuel and Joseph), three sisters (Lizzie, Eliza and Flora). Educated at Elmore

Green School. Single. Currier employed by T.B. Buxton & Company of Queen Street, Walsall. **Enlisted in January 1917** in Walsall. **204065, Gunner, 'C' Battery, 235th Brigade, Royal Field Artillery, (47th '2nd London' Division).** *Unit History* – landed in France in January 1918. Kaiserschlacht – Somme, 21-23/3/18 Battle of St. Quentin; 24-25/3/18 1st Battle of Bapaume; 5/4/18 Battle of the Ancre. Advance to Victory – 2nd Somme, 22-23/8/18 Battle of Albert; 31/8-3/9/18 2nd Battle of Péronne-Bapaume. **Killed in action (age 20) on Monday, 2nd September 1918** at the 2nd Battle of Bapaume on the Somme. **Buried** in plot II. E. 38 of **Combles Communal Cemetery Extension**, Somme, France. **Entitled** to the British War Medal and Victory Medal (Medal Roll – RFA/290B, p.38042). Commemorated on the Elmore Green School Roll of Honour (formerly located in the T.P. Riley School library) and on the Bloxwich Roll of Honour. **Family** – One brother served; three cousins served of whom one was wounded and one was gassed.

James SMITH

Born on 26th August 1898 in Essington, the son of coal miner Arthur (died in 1905) and Florence Smith of 14, Elmore Green Road (1901), Bloxwich. Mother remarried by 1906 – Charles Cash. Educated at Elmore Green Schools (from 21/08/05). Family lived at 41, Alfred Street, Bloxwich. Two older brothers (Arthur and Alfred) and one younger brother (Edward); one older sister (Annie). Single. Miner employed at the Holly Bank Colliery. **Enlisted in August 1916** in Walsall. **201540, Private, 2nd Battalion, the South Staffordshire Regiment (6th Brigade, 2nd Division).** *Unit History* – . Arras, 12-14/4/17 Battle of Vimy Ridge (1st Battle of the Scarpe); 28-29/4/17 Battle of Arleux; 3/5/17 3rd Battle of the Scarpe. Cambrai, 27-28/11/17 Capture of Bourlon Wood; 30/11-3/12/17 German Counter-Attacks. **Killed in action (age 19) on 3rd February 1918** under artillery bombardment in Havrincourt Wood Camp. **Buried** in plot II. G. 17 of **Metz-en-Couture Communal Cemetery British Extension**, near Bapaume, France. **Entitled** to the British War Medal and Victory Medal (Medal Roll – F/101B18, p.2334). **Family** – Three brothers served; 31332, Sergeant Arthur Smith of 10th Battery, 82nd Brigade, RFA was killed in action on 28/5/17 at Arras after two years at the front. Alfred Smith was a pioneer in the 9/South Staffordshire and was gassed in September 1918 but survived – he was a miner at Holly Bank Colliery. Another brother, Edward, was a Private in 1/South Staffordshire in Italy, 1917-18.

Ambrose SQUIRE

Born in 1897 or 1898 in Bloxwich and lived first at The Park, Bloxwich and later at 25, Blakenall Lane, Leamore. Son of Silas [a leather worker who predeceased his son] and Sarah Ann Squire (née Jones) of the same address. One of ten children in 1911 – eldest of four boys (himself, Jack, Harry and Robert); six sisters (Edith, May, Violet Evelyn, Daisy, Agnes and Bertha). Educated at Elmore Green and Leamore Schools. Single. Employed initially by a motor fittings company, then later by Boak Limited of Station Street, Walsall.

Enlisted in September 1916 in Walsall. 47874, Private, Yorkshire Regiment. Transferred to…, **199353, Pioneer, 419th Field Company, Royal Engineers, (55th '1st West Lancashire' Division).** *Unit History* – Landed in France in September 1917. Kaiserschlacht – Lys, 9-11/4/18 Battle of Estaires; 12-15/4/18 Battle of Hazebrouck. **Killed in action (age 23) on Saturday, 13th April 1918** in the Battle of Hazebrouck during the German Spring Offensive. **Commemorated** on panels 4 & 5 of the **Loos Memorial to the Missing**, near Lens, France. **Entitled** to the British War Medal and Victory Medal (Medal Roll – RE/101B216,p.53109). Commemorated on the Elmore Green School Roll of Honour (formerly located in the T.P. Riley School library).

Albert Victor WILKES

Born in 1896 or 1897 in Bloxwich. Son of Albert and Gertrude Annie Wilkes (née Perry) and lived with his parents, first at 40, New Street, Bloxwich and then later at 'Primrose Villa', 36, New Street, Bloxwich. Educated at Elmore Green School. One of six children in 1911 – elder of two brothers (Albert Victor and Gilbert C.J.) and four younger sisters (Jennie G., Grace L., Florence M., Ivy L.). Single. Assistant to his father in his brass casting business. He was a member of the Walsall and Birchfield Harrriers in his spare time. **Enlisted on 6th May 1916 (enlisted in the ranks and later commissioned on 30th October 1917).** 202141, Private, 2/5th (Territorial Force) Battalion, South Staffordshire Regiment, (176th Brigade, 59th '2nd North Midland' Division), Then commissioned and transferred to…, **2nd Lieutenant,** 1/7th (Territorial Force) 'Robin Hood' Battalion, Sherwood Foresters Regiment, (139th Brigade, 46th '1st North Midland' Division) (to 31/1/18) then absorbed 2/7th Battalion and became…, 7th (Territorial Force) Battalion, Sherwood Foresters Regiment, (178th Brigade, 59th '2nd North Midland' Division), (To cadre from 7/5/18. Attached to…), **1/5th**

(Territorial Force) Battalion, Sherwood Foresters Regiment, (139th Brigade, 46th '1st North Midland' Division). *Unit History* – [59th Division] landed at Le Havre, France on 25th February 1917. 1-13/3/17 Operations on the Ancre including the Occupation of the Gommecourt Defences (4/3/17) and the Attack on Rettemoy Graben (12/3/17). 14/3/17-22/3/17 German Retreat to the Hindenburg Line. 18/4/17 to 15/6/17 Lens sector (Cité St. Pierre). [59th Division] Kaiserschlacht – Somme, 21-23/3/18 Battle of St. Quentin; 24-25/3/18 1st Battle of Bapaume. 13-19/4/18 Kaiserschlacht – Lys, 13-15/4/18 Battle of Bailleul; 17-19/4/18 1st Battle of Kemmel. [46th Division] May 1918 – Locon, near Béthune. **Killed in action (age 21) on Friday, 24th May 1918** during preparations for a trench raid close to Le Quesnoy in the Locon sector. **Commemorated** on panels 87-89 of the **Loos Memorial to the Missing**, near Lens, France. **Entitled** to the British War Medal and Victory Medal (Medal Roll – Notts & Derby Officers 162, p.232; also on F/101B22 II, p.2923). Commemorated on the Elmore Green School Roll of Honour (formerly located in the T.P. Riley School library). His name appears on the Bloxwich Roll of Honour in the *'Walsall Peace Celebrations'* Book, on the Walsall and Bloxwich Rolls of Honour and also on the Roll of Honour in All Saints Church, Bloxwich; there is also a separate, personal monument to him inside the latter church. **Family** – Two uncles and a cousin served – the latter was killed in action.

Chapter Fourteen

1919-1920:

'Home to a Battle Unfinished...'

Demobilisation

Frank LLOYD

Alfred MAIN

Leonard BEECH

Silver War Badge (SWB) holders

From Elmore Green School to Bloxwich Cemetery

Frank Lloyd, Leon Beech and Alfred Main – brothers-in-arms who were post-war victims of the conflict.

363

Demobilisation

With hostilities suspended, most lucky survivors were desperate to see an end to army life and return to their families. However, to demobilise millions of servicemen was a complex task and had to be executed with the needs of the nation in prime focus. While their continued reluctant service elicited sympathy, it was a situation preferable to that of the 750,000 British servicemen who would never go home and also to that of men whose war wounds,[147] physical or psychological, rendered them unable to work post-war.

The most immediate commitments of the army included providing the Army of Occupation of the Rhine (2nd Division marched to the German border and formed part of Second Army's force to occupy the Rhineland in line with the terms of the Armistice), the re-garrisoning of the outposts of Empire (particularly those far-flung areas that had remained essentially peaceful during the Great War) and the provision of several fully-equipped divisions to support the anti-Bolshevik 'White Army' in Russia.

A number of other factors had to be taken into consideration, salient amongst which was to effect the transition from an economy geared to full-scale warfare to a peacetime economy. This raised the obvious questions of how best to get the country back on its feet and how to channel ex-servicemen back into employment. To achieve this, men were largely discharged in 'industry groupings', and since Britain's pre-war economy had been highly reliant upon primary industries, agricultural workers and miners were afforded a high degree of priority. Men with scarce industrial skills, including miners, were released early; those who had volunteered early in the war were given priority treatment, leaving the conscripts – particularly the 18 year olds of 1918 – until last. Even so, most of the war service men were back in civilian life by the end of 1919, though most remained in the *Class Z Army Reserve*.

Class Z Army Reserve was authorised by an Army Order of 3rd December 1918 as there were fears that Germany would not accept the terms of any peace treaty and therefore the British Government decided it would be wise to be able to quickly recall trained men in the eventuality of the resumption of hostilities. Soldiers who were being demobilised, particularly those who had agreed to serve *'for the duration'*, were at first posted to *Class Z Army Reserve*. They returned to civilian life but with an obligation to return if called upon. Following the Paris Peace Settlement of 1919, the *Class Z Reserve* was eventually abolished on 31st March 1920.

Gradually, those who had survived the Great War were demobilised and returned to their homes. Sadly, the stories of many Elmore Green lads will

---

147 In excess of 2 million British servicemen sustained wounds (some more than once) during the Great War.

never be told – not because the part they played was any less worthy than those who are recorded here but on account of the fact that sources of information in respect of casualties are more numerous and detailed. Thus the survivors mentioned here are often related to casualties who are commemorated on the Elmore Green Memorial. Servicemen who were wounded during the course of the war and those who were awarded gallantry medals often appeared in newspaper reports and photographs. Otherwise, beyond family recollections and medal collections it is difficult to establish details of war service.

Frank Lloyd was one of the few Bloxwich men who were serving prior to the outbreak of the Great War on 4th August 1914 and who managed to survive to its end on 11th November 1918. When the South Staffordshire Territorials were mobilised and invited to serve overseas[148], Frank was already a sergeant, most likely one of the sixteen Non-Commissioned Officers in 'D' (Bloxwich) Company under Captain H. Lord and Lieutenant L. Cozens, thus he would have played an important part in shaping the expanded 1/5th Battalion that was based at Walsall Drill Hall. Frank went out to the Western Front in early March 1915 with his battalion and, as far as is known, fought in all of the 137th 'Staffordshire' Brigade's battles, including at the Hohenzollern Redoubt near Loos, the first day of the Somme, the German Retreat to the Hindenburg Line and the fight for Hill 70 at Ypres. During his time with the South Staffordshire **Sergeant Frank Lloyd** had proved himself an outstanding, brave soldier, earning the Military Medal on two separate occasions. According to *'Honours & Awards of The South Staffordshire Regiment, 1914-1918'* by Jeff Elson, Frank Lloyd's first M.M. was awarded for his actions at Hulluch on 13th October 1915 during the Battle of Loos and was posted in the *'London Gazette'* supplement edition of 11th November 1916, page 10926; Frank was awarded the Bar to his M.M. (a second M.M.) for his actions at Bucquoy in 1917 and was posted in the *'London Gazette'* supplement edition of 21st December 1917, page 12449. Frank served in 1/5 South Staffordshire until late 1917 when, in the light of his leadership qualities and impressive example, he was sent to officer cadet school to train for a commission, eventually being gazetted **2nd Lieutenant** to the 6/Worcestershire on 29th January 1918. 6th Battalion had previously been on duty in the Harwich defences on the east coast but a reduction in strength following the dispatch of troops to France led to the battalion being temporarily amalgamated with the 5th Battalion of the Worcestershire. On

---

148 Under the terms of his attestation papers, a Territorial Force soldier was only required to serve within the United Kingdom. By signing Army Form E.624 (also known as the Imperial Service Obligation), a Territorial accepted '…*liability, in the event of national emergency, to serve in any place outside the United Kingdom.'* The vast majority of Territorials signed this, although just a few resisted until conscription was introduced early in 1916.

the 23rd February 1918 the amalgamated 5th/6th Battalion had moved to Newcastle-on-Tyne and it was there that Frank Lloyd joined his new unit.

Yet even now **Frank Lloyd** seemed not to be satisfied with his own contribution and so on Friday, 5th July 1918 Frank transferred to the recently-formed Royal Air Force, joining 61 Squadron on graduating as a pilot[149]. It is not known whether he flew in the wartime service, though this might later be established from his officer's papers in the National Archives at Kew. It is quite ironic that, after surviving the most terrible war in history, Frank Lloyd should die in a flying accident in England. On Monday, 7th October 1918 he had been sent to 61 (Fighter) Squadron that was based at RFC Rochford [an area that is now Southend Airport] and flying Sopwith Camels but was in the process of converting from Camels to the Sopwith Snipe and S.E.5. In 'Sagittarius Rising', the Great War memoirs of Cecil Lewis, there appears a first-hand description of Rochford Aerodrome in its wartime role. Lewis, a pilot from the early days of the Royal Flying Corps (RFC), went to France in March 1916 and served throughout the Somme campaign; having flown three tours of duty on the front line, he was posted to south-east England to protect the civilian population against the burgeoning bombing threat posed by Zeppelins and later, the huge Gotha bombers during the first 'Blitz':

> *"Rochford was a magnificent aerodrome, almost a mile square. No.61, the Home Defence squadron to which I had been transferred, was quartered on one side of it, while up at the other end were a couple of training squadrons. Rochford village was about two miles from Southend, and the squadron formed part of the ring of the outer defences of London. 61 Squadron was equipped with Pups, another lovely Sopwith scout; but its performance and armament were not good enough to deal with Gothas, so the squadron was changing over to S.E. 5's." [from 'Sagittarius Rising', Cecil Lewis].*

On Saturday, 18th January **1919**, just two weeks before Frank was killed, he married Margaret Mary Fulcher at Rochford Register Office, his address then being 22, Windsor Road, Westcliff-on-Sea, having previously lived at 3, Cumberland Terrace, Rochford. A fortnight later, on Saturday, **1st February, 2nd Lieutenant Frank Lloyd** took off in his Sopwith Camel, H799, a machine that 61 Squadron at Rochford had taken on its strength on 23rd October 1918.

It had previously been damaged in an accident during December but had been repaired on station. It would appear that Frank was 'volplaning' (gliding

---

149 The R.A.F. was formed on 1st April 1918 from the amalgamation of the Royal Flying Corps (a corps of the army) and the Royal Naval Air Service (administered by the Admiralty).

A Sopwith 'Camel'

with the engine turned off) and banking when the wing of his aircraft touched a live electric wire on the tramway system on the London Road. His aircraft immediately burst into flames and crashed to the ground. When rescuers reached Frank they found him to be dead, presumably having been electrocuted. He was just 23 years of age, had fought through the entire Great War and had recently married. Local newspapers reported that Frank was flying *'rather low'* and, to avoid a collision with a full tramcar, had then collided with an electric tram-standard. At the inquest into the accident, held on Tuesday, 4th February 1919, Mr. H.J. Jeffries, the Coroner, recorded the cause of death as:

> *'a smashed skull due to…accidentally colliding with an electric standard in an aeroplane.'*

The place of death was given as:

> *"….opposite Fairmead Avenue, London Road, Westcliff-on-sea."*

As the accident occurred in peacetime **Frank Lloyd**'s body was returned home to the Midlands where he had so many connections. The funeral service for the former mining engineer who worked at Holly Bank Colliery was held in the Bloxwich Wesleyan Church and was conducted by the Reverend M.F. Ryle. Frank now lies buried in Bloxwich Cemetery. His widow, Margaret, remarried in April 1927 becoming Mrs. Sydney James William Baldwin and she lived until 1997.

It appears that **Alfred Main** served two or three years in the army before the war erupted, most likely in the Special Reserve battalion of the South Staffordshire Regiment. Early in the war, himself a trained soldier, he was most likely used to train new recruits and was not drafted to France until 25th May 1915, whereupon he arrived as a replacement for some of those men who had become casualties with 2/South Staffordshire during the Battle of Festubert. Alfred lived through the Battle of Loos in September and the follow-up actions at the Hohenzollern Redoubt in mid-October. For the first six months of 1916, 2/South Staffordshire was not involved in any major set-piece battles but all changed with the opening of the Somme offensive on 1st July. Although not in battle for the first three weeks of July, 2/South Staffordshire was sent into the bloody struggle for Delville Wood from 25th July and it was there, near Montauban, that **Alfred Main** was wounded for the first time. He was sent down the line and the decision was taken to send him back to 'Blighty' for treatment. Following his recovery and convalescence, Alfred returned to France but was posted to the 7/South Staffordshire, a battalion that itself had been heavily committed in the Somme sector. With the 7th, Alfred fought in the Ancre valley in early 1917, at Messines Ridge in June 1917 and at 3rd Ypres in the summer and autumn of 1917, suffering his second wound at Broodseinde near Ypres on Thursday, 4th October 1917. On that occasion, his battalion attacked near Poelcappelle, the attack commencing at 6 a.m. with tanks of "D" Battalion, 1st Tank Brigade, deployed to assist. There was little opposition to the advance other than a pocket of Germans hidden under a derelict tank and small groups in shell holes. Near to Poelcappelle Church, a concrete bunker was taken and consolidation commenced in spite of the snipers in the area. Alfred's bravery during the battle was recognised by his being offered a commission and subsequently being gazetted 2nd Lieutenant with 5th Battalion, the Worcestershire Regiment. Having received his commission on 29th May 1918, Alfred never served abroad again prior to the armistice and yet survived less than a year beyond the war, dying from complications resulting from earlier exposure to poison gas on the Western Front. He developed consumption [now known as Tuberculosis] and was treated in Sunderland Military Hospital (formerly Women's Block, Sunderland Poor Law Institution) where **Second Lieutenant Alfred Main** died, aged twenty-two, on Friday, **3rd October 1919**. Like Frank Lloyd, Alfred Main was returned to Bloxwich for his funeral that was conducted by the Reverend J.C. Hamilton. An Old Boy of Elmore Green School and a former miner at Huntington Colliery, near Cannock, Alfred was buried locally in Bloxwich Cemetery.

Leonard Beech, who served in 2/5 South Staffordshire during the Great War, survived longer than any other Old Boy whose name appears on the Elmore Green School memorial. Leon, who had two brothers, was born in February 1894 and was educated at Elmore Green School. His father, Titus Beech senior, owned an awl blade and needle manufacturing company that was based at the family home at 65, Field Street (and from 1923 in a large house 'The Poplars' on Lichfield Road, standing in the grounds of the now St. Peter's RC School.) Leonard was employed in the family business as an awl blade grinder. In late February 1917, **Second Lieutenant Leonard Beech** of 2/5 South Staffordshire landed with his battalion at the French port of Le Havre.

The Staffords were soon into the line, pursuing the Germans in their withdrawal to the Hindenburg Line during March and April. July to September saw the battalion fighting in the Ypres Salient before playing a part in the Battle of Cambrai. In the reorganization of brigades at the end of January 1918, 2/5 South Staffordshire was disbanded and there is no clear evidence

IN UNDYING LOVE AND
AFFECTIONATE REMEMBRANCE

— OF —

LEONARD,

The son of

TITUS V. AND ELIZA BEECH,

Born February 18th, 1894.
Died December 13th, 1920.

AGED 26 YEARS.

Interred in Bloxwich Cemetery December 16th, 1920.

He fought and died for his country.

R. I. P.

Leon Beech, 'In Memoriam' card

as to what happened to Leonard Beech. As an officer, it is likely that he was transferred to another battalion within 59th Division; it is also possible that he was transferred to 1/5 South Staffordshire in 46th Division. However, it is certain that **Second Lieutenant Beech** survived to the November 1918 Armistice and returned to his family in England. According to his younger brother Titus, Leonard was gassed and injured during his army service and, like many former soldiers, his resistance to the Spanish Influenza was fatally impaired. The influenza pandemic is estimated to have killed in excess of 50 million people worldwide – a death-toll that exceeded that of the fighting during the Great War. Once influenza had taken hold, the effects of gas would have made his respiratory system increasingly susceptible to infection and twenty-six year-old **Leonard Beech** died in hospital in England on Monday, **13th December 1920**. He was buried in Bloxwich Cemetery on Thursday, 16th December 1920.

Leonard Beech, Alfred Main and Frank Lloyd possibly knew each other from their schooldays; their paths may well have crossed in the army as they all served in the South Staffordshire Regiment, though in different battalions; they certainly share the same consecrated ground in Bloxwich.

Silver War Badge awards

Six lads, each related to at least one Old Boy on the Elmore Green School War memorial, were discharged from the army on the grounds of wounds or sickness incurred as a direct result of their war service. In recognition of their service and sacrifice, each was awarded the Silver War Badge (SWB shown right and worn on the right lapel of civilian dress) and the appropriate certificate.

9134 **Private Ernest LAVENDER** 2/ South Staffordshire Regiment
Enlisted 19/04/12 Discharged 08/01/17 (wounds)
SWB number 212558 Age 24, overseas
[Uncle to Alfred James Bushnell, killed in action on 06/07/15 and
George Bernard Bushnell, killed in action on 13/10/15. Brother of Wm
'Coxy' Lavender killed in action on 07/11/14].

9586 **Private James JONES** 1/South Staffordshire Regiment
Enlisted 12/08/14 Discharged 08/05/18 (sickness)
SWB number 363923 Age 25 years, overseas
[Brother of Edward Jones, killed in action on 27/11/16]

260049 **Corporal Jonah GILL** 6/ King's Liverpool Regiment
Enlisted 31/12/14 Discharged 27/11/18 (wounds)
SWB number B209952 Age 23 years, overseas
[Brother of Bertie Gill who died of wounds 27/04/16].

43618 **Private Edward PARTON** Lincolnshire Regiment
Enlisted 27/09/15 Discharged 14/12/18 (sickness)
SWB number B250949 Age 22 years, overseas
[Brother of Jack Parton, killed in action on 13/10/15].

242475 **Private Benjamin HAYCOCK** South Staffordshire Regiment
Enlisted 07/03/14 Discharged 10/03/19 (sickness)
SWB number B268948 Age 21 years, overseas
[Brother of Bill Haycock, killed in action on 09/08/18].

242535 **Private Joseph STYCH** 1/6 South Staffordshire Regiment
Enlisted 14/06/10 Discharged 12/09/19 (wounds)
SWB number B308723 Age 27 years, overseas
[Brother of Albert Stych, killed in action on 28/04/17 and also of
Samuel Henry Stych, killed in action on 09/03/16]

Chronological Roll of Honour for 1919-20

England 1919

February 1st	Frank	LLOYD, M.M.	Flying accident
October 3rd	Alfred	MAIN	Consumption

England 1920

December 16th	Leon	BEECH	Influenza (gassed)

Alphabetical Roll of Honour for 1919-20

Leonard BEECH

Born on 18th February 1894 in Bloxwich, Leonard was the fourth child of Titus Vincent and Eliza Beech (both 41 years old in 1901) of 37, Park Road, Bloxwich and later (at time of 1901 and 1911 Censuses) of 65, Field Street, Bloxwich. By the 1901 Census, Leonard had at least four sisters (Ellen 18 and an elementary-school teacher (Walsall Education Committee), Elizabeth Mary 12, Catherine Mary 4 and Agnes 1 – all born in Bloxwich, as was their father) and two brothers (Titus Vincent 8, and Charles Henry, 5) – in 1901, his 10 year-old French-born cousin, Henri, was staying with the family (Henri Beech was a British subject). Eight of ten children survived beyond their early years. Titus senior  owned an awl blade and needle manufacturing company that was based at the family home in Field Street (and from 1923 in a large house 'The Poplars' on Lichfield Road, standing in the grounds of the now St. Peter's RC School.) Leonard was employed in the family business as an awl blade grinder.

Second Lieutenant, 2/5th (Territorial Force) Battalion, South Staffordshire Regiment, (176th Brigade, 59th '2nd North Midland' Division). *Unit History* – 25/2/17 landed at Le Havre, France. 14/3-5/4/17 German Retreat to the Hindenburg Line. 3rd Ypres ('Passchendaele'), 20-25/9/17 Battle of the Menin Road; 26/9-3/10/17 Battle of Polygon Wood. Cambrai, 30/11-3/12/17 German Counter-Attacks. Disbanded 30/1/18. **Died post-war (age 26) in England on Monday, 13th December 1920**. Leonard was gassed and injured during his army service and, like many former soldiers, his resistance to the Spanish Influenza was fatally impaired. The influenza pandemic (an epidemic on a worldwide scale) is estimated to have killed in excess of 50 million people – a death-toll that exceeded that of the fighting during the Great War. **Buried** in Grave M. 2. 223 of **Bloxwich Cemetery**, Walsall, on Thursday, **16th December, 1920**. **Entitled** to the British War Medal and Victory Medal. Commemorated on the Elmore Green School Roll of Honour (formerly displayed in T.P. Riley School library) and on the Bloxwich Roll of Honour.

Frank LLOYD, MM and Bar

Frank was born in 1895 or 1896 in Bloxwich, the son of Thomas and Elizabeth Lloyd (née Grant) of 17, Little Bloxwich Lane, Bloxwich; his father, who predeceased him, was a colliery railway platelayer. Elizabeth married Jonah Ray at Walsall in 1912 and then resided at 15, Lichfield Road, Bloxwich with her family; at the outbreak of war Frank lived with his mother and stepfather. He had seven brothers and sisters and was educated at Elmore Green School. In 1911 he was working as a cinder hewer at a blast furnace but by the outbreak of war he was employed as a mining engineer at Holly Bank Colliery, Essington. Single throughout the war, Frank was married just two weeks prior to his death. **Mobilised from the Territorial Force in August 1914.**

8424>200276, Sergeant, 'D' Company, 1/5th (Territorial Force) Battalion, South Staffordshire Regiment. To…, 8424>200276, Sergeant, 6th Battalion, Worcestershire Regiment (29/1/18). To…, **2nd Lieutenant, 61st Squadron, Royal Air Force.** *Unit History* – [1/5th South Staffordshire] 5th March 1915 landed at Le Havre, France. From 4/4/15 at Neuve Eglise/ Wulverghem. 7/15 to 2/10/15 Hill 60, Ypres.
13-15/10/15 Battle of Loos (Hohenzollern Redoubt and Hulluch Quarries). January 1916 to Egypt. February 1916 to France. From 19/3/16 Neuville St. Vaast/Ecoivres. May/June 1916 Fonquevillers sector of the Somme. Somme, 1/7/16 Battle of Gommecourt. 3/7/16 to 28/10/16 Berles-au-Bois and Bailleulmont sector on the Somme. 1-13/3/17 Operations on the Ancre including the Occupation of the Gommecourt Defences (4/3/17) and the Attack on Rettemoy Graben (12/3/17). 14/3/17-22/3/17 German Retreat to the Hindenburg Line. 18/4/17 to 15/6/17 Lens sector (Cité St. Pierre). 3/6/17-26/8/17 Lens sector including the attack on Liévin (1/7/17); 15-25/8/17 Battle of Hill 70. [Late 1917, he was sent to officer cadet school to train for a commission, subsequently being gazetted to 6/Worcestershire on 29/1/18] Newcastle-upon-Tyne. [To **Royal Air Force** on 5th July 1918] – attended flying-cadet training school; 7th October 1918, posted to RAF Rochford in Essex as a 2nd Lieutenant with 61 Squadron. **Killed (age 23) on Saturday, 1st February 1919** in a flying accident when his aircraft hit a live tram wire near Westcliff-on-Sea. **Buried** in plot M. 1. 30 of **Bloxwich Cemetery**. Entitled to the Military Medal, awarded for his actions at Hulluch on 13th October 1915 during the Battle of Loos (posted in the 'London Gazette' supplement edition of 11th November 1916, page 10926) and a bar (effectively

a second M.M.) was added to his Military Medal for his actions at Bucquoy in 1917 (posted in the 'London Gazette' supplement edition of 21st December 1917, page 12449). **Entitled** to the 1914-15 Star (Medal Roll – F/12B, p.612), British War Medal and Victory Medal (Medal Roll – F/101B22/2, p.2916). Commemorated on the Elmore Green School Roll of Honour (formerly located in the T.P. Riley School library), on the Walsall and Bloxwich Rolls of Honour and on the Roll of Honour in All Saints Church, Bloxwich. [Note: The Walsall Roll of Honour does not correctly record him serving in the R.A.F nor does it give the correct rank.] **Family** – left a widow, Margaret Lloyd of 22, Windsor Road, Westcliff-on-Sea, Essex. They had been married for just two weeks. Margaret remarried in April 1927 becoming Mrs. Sydney James William Baldwin; she died in 1997.

Alfred Leonard MAIN

Born in 1896 or 1897 in Bloxwich to Alfred (a colliery banksman) and Mary Jane Main (née Merricks) of 70a, Sandbank, Bloxwich. Mary Jane passed away in 1909 and the following year Alfred married Alice Courtney. The family then lived at 112, Parker Street and later at 2, Bell Lane, Bloxwich. In 1911, Alfred was one of ten children in the extended family (three brothers – Thomas, George and Jack; one sister – Emily; five step-sisters – Florence, Selina, Dora, Polly and Winifred). Young Alfred (the second oldest of the brothers) served at least three years in the army before the war, possibly in the Special Reserve battalion of the South Staffordshire Regiment. During this time, Alfred was employed at the Huntington Colliery, just north of Cannock. **Called up from the Army Reserve at the outbreak of war (5th August 1914).** 9164 > 20002, Private, 2nd (Regular) Battalion, South Staffordshire Regiment. (6th Brigade, 2nd Division) Transferred to…, 7th (Service/New Army) Battalion, South Staffordshire Regiment, (33rd Brigade, 11th 'Northern' Division) Commissioned to…, **Second Lieutenant, 5th (Reserve) Battalion, Worcestershire Regiment** (from 29th May 1918). *Unit History* – landed in France on 25th May 1915. [2/South Staffordshire] 25/9/15-4/10/15 Battle of Loos. 13-19/10/15 Hohenzollern Redoubt (Loos). Wounded. [7/South Staffordshire] Somme, 15-22/9/16 Battle of Flers-Courcelette; 26-28/9/16 Battle of Thiepval. 11-19/1/17 Operations on the Ancre. 9-14/6/17 Battle of Messines. 3rd Ypres ('Passchendaele'), 16-18/8/17 Langemarck; 19/8, 22/8 and 27/8/17 Fighting Around St. Julien; 26/9-3/10/17 Polygon Wood; 4/10/17 Broodseinde. Wounded. Commissioned. [5/Worcestershire] Harwich Garrison, east of England. **Died (age 22) post-war in England on Friday, 3rd October 1919** in Sunderland Military

Hospital (formerly Women's Block, Sunderland Poor Law Institution) from consumption, a consequence of being gassed while in France. **Buried** in plot M. 2. 109 of **Bloxwich Cemetery**; the service was conducted by the Reverend J.C. Hamilton. **Entitled** to the 1914-15 Star (Medal Roll – F/12B, page 600); British War Medal, Victory Medal (Medal Roll – F107B22, page 2882). Alfred is commemorated on the Bloxwich Roll of Honour and on the Roll of Honour in All Saints Church, Bloxwich. **Family** – a brother, George Main, served in the army.

Known Survivors of the Great War
(with Elmore Green School or family links)

BRYAN (unknown forename)

Son of Joseph (a puddler in an ironworks but deceased prior to 1911) and Elizabeth Bryan (née Sanders) of the same address. **Family** – An older brother of 352832, Private James Bryan 1/9th (Territorial Force) 'Highlanders' Battalion, Royal Scots Regiment, who was killed in action (age 23) near Chambrécy on Saturday, 20th July 1918. No further details of service discovered. Survived the war.

John BULLOCK *One of the 'Old Contemptibles'*

Son of John (a bricklayer's labourer) and Ruth Bullock (née Henden) of 28, New Street, Bloxwich. One of eleven children – nine brothers (Alfred Charles, Joseph Henry, William Amos, Frank, Lilias, George Edward, Leonard, Herbert, Harold) and one sister (Amy Gladys). **7745, Private, 1st (Regular) Battalion, the South Staffordshire Regiment, (22nd Brigade, 7th Division)**. 4th October 1914 landed at Zeebrugge in Belgium. 9-10/10/14 Antwerp Operations (Bruges). 1st Ypres, 21-24/10/14 Battle of Langemarck; 29-31/10/14 Battle of Gheluvelt. Taken prisoner of war at the beginning of November 1914 and held in Germany until the Armistice. **Entitled** to the 1914 'Mons' Star (Medal Roll – F/2/4 p.16), British War Medal and Victory Medal (Medal Roll – F/101B2, p.165). Returned home after release. **Family** – Two brothers died – R/16384, Rifleman William Amos Bullock, 1 Company, 16th (Service/New Army) 'Church Lads Brigade' Battalion, King's Royal Rifle Corps was killed in action (age 22) near Arras on Monday, 23rd April 1917 on the first day of the 2nd Battle of the Scarpe. 200822, Private Alfred Charles Bullock, 1/5th (Territorial Force) Battalion, the South Staffordshire Regiment died (age 23) on 10th June 1917 of wounds sustained two days earlier, near Lens.

Joseph Henry BULLOCK *One of the 'Old Contemptibles'*
Son of John (a bricklayer's labourer) and Ruth Bullock (née Henden) of 28, New Street, Bloxwich – nine brothers (John, William Amos, Alfred Charles, Frank, Lilias, George Edward, Leonard, Herbert, Harold) and one sister (Amy Gladys). **9285, Private, 2nd (Regular) Battalion, the South Staffordshire Regiment, (6th Brigade, 2nd Division). 1914** 12th August 1914 landed at Le Havre, France. Battle of Mons, Retreat from Mons, Battle of the Marne; Battle of the. 1st Ypres Battle of Langemarck, Battle of Gheluvelt, Battle of Nonne Bosschen. **1915** [La Bassée sector all year] Affairs of Cuinchy, Battle of Festubert, Battle of Loos – Hohenzollern Redoubt (Loos). **1916** Somme Battle of Delville Wood, Attack on Waterlot Farm near Guillemont, Battle of the Ancre. **1917** Operations on the Ancre. German Retreat to the Hindenburg Line. Arras Battle of Vimy Ridge (1st Battle of the Scarpe), Battle of Arleux, 3rd Battle of the Scarpe. Cambrai Capture of Bourlon Wood, German Counter-Attacks. **1918** Spring Offensives – Somme Battle of St. Quentin, 1st Battle of Bapaume (Flesquières Salient), 1st Battle of Arras. 2nd Somme Battle of Albert, 2nd Battle of Bapaume and the Assault on the Drocourt-Quéant Line. Battles of The Hindenburg Line Battle of Havrincourt, Battle of the Canal du Nord, Capture of Mont sur l'Oeuvre, Battle of Cambrai and the Capture of Forenville. Final Advance in Picardy Battle of the Selle. **Sometime transferred (date unknown) to the Labour Corps, maybe as a result of wounding or illness – 403898/40898, Private, Labour Corps. Entitled** to the 1914 'Mons' Star (Medal Roll – F/2/5, p.17), British War Medal and Victory Medal (Medal Roll – LC/101B144, p.14677). Returned home. **NOTE**: Out of respect for a soldier who survived the entire war, Joe's story has been told as if he served in 2/South Staffordshire throughout. **Family** – Two brothers died: R/16384, Rifleman William Amos Bullock, 1 Company, 16th (Service/New Army) 'Church Lads Brigade' Battalion, King's Royal Rifle Corps was killed in action (age 22) near Arras on Monday, 23rd April 1917 on the first day of the 2nd Battle of the Scarpe. 200822, Private Alfred Charles Bullock, 1/5th (Territorial Force) Battalion, the South Staffordshire Regiment died (age 23) on 10th June 1917 of wounds sustained two days earlier, near Lens.

Ernest William COPE
Born in Hednesford, Staffordshire and lived at Belt Road, Chadsmoor, Cannock and the family later moved to Bloxwich, residing first in Bell Lane and later at 33, The Flats, Bloxwich. Son of a coal-miner, Isaac, and Mary Ann Cope (née Gaunt) of Bloxwich. One of seven children (six living at home in 1911) – two younger brothers (John Henry and Isaac) and four sisters (Lucy, Julia, Annie and Beatrice May). Single. Miner employed at Huntington

Colliery. **Volunteered** in **August 1915** in Hednesford, on the same day as his 17-year-old brother, John Henry Cope – they served in 9/South Staffordshire together and their regimental numbers were consecutive. **19804, Private, 'C' Company, 9th (Service) Battalion, South Staffordshire Regiment, (Pioneer Battalion, 23rd Division)**. The battalion shipped to Boulogne, France on 24th August 1915. Following his period of training, Ernest Cope would probably have crossed the Channel to join his unit around the turn of the year 1915/1916. **1916** Somme Battle of Albert and the Capture of Contalmaison (10/7/16), Battle of Bazentin, Battle of Pozières, Battle of Flers-Courcelette, Battle of Morval, Battle of Le Transloy including the Capture of Le Sars (7/10/16). **1917** Battle of Messines. 3rd Ypres ('Passchendaele') Battle of the Menin Road, Battle of Polygon Wood, 1st Battle of Passchendaele, 2nd Battle of Passchendaele. November 1917 to Italian Front – arrived near Mantua. **1918** Battle of the Piave The Fighting on the Asiago Plateau. Battle of Vittorio Veneto and the passage of the Piave River and Passage of the Monticano River. **Entitled** to the British War Medal and Victory Medal (Medal Roll – F/101B9, p.1027). Returned to England. **Family** – two younger brothers died, each in a separate war: 19803, Private John Henry Cope, 'C' Company, 9th (Service) Battalion, South Staffordshire Regiment died (age 18) in hospital, on Wednesday, 23rd February 1916, from the effects of shrapnel wounds to his legs, sustained near Armentières on 21st February 1916. His youngest brother, 5057631 Private Isaac Cope, 5/Devonshire, was killed in Germany during the Second World War.

Charles DAWSON
Born in Blakenall in 1890 or 1891 and lived first at 35, Chapel Row, Blakenall Heath and later at 4, Blakenall Heath. Son of John and Hannah Dawson. One of eight children – five brothers (George, James, Howard, Leonard and Thomas) and two sisters (Elizabeth and Mary). Employed as a miner. **Volunteered** in **1915**. [Most likely] **17321, Private, 7th (Service) Battalion, the South Staffordshire Regiment, (33rd Brigade, 11th 'Northern' Division)**. Landed in Egypt on 5th December 1915. **Entitled** to the British War Medal and Victory Medal (Medal Roll – F/101B9, p.1027). **Family** – a younger brother, 9451, Lance-Corporal James Dawson, 'C' Company, 2nd (Regular) Battalion, South Staffordshire Regiment was killed in action (age 24) on Monday, 13th November 1916 attacking the Quadrilateral strongpoint on Redan Ridge during the Battle of the Ancre on the Somme. Brothers George and Howard Dawson both served and survived. All four of the Dawson brothers served in battalions of the South Staffordshire Regiment.

George DAWSON

Born in Blakenall in 1888 or 1889 and lived first at 35, Chapel Row, Blakenall Heath and later at 4, Blakenall Heath. Son of John and Hannah Dawson. One of eight children – five brothers (Charles, James, Howard, Leonard and Thomas) and two sisters (Elizabeth and Mary). Employed as a miner at the Fair Lady Colliery. **Volunteered** for army service in **1914**. [Most likely] **215>201036, Private, 1/5th or 1/6th (Territorial Force) Battalion, the South Staffordshire Regiment.** Landed in France on 28th August 1915. Wounded in the neck and left thigh on 30th September 1918 – invalided to England and treated at Southmead Hospital, Bristol. **Entitled** to the 1914-15 Star (Medal Roll, F/2B2, p.104), British War Medal and Victory Medal (Medal Roll, F/101 B18, p.2304). Demobilised 4th January 1919. **Family** – a younger brother, 9451, Lance-Corporal James Dawson, 'C' Company, 2nd (Regular) Battalion, South Staffordshire Regiment was killed in action (age 24) on Monday, 13th November 1916 attacking the Quadrilateral strongpoint on Redan Ridge during the Battle of the Ancre on the Somme. Brothers Charles and Howard Dawson both served and survived. All four of the Dawson brothers served in battalions of the South Staffordshire Regiment.

Howard DAWSON

Born in Blakenall in 1899 or 1900 and lived first at 35, Chapel Row, Blakenall Heath and later at 4, Blakenall Heath. Son of John and Hannah Dawson. One of eight children – five brothers (George, Charles, James, Leonard and Thomas) and two sisters (Elizabeth and Mary). **Enlisted** in **late 1917 or early 1918** – the youngest of the four Dawson brothers to serve in the war. **South Staffordshire Regiment**. Landed in France in 1918. **Entitled** to the British War Medal and Victory Medal – details unknown. **Family** – an older brother, 9451, Lance-Corporal James Dawson, 'C' Company, 2nd (Regular) Battalion, South Staffordshire Regiment was killed in action (age 24) on Monday, 13th November 1916 attacking the Quadrilateral strongpoint on Redan Ridge during the Battle of the Ancre on the Somme. Brothers Charles and George Dawson both served and survived. All four of the Dawson brothers served in battalions of the South Staffordshire Regiment.

Elijah DUNN

Prior to volunteering for the tunnellers, he was employed as a miner in Yorkshire. **Tunnelling Company, Royal Engineers**. **Entitled** to the 1914-15 Star, the British War Medal and the Victory Medal (details unknown). **Family** –

His brother, 50614, Sapper Thomas H. Dunn of 89th Field Company, Royal Engineers, was accidentally killed (age 35) on Sunday, 12th March 1916 by an earth slip whilst digging a gun-pit in the Arras sector. Thomas Dunn's stepson, 30578, Private Ernest Haywood, 'B' Company, 8th (Service) Battalion, the South Staffordshire Regiment was killed in action (age 20) on Tuesday, 17th April 1917 at Arras.

Joseph or John EVANS

Older brothers of Thomas Evans – in 1914, Joseph was 32 and a coal miner; John was 30 and an iron-founder. Both were born in Walsall to Thomas and Elizabeth Evans of 62, Reeves Street, Bloxwich; their father worked as a coal miner. One of Thomas's two brothers served in the army. No other details have been uncovered.

Jonah GILL

Born on 10th July 1898 in Bloxwich and lived at 100, Parker Street, Bloxwich. Son of a coal-miner, Jonah, and Lydia Gill (née Dean) of the same address. One of five children in 1911 – four brothers (Bertie, Norman Victor, Alexander and Arthur). Educated at Elmore Green School from 27/06/10. Single. **Volunteered** on 31st December 1914. **2/5th (TF) Battalion, South Staffordshire** transferred to **260049, Corporal, 1/6th (Territorial Force) Battalion, the King's (Liverpool) Regiment, (165th Brigade, 55th 'West Lancashire' Division)**. First saw service in the Irish rebellion with the 2/5th Battalion, the South Staffordshire Regiment. Drafted to France in 1916, he transferred to The King's (Liverpool). Served in two battles of 3rd Ypres, at Cambrai and in the Battles of the Lys in 1918 where he was badly gassed on Friday, 24th May. Jonah was discharged from the Army on Wednesday, 27th November 1918, probably as a result of wounds and gas. He was awarded the Silver War Badge number B209952. **Entitled** to the British War Medal and Victory Medal – (Medal Roll, H/2/102B34, p.4681; SWB List, H/2473/2). **Family** – an older brother, 75940, Gunner Bertie Gill, 94th Battery, 18th Brigade, Royal Field Artillery, (3rd Canadian Division) died of wounds (age 22) on 27th April 1916, having been severely wounded near Poperinghe by counter-battery fire on 10th April 1916.

Fred GOODALL

Born in 1896 or 1897. Son of William and Charlotte Goodall. Lived at 699, Bloxwich Road and at 13, Church Street, Bloxwich. Single. Prior to enlisting, he was employed at Brockley's Brickyard. **Enlisted** on **October 22, 1914**. **9806, 20094, 242538, Private, 1/5th or 1/6th (Territorial Force)**

Battalion, the South Staffordshire Regiment, (137th Brigade, 46th '1st North Midland' Division). Landed in France on 18th August 1915. **1915** Hill 60, Ypres. Battle of Loos (Hohenzollern Redoubt and Hulluch Quarries). **1916** January 1916 to Egypt. February 1916 to France. Neuville St. Vaast/Ecoivres near Arras. Fonquevillers sector of the Somme. Somme 1/7/16 Battle of Gommecourt. Berles-au-Bois and Bailleulmont sector on the Somme. **1917** Operations on the Ancre including the Occupation of the Gommecourt Defences (4/3/17) and the Attack on Rettemoy Graben (12/3/17). German Retreat to the Hindenburg Line. Lens sector (Cité St. Pierre). Lens sector including the attack on Liévin (1/7/17); Battle of Hill 70. **1918** March 1918 Cuinchy (near Béthune). Battles of The Hindenburg Line, Battle of St. Quentin Canal including the Passage at Bellenglise (29/9/18); Battle of Beaurevoir; Battle of Cambrai. Pursuit to the Selle. Final Advance in Picardy, Battle of the Selle (including the Action of Riqueval Wood). Battle of the Sambre. Suffered a gunshot wound between the eyes by on July 1st 1916, when he was nineteen. **Entitled** to the 1914-15 Star (Medal Roll, F/2B2, p.154). British War Medal and Victory Medal – (Medal Roll, F/101B22, p.2828). Discharged on 14/12/18. **Family** – two brothers served, one at Salonika and the other in France, while five cousins also served with the forces.

Robert HANDY, DCM

Born in 1879 or 1880 in Burntwood, Staffordshire. Son of Edwin (a miner) and Matilda Handy. Lived at 72, Reeves Street, Bloxwich in 1901. At least three brothers – Edwin (14 years older), H. Joseph (12 years older), John (6 years older); and at least five sisters – Sarah A. (8 years older), Fanny (4 years older), Emily (2 years older), Matilda (3 years younger) and Elsie (nine years younger). Single. Coal-miner employed at a pit in Yorkshire. Boarder in 1911 (with Frank and MaryAnn Hough) at 47, King St., South Kirkby, near Wakefield, Yorkshire. **Volunteered in late 1914 or early 1915. 13628, Acting Company Sergeant-Major, 8th (Service) Battalion, the South Staffordshire Regiment, (51st Brigade, 17th 'Northern' Division).** *Unit History* – landed at Boulogne, France on 14/7/15. **1915** Action of Hooge. **1916** Actions of the Bluff (Ypres). Somme, Battle of Albert including the Capture of Fricourt; Battle of Delville Wood. **1917** Arras, 1st Battle of the Scarpe; 2nd Battle of the Scarpe. Capture of Roeux and its subsequent defence. 3rd Ypres ('Passchendaele'), 1st Battle of Passchendaele; 2nd Battle of Passchendaele. **1918** Kaiserschlacht – Somme, Battle of St. Quentin; 1st Battle of Bapaume. Advance in Picardy, Battle of Amiens; 2nd Somme, Battle of Albert; 2nd Battle of Bapaume. Battles of The Hindenburg Line, Battle of Havrincourt; Battle of Epéhy; Battle of Cambrai. Pursuit to the Selle. Final

Advance in Picardy, Battle of the Selle; Battle of the Sambre. Awarded the **DCM** – *'London Gazette'* Supplement, issue 30188, 18/7/17, p.7265. **Entitled** to the 1914-15 Star (Medal Roll – F/2B2, p. 171) & BWM/VM (Medal Roll – F/101B6, p.671). Discharged to Class 'Z' Army Reserve on 23.1.19. **Family** – uncle of twenty-two year-old 200088, Corporal Joseph Henry Handy (brother Edwin's son) who was killed in action with 'B' Company of 1/5 South Staffordshire attacking Bucquoy village on 14th March 1917.

William HARPER
Born in 1888 or 1889 in Bloxwich. Son of a bricklayer's labourer (and later a colliery boilerman) Frederick William, and Eliza Harper (née Stokes) of 6, Elmore Green Road. One of nine children in 1911 – the seven brothers were William, Charles, George, Fred, Harry, Philip and Ernest) and two sisters (Louie and Harriet). Single. Employed as a file-maker in 1911. No details of military service yet traced. **Family** – 3 brothers served (see below) – 42192, Private Fred Harper of 2/6 Sherwood Foresters was killed in action (age 23) on Wednesday, 26th September 1917 when the battalion captured several German blockhouses near Gravenstafel on the first day of the Battle of Polygon Wood during 3rd Ypres ('Passchendaele').

Two Harper brothers from the following three served:

Charles HARPER
Born in 1890 or 1891 in Bloxwich. Single. Employed as a coal-miner. Other details as for William Harper. No details of military service yet traced.

George HARPER
Born in 1892 or 1893 in Bloxwich. Single. Employed as an awl-blade maker. Other details as for William Harper. No details of military service yet traced.

Harry HARPER
Born in 1897 or 1898 in Bloxwich. Single. Employed as a brickyard labourer. Other details as for William Harper. No details of military service yet traced.

Joseph HARRISON
Born in 1895 or 1896 in Bloxwich and lived with his parents at 6, Bullock's Fold, Bloxwich and later at 85 and then 19, Field Street, Bloxwich. Son of a coal-miner (at Hawkins Colliery), Samuel George, and Sarah Louisa Harrison (née Dean) of the same address. One of five children in 1911 – one younger brother (Samuel George) and three sisters (Fanny, Elizabeth and Lydia). Single.

No details of military service yet traced. **Family** – his brother, 242568, Private Samuel George Harrison of 1/6 South Staffordshire was killed in action (age 20) on Sunday, 29th September 1918 attacking the Hindenburg Line during the Battle of the St. Quentin Canal.

Alfred HARVEY

Born between 1887 and 1890 in Bloxwich; lived at 50, Blakenall Lane. Son of Eli and Zillah Harvey (née Glover) of the same address; (at one time his father, Eli, had owned a greengrocery shop situated at 92, Parker Street, Bloxwich but was later employed as an insurance agent. Eli had, for about 20 years, been a checkweighman at Cannock Lodge Colliery). One of eight children in 1911 – three older brothers (Oscar E., Bernard G., Frank and Thomas Ralph) and three sisters (Wallena, Florence M. and Edith Billiah). **Attested under the Lord Derby scheme, late in 1915.** Wounded at least once during his war service. No details of his regiment or corps. **Entitled** to the British War Medal and the Victory Medal. **Family** – a younger brother 8632, Private Frank Harvey of 2nd Battalion, South Staffordshire Regiment was killed in action (age 22) on Wednesday, 24th November 1915 on regular trench duty in the Cambrin sector near Loos. His father, Eli, worked in a munitions factory.

Benjamin HAYCOCK

Born on 21st September 1897 in Rugeley and lived at 38, Bell Lane, Bloxwich. Son of an London & North-Western Railway platelayer, Albert Israel, and Elizabeth Haycock (née Powis) of the same address. One of five children, of whom four were living at home in 1911 – two brothers (William Albert and Jasper J.H.) and a sister (Celia). Educated at Elmore Green School (from 04/05/08). Single. Later lived at Station Gates, Bloxwich. Employed in a timber-yard. **Enlisted pre-war on 7th March 1914. 242475, Private Benjamin Haycock, South Staffordshire Regiment.** Served overseas – landed in France in March or April 1916. Severely gassed on 23rd May 1918 and was invalided to Stepping Hill Hospital, Hazelgrove, Stockport. Discharged the army due to sickness on 10th March 1919 and was awarded the Silver War Badge number B268948. **Entitled** to the British War Medal and the Victory Medal. **Family** – an older, married brother, 203479, Sergeant Bill Haycock of 1st Battalion, South Staffordshire Regiment, was killed in action (age 26) on Friday, 9th August 1918 during a raid on the village of Canove in Northern Italy.

James HAYWARD

Born in 1892 or 1893 in Coalpool, Walsall to James (a coalminer) and Fanny Hayward who originally lived at 5, William Street, Fenton, Stoke on Trent and later at 44 and 46, High Street, Bloxwich. Siblings – William b. 1876, George b. 1882, Eliza and Aaron b. 1890. Employed as a colliery banksman. **Volunteered in late 1914 or early 1915**. **2316, Private, Royal Army Medical Corps.** Served first in a hospital in Wales. Landed in the Balkan theatre on 10th August 1915. **Entitled** to the 1914-15 Star (Medal Roll – RAMC/11B, p.881), British War Medal and Victory Medal (Medal Roll – RAMC/101/B50, p.3620). Disembodied 3rd September 1919. **Family** – an older brother, 7979, Private Aaron Hayward, [possibly 'D' Company], 1st Battalion, South Staffordshire Regiment died of wounds (age 24) in a Lille hospital on Monday, 2nd November 1914 behind enemy lines – one of the *'Old Contemptibles'*.

Charles Henry HEELEY

Born before 1887 in Blakenall and lived at 23, Cope Street, Leamore. Son of a coal-miner, John, and Prudence Heeley (née Simmons). One of twelve children, of whom ten were living at home in 1911 – at least five brothers (John, Arthur, James, Victor and Norman) and at least five sisters (Lily, Ethel, Emma, Agnes and Florrence M.). Possibly married. His mother passed away on Tuesday, 5th March 1912. **T/344176, Private, Army Service Corps.** Landed in France in 1916. **Entitled** to the British War Medal and Victory Medal. **Family** – a younger brother, 56837, Lance-Corporal James Heeley of 14th Durham Light Infantry was killed in action (age 20) on Monday, 3rd December 1917 in the German Counter Attacks at Cambrai.

HOOPER brothers

Two brothers of Bernard Hooper served, most likely **Sidney Hooper** and **Leonard Hooper**. Both were born in Bloxwich. Details are difficult to trace as Census information for 1891, 1901 and 1911 shows that the given names are not consistently recorded. **Family** – 37061, Lance-Corporal Bernard Hooper of 8th Battalion, the Gloucestershire Regiment was killed in action (age 21) by a shell burst on Saturday, 28th July 1917 at Oosttaverne near Ypres.

James 'Jimmy' JONES

Born on 20th October 1895 in Bloxwich and lived at 55, Marlborough Street, Bloxwich. Son of a coal-miner, Thomas, and Ann Maria Jones of 21, Elmore Row, Bloxwich and later of 55, Marlborough Street, Bloxwich and 95, Church Street. One of eight children – four brothers (Edward, William, David and

Thomas Edward) and three sisters (Flora, Mabel and Hetty). Educated at Elmore Green School from 20/08/06. Single. Miner. **Volunteered on 12th August 1914. 9586, Private, 1st (Regular) Battalion, the South Staffordshire Regiment, (22nd>91st Brigade, 7th Division).** Landed at Zeebrugge, Belgium, on 17th December 1914. [**22nd Brigade,**

7th Division] 1914 Antwerp Operations (Bruges). 1st Ypres, Battle of Langemarck; Battle of Gheluvelt. Rouges Bancs – Well Farm Attack. **1915** Battle of Neuve Chapelle. Battle of Aubers (Fromelles). Battle of Festubert. Action of Givenchy. Battle of Loos. [**91st Brigade, 7th Division] 1916** Somme, Battle of Albert including the Capture of Mametz; Battle of Bazentin; Attack on High Wood; Battle of Delville Wood. Battle of Guillemont. **1917** Operations on the Ancre. German Retreat to The Hindenburg Line. Arras, Flanking Operations around Bullecourt including Battle of Bullecourt; Actions on The Hindenburg Line. 3rd Ypres ('Passchendaele'), Battle of Polygon Wood; Battle of Broodseinde; Battle of Poelcapelle; 2nd Battle of Passchendaele. November 1917 to the Italian Front. Arrived Legnago (on the R. Adige). Discharged the army sick on 8th May 1918; awarded the Silver War Badge number 363923. **Entitled** to the 1914-15 Star (Medal Roll – F/2B3, p.220), British War Medal and Victory Medal (Medal Roll – F/101B4, p.39513 or 395B). **Family** – a younger brother, 40171, Private Edward Jones, 'D' Company, 7th (Service) Battalion, the South Staffordshire Regiment was killed in action (age 21) on Monday, 27th November 1916 in the Ancre Valley on the Somme.

Ernest 'Ernie' LAVENDER   *'One of the 'Old Contemptibles'*
Born in 1892 or 1893 in Bloxwich. Son of William and Mary Lavender of 19, Little Bloxwich Lane and later at 7 Court, 3 Sneyd Lane (1911). Had at least two brothers, William, Henry 'Harry' (both older), Thomas and James (both younger), and at least three sisters, Alice, Dora and Florence (all younger). Single. Formerly a coal-miner. **Enlisted as a regular soldier on 19th April 1912. 9134, Private, 2nd (Regular) Battalion, the South Staffordshire Regiment, (6th Brigade, 2nd Division).** *Unit History* – 12/8/14 landed at Le Havre, France. **1914** Battle of Mons. Retreat from Mons, Rearguard Actions of Villers Cottérêts. Battle of the Marne; Battle of the Aisne including the Passage of the Aisne and the Actions on the Aisne Heights. 1st Ypres,

Battle of Langemarck; Battle of Gheluvelt; Battle of Nonne Bosschen. **1915** [La Bassée sector all year] Affairs of Cuinchy. Battle of Festubert. Battle of Loos. Hohenzollern Redoubt (Loos). **1916** Somme, Battle of Delville Wood including the Capture and Consolidation of the Wood; Attack on Waterlot Farm near Guillemont; Battle of the Ancre. Wounded on three separate occasions between August 1914 and May 1916; discharged the army (to Reserve, Class 'P') as a result of his injuries, on 8th January 1917 and awarded the Silver War Badge number 212558. A member of the *'Old Contemptibles'*. **Entitled** to the 1914 'Mons' Star (Medal Roll – F/2/5/p.61), BWM and VM (Medal Roll – F/101B3, p.308). He was one of the *'Old Contemptibles'*. **Family** – an older brother, 14114, Private William 'Coxy' Lavender, 1st Battalion, the Lincolnshire Regiment, was killed in action (age 28) on 1st November 1914 near Wytschaete in the Ypres Salient. William, like Ernest, was one of the *'Old Contemptibles'*. Another older brother, Henry 'Harry' served before the war as a regular soldier in South Africa and Gibraltar with 1/South Staffordshire; in the Great War he served in Ireland and Egypt as 1181, Acting Sergeant, Military Foot Police. A younger brother, Charles, possibly served in the South Staffordshire Regiment.

Henry 'Harry' LAVENDER

Born in 1892 or 1893 in Bloxwich. Son of William and Mary Lavender of 19, Little Bloxwich Lane and later at 7 Court, 3 Sneyd Lane (1911). Had at least two brothers, William (older), Ernest, Thomas and James (all younger), and at least three sisters, Alice, Dora and Florence (all younger). Enlisted as a regular soldier in about 1906-07 and served in the capacity of Military Policeman with 1/South Staffordshire in South Africa and Gibraltar. Returned to civilian life and joined the Police Force. Re-enlisted for the duration of the war, serving in Ireland and also in Egypt. He was awarded the Meritorious Service Medal. **Entitled** to the British War Medal and the Victory Medal. **Family** – an older brother, 14114, Private William 'Coxy' Lavender, 1/Lincolnshire Regiment, was killed in action (age 28) on 1st November 1914 near Wytschaete in the Ypres Salient. William, like Ernest, was one of the *'Old Contemptibles'*. A younger brother, 9134, Private Ernest Lavender, served in the BEF with 2/South Staffordshire from August 1914 until his discharge in January 1917 as a result of wounds. He was awarded the Silver War Badge. Another younger brother, Charles, possibly served in the South Staffordshire Regiment. **Post-war note**: after the war, Harry Lavender rose to the rank of chief of police in Walsall.

Edward 'Ted' LESTER

Born in 1889 or 1890 in Bloxwich and lived at 11, Sand Bank, Bloxwich. Son of an awl-blade maker, Edward, and the late Elizabeth Lester (née Handy) of the same address. One of eight children – four brothers (Herbert, Frank, Fred and Charles Henry) and three sisters (Elizabeth, Olive and Nellie). Single. Employed as an awl-blade maker. Enlisted after the end of 1915. **30921, Private, South Staffordshire Regiment** then **146515, Private, Royal Army Medical Corps.** No details of service beyond those given. **Entitled** to the British War Medal and the Victory Medal (Medal Roll – RAMC101B57, p.4229). **Family** – a younger brother, 41279, Private Fred Lester of 15th Battalion, the Highland Light Infantry was killed in action (age 22) on Tuesday, 16th January 1917 by shell fragments while carrying rations up the line in the Serre sector of the Somme. Another younger brother, 9814, Private Frank Lester (see below) of 69th Machine Gun Company was wounded on the Somme but survived the war.

Frank LESTER

Born on 7th February 1892 in Bloxwich and lived at 11, Sand Bank, Bloxwich. Son of an awl-blade maker, Edward, and the late Elizabeth Lester (née Handy) of the same address. One of eight children – four brothers (Herbert, Frank, Fred and Charles Henry) and three sisters (Elizabeth, Olive and Nellie). Single. Employed as a needle-maker. **Enlisted on 13th December 1915 in Walsall** (for seven years with the Regular Army). **20633, Private, 3rd Battalion, the South Staffordshire Regiment** then transferred on 12th February 1916 to **9814, Private, 69th Machine Gun Company, (69th Infantry Brigade, 23rd Division).** Arrived on the Western Front in May 1916. Suffered a gunshot wound to his right thigh on 6th July 1916 near Contalmaison on the Somme; evacuated to England, he was treated in hospital in Leeds. Returned to 69/MGC in France on 29th January 1917. Invalided back to England (aboard S.S. 'St. David') on 7th July 1917 suffering from trench fever. Posted to Egypt, 9th December 1917, disembarked Alexandria on 3rd January 1918 – to 155 Company MGC. Returned to BEF on 17th April 1918. Returned to hospital in Warrington, England on 27th August 1918. Home service for the remainder of the war. Stayed in the post-war Regular Army with 11th Battalion, MGC – 14th November 1919 disembarked in Bombay, India. 27th October 1920, attached to Royal Welsh Fusiliers as an instructor. Returned to UK on 25th March 1921. Discharged on 14th June 1921 (described as, 'honest, sober and reliable'). **Entitled** to the British War Medal and the Victory Medal (Medal Roll – MGC/101B6, p.575). **Family** – a younger brother, 41279, Private Fred Lester of 15th Battalion, the Highland Light Infantry was killed in action (age

22) on Tuesday, 16th January 1917 by shell fragments while carrying rations up the line in the Serre sector of the Somme. An older brother, 146515, Private Ted Lester of the Royal Army Medical Corps, served on the Western Front and survived the war.

[One of...] John, Joseph or Alfred LINNELL

John was a general labourer, 26 years old in 1914; Joseph was a general labourer, 24 years old in 1914; Alfred was a carpenter, 18 years old in 1914. All were born in Bloxwich, sons of boat-builder, Joseph, and Mary Linnell (née Woolley) of 119, Green Lane, Walsall and later of 89, Hatherton Lane, Leamore. Family of eleven children, of whom six were living at home in 1911 – brothers (John, Joseph, Arthur, Alfred and Ernest) and one sister (Amy). Single. No details of which brother served, thus no military record apart from the fact that he served in France and would have qualified for the British War Medal and the Victory Medal. **Family** – a brother, 200373, Sergeant Arthur Linnell M.M. of 1/5th Battalion, the South Staffordshire Regiment was killed in action (age 24) on Wednesday, 14th March 1917 at Bucquoy in a night attack during the German Retreat to the Hindenburg Line.

George MAIN

Born in 1898 or 1899 in Bloxwich to Alfred (a colliery banksman) and Mary Jane Main (née Merricks) of 70a, Sandbank, Bloxwich. Mary Jane passed away in 1909 and the following year Alfred married Alice Courtney. The family then lived at 112, Parker Street and later at 2, Bell Lane, Bloxwich. In 1911, George was one of ten children in the extended family. Three full brothers – Thomas [born on 3rd April 1895 and educated at Elmore Green School from September 1908], Alfred [born 1897 or 1898] and Jack [born 1901 or 1902]; one full sister – Emily; five step-sisters – Florence, Selina, Dora, Polly and Winifred). **Enlisted in late 1915 or early 1916. 42282, Private, 1/23 London Regiment then 61862, Private, South Staffordshire. Entitled** to the British War Medal and the Victory Medal (Medal Roll – F/101B17, p.2201). **Family** – Alfred Leonard Main (the second oldest of the brothers) served at least three years in the army before the war, possibly in the Special Reserve Battalion of the South Staffordshire Regiment. Called up from the trained reserve – served initially as 20002, Private, 2/South Staffordshire Regiment and was wounded on 4th October 1917 in the Battle of Broodseinde (Third Ypres) but was later commissioned Second Lieutenant (in May 1918) and served in 5/Worcestershire. He survived the war only to die, aged 22, in England on Friday, 3rd October 1919 in Sunderland Military Hospital from consumption (he was more susceptible as a consequence of being gassed while serving in France).

John ORGILL

Born on 7th November 1896 in Pelsall. Son of John and Letitia 'Letty' Orgill (née Bramwell) of 62, New Street, Bloxwich; his father, a stationary engine driver, predeceased him prior to 1911. Educated at Elmore Green School (from 4th May 1908). Had at least six siblings – at least two brothers, Joseph and George Henry; one sister, Gladys Maude, was living at home in 1911 – his 'next-of-kin' was listed as 'Miss G.M. Orgill of 107, Station Street, Bloxwich. John's mother died in 1917, a victim of influenza. Married to May Maria Orgill (née Crowther), had one son (John) pre-war and lived at 18, Church Street, Bloxwich. Colliery horse-keeper (underground). Pre-war, John volunteered for the Territorials of 'D' Company, 1/5th Battalion, South Staffordshire Regiment, holding service number 9009 and served for five years. Accepted overseas service. Landed in France on Wednesday 3rd March 1915 with 46th '1st North Midland' Division but In September 1915 (time-expired from the TF) he volunteered 'in the field' for the Royal Engineers (he was a mine engine operator in civilian life). John transferred to the 172nd Tunnelling Company, Royal Engineers on Friday, 15th October 1915 with service number **137606**, the rank of **Sapper** and designated as 'Tunneller's mate'. On New Year's Day 1917, John was posted to **174th Tunnelling Company, R.E. Entitled** to the 1914-15 Star (Medal Roll – RE/2C2, p.124); British War Medal and the Victory Medal (Medal Roll – RE/101/B74, p.15713). He survived the war and was discharged from the Army on Tuesday, 28th January 1919 (to 'Z' Reserve). John Orgill's service record exists. **Family** – Two brothers served in France. 33146, Corporal Joseph Orgill, 'B' Company, 2nd Field Ambulance, Canadian Army Medical Corps was killed in action on Saturday, 3rd November 1917 (age 25) in the Ypres Salient. George Henry Orgill (ten years older) also served.

PARKES brothers

Edward   25 years old in 1914,
Thomas   20 years old in 1914,
Joseph   18 years old in 1914

All three lads were born in Bloxwich to John and Matilda Parkes (née Turner) of 40, Providence Lane, Blakenall Heath and later of 4, May Street, Leamore, their father being employed as a coal miner. A family of nine children in 1901, five brothers (William, Edward, Thomas, Joseph and Arthur) and four sisters (Eliza A., Matilda, Kate and Elsie). Of the brothers, Arthur was educated at Elmore Green High School (from 28/08/11). No detail of their military service (except for William and Arthur) has yet been traced. **Family** – two brothers (the oldest and the youngest of the five brothers) died in battle – 40801, Private William Parkes of 6/Lincolnshire died (age 31) on Sunday, 10th June 1917 during the Battle of Messines. 202649, Corporal Arthur Parkes of 1st Battalion, the Bedfordshire Regiment died (age 19) on Friday, 27th September 1918 near Beaucamp during the Battle of the Canal du Nord on the Hindenburg Line.

Edward PARTON Elmore Green School
Born on 2nd February 1893 in Walsall and lived first at 50, Green Lane, Bloxwich and later at 33, Cope Street, Leamore. Son of a bridle-bit filer, Edwin Alfred, and Clara Parton (née Webb) of the same addresses. One of seven children of whom five were living at home in 1911 – at least four brothers (Stephen, Jonah Thomas, Edward and Frank [b. 04/05/96; EGS from 01/08/07]). Educated at Elmore Green School [from 28/08/05]. Employed at the Talbot Stead Tube Works. **Enlisted on 27th September 1915.** 1194, Private South Staffordshire Regiment ..then… **43618, Private, Lincolnshire Regiment.** Entitled to the British War Medal and the Victory Medal (Medal Roll – F/105/B16, p.2165). Discharged sick on 14th December 1918 and was awarded the Silver War Badge (number B250949) in December 1918. Family – four brothers served in the army. 18 year-old John (Jack), 9441, Private, 'A' Company, 1/5th Battalion, South Staffordshire Regiment was killed in action on 13th October 1915 attacking the Hohenzollern Redoubt during the Battle of Loos. 30579, Private (Jonah) Thomas of 8th (Service) Battalion, the South Staffordshire Regiment was killed in action on 23rd April 1917 near Roeux during the Second Battle of the Scarpe. Stephen served as a Corporal (59712) in the Royal Welsh Fusiliers, surviving the war; Frank served as a Private (11637) in the Machine Gun Corps and survived the war.

Frank PARTON Elmore Green School
Born on 4th May 1896 in Walsall and lived first at 50, Green Lane, Bloxwich and later at 33, Cope Street, Leamore. Son of a bridle-bit filer, Edwin Alfred, and Clara Parton (née Webb) of the same addresses. One of seven children of whom five were living at home in 1911 – at least four brothers (Stephen, Jonah Thomas, Edward and John. Educated at Elmore Green School (from 01/08/07). In 1911 he was employed as an errand boy to a bridle-maker. **Enlisted late in 1915 or early 1916.** 20383, Private South Staffordshire Regiment..then… **11637, Private, Machine Gun Corps** (Company or battalion unknown). **Entitled** to the British War Medal and the Victory Medal (Medal Roll – MGC/101B7, p.718). **Family** – four brothers served in the army. 18 year-old John (Jack), 9441, Private, 'A' Company, 1/5th Battalion, South Staffordshire Regiment was killed in action on 13th October 1915 attacking

the Hohenzollern Redoubt during the Battle of Loos. 30579, Private (Jonah) Thomas of 8th (Service) Battalion, the South Staffordshire Regiment was killed in action on 23rd April 1917 near Roeux during the Second Battle of the Scarpe. Stephen served as a Corporal (59712) in the Royal Welsh Fusiliers, surviving the war; Edward served as a Private (43618) in the Lincolnshire Regiment and was discharged sick and awarded the Silver War Badge in December 1918.

Stephen PARTON

Born in 1888 or 1889 in Walsall and lived first at 50, Green Lane, Bloxwich and later at 33, Cope Street, Leamore. Son of a bridle-bit filer, Edwin Alfred, and Clara Parton (née Webb) of the same addresses. One of seven children of whom five were living at home in 1911 – at least four brothers (Jonah Thomas, Edward, Frank and John. In 1911 he was employed as a brick-maker. **Enlisted late in 1915 or early 1916. 59712, Corporal, Royal Welsh Fusiliers. Entitled** to the British War Medal and the Victory Medal (Medal Roll – J/2/102B22, p.7302). **Family** – four brothers served in the army. 18 year-old John (Jack), 9441, Private, 'A' Company, 1/5th Battalion, South Staffordshire Regiment was killed in action on 13th October 1915 attacking the Hohenzollern Redoubt during the Battle of Loos. 30579, Private (Jonah) Thomas of 8th (Service) Battalion, the South Staffordshire Regiment was killed in action on 23rd April 1917 near Roeux during the Second Battle of the Scarpe. Frank served as a Private (11637) in the Machine Gun Corps and survived the war; Edward served as a Private (43618) in the Lincolnshire Regiment, was discharged sick and was awarded the Silver War Badge in December 1918.

Simeon Frank PERKS

Born in 1899 or 1900 in Bloxwich and lived with his parents at 80, Revival Street, Bloxwich and later at 199, High Street, Bloxwich, and at 99, Harrison Street, Bloxwich. Son of colliery stallman Henry, and Gertrude Jane Perks (née Burgess) of the same address; at least one brother, Simeon Frank. Educated at Elmore Green School. Single. **Called up** with his age group in **late 1917 or early 1918. Private, 'A' Company, 1/5th Battalion, the South Staffordshire Regiment.** Landed in France in 1918. **Entitled** to the British War Medal and Victory Medal (details unknown). **Family** – An older brother, 238021, Private Harry Perks, who served in 1st Battalion, the Worcestershire Regiment was killed in action (age 23) near Auby on Monday, 14th October 1918 – the 852nd anniversary of the Battle of Hastings.

Harold PICKIN

Born in 1897 or 1898 in Bloxwich and lived at 88, Field Street, Blakenall Heath and later of 57, Marlborough Street, Bloxwich (1911) and at Back 158, High Street, Bloxwich (back of the old picture house). He was the son of a coal-miner, Richard, and Martha Alice Picken (née Johnson) of the same address. One of eight children – at least one older brother (William Edward) and at least five sisters (Lydia, Florence, Edith, Maud and Gertrude). **Enlisted** (probably) **in 1917**. Single. 38312, Private, the South Staffordshire Regiment… then…172144, Private, the Machine Gun Corps (no details of company or battalion). Wounded by a gas shell in January 1918. **Entitled** to the British War Medal and Victory Medal (Medal Roll – MGB/101B112, p.9338). **Family** – an older brother, 200823, Private (William) Edward Pickin, of 2/5th Battalion, the South Staffordshire Regiment was killed in action (age 21) on Thursday, 27th September 1917 by shellfire near Gravenstafel during the Battle of Polygon Wood.

Alfred or Richard REVITT

One of eight children born to Richard and Elizabeth Revitt (née Allen) of 41 and 58, Reeves Street, Bloxwich, and later at 10, High Street, Bloxwich (1911), the father making his living as a bricklayer. At least two brothers: Alfred – 39 and overage for military service at the outbreak of war in 1914; employed as a harness-maker. Richard – 23 in 1914. At least five sisters (Susannah, Emma, Sarah, Minnie and Edith). All the children were born in Bloxwich. No details of military service have been discovered. **Family** – a married younger brother, 25383, Private Harold Revitt of 2nd (Regular) Battalion, the South Staffordshire Regiment was killed in action (age 21) on Sunday, 24th March 1918 in the Flesquières Salient sector during the 1st Battle of Bapaume during the German Spring Offensive.

Edward ROWBOTHAM M.M.

Born in 1890 in Bloxwich to parents Edward (a coal-miner) and Eliza Jane Rowbotham of 84, Reeve Street (1891) and 50, then later 60, Church Street, Bloxwich in 1911. One of fourteen children – Henry E. 'Harry', Leonard Arthur 'Len', (Wm.) Albert, Ernest, Ada Martha, Edith, Edward, Gertrude, John Thomas 'Tom', Edgar, Hilda Annie, Evelyn Alice (Nellie), Frank, (Frederick) George. Employed as a coal-miner. Single. **Enlisted in November 1915** in Walsall. 20331, Private, 1/5 South Staffordshire…then…**6470, Sergeant, No.2 Section, 71st Company, Machine Gun Corps, (71st Infantry Brigade, 6th Division).** *Unit History* – landed at Le Havre, France in March 1916. **1916** Somme – Battle of Flers-Courcelette; Battle of Morval;

Battle of the Transloy Ridges. **1917** Hill 70, Lens. Battle of Cambrai – Tank Attack; Bourlon Wood; German Counter-Attacks. **1918** On 1st March 1918, 6th Division's three Machine Gun Companies (16th, 18th and 71st) were combined and renamed **No.6 Battalion, MGC**. German Spring Offensives – The Somme, Battle of St. Quentin. The Lys – Battle of Bailleul; First Battle of Kemmel; Second Battle of Kemmel; Battle of the Scherpenberg. [Wounded by a sniper in August 1918.] Hindenburg Line – Battle of Epehy; Battle of the St. Quentin Canal; Battle of Cambrai. Final Advance – Battle of the Selle. Awarded the Military Medal for bravery and **entitled** to the British War Medal and Victory Medal (Medal Roll – MGC 101/B3, p.295). **Family** – A younger brother, twenty-three year-old Tom Rowbotham, was drowned while serving in the Royal Naval Volunteer Reserve aboard the S.S. *'Kilmaho'* that was torpedoed by a German submarine on 17th May 1917 off the Cornish coast. Edward pledged to kill seven German soldiers in revenge for his brother Tom's death at sea. He kept his promise. (For an excellent account of Edward Rowbotham's war service it is well worth reading his evocative book/diary, *'Mud, Blood and Bullets – Memoirs of a Machine Gunner on the Western Front'*, edited by his grand-daughter, Janet Tucker).

Fred SANDERS
Sergeant, Royal Engineers. **Family** – Uncle of the Bushnell brothers, Alfred and George. No further details have been uncovered.

Harry SARGENT
Born in 1895 or 1896 in Bloxwich, the son of William and Alice Sargent of 14, Tudor Place, Bloxwich and later of 60, Parker Street, Bloxwich. One of six children (five living with parents in 1911). At least two brothers, George and William, as well as two sisters, Susan and Alice. George, like his father, was employed as a miner at the Holly Bank Colliery, Essington prior to enlistment. Military service record untraced. **Family** – an older brother, 6745, Private George Sargent, 'D' Company, 1/5th Battalion, the South Staffordshire Regiment who was killed in action (age 24) on Wednesday, 13th October 1915 attacking the Hohenzollern Redoubt during the Battle of Loos.

[One from…] **John Thomas, Josiah, Joseph or Samuel SHARRATT**
All were born in Bloxwich to parents Josiah (a stirrup forger) and Sarah Jane Sharratt (née Morris), who lived at 63, Leamore Lane, Blakenall Heath and

later at 23, Blakenall Lane, Bloxwich. Eight children in 1911 – five males (John Thomas, 34 in 1914, Josiah 32, Samuel 18, and Joseph 13); three sisters (Lizzie, Eliza and Flora). **Family** – one of the younger brothers, 204065, Gunner William Sharratt of 'C' Battery, 235th Brigade, Royal Field Artillery, was killed in action (age 20) on Monday, 2nd September 1918 at the 2nd Battle of Bapaume on the Somme.

Arthur SHINGLER

Served in a Signals company, Royal Engineers – no further details of his military service have been discovered. Family – an uncle of 20386, Private William Henry Lawley of 2nd Battalion, the Grenadier Guards who died (age 20) in No.4 General Hospital, Versailles, on Wednesday, 13th October 1915 of wounds sustained five days previously during the Battle of Loos.

William SHINGLER

Served in a Training Reserve battalion – no further details of his military service have been discovered. Family – an uncle of 20386, Private William Henry Lawley of 2nd Battalion, the Grenadier Guards who died (age 20) in No.4 General Hospital, Versailles, on Wednesday, 13th October 1915 of wounds sustained five days previously during the Battle of Loos.

Edward SMITH

Born in 1890 or 1891 in Bloxwich, the son of Edward and Elizabeth (née Newell) Smith of 94, Reeve Street, Bloxwich, his father being a stallman in a local colliery. One of seven children, Edward had two brothers (George and John) and four sisters (Frances, Eliza Ellen, Ruth and Elizabeth). The 1911 Census indicates that both parents died before 1911 (the eldest brother, George Smith, is shown as the head of the household at the family home of 94, Reeve Street, Bloxwich). By the outbreak of war in August 1914, brother George was living in Castleford, Yorkshire, presumably having moved north to obtain pit-work at the local colliery. Edward was a miner, originally at Holly Bank Colliery, Essington. Married to Annie and they had a daughter, Lily. He served with the pre-war Territorials of 5/South Staffordshire, though his 'time' expired in June 1914. **Enlisted on 5th February 1915** in Walsall in the West Yorkshire Regiment (the same regiment as his brother George, though they served in different battalions). **16510, Private, 10th Battalion, the West Yorkshire Regiment, (50th Brigade, 17th 'Northern' Division).** *Unit History* – landed in France on 10th September 1915. **1916** 14/2/16 and 2/3/16 Actions of the Bluff (Ypres). Somme, 1/7/16 Battle of Albert; 1-12/8/16 Battle of Delville Wood. **1917** Arras, 12-14/4/17 1st Battle of the Scarpe; 23-24/4/17 2nd Battle of the Scarpe. 13-16/5/17 Capture of Roeux and its subsequent defence. 3rd Ypres ('Passchendaele'), 12/10/17 1st Battle of Passchendaele; 8-10/11/17 2nd Battle of Passchendaele. **1918** Kaiserschlacht – Somme, 21-23/3/18 Battle of St. Quentin; 24-25/3/18 1st Battle of Bapaume. Advance in Picardy, 8-11/8/18 Battle of Amiens; 2nd Somme, 21-23/8/18 Battle of Albert. Edward was wounded three times:- on 2nd October 1915, a gunshot wound to his right thigh; on 1st July 1916 on the Somme he received a gunshot wound to his finger and was treated at the 1st Australian General Hospital in Rouen; on 24th August 1918, another gunshot wound effectively ended his war. On recovery, he was posted first to the Depot Battalion, then to the 3rd 'Reserve' Battalion. Unlike his brother, Edward survived the war to return to his wife and daughter in Little Bloxwich. **Entitled** to the 1914-15 Star (Medal Roll – O/2/1B, p. 670) and British War Medal and Victory Medal (Medal Roll – O/2/104B12, p.1456). **Family** – his older brother, 14757, Private George Smith of 12th Battalion, the West Yorkshire Regiment was killed in action on Friday, 14th July 1916 (aged 26 years) attacking Bazentin-le-Grand on the Somme.

George STYCH

Born on 7th March 1898 in Short Heath, Willenhall to Richard Henry 'Harry' (a coal miner) and Agnes Stych (née Simmons) of Back Lane, Short Heath. The family later resided at 53, Marlborough Street and at 78 and 102, Parker Street, Bloxwich. Father, Richard Henry, died during the war years. One of nine children in 1911 – had at least six brothers (Samuel Henry, Joseph, Albert, George [born 07/03/98; Elmore Green School from 04/12/05], John, David and Harry – all miners to and including Albert; all born in Short Heath except Harry, who was born in Bloxwich) and at least two sisters (Martha and Maryann). Educated at Elmore Green School (from 4th December 1905). Single. Like all the Stych men of working-age, George was a miner – at Allens Rough Colliery. **Enlisted in May 1914. 9486, Private, 2nd Battalion, the South Staffordshire Regiment, (6th Brigade, 2nd Division)** transferred to **48753, Private, King's Shropshire Light Infantry** (battalion unknown). *Unit History* – Landed in France on 25th May 1915. 25/9/15-4/10/15 Battle of Loos. 13-19/10/15 Hohenzollern Redoubt (Loos). Record unknown as date of transfer to KSLI is unknown. Wounded in the foot. Discharged to Army Reserve class 'Z' from 18/3/19. [According to the local newspaper, George served on the Italian Front in 1918 but neither 2/South Staffordshire nor any of the KSLI battalions served in Italy.] **Entitled** to the 1914-15 Star (Medal

Roll – F/2/B5, p.376) and to the British War Medal and Victory Medal (Medal Roll – J/1/102B15, p.4601). **Family** – Three of George's brothers served; a younger brother, 40593, Lance-Corporal Albert Stych of 7th Battalion, the Suffolk Regiment won the Military Medal in 1916 and was killed in action (age 21) on Saturday, 28th April 1917 during the Battle of Arleux at Arras. A third older brother, 242535, Private Joseph Stych of 1/6th Battalion, the South Staffordshire Regiment survived the war despite being twice wounded and also suffering a form of trench fever in 1917.

Joseph STYCH

Born in 1891 or 1892 in Short Heath, Willenhall to Richard Henry (a coal miner) and Agnes Stych (née Simmons) of Back Lane, Short Heath. The family later resided at 53, Marlborough Street and at 78 and 102, Parker Street, Bloxwich. Father, Richard Henry, died during the war years. One of nine children in 1911 – he had at least six brothers (Samuel Henry, Albert, George, John, David and Harry) and at least two sisters (Martha and Maryann). Single. Like all the Stych men of working-age, Joseph was a miner (at Holly Bank Colliery). Enlisted in the local Territorial Force on 5th July 1910. **Volunteered for overseas service in 1914.** 5 feet 2 inches tall. **7645>20091>242535, Private Joseph Stych** of [1/5th, 3/5th] **1/6th Battalion, the South Staffordshire Regiment (137th Brigade, 46th '1st North Midland' Division)**. [According to Joseph's army pension service record that, though damaged by fire still exists, Joseph was twice wounded (once at the Hohenzollern Redoubt) and once hospitalised with probable trench fever. He served in France from March 1915 to October 1915 and from November 1916 to August 1918. His wounds caused him to be discharged the army on 12th September 1919 when he was awarded the Silver War Badge (number B308723)]. **Entitled** to the 1914-15 Star [Medal Roll – F/2.B.5, P.376], British War Medal and Victory Medal [Medal Roll – F/101 B22, P.2828]. **Family** – Three of Joseph's brothers served; his older brother, 17/1041, Private Samuel Henry Stych of 17th Battalion, the West Yorkshire Regiment (and who was a former miner at Hollybank Colliery, aged 26 and married with three children) was killed in action with on 9th March 1916 near Festubert. A second but younger brother, 40593, Lance-Corporal Albert Stych of 7th Battalion, the Suffolk Regiment won the Military Medal in 1916 and was killed in action (age 21) on Saturday, 28th April 1917 during the Battle of Arleux at Arras. Another younger brother, 242535, Private George Stych 2nd Battalion, the South Staffordshire Regiment and later of the King's Shropshire Light Infantry survived the war despite being wounded in his foot.

PART IV

'Tribute to a lost generation...'

Chapter Fifteen

The School community and the rededication ceremony

WHEN JANE Humphreys, the head-teacher of Elmore Green Junior School, heard about the long-lost Old Boys' war memorial needing a new home, she immediately considered the idea of bringing the memorial 'home' to Elmore Green. In many respects it made good sense to return the memorial to its origins in tribute to those lads who had paid for their military service with their lives. For Jane Humphreys there was a tie even closer than bringing the memorial back to its 'home' – one of the lads named on the memorial, Pioneer Ambrose Squire who was killed in April 1918, was her great-uncle. Even more, the pupils in the school were enthused by the staff to produce some outstanding project work based on the experiences of the pupils' school predecessors. Much of this work was on display in the school hall when the rededication took place and two outstanding pieces, by Luke Little and Camille Sutton, were read by the two students as part of the ceremony.

Elmore Green Primary School on Friday, 11th November at 2:00 p.m:

- Arrival: Vaughan Williams – *Symphony No.3, 'Pastoral'*.
- Welcome by Jane Humphreys to explain that this dedication will include many features of the original dedication.
- Outline of the Great War (context): (Reverend Phil Hoar)
- Hymn: *'For All the Saints Who from Their Labours Rest'*.
- Pupils' writing and poems about the war based on their topic work:-

  i) Poem by Luke Little.

  ii) A soldier's diary by Camille Sutton.

  [Many other related pieces of pupils' topic work adorn the hall.]
- Outline of the history of the war memorial plaque – (Jane Humphreys).
- Prayer: To remember the fallen – (Reverend Phil Hoar / Reverend Roger Williams).
- Reading: *Wisdom* iii, 1-6 and v 15-16. (Reverend Phil Hoar / Reverend Roger Williams).
- Roll of honour: Pupils to read out the names of all the servicemen on the memorial. (Jane Humphreys & Reverend Phil Hoar).
- Songs from the trenches. *'Keep the home fires burning.'* (Pupils)
- Unveiling of the memorial, the cutting of the ceremonial ribbon and speech by the Mayor of Walsall, Garry Perry.
- Prayer of Dedication: (Reverend Roger Williams).
- *'The Last Post'*.
- Minute's silence.
- *'Reveille'*.
- Thanks: to the Reverend Phil Hoar and to the Reverend Roger Williams for their kind help in organising the service.

  …also to Derek Willets for playing the piano.

  …and to all those who contributed in any way to the occasion.
- The National Anthem.

Invitation to refreshments, to view the plaque and to take photographs.

Home at last

The rededicated Old Boys' Great War memorial after the unveiling ceremony – once again in pride of place in Elmore Green Junior School main hall.

The family connections on the day:

Relatives of the following men were able to attend the rededication:

Leonard Beech

Alfred Bushnell (family connection to George Bushnell and Timothy Taylor).

James Dawson (family connection to Charles, George and Howard Dawson)

Thomas Eccleston M.M.Bertie Elks

Edgar Goodall (family connection to J. William, Harold, David, John and Samuel Goodall).

J. William Groves (family connection to George Groves, Ernest Lavender and William 'Coxy' Lavender).

Frank Groom   William 'Bill' Haycock   Horace Jordan

Arthur Kitson   Arthur Linnell   M.MFrank Lloyd M.M. & Bar

Alfred Main   Edward PickenJ.T. 'Tom' Rowbotham

Ambrose Squire

Relatives and friends of the several other men were prevented by illness or other circumstances from attending the rededication, among them:

John Bate

Harold Baugh

Edward 'Ted' Jones and James 'Jimmy' Jones

Chapter Sixteen

Re-Dedication Ceremony of the Old Boys' War Memorial

Elmore Green School Hall, 11 November 2011

By Stuart Williams
(transcribed from the *"Bloxwich Telegraph"*).

'TODAY IN Bloxwich Armistice Day was marked in a particularly poignant manner by the rededication of a school war memorial which commemorates the sacrifice made by former pupils of Elmore Green School in the Great War. The memorial, listing sixty-seven 'old boys' of what was then Elmore Green Central School, later High School, who gave their young lives in "the war to end all wars", had been moved in 1958 when the secondary functions of Elmore Green High were transferred to the new T.P. Riley Comprehensive, not far away in Lichfield Road.

The memorial quietly became part of the life of the new school until, in 2001, T.P. Riley was demolished and replaced by the present Walsall Academy, which opened in 2003. It was around this time that the finely carved marble sculpture by Bloxwich-born Frederick T. Perry "disappeared" from the public eye. In fact, it had gone into storage, but had been forgotten.

Over the following years, various people including Bloxwich local historians Edna Marshall, Barry Crutchley and ex-T.P. Riley history teacher Ken Wayman, had tried to find and raise the profile of the missing memorial and eventually, following convoluted enquiries via the Academy and within Walsall Council departments, in late 2010 it was tracked down to the premises of monumental masons A. Walker & Sons of Cannock, who had been storing it safely since the demolition of T.P. Riley years ago.

Following work done by Walsall Council officers Elaine Box and Mike Gaffney, funding was found from the Council to have the memorial returned to its original home in March of this year, when it was mounted on the wall of the school hall by the masons who had preserved it.

Today, the memorial finally came home in a spiritual sense, during a poignant and emotionally-charged Armistice Day service held at what is now Elmore Green Primary School, in the presence of the junior school children and staff, relatives of those listed on the memorial, local people, clergy from both Anglican and Methodist churches and the Mayor and Mayoress of Walsall.

In the bright and airy school hall, decorated with symbols and displays of remembrance made by pupils, who had taken the theme on as a class project, everyone gathered at 2pm to witness the formal rededication of the memorial. Jane Humphreys, Headteacher of Elmore Green School, welcomed one and all and presided over the event which, deliberately echoing the original service of dedication in March 1922, ran liked clockwork thanks to staff and children alike.

Reverend Phil Hoar of St John's Methodist Church first spoke eloquently of the history of the Great War of 1914-18, and was followed by the junior pupils singing the hymn, '*For all the Saints who from their labours rest,*' accompaniment on the piano being played throughout and later by Derek Willets.

Next, year 5/6 pupil Luke Little recited his own powerful poem about the soldiers' war and its horrors. He was followed in turn by Camille Sutton, also of year 5/6, with her thoughtful version of a soldier's war diary. Then Reverend Hoar led a prayer to remember the fallen, which was followed by a reading on Wisdom by Reverend Roger Williams of All Saints Parish Church. Following this, the junior pupils rose and turned, row on row, to recite names from the Roll of Honour to the assembled audience, after which pupils sang '*Keep the Home Fires Burning*'.

There was then a pause as the Mayor of Walsall, Councillor Garry Perry, accompanied by the Mayoress, Mrs. June Perry, stood to speak on the subject and symbolism of remembrance, of war, the fallen, the importance of learning from the past to shape a better future, and of the promise shown by the youngsters who had done such a fine job this afternoon. He was very proud of them, and proud to be a part of this rededication in Bloxwich, a true highlight of his year as Mayor.

The Mayor then cut a ceremonial ribbon across the war memorial, and Reverend Roger Williams conducted a Prayer of Dedication before the marble sculpture.

Finally, *'The Last Post'* was played, followed by a minute's silence, and all present sang the *National Anthem* before concluding remarks by the Headteacher. The service was over, and there was time for reflection, to view the memorial, and for refreshments before departing.

A rare privilege; we are unlikely to see such an event again, and what better way to mark Armistice Day in the ancient English village of Bloxwich?'

[*With thanks to Stuart Williams of Walsall Local History Centre who kindly granted permission for this article to be reproduced. The original article with photographs may be accessed at www.thebloxwichtelegraph.wordpress.com*].

THE FULL ROLL OF HONOUR

Commemorated on the memorial:

ANDREWS, I
BATE, J
BAUGH, H
BEECH, L
BRICKNALL, T(A)
BRYAN, J
BULLOCK, WA
BULLOCK, AC
BUSHNELL, AJ
BUSHNELL, GB
COCKAYNE, WC
COOPER, AE
COPE, JH
DAVI(E)S, JJ
DAWSON, J
DOWNES, H
ECCLESTON(E), TF
ELKS, BL
EVANS, T
FRANCE, H
GILL, B
GOODALL, E
GOODALL, JW
GOODALL, H
GRIMSLEY, WE
GROVES, GA
GROVES, JW
GROOM, FJ
HALL, AG
HARPER, F
HARVEY, F
HARRISON, SG
HANDY, JH
HAYCOCK, WA

HAYWARD, A
HAYWOOD, E
HEELEY, J
HILL, H
HOOPER, B
JONES, E
JORDAN, H
KITSON, A
LAWLEY, WH
LESTER, F
LINNELL, A.
LLOYD, F
MAIN, AL
MALPASS, L
ORGILL, J
PARTON, J
PERKS, HV
PICK(E)N, EW
REVITT, H
ROWBOTHAM, J.T.
SARGENT, G
SHARRATT, W
SIMMONS, AJ
SLEIGH, A
SMITH, J
SMITH, S
SMITH, G
SQUIRE, A
STYCH, A
SYLVESTER, R
WILKES, AV
WILLETT, JH
YATES, J
[67]

Note: There are a few errors on the memorial. Some surnames are mis-spelt, some initials are inaccurate and the alphabetical order is not quite right.

Old Boy missing from the memorial:
As far as has been ascertained, only one lad who was educated at Elmore Green School and who was killed in the Great War is missing from the memorial. He is:-

PARKES, A
[1]

Men killed during the Great War, related to those named on the memorial:

DUNN, TH
GOODALL, D
GOODALL, J
GOODALL, S
LAVENDER, W
PARKES, W
PARTON, JT
SMITH, A
STYCH, SH
TAYLOR, T
[10]

PART V

'Never again..?'

Chapter Seventeen

A land fit for heroes…?

'Peace! Peace! Peace!' – The Armistice in Walsall

'*P*EACE! PEACE! *Peace!*' ran the headline in the *'Walsall Observer'* following the signing of the armistice on Monday, 11th November 1918. The previous Thursday, someone from the Press Bureau had mistakenly reported that an armistice[150] had been signed. Officials quickly suppressed the message but it raised hopes that the end of the war was near. On Saturday, 9th November it was revealed that Kaiser Wilhelm had abdicated and crowds began to gather outside the *'Observer'* offices in the expectation that further news was imminent. Sunday morning brought the news that German peace envoys had reached Allied headquarters and it became apparent that negotiations were beginning.

It was shortly after 10.30 on Monday morning that the eagerly awaited telephone message confirming the agreed armistice was received at the *'Observer'* office – it was less than a quarter of an hour after the Prime Minister had made the historic announcement in London. A vivid yellow poster appeared in a first floor window inscribed in big, black lettering the single word, *'Peace'*. There was a curious, noticeable silence among the crowds on The Bridge in Walsall until realisation dawned and the cheers began. People crowded toward the *'Observer'* windows to read the full text of Lloyd George's message that the Allies' armistice terms had been finally accepted at 5 a.m. that morning and hostilities were to cease at 11 a.m. Two days later the Mayor of Walsall, Councillor Llewellen paid tribute to the orderliness and sobriety of Walsall's peace celebration. He expressed his satisfaction with the:

---

150 The armistice was a ceasefire, not a peace treaty – that would come later, during the summer of 1919.

> *"...extraordinarily orderly manner in which many thousands of artisan people had taken part in the rejoicing."* [151]

On Sunday, 17th November the Mayor of Walsall, the Town Clerk and other members of the Town Council attended a service at Bloxwich Parish Church. Along with a good number of discharged and demobilised sailors and soldiers, local Volunteers, Special Police and Women's Volunteer Reserves, and headed by the Bloxwich Imperial Prize Band, they marched from the Public Hall to the church where the vicar, the Reverend J. C. Hamilton, thanked God for the end of the war and said that the country would need men,

> *"...with clear brains, just and righteous in their decisions and with wisdom from on high, that they might have a right judgement in all things."* [152]

The offertory was taken for the Walsall General Hospital. At the end of the service the procession returned to the Public Hall where the Mayor thanked all who had taken part in the morning's proceedings.

Jobs for the boys who won the war?

The Government created a Ministry of Reconstruction in 1918 with plans for advances in education and housing but the more urgent need in Bloxwich was to welcome the 'demobbed' men home and get them back into employment. The politicians' plans to employ additional staff in the Employment Exchanges, many of whom would be discharged men, with a suitable proportion of war-disabled men amongst them, foundered on the problem of finding employers who could employ the returning lads.

At the Walsall War and Pensions Committee meeting in December 1918 it was said that the position of discharged men was becoming acute. There were a great many unemployed men in the town who received donation benefit and their numbers would increase over the next year. November had seen 1,099 applications and in December the monthly number had risen to 1,419. There were two or three men applying for every vacancy and the donation benefit could only be spread over six months.

---

151 *'Walsall Observer'*, 16th November 1918.
152 *'Walsall Observer'*, 23rd November 1918.

Welcome Home

The people of Bloxwich did their best to welcome home their returning servicemen. Special events were held as often as possible. In March 1919 there was a Monday evening procession of servicemen and ex-servicemen headed from the Swan Inn to the Central Hall led by the Bloxwich Imperial Prize Band. In front of a large and enthusiastic audience, the Mayor, Councillor A. J. Llewellen, presented three bravery medals won by Bloxwich men during the war. The recipients were, 5751, Corporal C. Knowles, DCM ('A' Company, 6/DCLI), Lance-Corporal Cartwright, MM and 6470, Sergeant Edward Rowbotham, MM (No.2 Section, 71st Company, MGC); each man also received a small monetary gift. There was a particular welcome for the returned prisoners of war from the whole borough of Walsall who were entertained at a supper and a concert at the Town Hall. The Prisoners of War Committee was able to make the acquaintance of men they had only previously known by name. There was also a suggestion at that time that each returning soldier should be presented with a token of recognition in the form of a certificate in a plain oak frame. A further suggestion that close relatives of the men buried on the Western Front should be taken to visit the graves of their husbands or sons was never taken up because the cost wouldhave been about £2 million.

Holly Bank Colliery

With the outbreak of war in 1914, coalmines had been taken under government control, providing a relatively good period for the miners as government control resulted in better safety standards and common pay rates across the country. Employment in local mines and output both often reached record rates.

Holly Bank Colliery had employed 924 men in 1906 but by 1917 the number had reached 1,265. However, after the war the mines returned to private ownership and trouble returned to the pits. By the end of February 1919 miners in the district voted heavily in favour of a strike on March 15th. Local miners' agent, Mr. F. Dean (who had been at the forefront of disputes pre-1914) hoped that the government would 'come forward' with an offer that would avert a strike. However, the Government was not keeping its promise to the men who went to fight as coal companies were employing retired men and boys at minimum wages leaving no work for the returning ex-servicemen. The Government responded with the Sankey Commission and within twenty days of its convening, the Commission had issued Part One of its report, promising a 'two shillings a day' increase in pay (now ten pence but then worth much more) backdated to January 9th and also a reduction of the working day by one hour for all underground workers. It is a reflection of the vulnerable state of the government at that time that it was willing to make these offers to the miners whose demands such as the re-nationalisation of the mines was left for Part Two of the report, by which time the momentum for strikes had died down and the Government was let off the hook. Holly Bank Miners went on strike again in August 1919 over the dismissal of Dan Cartwright a popular check-weighman who also acted as the miners' representative in discussions with the managers. He had been elected by his fellow miners to oversee the mine-owner's weighman who determined how much coal had reached the surface and therefore how much the miners were paid. Several summonses were brought before Willenhall magistrates accusing Mr. Cartwright of breaking company rules. After a protracted dispute the company won and the miners had to elect a new checkweighman.

In other ways little had changed in Bloxwich. If you wanted to fight on a Saturday night then Alfred Street (from 'Observer' reports) seemed to offer the most disputes. The younger generation was also causing concern as a report on 11th January 1919 reveals. Headlined, "…Bloxwich Boys Running Wild", the story tells of an incident on a Sunday afternoon the previous week. Five Bloxwich boys, aged from nine to fourteen were summonsed for damaging machinery belonging to Bloxwich Lock & Stamping Company to the value of thirty shillings. All pleaded not guilty except for the smallest boy who pleaded guilty. The four older boys pleaded that it was the little boy who did all the damage. Chief Constable Thomson mentioned that the smallest boy had been before the court before on a charge of stone-throwing in the streets. The Clerk of the Court declared that, "…he tells the truth at any rate. He seems to be the only one who can tell the truth." Harry Squires, representing the company, admitted that the workshop had been left unlocked that Sunday afternoon. The four older boys were put on probation for three months while the smallest boy was 'let off' because he had told the truth. A few months later four other Bloxwich boys, aged ten to twelve, were summonsed for entering the stables at Broad Lane Colliery and scattering a bag of oats, worth five shillings, onto the road. This offence also occurred on a Sunday. Magistrate T. A. Smith expressed the thought that the churches were getting hold of all the youngsters on Sundays but Magistrate Thickett replied, "...If the churches had got them, would they be any better?" Parents of the defendants were fined two shillings and sixpence and were advised to look after their children better.

More positive news concerned the girls of the town. Announcing that, "Bloxwich leads the way; recreative and educational club opened for girls," it was revealed that the Elmore Green Schools had the up-to-date and finely equipped premises suitable to be used for the proposed girls' club. It was hoped it would be a, "...counter-attraction to spending the evenings walking the streets or in other undesirable pursuits." The Central Hall could offer admirable dancing facilities with a rest room and canteen nearby. As well as being a social club it would provide classes in cookery, dressmaking, laundry, first aid and physical exercise. Prospective members were present in large numbers and in subsequent months the club became very successful. Even the seemingly innocuous pursuit of strolling up and down the High Street on a Sunday evening could have unforeseen consequences. On Tuesday 21st January 1919, five youths were ordered to pay five shillings each for 'obstructing the footpath' in High Street, Bloxwich on Sunday 12th. "It's becoming a perfect nuisance in the town not only on the part of some young men but girls as well!" said Mr. T. A. Smith, Magistrate, of the popular 'monkey run'.

In March 1919 you could buy a freehold business property on Wolverhampton Road with four cottages at the rear for £1,075, while a freehold cottage on Broad Lane could be bought for £150.

The August Bank Holiday brought, 'unfavourable weather' but the Bloxwich Wakes provided a fair that was the largest ever and over 12,000 people visited the grounds on the opening Saturday. As usual, the menagerie proved extremely popular with a magnificent collection of lions. There was a giant rat, alleged to have been captured in the trenches at the 'front'! There were monkeys and Mrs. Hengleur's performing dogs. Hughes' boxing saloon provided competitions and exhibitions for hundreds of spectators, with local males being encouraged to take on the travelling professionals. On Bank Holiday Tuesday Mr. Pat Collins, as was his usual custom, generously donated the entrance money and 'takings' from his own booths to the Walsall General Hospital.

Finally, Bloxwich Strollers lost the opening match of the 1919-1920 season at the Red Lion ground by three goals to two to Burton All Saints. Things were slowly returning to normal!

Chapter Eighteen

Reflections on the 'War to end War'

Mr. W.H. Brown and the Valour of the South Staffords
[extracted from the post-war *'Walsall Observer'*]

'A Bloxwich Peace celebration meeting in Elmore Green Schools, on Monday evening, was addressed by Mr. W.H. Brown of Leytonstone.

Councillor Pat Collins, presiding, said that if ever joy was justified in the heart of an Englishman it was today, and if ever pride was justified they could all be proud today.

The impossible, said Mr. Brown, had been accomplished, Prussianism had met its doom, and the Continent was freed. It had been a gigantic task but firmly convinced of the justice of our cause, we struggled on and patience, courage and resolve had won their reward. Walsall might indeed be proud of the part played by the men who have gone from its midst. Ever to be found in the forefront! Alike at the Salient of Ypres as at the costly struggle on the Somme, and later still at that memorable crossing of the Scheldt Canal, the rallying cry of the Staffords was the prelude to victory. And when, in place of offensive operations, conditions compelled them to remain on the defensive, none showed greater powers of endurance, none performed greater deeds of valour! Brave, indomitable souls! When the full story of their achievements was able to be told, it would furnish an epic greater by far than that of Horatius. Speaking of our debt to the wounded and discharged, Mr. Brown added:

"In this, the hour of glorious triumph, let the government and the country reconsider its obligations. Already we anticipated the coming demobilisation and we must not tolerate any unnecessary delay. The front places in trade must be available for the men from the Front. Let us start making Blighty worthy of their work."'

Yet this makes difficult reading when one has the benefit of hindsight. One can understand the surge of relief where a family had avoided tragic loss; one might understand the resentment of the militaristic 'Prussianism' that appeared to many to have led to a war that deprived so many families of husbands, fathers, sons, brothers, uncles in so violent a manner. 'Lionising' the winners in war has always been common – much local history dates back to the Norman Conquest, when the winners re-told (and of course justified) their actions in shaping history to their own requirements – thus we have the Bayeux Tapestry. Unfortunately, anger, resentment and triumphalism foster a spirit of revenge but do not make for good peace-making. The lads in the 'Bloxwich Peace Celebrations' photograph [shown below] seem happy simply to have survived and to have returned to a way of life that they recognised.

Local peace celebrations in 1919: Bloxwich ex-servicemen in fancy dress, outside the Thatched House Tavern opposite Elmore Green School. They were raising funds for ex-servicemen through a football match between the Bloxwich 'D.D.S.S. Comic Footballers' and the 'Wild Warriors of the Mop'. [Courtesy of Stuart Williams]

The second descent into war, 1936-1939

Throughout the 1920's jobs became harder to find until the Wall Street Crash in 1929 America gave rise to the Great Depression of the 1930's. The economic crisis in the Thirties hit the United Kingdom hard but Germany, saddled with war reparations after the peace treaties, was hit even harder. Extremists such as the National Socialists and Communists struggled for power with the outcome that is well-known to history – Adolf Hitler taking the powers of dictator and launching a foreign policy that unnerved the rest of Europe. Hitler secretly re-armed Germany at a time when the rest of the world was pursuing peace policies and disarmament – between 1936 and 1939 Hitler set abut dismantling the terms of the Versailles Treaty that most rankled with the German people. None of the treaty signatories, notably France and Britain, appeared willing to use military force to deter Hitler's remilitarisation of the Rhineland in 1936, nor his invasion of Austria (the 'Anschluss') on a thin pretext, nor the re-taking of the Sudetenland and subsequent invasion of Czechoslovakia. It was not until Hitler's troops invaded Poland, again on a thin pretext, that Britain and France dug their heels in and saw Hitler's actions for what they really were.

At 11.15 a.m. on 3rd September, 1939, Prime Minister Neville Chamberlain broadcast to the nation the following statement announcing that a state of war existed between Britain and Germany:.

> *"This morning the British Ambassador in Berlin handed the German Government a final note stating that, unless we heard from them by 11 o'clock that they were prepared at once to withdraw their troops from Poland, a state of war would exist between us.*
>
> *"I have to tell you now that no such undertaking has been received, and that consequently this country is at war with Germany."*

It seems that before wars, politicians play the gambler's games of 'diplomatic bluff'. And when they lose, they then require servicemen and civilians to pay the price for those errors of political judgment. Subsequently, after wars, the talk is of glory and sacrifice, of homes fit for heroes, of jobs kept 'open'.

The many war memorials across so many communities suggest that reality always seems to turn out differently from the rhetoric.

Appendix One

*Burials &
Commemorations*

BELGIUM [11]

Lijssenthoek Military Cemetery, near Poperinge, Belgium. **(2)**

7993, Private Horace DOWNES, South Staffordshire Regiment, plot III.B.11A

37996, Private Bertram Laurence ELKS, South Staffordshire Regiment, plot XXVI.HH.2

Menin Gate Memorial to the Missing, Ypres. **(4)**

8605, Private John William GROVES, one of the *'Old Contemptibles'*. South Staffordshire Regiment, addenda panel 60

14114, Private William Lavender, one of the *'Old Contemptibles'*. Lincolnshire Regiment, panel 21

33146, Corporal Joseph ORGILL, Canadian Army Medical Corps, panel 32

40801, Private William Parkes, Lincolnshire Regiment, panel 21

Ploegsteert Memorial to the Missing, near Ypres. **(1)**

36920, Lance-Corporal William Ernest GRIMSLEY, South Staffordshire Regiment, panel 6

Poelcapelle British Cemetery, near Ypres. **(1)**

T/37306, Driver, Samuel SMITH, Army Service Corps, LATER 28503, Private, Loyal North Lancashire Regiment, plot XLII.D.5

Tyne Cot Memorial to the Missing, near Ypres. **(3)**

42192, Private Fred HARPER, Sherwood Foresters Regiment, panels 99-102 and 162, 162A

719, Private Bernard (Clarence) HOOPER, South Staffordshire, LATER 37061, Lance-Corporal, Gloucestershire Regiment, panels 72-75

200823, Private (William) Edward PICKIN, South Staffordshire Regiment, panels 90-92 and 162, 162A

FRANCE [59]

Armentières/Béthune (9)

Bailleul Communal Cemetery Extension, France. **(1)**

19803, Private John Henry COPE, South Staffordshire Regiment plot II.C.172
Béthune Town Cemetery, (2)
19038, Lance-Corporal John Henry WILLETT, Grenadier Guards, plot IV.F.44
12689, Private John YATES, South Staffordshire Regiment, plot IV.A.65
Le Touret Memorial to the Missing, near Festubert. **(2)**
8931, Private James William GOODALL, South Staffordshire Regiment, panel 21 or 22.
9523, Private Timothy Taylor, South Staffordshire Regiment, panel 21 or 22.
Locre Hospice Cemetery, south of Ypres. **(1)**
9543, Private Robert SYLVESTER, South Staffordshire Regiment, LATER 37046, Private, Gloucestershire Regiment, plot I.A.23

Noeux-les-Mines Communal Cemetery, south of Béthune. **(2)**
9725>200822, Private (Alfred) Charles BULLOCK, South Staffordshire Regiment, plot II.A.3
11456, Private Edgar GOODALL, South Staffordshire Regiment, LATER 86336, Sapper, 173rd Tunnelling Company, Royal Engineers, plot I.M.27
Rue-du-Bacquerot No.1 Military Cemetery, Laventie. **(1)**
17/1041, Samuel Henry Stych, plot II.F.1

Lens/Loos/Lille areas (10)
Lille Southern Cemetery. (2)
2337>836120, Bombardier Thomas Frederick ECCLESTON, M.M, Royal Field Artillery, plot I.B.21
7979, Private Aaron HAYWARD, one of the *'Old Contemptibles'*. South Staffordshire Regiment, plot III.A.10
Loos British Cemetery, near Lens, France. **(1)**
20667, Private Thomas Vaughan BRICKNALL, South Staffordshire Regiment plot XVIII.B.24
Loos Memorial to the Missing, near Lens. **(6)**
9440, Private George Bernard BUSHNELL, South Staffordshire Regiment panels 73-76
8632, Private Frank HARVEY, South Staffordshire Regiment, panels 73-76
9441, Private John 'Jack' E.W. PARTON, South Staffordshire Regiment, panels 73-76
6745, Private George SARGENT, South Staffordshire Regiment, panels 73-76
47874, Private Ambrose SQUIRE , Yorkshire Regiment, LATER 199353, Pioneer, Royal Engineers, panels 4 and 5

2nd Lieutenant Albert Victor WILKES, Sherwood Foresters Regiment, panels 87-89

Orchard Dump Cemetery, Arleux-en-Gohelle. **(1)**

1952, Private Harry Virginus PERKS, Royal Army Medical Corps, LATER 248693, Private, Army Service Corps, LATER 47821, Private, Royal Welch Fusiliers, LATER, Worcestershire Regiment, plot VI.C.42

Arras area (15)

Arras Memorial to the Missing. **(6)**

R/16384, Rifleman William Amos BULLOCK, King's Royal Rifle Corps, bay 7

28737, Lance-Corporal Thomas EVANS, Leicestershire Regiment, bay 5

16677, Private David Goodall, South Staffordshire Regiment, bay 6

30579, Private Jonah Thomas Parton, South Staffordshire Regiment, bay 6

25383, Private Harold REVITT, South Staffordshire Regiment, bay 6

8281, Private Albert STYCH, M.M, South Staffordshire Regiment, LATER 40593, Lance-Corporal, Suffolk Regiment, bay 4

Cambrai Memorial to the Missing, Louverval. **(1)**

422 >35073, Private James HEELEY, South Staffordshire Regiment, LATER 56837, Lance-Corporal, Durham Light Infantry, panel 10

Dainville Communal Cemetery, near Arras **(1)**

50614, Sapper Thomas Henry Dunn, Royal Engineers, plot A.4

Estaires Communal Cemetery, near Merville. **(1)**

930, Gunner Horace FRANCE, Machine Gun Corps, Motor Machine Gun Service, Royal Field Artillery plot III.G.5

Fifteen Ravine British Cemetery, Villers-Plouich **(1)**

205934, Corporal Arthur Parkes, Bedfordshire Regiment, plot II.G.20

St. Catherine British Cemetery, Arras. **(1)**

30578, Private Ernest HAYWOOD, South Staffordshire Regiment, plot J.21

St. Martin Calvaire British Cemetery, near St. Martin-sur-Cojeul, **(1)**

31332, Sergeant Arthur Smith, Royal Field Artillery, plot I.B.4

Tilloy British Cemetery, Tilloy-les-Mofflaines. **(1)**

185228, Gunner Alfred SLEIGH, Royal Field Artillery, plot I.B.3

Vis-en-Artois Memorial to the Missing, Haucourt. **(1)**

47918, Lance-Corporal William Charles COCKAYNE, Leicestershire Regiment panel 5

Wancourt British Cemetery, south east of Arras. (1)

352832, Private Isaac ANDREWS, Royal Scots, plot I.B.53

Somme area (20)

Abbeville Communal Cemetery Extension, Somme. **(1)**
38357, Private Albert James SIMMONS, South Staffordshire Regiment, plot III.F.3

Ancre British Cemetery, Beaumont-Hamel, Somme. **(1)**
40171, Private Edward JONES, South Staffordshire Regiment, plot VI.C.45

Bellicourt British Cemetery, east of Péronne. **(1)**
1201>>20124>242568, Private Samuel George HARRISON, South Staffordshire Regiment, Special Memorial A.4

Brie British Cemetery, south of Péronne. **(1)**
201723, Private Horace HILL, South Staffordshire Regiment, plot V.B.12

Caterpillar Valley Cemetery, Longueval, Somme. **(1)**
14757, Private George SMITH, West Yorkshire Regiment, plot XV.C.17

Combles Communal Cemetery Extension, Somme. **(1)**
204065, Gunner William SHARRATT, Royal Field Artillery, plot II.E.38

Daours Communal Cemetery Extension, east of Amiens. **(1)**
61223, Private Frank James GROOM, North Staffordshire Regiment, LATER G/62991, Private, London Regiment, plot VIII.B.39

Doullens Communal Cemetery Extension No.1. **(2)**
8605, Private George Alexander GROVES, South Staffordshire Regiment, plot II.B.11
35447, Corporal Horace JORDAN, South Staffordshire Regiment, plot V.A.75

Euston Road, Cemetery, Colincamps, Somme. **(1)**
23707, Private Fred LESTER, South Staffordshire Regiment, LATER 41279, Private, Highland Light Infantry, plot I.H.27

La Baraque British Cemetery, Bellenglise, near St. Quentin, France. **(1)**
18363, Private Harold BAUGH, Leicestershire Regiment, plot B.11

Metz-en-Couture Comm CemBritish Extension, near Bapaume. **(1)**
201540, Private James SMITH, South Staffordshire Regiment, plot II.G.17

Rossignol Wood Cemetery, Hébuterne, Somme. **(1)**
7821>200088, Corporal Joseph Henry HANDY, South Staffordshire Regiment, plot B.III

Serre Road Cemetery No.2, Somme. **(1)**
9451, Lance-Corporal, James DAWSON, one of the *'Old Contemptibles'*. South Staffordshire Regiment, plot II.D.13

Shrine Cemetery, Bucquoy. **(1)**
8706>200373, Sergeant Arthur LINNELL, MM, South Staffordshire Regiment, plot I.A.23

APPENDICES

Thiepval Memorial to the Missing, Somme. **(5)**
25095, Guardsman John BATE, Grenadier Guards, pier and face 8D
200630 Private Joseph James DAVIES, South Staffordshire Regiment, pier and face 7B
19972, Private John Goodall, South Staffordshire Regiment, pier and face 7B
15590, Private Samuel Goodall, Northumberland Fusiliers, pier and face 10B, 11B and 12B.
18399, Lance-Corporal Arthur KITSON, Royal Welch Fusiliers, pier and face 4A

Channel Coastal (2)
Boulogne Eastern Cemetery (1)
7822, Private Leonard MALPASS (MORRIS), South Staffordshire Regiment, plot VIII.B.75
Etaples Military Cemetery. (1)
75940, Gunner Bertie GILL, Royal Field Artillery, plot V.B.15A

Paris area (1)
Les Gonards Cemetery, Versailles, near Paris. **(1)**
20386, Private William Henry LAWLEY, Grenadier Guards, plot 5.28

Reims area (2)
Marfaux British Cemetery, Reims, France. **(1)**
202609, Private James BRYAN, Duke of Wellington's West Riding Regiment, plot VII.I.7/9
Solesmes British Cemetery, south of Valenciennes. **(1)**
1205, Private, Archie George HALL, C de G, South Staffordshire Regiment. LATER 26772, Private, Hampshire Regiment, LATER 205143, Private, King's Shropshire Light Infantry, plot I.C.13

TURKEY [1]

Gallipoli
Twelve Tree Copse Cemetery, Krithia, Gallipoli. **(1)**
19008, Alfred James BUSHNELL, King's Own Scottish Borderers, Special Memorial A.55

ITALY [2]

Treviso
Giavera Memorial, Treviso. (1)
203479, Sergeant William Albert HAYCOCK, South Staffordshire Regiment

Vicenza
Montecchio Precalcino Communal Cemetery Extension, South of Sanango, Vicenza. **(1)**
35429, Private Albert Ernest COOPER, South Staffordshire Regiment. LATER TR/5/13991, 4th Training Reserve Battalion. LATER Northumberland Fusiliers LATER 78533, Durham Light Infantry, plot 4.B.5

ENGLAND [5]

Bloxwich
Bloxwich Cemetery, Walsall, West Midlands. **(3)**
2nd Lieutenant Frank LLOYD, MM and Bar, Worcestershire Regiment (29/1/18). LATER 61st Squadron, Royal Air Force, plot M. 1. 30
9164 > 20002, Private Alfred Leonard MAIN, South Staffordshire Regiment. LATER Commissioned to…2nd Lieutenant, Worcestershire Regiment, plot M.2.109
2nd Lieutenant Leonard BEECH, South Staffordshire Regiment, plot M.2.223.

Plymouth
Royal Naval Memorial, Plymouth, Devon. **(2)**
Bristol Z/10064, Able Seaman Harold GOODALL, S.S. *'Ottokar'*, Royal Naval Volunteer Reserve, panel 24
Bristol Z/9639, Able Seaman (John) Thomas ROWBOTHAM, S.S. *'Kilmaho'*, Royal Naval Volunteer Reserve, panel 24.

Total = 78 servicemen died.
67 names on the memorial
11 related

Appendix Two

Campaign, Bravery, Wound & Memorial Awards 1914-1919

Campaign Awards

1914 'Mons' Star

The 1914 Star was awarded to all officers, non-commissioned officers and men of the British Expeditionary Force and sailors serving ashore, serving under fire in France or Belgium between 5th August 1914 and midnight 22nd-23rd November 1914. Most recipients were men of the pre-war British army or *'Old Contemptibles'*, who took part in the Retreat from Mons, hence the nickname, 'Mons' Star.

It is a bronze, four-pointed star faced by two crossed swords and inscribed with a scroll that reads, *'1914'*, with *'AUG'* above and *'NOV'* below. The ribbon is red white and blue, shaded left to right. Approximately 378,000 were issued to the BEF.

Seven men whose names appear in the Elmore Green war memorial story were entitled to the 1914 'Mons' Star.

1914-1915 Star

The 1914-1915 Star was awarded to all those who served in any theatre of war against the Central Powers between 5th August 1914 and 31st December 1915, unless eligible for the 1914 Star.

The design is the same as the 1914 Star, except that on the obverse is a scroll with *'1914-1915'*. The ribbon is also red white and blue, shaded left to right. The award was authorised in December 1918 and 2,366,000 were issued. It was always issued with the British War Medal and the Victory Medal.

At least thirty men whose names appear on the memorial were entitled to the 1914-1915 Star.

Note: The 1914 Star and the 1914-1915 Star were mutually exclusive awards. Either of the stars plus the British War Medal and Victory Medal were colloquially known as 'Pip, Squeak and Wilfred' after a popular *'Daily Mirror'* comic strip of the time.

British War Medal

This medal was awarded for service abroad in recognition of the successful conclusion of the Great War but was later extended to include the period 1919-1920.

It is a circular, silver medal, the obverse showing King George V and the reverse showing St. George and the dates '1914-1918'. The ribbon, displaying an orange centre stripe, is progressively edged by white, black and blue stripes. The medal was authorised on 26th July 1919 and 6,500,000 were issued in silver, 110,000 in bronze.

All sixty-seven of the men whose names appear on the memorial (as well as the fifteen related men whose stories are told) were entitled to the British War Medal.

Victory Medal

This medal was awarded to all military ranks and civilians who served in a theatre of war between 5th August 1914 and 11th November 1918. It was never issued alone and was also known as the Allied War Medal.

It is a circular, copper medal, lacquered bronze; the obverse shows the winged figure of Victory and the reverse shows the inscription, *'The Great War For Civilisation, 1914-1919'*. The ribbon has a red centre stripe, edged progressively outwards by yellow, green and blue. The medal was authorised on 1st September 1919 and 5,725,000 were issued.

All sixty-seven of the men whose names appear on the memorial (as well as the fifteen related men whose stories are told) were entitled to the British War Medal.

Bravery Awards

Military Medal (MM)

The Military Medal was instituted in 1916 for other ranks – officers were awarded the Military Cross. On the obverse of the medal is a royal effigy and on the reverse are the words, *'For Bravery in the Field'*, encircled by a wreath surmounted by the royal cipher and a crown. The ribbon is dark blue; in the centre are three white and two red stripes alternating. The medal was authorised in April 1917.

Four soldiers whose names appear on the memorial were awarded the Military Medal, one of whom won it twice. They were, in alphabetical order, Thomas Frederick Eccleston MM, Arthur Linnell MM, Frank Lloyd MM &

Bar and Albert Stych MM. Note: Although Frank Lloyd ended the war as an officer, he won the MM whilst still a sergeant.

Distinguished Conduct Medal (DCM)

The Distinguished Conduct Medal was instituted in December 1854 for other ranks. Circular and cast in silver, it bears a ribbon that is crimson with a dark blue central stripe. On the reverse is inscribed, *'For Distinguished Conduct in the Field'*.

No soldier whose name appears on the memorial was actually awarded the Distinguished Conduct Medal, despite at least one being recommended for it.

Croix de Guerre (C de G)

This was a French military decoration instituted in 1914 and similar to the British 'Mention in Despatches' award. In 1918, Archie Hall's battalion, 1/4 King's Shropshire Light Infantry, was awarded the Croix de Guerre for their commendable collective action during the German offensive on the Aisne.

Wound and Memorial Awards

Silver War Badge (SWB)

The SWB was awarded for retirement or discharge due to sickness or wounds caused by war service at home or abroad after 4th August 1914. It is circular and its rim bears the inscription, *'For King and Empire – Services Rendered.'* As far as can be ascertained, at least seven Elmore Green soldiers qualified for the Silver War Badge:

9134 **Private Ernest LAVENDER** 2/ South Staffordshire Regiment
Enlisted 19/04/12   Discharged 08/01/17 (wounds)
SWB number 212558   Age 24, overseas
[Uncle to Alfred James Bushnell, killed in action on 06/07/15 and George Bernard Bushnell, killed in action on 13/10/15. Brother of Wm 'Coxy' Lavender killed in action on 07/11/14].

9586 **Private James JONES**   1/South Staffordshire Regiment
Enlisted 12/08/14   Discharged 08/05/18 (sickness)
SWB number 363923   Age 25 years, overseas
[Brother of Edward Jones, killed in action on 27/11/16]

260049 **Corporal Jonah GILL**   6/ King's Liverpool Regiment
Enlisted 31/12/14   Discharged 27/11/18 (wounds)
SWB number B209952   Age 23 years, overseas
[Brother of Bertie Gill who died of wounds 27/04/16].

43618 Private Edward PARTON   Lincolnshire Regiment
 Enlisted 27/09/15   Discharged 14/12/18 (sickness)
 SWB number B250949   Age 22 years, overseas
 [Brother of Jack Parton, killed in action on 13/10/15].

242475 Private Benjamin HAYCOCK South Staffordshire Regiment
 Enlisted 07/03/14   Discharged 10/03/19 (sickness)
 SWB number B268948   Age 21 years, overseas
 [Brother of Bill Haycock, killed in action on 09/08/18].

242535 Private Joseph STYCH   1/6 South Staffordshire Regiment
 Enlisted 14/06/10   Discharged 12/09/19 (wounds)
 SWB number B308723   Age 27 years, overseas
 [Brother of Albert Stych, killed in action on 28/04/17 and also of
 Samuel Henry Stych, killed in action on 09/03/16]

Memorial Plaque[153]

A 'Dead Man's Penny', this one for a Pelsall man

A bronze memorial plaque was awarded to the next-of-kin of those who lost their lives on active service during the Great War. The plaque shows Britannia and the full name of the dead with the inscription, *'He died for freedom and honour'*. A parchment scroll was issued with each plaque, showing the man's name and unit. The award was authorised in 1919 and 1,355,000 were issued. The families of all sixty-seven soldiers whose names appear on the memorial (as well as the fifteen related servicemen who died) were entitled to Bronze Memorial Plaques.

---

153 This was colloquially known as 'the dead man's penny.'

Appendix Three

Tracing the servicemen and their descendants

The first efforts to trace the stories of the men on the war memorial were made during the 1980s by Paul Jones, an historian at T.P. Riley School, prior to taking a group of fifteen-year-old history students to Ypres in order to gain knowledge of the Great War and its local connections. In those pre-internet days, Paul sought information on the servicemen from the *'Walsall Observer'* and from individual families whose youngsters attended T.P. Riley School at that time.

The process was revived when the alabaster memorial was finally run to earth in 2011 (please see the Introduction for details of the search for the 'missing' memorial) and the decision was made to reinstate it in Elmore Green Primary school and to hold a re-dedication ceremony, drawing together school, memorial, relatives of the fallen, present-day pupils and the original dedication ceremony of 1922.

Ken Wayman and Barry Crutchley felt that it would be an appropriate tribute (and draw further attention to the memorial) to make a search for the full stories of the named Old Boys, employing all the resources that had not been available to Paul Jones' initial search nearly thirty years earlier.

Working from the list of names and initials shown on the war memorial itself, the obvious starting point was the Internet and the Commonwealth War Graves Commission (CWGC), casualty database. The more detailed records immediately identified a fair number of the lads on the memorial, though many surnames were such that further clues were essential before identification could effectively be made. The next port of call was, logically, the local press reports from the time of the Great War. By now the *'Walsall Observer'* was available on microfilm, giving access to the casualty and bravery reports as well as photographs of many of the lads. As Ken and Barry both live in Pelsall, it was very convenient that the excellent Pelsall Local History Centre in Church Road, Pelsall, had recently obtained the *'Walsall Observer'* microfilm records and a film-reader. Andrew Weller, a good friend who runs the Centre, made us very welcome and so began the real search. Much time was saved by referring to Sue Satterthwaite's book, *'Walsall Servicemen 1914-1918 – A Guide to Research'*.

Now armed with starting details for many of the Old Boys, we were able to make more effective use of the CWGC website; these results we cross-referenced with the excellent *'Soldiers Died in the Great War'*, CD-Rom, searchable database. We were fortunate in that some of the servicemen's records were available among the twenty-five per cent that survived Hitler's bombs during the Second World War; every man's medal entitlement is also obtainable online, offering in some cases the date when a man first arrived in a theatre of war. Once a man's army unit was established, it was possible to consult that unit's war diary in the National Archives at Kew, London. This revealed the day-to-day record of the unit and showed in which area a soldier was when he was killed or mortally wounded.

As the picture was gradually built up, the broader context of the man's unit and its actions could be traced in the Official Histories of the Great War on the land, at sea and in the air (please see the bibliography for specific details). This information was expanded by consulting a wide range of divisional, regimental and battalion histories.

Tracing the family background of the many Old Boys also began in many cases with the reports and photographs available in the local newspapers[154]. These could be expanded by consulting an invaluable book, *'Walsall Peace Celebrations, 1919'*, that offers numerous clues to a man's place of work and connected memorials. Family information, in terms of parents and siblings, along with birthplace and residences at various times were obtained by consulting online the National Census returns from 1841 to 1911.

Information was also available on a number of other war memorials, apart from that produced by Elmore Green School. Relevant names appear on such memorials as those in All Saints Church, Bloxwich, in St. Peters (Roman Catholic) Church, Bloxwich, on the Walsall War memorial plaques in the Town Hall and on several other memorials in the borough and around the country.

As the research progressed, we were fortunate to benefit from the help afforded by local newspapers in providing publicity for our quest. In particular Deborah Stewart, writing in the Express & Star, put out appeals for information from and for contact with descendants of the servicemen named on the memorial. These articles prompted numerous family members to contact the authors, offering help in the shape of factual and documentary details, family stories in respect of their ancestor, treasured photographs and a wide range

---

154 In addition to the *'Walsall Observer'*, information may also be gleaned from, *'The Pioneer'*, that may be accessed at Walsall Local History Centre in Essex Street.

of other memorabilia. The families' help and support for the project has been invaluable and has encouraged us in our efforts to turn a list of revered names into a properly-researched (we hope!) tale of courage and tragedy in equal measure.

Of the sixty-seven names engraved on the memorial, some were easier to trace than others. For a few of the lads, several family descendants quickly made contact with researchers following the articles in the local newspapers and were instrumental in resolving what had hitherto proved to be something of a 'minefield'; prime examples included 'Jones, E.', whose identity was swiftly revealed as 'Edward' by descendant Trevor Jones who now lives in Manchester. Trevor happily provided a range of memorabilia that included personal photos of Edward in uniform, photos of Edward's medals and a copy of the original scroll of thanks awarded by the people of Walsall. For a small minority of lads, finding the correct identity long remained almost impossible and three in particular, 'Hill H., Smith, J. and Yates, J.' remained remarkably elusive. For each of the three lads, a number of credible candidates existed; however, until a conclusive piece of evidence presented itself, it was possible only to offer the various alternatives. However, as we have discovered throughout the researching of the story, a saviour came to our rescue. Paul Ford, archivist at Walsall Local History Centre in Essex Street, responded to an appeal on the Walsall Council website by contacting us with the results of his investigation of the three 'difficult' names. As a professional, he knew *where* to look and *how* to link the possible sources. Needless to say, Paul solved the problem and the last three unidentified lads were 'brought in from the cold'.

Tracing the stories of the sixty-seven lads on the memorial has, through the process itself, expanded to tracing sixty-seven plus one lad whose name was inexplicably omitted from the memorial (Arthur Parkes) and also eleven close relatives (fathers, brothers and some cousins) in order to tell the story more fully. For the story of the Elmore Green memorial is not simply a tragic and heroic story of *individuals* but of Bloxwich *families* that suffered during the war and in consequence of it.

Appendix Four

Battlefront Chronology of Elmore Green Memorial War Deaths

Note: ** and name in lower case – indicates a serviceman related to those that appear on the Elmore Green School Old Boys War Memorial.

Ypres/Ploesteert/Bailleul/Lille area [15]

01/11/14	Lavender, W**	Menin Gate Memorial [panel 21]
02/11/14	HAYWARD, A	Lille Southern Cemetery [III.A.10]
07/11/14	GROVES, JW	Menin Gate Mem. [addenda panel 60]
17/07/15	DOWNES, HD	Lijssenthoek Military Cemetery [III.B. 11A]
23/02/16	COPE, JH	Bailleul Communal Cemetery Extension [II.C.172]
10/06/17	Parkes, W**	Menin Gate Memorial [panel 21]
10/07/17	SYLVESTER, R	Locre Hospice Cemetery [I. A. 23]
28/07/17	HOOPER, BC	Tyne Cot Memorial [panels 72-75]
26/09/17	HARPER, F	Tyne Cot Memorial [panels 99-102 and 162, 162A]
27/09/17	PICKIN, WE	Tyne Cot Memorial [panels 99-102 and 162, 162A]
26/10/17	SMITH, S	Poelcapelle British Cemetery [XLII. D. 5]
03/11/17	ORGILL, J	Menin Gate Memorial [panel 32]
10/04/18	GRIMSLEY, WE	Ploegsteert Memorial to the Missing [panel 6]
13/04/18	ELKS, BL	Lijssenthoek Military Cemetery [XXVI.HH.2]
17/11/18	ECCLESTON, TFMM	Lille Southern Cemetery [I.B.21]

Loos/Lens/Béthune/Festubert area [14]

10/03/15	GOODALL, JW	Le Touret Memorial, Festubert [panels 21 & 22]
12/03/15	YATES, J	Béthune Town Cemetery [IV.A.65]
13/10/15	BUSHNELL, GB	Loos Memorial [panels 73-76]
13/10/15	PARTON, JE	Loos Memorial [panels 73-76]
13/10/15	SARGENT, G	Loos Memorial [panels 73-76]
18/10/15	WILLETT, JH	Béthune Town Cemetery [IV.F.44]
24/11/15	HARVEY, F	Loos Memorial [panels 73-76]
09/03/16	Stych, SH**	Rue-du-Bacquerot No.1 Mil Cem [II.F.1]
15/05/16	BRICKNALL, TV	Loos British Cemetery [XVIII.B.24]
16/05/15	Taylor, T**	Le Touret Memorial, Festubert [panels 21-22]
24/05/16	GOODALL, E	Noeux-les-Mines Communal Cemetery [I.M.27]
10/06/17	BULLOCK, AC	Noeux-les-Mines Communal Cemetery [II.A.3]
13/04/18	SQUIRE, A	Loos Memorial to the Missing [panels 4 and 5]
24/05/18	WILKES, AV	Loos Memorial to the Missing [panels 87-89]
14/10/18	PERKS, HV	Orchard Dump Cemetery [VI.C.42]

Arras area [15]

20/09/15	FRANCE, H	Estaire Communal Cemetery, Merville [III.G.5]
12/03/16	Dunn, TH**	Dainville Comm Cem [A.4]
18/06/16	GROVES, GA	Doullens Communal Cemetery Extension No.1 [II.B.11]
17/04/17	HAYWOOD, E	St. Catherine British Cemetery [J.21]
23/04/17	BULLOCK, WA	Arras Memorial [bay 7]
23/04/17	Parton, JT**	Arras Memorial [bay 6]
28/04/17	STYCH, A MM	Arras Memorial [bay 4]
12/05/17	Goodall, D**	Arras Memorial [bay 6]
15/05/17	SLEIGH, A	Tilloy British Cemetery, Tilloy-les-Mofflaines [I.B.3]
28/05/17	Smith, A**	St. Martin Calvaire Brit Cem [I.B.4]
23/10/17	ANDREWS, I	Wancourt British Cemetery [I.B.53]
21/03/18	EVANS, T	Arras Memorial [bay 5]
24/03/18	REVITT, H	Arras Memorial [bay 6]
25/03/18	JORDAN, H	Doullens Communal Cemetery Extension No.1 [V.A.75]
24/09/18	COCKAYNE, WC	Vis-en-Artois Memorial [panel 5]

Cambrai [2]

03/12/17	HEELEY, J	Cambrai Memorial [panel 10]
27/09/18	Parkes, A**	Fifteen Ravine British Cem [II.GG.20]

Somme area [18]

14/07/16	SMITH, G	Caterpillar Valley Cemetery, Longueval [XV. C. 17]
18/07/16	Goodall, S**	Thiepval Memorial [pier/face 10B,11B & 12B]
29/07/16	Goodall, J**	Thiepval Memorial [pier/face 7B]
27/08/16	KITSON, A	Thiepval Memorial [pier/face 4A]
25/09/16	BATE, J	Thiepval Memorial [pier/face 8D]
13/11/16	DAWSON, J	Serre Road Cemetery No.2 [II. D. 13]
27/11/16	JONES, E	Ancre British Cemetery, Beaumont Hamel [VI. C. 45]
16/01/17	LESTER, F	Euston Road, Cemetery, Colincamps [I. H. 27]
14/03/17	DAVIES, JJ	Thiepval Memorial [pier/face 7B]
14/03/17	HANDY, JH	Rossignol Wood Cemetery, Hébuterne [B. III]
14/03/17	LINNELL, A MM	Shrine Cemetery, Bucquoy [I. A. 23]
06/12/17	SIMMONS, AJ	Abbeville Communal Cemetery Extension [III. F. 3]
03/02/18	SMITH, J	Metz-en-Couture CCBE [II.G.17]
01/09/18	GROOM, FJ	Daours Communal Cemetery Extension, east of Amiens [VIII. B. 39]
02/09/18	SHARRATT, W	Combles Communal Cemetery Extension [II. E. 38]
29/09/18	BAUGH, H	La Baraque British Cemetery, Bellenglise [B. 11]
29/09/18	HARRISON, SG	Bellicourt British Cemetery, east of
04/10/18	HILL, H	Brie British Cemetery [V.B.12]

Champagne area [2]

20/07/18	BRYAN, J	Marfaux British Cemetery [VII. I. 7/9]
21/11/18	HALL, AG CdeG	Solesmes British Cemetery, south of Valenciennes [I. C. 13]

Etaples (base hospital) [1]

27/04/16	GILL, B	Etaples Military Cemetery [V. B. 15A]

Boulogne (base hospital) [1]

30/08/15	MALPASS, L	Boulogne Eastern Cem. [VIII.B.75] (MORRIS, L)

Paris (base hospital) [1]

13/10/15   LAWLEY, WH   Les Gonards Cemetery, Versailles [5.28]

Italy [2]

16/06/18   COOPER, AE   Montecchio Precalcino Communal Cemetery
                               Extension, Vicenza [4. B. 5]
09/08/18   HAYCOCK, WA   Giavera Memorial to the Missing, Treviso

Turkey [1]

06/07/15   BUSHNELL, AJ   Twelve Tree Copse Cem., Krithia [Sp.Memorial
                               A.55]

England [5]

17/05/17   ROWBOTHAM, JT Plymouth Naval Memorial [panel 24]
11/12/17   GOODALL, H   Plymouth Naval Memorial [panel 24] 01/02/19
                               LLOYD, F MM & Bar
                               Bloxwich Cemetery [M. 1. 30]
03/10/19   MAIN, AL   Bloxwich Cemetery [M. 2. 109]
16/12/20   BEECH, L   Bloxwich Cemetery [M. 2. 223]

67 men on the war memorial
11 related to the memorial men
TOTAL = 78

Appendix Five

Elmore Green Servicemen Units and Service Dates

Division	Regiment or Unit	Service Dates	Brigade	Name
2nd	2nd S Staffs	8/14 to 10/3/15	6th	Goodall, JW
2nd	2nd "	8/14 to 12/3/15	6th	Yates, J
2nd	2nd "	1914 to 24/11/15	6th	Harvey, F
2nd	2nd "	2/16 to 15/5/16	6th	Bricknall, TV
2nd	2nd "	Early '15-29/7/16	6th	Goodall, J**
2nd	2nd "	8/13 to 13/11/16	6th	Dawson, J
2nd	2nd "	8/16 to 3/2/18	6th	Smith, J
2nd	2nd "	5/16 to 24/3/18	6th	Revitt, H
3rd	1st Lincs	8/14 to 1/11/14 8/14	9th	Lavender,W**
3rd	12th WYR	to 14/7/16	9th	Smith, G
3rd	129(H)RFA	14/10/16-15/5/17	42Bde,RFA	Sleigh, A
5th	1st Bedford	11/15 to 27/9/18	15th	Parkes, A**
6th	14th DLI	5/5/16 to 3/12/17	18th	Heeley, J
6th	1st Leics	3/7/16 to 21/3/18	71st	Evans, T
6th	1st Leics	3/17 to 24/9/18	71st	Cockayne, WC
7th	1st S Staffs	1907 to 2/11/14	22nd	Hayward, A
7th	1st "	1909 to 7/11/14	22nd	Groves, JW
7th	1st "	3/14 to 16/5/15	22nd	Taylor, T**
7th	1st RWF	11/14 to 27/8/16	22nd	Kitson, A
7th	1st S Staffs	Early '15-12/5/17	91st	Goodall, D**
7th	1st S Staffs	8/14 to 9/8/18	91st	Haycock, WA
8th	1st Worcs	14/9/14-14/10/18	24th	Perks, HV
11th	7th S Staffs	8/14 to 27/11/16	33rd	Jones, E
11th	6th Lincs	8/16 to 10/6/17	33rd	Parkes, W**

12th	7th Suffolk	22/4/13 to 28/4/17	35th	Stych, A
14th	89 Fld Coy	9/14 to 1/3/16		Dunn, TH**
17th	8th S Staffs	28/8/16 to 17/4/17	51st	Haywood, E
17th	8th S Staffs	1916 to 23/4/17	51st	Parton, JT**
18th	18 Bty	12/14-28/5/17	82Bde RFA	Smith, A**
19th	8th Gloucs	9/14 to 10/7/17	57th	Sylvester, R
19th	8th Gloucs	8/15 to 28/7/17	57th	Hooper, BC
19th	1/4th KSLI	11/10/15-21/11/18	56th	Hall, AG
20th	14/MGC	5/15 to 20/9/15	MMGS/RFA	France, H
21st	13th N. Fus.	1914 to 18/7/16	62nd	Goodall, S**
23rd	9th S. Staffs	8/15 to 23/2/16	Pioneers	Cope, JH
23rd	12th DLI	26/2/17 to 16/6/18	68th	Cooper, AE
25th	4th S. Staffs	2/17 to 25/3/18	7th	Jordan, H
25th	4th "	Unkn to 10/4/18	7th	Grimsley, WE Elks,
25th	4th "	4/17 to 13/4/18	7th	BL
29th	1st KOSB	8/14 to 6/7/15	87th	Bushnell, AJ
32nd	1st HLI	4/16 to 16/1/17	14th	Lester, F
33rd	16th KRRC	6/12/15 to 23/4/17	100th	Bullock, WA
35th	17th WYR	Late 1915-9/3/16	106th	Stych, SH**
46th	1/5thS.Staffs	8/14 to 17/7/15	137th	Downes, HD
46th	1/5th "	8/14 to 30/8/15	137th	Malpass, L
46th	1/5th "	10/14 to 13/10/15	137th	Bushnell, GB
46th	1/5th "	9/14 to13/10/15	137th	Parton, JE
46th	1/5th "	8/14 to 13/10/15	137th	Sargent, G
46th	1/5th "	1914 to 18/6/16	137th	Groves, GA
46th	1/5th "	9/14 to 14/3/17	137th	Davies, JJ
46th	1/5th "	2/12 to 14/3/17	137th	Handy, JH
46th	1/5th "	8/14 to 14/3/17	137th	Linnell, A
46th	1/5th "	10/14 to 10/6/17	137th	Bullock, AC
46th	1/5thSh. For.	6/5/16 to 24/5/18	139th	Wilkes, AV
46th	1/4th Leics	Unkn to 29/9/18	138th	Baugh, H
46th	1/6thS.Staffs	5/10/15 to 29/9/18	137th	Harrison, SG
46th	1/6thS.Staffs	1916 to 4/10/18	137th	Hill, H
47th	235th RFA	1/17 to 2/9/18	'C' Bty	Sharratt, W
51st	1/9thRScots	10/16 to 23/10/17	154th	Andrews, I
55th	419 Fd Coy	9/16 to 13/4/18	RE	Squire, A
57th	2/4th LNL	12/15 to 26/10/17	170th	Smith, S
58th	7th London	4/18 to 1/9/18	174th	Groom, FJ
59th	2/5thS.Staffs	4/17 to 6/12/17	176th	Simmons, AJ
59th	2/5thS.Staffs	10/14 to 27/9/17	176th	Pickin, WE
59th	2/6th Sh For	14/4/16 to 26/9/17	178th	Harper, F
59th	2/5thS.Staffs	Unkn to 16/12/20	176th	Beech, L
62nd	2/4thDWR	4/16 to 20/7/18	186th	Bryan, J

Guards	2nd Gren G	1914 to 13/10/15	1st Gds	Lawley, WH
Guards	3rd Gren G	8/14 to 18/10/15	2nd Gds	Willett, JH
Guards	4th Gren G	11/15 to 25/9/16	3rd Gds	Bate, J
-	5 Res.Worcs	5/8/14 to 3/10/19	+2/S.Staffs	Main, AL
Tunnellers	173rd RE	8/14 to 24/5/16	-	Goodall, E
AFA	242 RFA	15/4/15-17/11/18	'B' Bty	Eccleston, TF
1st Can.	2nd FdAmb	1915 to 3/11/17	-	Orgill, Jos
3rd Can.	94 Bty	11/1/15 to 27/4/16	18 BdeRFA	Gill, B
RAF	61 Sq.	8/14 to 1/2/19	Also 1/5 S. Staffs	Lloyd, F
RNVR	'Kilmaho'	7/9/16 to 17/5/17	-	Rowbotham, T
RNVR	'Ottokar'	3/10/16-11/12/17	-	Goodall, H

** Indicates a name related to those that appear on the Elmore Green School Old Boys War Memorial.

Notes:

- The **Machine Gun Corps** (MGC for short) came into existence as a separate corps in February 1917. Prior to that time, the machine-gunners were an integral part of each battalion. The MMGS was the **Motorised Machine Gun Service** that employed motorcycle 'combinations'.

- **RFA** is the shortened version of the 'Royal Field Artillery'.

- **RE** is the shortened form of 'Royal Engineers'.

- The **Tunnellers** or a **Tunnelling Coy** (or Company) of the RE was a specialist unit consisting of miners and mining engineers whose task was to mine under the enemy lines, placing explosives and detonating them. In some areas, both sides mined and counter-mined intensively; for the men underground, hard toil often came accompanied by sudden death.

- A **'pioneer'** battalion, such as the 9th Battalion, the South Staffordshire Regiment (23rd Division), was attached to each division from 1916 onwards. Pioneer battalions performed construction tasks in the forward area not requiring the specialist equipment of the RE, such as constructing trenches and dugouts although the pioneers occasionally acted in the engineer role of tasks such as the construction of bridges. These battalions contained a large proportion of tradesmen and were organised along the same lines as infantry battalions. The **Guards Division** came into being in August 1915. Prior to that time, battalions of the Guards regiments were distributed among the regular army divisions.

- **L.I.** is the shortened form of **'Light Infantry'** (as in King's Shropshire Light Infantry or KSLI); the term refers to the fact that such units were lightly-equipped, fast-moving troops, though their effectiveness in previous wars was obviously greatly limited in trench warfare.

- **Canadian Divisions** – in August 1914, Canada, in support of Great Britain, decided to mobilise an expeditionary force of one division along with support units.

Glossary of terms, expressions and nicknames

Note on 'old' money: Until the early 1970's, one pound (£1-00) consisted of 240 pennies; it could be divided into 20 shillings (each worth 12 pennies). Prices were shown in pounds (£), shillings (s) and pence (d). Today, one pound (£1-00) consists of 100 pennies or pence – much simpler! So, one new penny is the same as 2.4 old pennies, except that inflation (we won't go there!) means that money was worth much more in 1914. For example, in 1899 the upper limit of a family's 'poverty line' was judged to be £1 " 1s. per week.

Adjutant = senior administrative officer in a battalion; responsible for writing up the battalion war diary.

Armistice = an armistice is a ceasefire; it is not a treaty but does stop the fighting. An Armistice was agreed and implemented from 11 a.m. on 11th November 1918. If it had been 'broken', the fighting would have re-commenced.

Army Reserve = following military service, most men who were demobilised were placed on the Army Reserve, in case of emergency.

A.S.C. = Army Service Corps (nicknamed 'Ally Sloper's Cavalry'). The ASC's role was to re-supply the troops in the field. Their job was often carried out under fire, was under-appreciated but vital.

Artillery duel = a term used when the artillery of both sides attempted to neutralise each other. The infantrymen in their trenches were frequently caught in the hail of shells.

Attestation form = this was an army form used to 'enlist' a new recruit. It was signed by the recruit who then underwent a medical examination prior to acceptance.

Balloon, observation = tethered balloons were used for observing enemy troop movements and for observing the fall of artillery shells. Such balloons were, of course, very vulnerable.

Barbed wire (also, the wire, wiring-party, re-wiring) = huge amounts of barbed wire were used in No Man's Land to protect the parapet of trenches. Damage to the 'wire' had to be repaired under the cover of darkness – it was a dangerous and unpopular duty.

Barrage (also artillery…, machine-gun…; creeping…, lifting…) = a barrage was another name for a bombardment. A 'creeping' barrage gradually extended the range of the artillery; a 'lifting' barrage moved forward in pre-arranged steps or lifts ahead of infantry, e.g. 100 yards forward every minute.

B.E.F. = British Expeditionary Force. The name for the British army that was sent to France and Belgium from August 1914. The name was retained throughout the war

Big push = a major, set-piece attack such as at Arras in April 1917.

'Blighty' (also 'Blighty one') = Army slang originating on Indian service; possibly from an Urdu word meaning foreign or European. By association it came to mean 'home' or 'UK'. To 'cop a Blighty one' meant to suffer a wound serious enough to be invalided to UK but not serious enough to maim or kill.

'Boys in blue' (also **'hospital blues'**) = wounded or very sick men who were evacuated to hospital in the UK, wore a distinctive blue garb once they had improved sufficiently to leave their beds and get dressed.

Burst (also 'air burst', ground burst') = an artillery shell carried a fuze that could be set to detonate at various distances, thus it might explode on impact or, especially in the case of shrapnel shells, might be set to explode at several hundred feet above a trench or above attacking troops.

Casualty = a term covering any soldier who was put out of action, from 'walking wounded' to killed in action. Casualty 'figures' included those men who were ill, wounded, missing in action or killed. To a battalion, a casualty was, to put it bluntly, a man who could not carry out his military duty.

C.C.S. = Casualty Clearing Station where casualties were assessed, initially treated and sent 'down the line' for further treatment as necessary.

Chantilly Conference = Allied war leaders' conference held in December 1915 to decide on military priorities for 1916.

Civvy Street = life outside the military.

C.O./O.C. = Commanding Officer/Officer Commanding.

Communication trench = a trench that linked fire-trench, reserve trench and support trench. The communication trench followed a zig-zag pattern to avoid enemy fire 'enfilading' the length of the trench. The communication trench was used for moving troops back and forth, re-supplying the front-line and evacuating casualties.

Counter-attack = to carry out an attack in response to being attacked. German forces in particular were always expected to counter-attack.

'Cushy number' = an easy, less dangerous duty. Derives from a Hindustani word for 'pleasure'.

D.A.C. = Divisional Ammunition Column, employed on re-supplying the guns with ammunition. Also re-supplied small arms ammunition (S.A.A.).

'Daily hate' = even when a sector was relatively quiet, both sides usually fired a few shells at each other. This was regular and was referred to as the 'daily hate.'

Demobilisation = the complex process of returning servicemen to civilian life.

Diversionary attack = a minor attack to divert the enemy's attention from a main assault elsewhere. On 1st July 1916, the attack on Gommecourt by 46th Division was intended to divert enemy resources from the major targets in the northern sector of the Somme front-line.

Divisional boundary (also corps… and army…) = official orders always specified the boundary between major units. This was done to avoid troops becoming inter-mingled during attacks.

Drumfire (also barrage fire) = known to the Germans as *'trommelfeuer'*, this referred to near-continuous, heavy shellfire. Prior to the start of the Somme offensive, this drumfire lasted for several days without respite.

Dump (also ammunition…, supply…) = a dump was an open-air supply store, whether weapons, ammunition, food, clothing or any other of the necessities of war. From the supply port, stores were moved usually by rail (standard then narrow gauge) to main dumps at the Corps or Divisional railhead; they were then moved on to brigade or battalion dumps by motorised or horse-drawn wagons. Each unit's were then collected by sections of each division's ASC units.

'Duration' man = soldier who enlisted for the 'duration of the war.'

Eastern Front = the fighting front-line between Germany, Austria and the Russians in Eastern Europe.

Enfilading fire = firing down the length of an enemy trench, thus causing maximum casualties.

Entraining procedures = the process of moving say, a battalion from barracks to a railhead, boarding a military train and reversing the process at the destination. Practice decreased the time needed to put a unit into action.

Fire-step (also reversing the…) = below the trench parapet was a fire-step cut into the earth of the trench, enabling infantry to fire over the top of the sandbags when under enemy attack.

Flank (also outflank) = military term referring to the vulnerable 'sides' of a unit. To outflank meant to partly surround and enemy.

Front line (also the line, up the line, into the line) = front-line fighting trenches; came to mean 'in harm's way'.

Fuze settings = at the point of an artillery shell was a carefully-milled, adjustable brass fuze. This determined in what position the explosive was detonated.

Gallows humour = the dark humour of the Tommies, very pessimistic in nature – making jokes at their own situation's expense.

'Go over the top' = to climb over the sand-bagged parapet of a trench to cross No Man's Land to attack enemy lines.

Gun-lines = the gun-line was the 'front-line' for the artillery. The lighter the artillery piece battery, the further forward its gun-line. This depended on the range of the gun/howitzer and the time it took to withdraw the weapon from harm's way. Each gun/howitzer was dug in to its own **gun-pit**.

Gun-pit = a single position from which to fire an artillery piece; carefully sited, camouflaged and the guns dug-in, often reinforced by steel, timber and dozens of sandbags. Usually part of the 'gun-line'.

Hand grenade or 'bomb' = hand-held, small iron 'ball', filled with explosive and detonated several seconds after a securing pin had been removed from the top of the grenade. Commonly referred to as a 'bomb', hence a 'bomber' was really a grenadier. The alternative name of 'bombers' was coined when the Grenadier Guards objected to 'lesser' units being called grenadiers.

Hand-to-hand fighting = close-quarter fighting with bayonet or any makeshift weapon that came to hand when under attack.

Headquarters (also H.Q.) = each army unit on active service had its own HQ, from General Headquarters (Haig's was a Montreuil for much of the war), through Army, Corps, Division, Brigade and Battalion down to Company at the lowest level.

H.E. = high explosive.

Hindenburg Line/Siegfried Stellung (German name) = powerful, defensive line constructed by the Germans in 1916-17. It shortened and strengthened their front line from Arras to south of the Somme River.

Hospital = base or stationary hospitals were located far back from the front-line. Unlike Casualty Clearing Stations, base and stationary hospitals did not move in reaction to the front-line.

Howitzer = a short-barrelled, usually heavy, gun that fired a shell in a high trajectory; from a German word for catapult

'Kitcheners' = logical nickname given to lads who joined the 'New Army' that was raised by Lord Kitchener.

Lewis Gun = a British-developed light machine-gun that greatly increased the potential effectiveness of infantry.

Light railway = a quickly-built, narrow gauge railway that linked standard-gauge track to positions closer to the front.

Logistical problems = supply problems, such as ammunition, food, water, kit, medical supplies, tools, R.E. stores; often in the hands of the Army Service Corps (ASC).

Machine-guns (Lewis light m/gun, Vickers heavy m/gun) = on 30th November 1915 machine-gun changes were introduced – 4 Lewis Guns per battalion, while the Vickers Guns formed M/gun Companies and were allocated one per brigade – each company comprised 4 sections, 2 m/guns per section (one m/gun was valued at approximately 30 rifles).

Mesopotamia = modern Iraq.

'Mills' bomb = hand grenade that became standard issue in the British army.

Minenwerfer = a German-developed, short-range mine-launcher. The 25cm muzzle-loading mortar was as effective as a mortar ten times its weight. The *'Moaning Minnie'* (nicknamed by the Tommies for the sound it made) was an important weapon in trench warfare.

Missing in action = when the roll-call was taken after a battle, any man not definitely accounted for as killed or wounded might well be posted as 'missing in action'. Such men might have been captured or killed in action. The effects of shelling often made identification of the dead impossible. These men are commemorated all along the battlefronts on Memorials to the Missing, such as the Menin Gate at Ypres and the Thiepval Memorial on the Somme.

New Army = the 'civilian' army raised by Lord Kitchener became known as Kitchener's 'New Army', battalions of which were classified as 'Service' battalions.

No Man's Land = the logical name for the area of land between the two front-lines as no-one could control it.

Objective (also first…, second…final…) = specified targets for each step of an attack.

Offensive = a major, planned battle, attack, assault or a series of these. For example, the Arras Offensive, the Somme Offensive, the German Spring Offensive.

On home leave = being granted a brief, official break from military duty. A serviceman was provided with travel warrants, official passes (for absence from his unit) and a specific time and date for his return to duty. Failure to return on time was described as 'absent without leave', commonly known as going 'AWOL'.

Patrol = patrols, comprising a few men and an officer, were often sent into No Man's Land in order to gain information on the enemy. It also gave the patrolling side the impression that they were 'dominating' No Man's Land.

Pioneer = from early in the war, each division was allocated a pioneer battalion (such as 9/South Staffordshire of 23rd Division). Many such battalions were specially raised and contained men whose skills often complemented those of the Royal Engineers.

Poison Gas (also gas shells/gas cylinders/Special Gas Companies) = both sides feared chemical warfare and the introduction of poison gases terrified many of the soldiers on the receiving end. Initially delivered by opening valves on gas cylinders, special gas shells made the delivery of gas easier for the attackers. The main gases employed were tear gas, chlorine gas, phosgene gas and the most devastating, mustard gas that blistered skin and remained effective for a long time.

Preliminary bombardment = most infantry attacks were preceded by a preliminary or preparatory artillery bombardment that was intended to destroy enemy positions, soldiers and communications. However, such a bombardment also announced an attack to the enemy. The preliminary bombardment on the Somme in July 1916 lasted for seven days, firing more than a million shells.

'Puttying-up' = a flexible support role devised by Corps Commander, General Sir Douglas Haig in 1914. In effect, the battalions of the support brigade were directed wherever the need was most pressing. This made most effective use of limited resources.

Railhead = each main section of the front-line had a major railway centre to which were delivered, men, ammunition, supplies and weaponry. From the railhead, wagons and narrow-gauge railways delivered all of the above to Corps and Divisional dumps for onward movement.

RAMC = the Royal Army Medical Corps had the major responsibility for organising the transportation and treatment of wounded and sick men, from front-line to Military Hospitals back in the United Kingdom..

Retreat = a retreat usually seems to suggest defeat but a tactical withdrawal saved many an army unit to fight another day. One of the best Great War examples was the Retreat from Mons in August/September of 1914.

RFC/ RNAS/RAF = the single service, the Royal Air Force, was not created until 1st April 1918. Prior to that date, there existed two air services, one controlled by the Army (Royal Flying Corps or RFC) one controlled by the Royal Navy (Royal Naval Air Service or RNAS).

Rifles 'at the port' = to carry a rifle at 45° to the vertical, held across the chest. It indicated that immediate opposition was not expected. The men who attacked on the Somme on 1st July were ordered to carry their rifles in this manner across No Man's Land – they were led to believe it would be a 'walkover'.

Rifle grenade = a metal rod attached to a standard hand grenade; was fired from a rifle using a blank cartridge. It increased the range of the grenade but quickly ruined the standard rifle in its normal role.

S.A.A. = Small Arms Ammunition i.e. ammunition for hand-held weapons.

Salient = on a map a salient appeared as a bulge in the front-line, pressing into the enemy's line. A salient was vulnerable as it could be fired upon from three sides. The best-known were at Ypres in Flanders and at Flesquières to the south of Arras.

Salonika = in October 1915 an Anglo-French force landed at the Greek port of Salonika, with the intention of aiding Serbia against Bulgaria. The Allied presence remained there until the final year of the war.

Sapper = this was the lowest rank in the Royal Engineers.

Service record, Pension record = every serviceman who served his country had a written service record. Those who were invalided from their service were granted a small pension, according to the severity of their injuries. During the Second World War, the records for men from the Great War were for the most part destroyed by incendiary bombs that hit the buildings housing the records. Only about 25% of the records survive in any shape or form.

Shell calibres = guns were rated according to the diameter (in inches or millimetres) or weight (in pounds) of the shells that they fired. The standard British field-gun in 1918 was the 18-pounder while the standard French field-gun was the 75 mm (known as the *Soixante-Quinze*).

Shell types = many artillery pieces could fire a range of shells, according to the purpose of the firing. High explosive was used to destroy buildings, gun-emplacements and trenches; shrapnel shells were especially useful against enemy personnel while early in the war shrapnel was used to destroy barbed-wire (rather unsuccessfully;) gas shells were more effective and accurate than the initial method of releasing the gas from iron cylinders.

Shrapnel – some shells were packed with small, iron balls; when this shell burst above troops it caused numerous wounds. Shrapnel also refers to the iron casing when it exploded into fragments, causing 'rip' injuries to flesh.

Siege gun = these were heaviest and/or longest-ranged guns on the battlefield. The British used a small number of 15-inch naval guns mounted on railway wheels. The Germans used a huge, 42 cm. howitzer built by Krupps Armaments, and known as *'Dicke Bertha'*. The Germans' legendary *'Paris gun'*, used against the French capital in the summer of 1918, had the longest barrel used in the Great War. It fired 210-pound shells a distance of eighty miles and reached a maximum height of 25 miles on its journey. Needless to say, its use against Paris was as a terror weapon.

Smoke candles = smoke candles were used to create an artificial fog to mask the advance of troops across No Man's Land. In the early use of poison gas, smoke candles were burned to intensify the natural 'fog' created by cylinder-released gas.

Sniper = this was a specialist marksman used by both sides in the war. A sniper needed to be an excellent shot, have good anticipation and be remarkably patient. Snipers were most effective where trenches were shallow or damaged. Many snipers were experts in camouflage.

Southern Front = this was the battlefront between the Italian army and its Austrian and German enemies. In 1917, the Italians were under huge pressure so several British and French divisions were sent to the Southern Front. At least two Elmore green lads served on the Southern Front.

Stand to (also 'stood to') = every available infantryman had to 'stand to' on the fire-step in his trench at dawn and again at dusk as these were considered the most likely times for the enemy to launch an attack. When the danger time was thought to be over, the men were 'stood down'. Whenever danger threatened at any time of day or night a man would be ordered to 'stand to'.

Stokes gun/trench mortar = this was a metal tube affixed to a base-plate; at the bottom of the barrel was a fixed firing-pin. A mortar shell, with fins for stability, was dropped down the barrel onto the pin, thus firing the shell in a high arc over No Man's Land. The firing-point or mortar-pit was easily traced by the enemy and so the mortar teams quickly moved on, leaving the infantry to face the retaliation. Unsurprisingly, mortar teams were unpopular with the foot-soldiers.

Storm troopers = German elite troops, specially trained, lightly-equipped and capable of the rapid infiltration of enemy lines during an offensive.

Strategic = in relation to the overall war plans and objectives. Long-term aims.

Tactical = in relation to immediate success on the present battlefield. Short-term aims.

'Time-expired' man = a soldier whose period of enlistment has ended or is about to end.

Tommy Atkins (also shortened to 'Tommy') = 'Thomas Atkins' or 'Tommy Atkins' was a name coined in the 19th Century by the Duke of Wellington for the ordinary soldier when asked for a name to write onto a sample pay-book.

Training (also basic…) = basic infantry training lasted six months but was reduced as the demands of replacing casualties increased. Training continued once a man reached his battalion; as the war went on, so each attack was practised beforehand on the training ground.

Trench lines = the standard trench pattern on the British side was of three roughly parallel trench-lines – firing, support and reserve – each connected by zig-zagged communication trenches.

Trench Mortar see Stokes gun, above.

Trench raids = a trench raid might involve any number of men up to company strength. The aim of such raids was to dominate No Man's Land and to raise morale; the objective might be to destroy a specific target, to cut enemy wire or to take prisoners for interrogation.

Troop transport = usually a troop-train or troopship, often requisitioned from civilian use.

War diary = during active operations, most units were required to keep a detailed record or diary of the unit's actions/involvement. A unit's war diary recorded orders, changes in personnel, changes of location, details of enemy contacts, casualty lists; generally, only officers were mentioned by name, although early in the war Territorial battalions tended to mention casualties by name regardless of rank. Keeping the war diary up to date was the responsibility of the adjutant or another specified officer. Copies of the unit's daily diary was sent up to Brigade, Division or Corps H.Q. in order to give senior officers a wider view of the front-line.

War Hospital = in the U.K., war hospitals were distributed throughout the country; wounded men returned to the U.K. were often treated far from their homes.

'Whizz-bang' = a type of German shell. The name derived from the sound it made, giving men in a trench little warning of its arrival.

'Wipers' = Tommy's pronunciation of Ypres.

Wire cutting bombardment = originally, shrapnel shells were used in the attempt to cut enemy wire prior to an attack but early failures led to High Explosive shells replacing shrapnel.

Ypres (Wallon-French) or Ieper (Flemish), battles of = Ypres/Ieper was an ancient town in Belgian Flanders and became the symbol of Allied resistance in the northern section of the Western Front. Major battles were fought in the Ypres Salient in 1914, 1915, 1917 and 1918. 3rd Ypres was notorious and the name of the village of Passchendaele, a final objective of that offensive, became synonymous with mud and slaughter on a huge scale.

Bibliography

A – Original documents:

Admissions Registers for Elmore Green School, 1890s-1912 [WLHC]

APPSA Committee – *'Army Pay and Pensions Separation Allowance, Walsall Districts, 1914-1918'.*

National Census of England – *1841, 1851, 1861, 1871, 1881, 1891, 1901, and 1911.*

National Archives, Kew, London –

- o *'Soldiers' Medal Index Cards and Medal Rolls – Great War'.*
- o *'Soldiers' Service Records, Great War – The Burnt Records'.*
- o *'Soldiers' Pension Records – Great War'.*
- o *Official War Diaries – WO95/1 to 5500 (inclusive).*

Public Records – *'War Graves of the British Empire.'* (This provides site maps for graves); *'Memorial Registers of British War Dead, 1914-1918'; 'Naval Memorial Registers, 1914-1918'; 'Walsall & District Roll of the Great War'; 'The Staffordshire Roll of Honour'*, original and facsimile in Lichfield Cathedral.

War Diaries (preceded by the National Archive reference):

WO95/1215 *'2nd Battalion, the Grenadier Guards'.*

WO95/1223 *'4th Battalion, the Grenadier Guards'.*

WO95/3005 *'1/7th (City of London) Battalion, the London Regiment'.*

WO95/2857 *'1/8th Battalion, the Royal Scots'.*

WO95/1665 *'1st Battalion, the Royal Welch Fusiliers'.*

WO95/1616 (18 brigade) *'2nd Battalion, the Sherwood Foresters Regiment'.*

WO95/1624 (71 brigade) *'2nd Battalion, the Sherwood Foresters Regiment'.*

WO95/3025 *'2/6th Battalion, the Sherwood Foresters Regiment'.*

WO95/1670 *'1st Battalion, the South Staffordshire Regiment'.*

WO95/1362 *'2nd Battalion, the South Staffordshire Regiment'.*

WO95/2244 *'4th Battalion, the South Staffordshire Regiment'.*

WO95/2686 *'1/5th Battalion, the South Staffordshire Regiment'.*

WO95/3021 *'2/5th Battalion, the South Staffordshire Regiment'.*

WO95/2687 *'1/6th Battalion, the South Staffordshire Regiment'.*

WO95/1816 (1) *'7th Battalion, the South Staffordshire Regiment'.*

WO95/4299 (2) *'7th Battalion, the South Staffordshire Regiment'.*

WO95/2007 *'8th Battalion, the South Staffordshire Regiment'.*

WO95/2178 *'9th Battalion, the South Staffordshire Regiment'.*

WO95/1852 *'7th Battalion, the Suffolk Regiment.'*

WO95/1723 *'1st Battalion, the Worcestershire Regiment'.*
WO95/3754 *'2nd Canadian Field Ambulance, Canadian Army Med. Corps'.*

B – Books, booklets and newspapers:
Banks, Arthur – *'A Military Atlas of the First World War'.* [1975, Heinemann Ltd; 2001 Reprint, Pen & Sword Books Ltd.]
Barrie, Alexander – *'War Underground – Tunnellers of the Great War'.* [1962; 1981 reprint, W.H. Allen.]
Becke, Major E. F. – *'Order of Battle of Divisions, 1914-1918 (Parts 1, 2A, 2B, 3A, 3B 5A)'.* [First published 1935, 1936, 1937, 1938 and 1945 respectively, HMSO; Reprinted 1989, 1989, 1988 and two undated, Ray Westlake Military Books]
Beckett, Ian F.W. – *'The First World War – The Essential Guide to Sources in the National Archives'.* [2002, Public Record Office.]
Bilton, David – *'The Home Front in the Great War'.* [2003, Leo Cooper]
Blore, J.E. and Sherratt, J.R. – *'Over There – The Old Leek Battery, 1908-1919 (46thDivision)'.* [1991, Martin Publicity]
Bridger, Geoff – *'The Great War Handbook'.* [2009, Pen & Sword]
Brown, Malcolm – *'Tommy Goes to War'.* [1978, J.M. Dent & Sons]
Butt, Roger – *'The National Schools, Bloxwich'.*
Cannock Chase Mining Historical Society – *'The Cannock Chase Coalfield'.*
Cherry, Niall – *'Most Unfavourable Ground – The Battle of Loos, 1915.'* [2005, Helion]
Coombs, Rose E. B. (Revised by Karel Margry) – *'Before Endeavours Fade.'*
Crossley, R.G. – *'Imperial Garrison of Natal'.* [Military History Journal, Vol. 2, No 5, June 1973, South African Military History Society,
Crown Stationery Office – *'War 1914 – Punishing the Serbs.'* [The 'Uncovered Editions', 1915 then abridged version 1999, TSO Publishing]
Edmonds, Brigadier-General Sir James – Official History, *'The Occupation of the Rhineland, 1918-1929.'* (1987, HMSO/Imperial War Museum).
Elson, J.C.J. – *'Index of Photos of Soldiers that appeared in the Walsall Pioneer,1/1/16 to 22/2/19'.* [Accession 713/1&2; Original Supplements at Location 36A]. *'Honours and Awards, The South Staffordshire Regiment, 1914-1918'. (Original work, Whittington barracks).*
Farmer, William – *'Under Bluer Skies'.*
Farndale, General Sir Martin, KCB – *'History of the Royal Regiment of Artillery – The Western Front 1914-18.'* [1986, The Royal Artillery Institution]

Farrar-Hockley, General Sir Anthony– *'Death of an Army'.* [Original 1967; reprint 1998, Wordsworth Editions Ltd]

Fowler, Will – *'Ypres 1914-15.'* [Battle Story series] [2011, Spellmount]

Gibbs, Philip –
- o *'The Battles of the Somme'.* [1917, Heinemann]
- o *'The War Dispatches'.* [1964, Times Press]

Gilbert, Martin – *'First World War Atlas.'* [1970, Weidenfeld & Nicolson]

Gliddon, Gerald – *'Battle of the Somme – a Topographical History'.* [1987, Gliddon Books]

Grieve, Capt. W. Grant & Newman, Bernard – *'Tunnellers (Tunnelling Companies, R.E., during the Great War).'* [Original 1936; reprint, Antony Rowe Ltd.]

Griffiths, Paddy (editor) – *'British Fighting Methods in the Great War'.* [1996, Cass]

Gudmundsson, Bruce –
- o *'The British Army on the Western Front, 1916'.* [2007, Osprey]
- o *'The British Expeditionary Force, 1914-15'.* [2005, Osprey]

Hardman, Robert – *'City Under the Slaughter.'* Excellent article on the Arras tunnels and caverns published in the Daily Mail on Saturday, 15th March 2008.

Haythornthwaite, Peter J. – *'Source Book of the First World War'.* [1992; 1998 edition, Brockhampton Press]

Henshaw, Trevor – *'The Sky Their Battlefield'.* [1995, Grub Street]

H.M.S.O. –
- o *'Military Operations, France and Belgium, 1914-1918, Maps',* (CD-Rom 2nd Edition, Naval & Military Press Ltd.).
- o *'Official History: Merchant Navy, volume III',* by Archibald Hurd.
- o *'Official History of the Great War – Principal Events, 1914-1918'.*
- o *'Official History – Military Operations in France and Belgium',* various volumes. [HMSO original; reprint by IWM with Battery Press]
- o *'Official History – Military Operations, Gallipoli, volumes 1 & 2.'* [HMSO original; reprint by IWM with Battery Press]
- o *'Official History – Military Operations – Italy.'* [HMSO original; reprint by IWM with Battery Press]
- o *'Official History of the Ministry of Munitions',* volumes 7, 8, 10 and 11. [HMSO original; reprint by IWM with Naval & Military Press]
- o *'Official History: Naval Operations, volume V',* by Henry Newbolt.
- o *'War Establishments, Part I, 1913'.*

Holding, Norman [4th edn. revised by Iain Swinnerton]– *'The Location of British Army Records, 1914-1918'. [1984; 4th edition 1999, Federation of Family History Societies Ltd.]*

Holmes, Richard – *'Tommy'.* [2004, HarperCollins Publishing]

Homeshaw, Ernest James – *'The Story of Bloxwich.'* [1955; reprinted 1988 [WLHC]

Hurst, Sidney C. – *'The Silent Cities – A Guide to the War Cemeteries and Memorials to the Missing in France & Flanders'.* [1929, Methuen & Co.; Modern reprint, undated, Naval & Military Press Ltd.]

IGN Maps – *'Institut Geographique National, Serie Verte (1 km to 1 cm)'.* Various sheets.

James, Brigadier E.A. –
   o *'British Regiments, 1914-1918'.* [1924, Gale & Polden Ltd; Modern reprint, Naval & Military Press Ltd.]
   o *'A Record of the Battles and Engagements of the British Armies in France and Flanders, 1914-1918'.* [First published in two volumes in 1969 & 1974; 1998 5th (single volume) edition, Naval & Military Press]

Jobson, Philip – *'Royal Artilllery - Glossary of Terms, Historical and Modern'.* [2008, The History Press]

Kelly's Directories – *'Kelly's Directory of Staffordshire, (1912 and 1916)'.* [WLHC]

Lomas, David & Dovey, Ed. – *'First Ypres, 1914'.* [1998, Osprey Publishing]

Matthews, Trevor – *'Hilton Main and Holly Bank Collieries'.*

MacPherson, Major-General Sir W.G., K.C.M.G., C.B., LL.D – *'Medical Services, General History, volumes I-4.'*

McCarthy, Chris –
   o *'The Somme, 1916 – the Day-by-Day Account'.* [1993, Arms & Armour Press]
   o *'Passchendaele, 1917 – the Day-by-Day Account'.* [1995, Arms & Armour Press]

McGreal, Stephen – *'The War on Hospital Ships, 1914-1918'.* [2008, Pen & Sword Maritime]

Messenger, Charles – *'Call to Arms – The British Army 1914-1918.'* [2005, Weidenfeld & Nicolson]

Middlebrook, Martin –
   o *'Your Country Needs You'.* [2000, Leo Cooper]
   o *'First Day on the Somme'.* [1971, Allen Lane]
   o *'The Somme Battlefields'.* [1994, Penguin Edition]
   o *'The Kaiser's Battle'.* [1978, Allen Lane]

Ministry of Pensions – *'Location of Hospitals and Casualty Clearing Stations, British Expeditionary Force, 1914-1919'.* [1923; Modern reprint, undated, Imperial War Museum]

Mitchell, Major T.J. – *'Medical Services, Casualties and Statistics.'*

Mitchinson, K. W. – *'Organised and Intelligent Labour - Pioneer Battalions in the Great War'.* [1997, Leo Cooper.]

Nicholls, Jonathan – *'Cheerful Sacrifice – Battle of Arras, 1917'.* [1995, Leo Cooper]

Ordnance Survey Maps – *'Landranger Series, sheets 179, 189 (1:50,000; 2008 editions).'*

Passingham, Ian – *'Pillars of Fire – the Battle of Messines Ridge, June 1917'.* [1998, Sutton Publishing]

Perry, F.W. – *'Order of Battle of Divisions, 1914-1918 (Part 5A)'.* [1992, Ray Westlake Military Books.]

Plumridge, John H. – *'Hospital Ships and Ambulance Trains'.* [1975,]

Ponting, Clive – *'Thirteen Days.'* [2002, Chatto & Windus].

Rawson, Andrew – *'Loos – Hohenzollern Redoubt', (Battleground Europe)*

Rinaldi, Richard A. – *'A Complete Order of Battle for the British Army in 1914'.* [2008, Ravi Rikhye]

Satterthwaite, Sue – *'Walsall Servicemen 1914-1918 – A Guide to Research'.* [1998, Walsall Local History Centre.]

Sheffield, Gary –
- *'The Somme'.* [2003, Cassell]
- *'Forgotten Victory'.*

Spencer, William – *'Army Service Records of the First World War'.*

Steel, Nigel & Hart, Peter – *'Passchendaele – The Sacrificial Ground'.* [2000, Cassell]

Thornton, Andrew – *'The Staffordshire Brigade's Assault on the Hohenzollern Redoubt, October, 1915'.* [Unpublished thesis].

The 'Times' – *'The Times Diary & Index of the War, 1914-1918'.*

Toland, John – *'No Man's Land - the Story of 1918'.*

Travers, Tim – *'Gallipoli 1915'.* [2002, Tempus Publishing Ltd.]

Walsall Local History Centre – *'Street names of Bloxwich and Pelsall.'* [1994]

Walsall Observer and South Staffordshire Chronicle – *'Walsall Observer, 1914-1922' (copies on microfilm).*

Walsall Peace Committee – *'Walsall Peace Celebrations Book'.*

War Office –
- *'Soldiers and Officers Died in the Great War'* – *(CD-Rom version, Naval & Military Press.'*
- *'Statistics of the Military Effort of the British Empire during the Great War, 1914-1920.'* [1922, War Office; 1999 reprint, Naval & Military Press.]

Wayman, Ken – *'The True and Faithful Men'.* [2004, 4Print Ltd.]

Wayman, Ken – *'Thank God I Am Trying to Do My Little Bit'.* [2008, Tommies Guides]

Webb, Dr. Eric – *'Military Medicine on the Western Front'* – *(major article in "Stand To!" volume 65, Journal of the WFA).*

Westlake, Ray –
- o *'British Battalions in France & Belgium, 1914'.* [1997, Leo Cooper]
- o *'British Battalions on the Western Front, January to June 1915'.* [2001, Leo Cooper]
- o *'British Battalions at Gallipoli'.* [1996, Leo Cooper]
- o *'British Battalions on the Somme, 1916'.* [1994, Leo Cooper]
- o *'Kitchener's Army'.* [1989, Spellmount Ltd.]
- o *'Order of Battle of Divisions – Index'.* [2008, Naval & Military Press (NMP)]

Wiggin, Maurice – *'The Memoirs of a Maverick.'*

Wilks, John & Eileen – *'The British Army in Italy, 1917-1918.'* [1998, Leo Cooper]

C – Divisional, Regimental and Battalion Histories:

Ashcroft, Major A.H., DSO – *'History of the 7th Battalion, the South Staffordshire Regiment'.*

Atkinson, C.T. – *'The Seventh Division, 1914-1918'.* [Orig. 1926; NMP reprint].

Atteridge, A. Hilliard – *'A History of the 17th (Northern) Division'.* [Orig. 1929; NMP reprint].

Baker, Chris – *'The Battle for Flanders – German Defeat on the Lys, 1918.'* [2011, Pen & Sword Military]

Beckett, Ian F.W. & Simpson, Keith (Editors) – *'A Nation in Arms.'* [1985>2004, Pen & Sword Select]

Bewsher, Major F.W., DSO, MC – *'History of the 51st Highland Division.'* [Orig.1920; NMP reprint]

Blair, Dale – *'The Battle of Bellicourt Tunnel (Hindenburg Line, 1918).'* [2011, Frontline Books, imprint of Pen & Sword Books].

Boraston, Lt.-Col. J.H. and Bax, Capt. E.O. – *'The Eighth Division, 1914-1918'.* [Orig.1926; NMP reprint 1999].

Bradbridge, Lt.-Col. E.U. – *'59th Division, 1915-1918.'* [Orig. 1928; NMP reprint].

Carrington, Lt. C.E. – *'War Record of the 1/5th Battalion the Royal Warwickshire Regiment.'*

Crosse, Rev. E.C., DSO, MC – *'The Defeat of Austria, as seen by the Seventh Division'.* [Orig. 1919' NMP reprint, 2007].

Coop, Rev. J.O., DSO – *'Story of the 55th West Lancashire Division.'* [Orig.1919; NMP reprint]

Headlam, Cuthbert, DSO – *'The Guards Division in the Great War, 2 volumes.'* [Orig. 1924; N & M Press reprint.]

Jones, James P. – 'History of the South Staffordshire Regiment (1705-1923)'.

Kincaid-Smith, Lt. Col. M. – '25th Division in France and Flanders'. [Orig. 1918; NMP reprint].

Kingsford, C. Lethbridge – 'Story of the Royal Warwickshire Regiment (formerly 6th Foot)'.

Macdonald, Alan – 'A Lack of Offensive Spirit – 46th (North Midland Division) at Gommecourt, 1st July 1916.' [February 2008, Iona Books]

Magnus, Laurie – 'West Riding Territorials in the Great War.' [Orig. 1920; NMP reprint]

Marden, Maj.-Gen. T.O., CB, CMG – 'A Short History of the 6th Division, 1914-1919'. [Orig. 1920; NMP reprint].

Maude, Alan H. – 'History of the 47th London Division, 1914-1919.' [Orig.1922; NMP reprint]

Murphy, Lt.-Col. C.C.R. – 'The History of the Suffolk Regiment, 1914-1927.' [Orig. 1928; NMP reprint].

Planck, C. Digby – 'The History of the 7th (City of London) Battalion, The London Regiment.' [Orig. 1946; NMP reprint].

Priestley, Maj. R.E., MC, RE – 'Breaking the Hindenburg Line: The Story of the 46th (North Midland) Division'. [Orig. 1919; NMP reprint].

Sandilands, Lt.-Col. H.R. – 'The 23rd Division, 1914-1919.' [Orig. 1925; NMP reprint].

Scott, Maj.-Gen. Sir Arthur B. and Brumwell, P. Middleton, MC, CF – 'The History of the 12th (Eastern) Division in the Great War, 1914-1918'. [Orig. 1923; NMP reprint].

Simpson, Maj.-Gen. Charles Rudyerd, CB – 'A History of the Lincolnshire Regiment, 1914-1918'. [Orig. 1931; NMP reprint].

Vale, Colonel W.L. – 'History of the South Staffordshire Regiment'.

Wyrall, Everard – 'The History of the Second Division, 1914-1918, 2 volumes.' [Orig. 1921; NMP reprint].

Wyrall, Everard – 'The Nineteenth Division, 1914-1918.' [Orig. c.1932; NMP reprint, 1999].

D – Websites (selected):

Commonwealth War Graves Commission – 'Debt of Honour –Casualties.' To be found at: **www.cwgc.org**

Long, Long Trail [Chris Baker] – 'Great War Forum.' To be found at: **www.1914-1918.net**

National Archives, Kew, London. Service records; battalion war diaries. To be found at: **www.nationalarchives.gov.uk**

The Bloxidge Tallygraph – now the Bloxwich Telegraph. Created and edited by Stuart Williams – an excellent site for 'all things Bloxwich'. To be found at: originally at **www.thebloxidgetallygraph.com** now found at **thebloxwichtelegraph.wordpress.com**

Western Front Association. To be found at: **www. westernfrontassociation.com**

World War One Cemeteries. A site of remembrance and comprehensive guide to the military cemeteries and memorials around the world. An excellent, user-friendly site created by Terry Heard and Brent Whittam. To be found at: **www.ww1cemeteries.com**

The Medal Roll Index Card:

An example of a soldier's Medal Roll Index Card (commonly referred to as an MIC). This shows that James Dawson, Private 9451 of 2nd Battalion, South Staffordshire Regiment, was a member of the British Expeditionary Force (BEF) that was sent to the Western Front in 1914. He disembarked on 12th August 1914. The card shows he was entitled to the 1914 'Mons' Star, the British War Medal and the Victory Medal; it also indicates that he was killed in action ('K. in A.') on 15th November 1916. The figures in the medal section refer to Medal Roll and Page numbers that link to microfilm held in the National Archives at Kew – the Rolls usually reveal further detail about the soldier. Unlike Great War service and pension records that were largely destroyed during the London Blitz, MIC records are largely intact and are especially useful in tracing soldiers who survived the conflict.